9WE 13

D1029713

Dialogue
and
Deconstruction

SUNY Series in Contemporary Continental Philosophy
Dennis J. Schmidt, Editor

Dialogue
and
Deconstruction

The Gadamer-Derrida
Encounter

Edited by

Diane P. Michelfelder
&
Richard E. Palmer

State University of New York Press

Published by
State University of New York Press, Albany

For information, address State University of New York
Press, State University Plaza, Albany, N.Y., 12246

Library of Congress Cataloging-in-Publication Data

Dialogue and deconstruction : the Gadamer-Derrida encounter / edited
   by Diane P. Michelfelder & Richard E. Palmer.
      p. cm. — (SUNY series in contemporary continental
   philosophy)
   Includes index.
   ISBN 0-7914-0008-5.   ISBN 0-7914-0009-3 (pbk.)
   1. Gadamer, Hans-Georg, 1900-   . 2. Derrida, Jacques
3. Hermeneutics—History—20th century.   4. Deconstruction—History.
I. Michelfelder, Diane P., 1953-   . II. Palmer, Richard E., 1933-   .
III. Series.
B3248.G34D53 1989
149—dc19   88-24792
                                                                   CIP

10 9 8 7 6 5 4 3 2 1

Contents

Acknowledgments   ix

Introduction   1

Part I: The Gadamer-Derrida Encounter: Paris, 1981

1. Text and Interpretation
Hans-Georg Gadamer   21
> translated by Dennis J. Schmidt and Richard Palmer

2. Three Questions to Hans-Georg Gadamer
Jacques Derrida   52
> translated by Diane Michelfelder and Richard Palmer

3. Reply to Jacques Derrida
Hans-Georg Gadamer   55
> translated by Diane Michelfelder and Richard Palmer

4. Interpreting Signatures (Nietzsche/Heidegger): Two Questions
Jacques Derrida   58
> translated by Diane Michelfelder and Richard Palmer

Part II: Gadamer Responds to the Encounter

Prelude
Hermeneutics and Deconstruction: Gadamer and Derrida in Dialogue
Fred Dallmayr   75

1. Letter to Dallmayr (1985)
Hans-Georg Gadamer   93
> translated by Richard Palmer and Diane Michelfelder

2. Destruktion and Deconstruction (1985)
Hans-Georg Gadamer   102
> translated by Geoff Waite and Richard Palmer

3. Hermeneutics and Logocentrism (1987)
Hans-Georg Gadamer   114
> translated by Richard Palmer and Diane Michelfelder

Part III: Commentaries

1. *Argument(s)*
   Philippe Forget 129
   translated by Diane Michelfelder

2. *Limits of the Human Control of Language: Dialogue as the Place of Difference between Neostructuralism and Hermeneutics*
   Manfred Frank 150
   translated by Richard Palmer

3. *Good Will to Understand and the Will to Power: Remarks on an "Improbable Debate"*
   Josef Simon 162
   translated by Richard Palmer

4. *The Two Faces of Socrates: Gadamer/Derrida*
   James Risser 176

5. *Imagine Understanding. . .*
   Charles Shepherdson 186

6. *Gadamer/Derrida: The Hermeneutics of Irony and Power*
   G. B. Madison 192

7. *All Ears: Derrida's Response to Gadamer*
   Herman Rapaport 199

8. *Dialogue and* Écriture
   Donald G. Marshall 206

9. *The Gadamer-Derrida Encounter: A Pragmatist Perspective*
   Richard Shusterman 215

10. *"Ashes, ashes, we all fall . . .": Encountering Nietzsche*
    David Farrell Krell 222

11. *Seeing Double:* Destruktion *and Deconstruction*
    Robert Bernasconi 233

12. *Interruptions*
    John Sallis 251

13. *Gadamer's Closet Essentialism: A Derridean Critique*
    John D. Caputo 258

14. *The Man with Shoes of Wind: The Derrida-Gadamer Encounter*
    Neal Oxenhandler   265

15. *The Privilege of Sharing: Dead Ends and the Life of Language*
    Gabe Eisenstein   269

List of Abbreviations   284
Contributors of Commentaries   292
Notes   295
Indices   317

Acknowledgments

The texts in Part I of this book first appeared in *Text und Interpretation,* edited by Philippe Forget (Munich: Wilhelm Fink Verlag, 1984), pp. 24–77. We would like to thank Wilhelm Fink Verlag for permission to reprint these pages in translation, as well as for permission to reprint in translation pp. 181–90 and 206–9 of Manfred Frank's essay, "Die Grenzen der Beherrschbarkeit der Sprache: Das Gespräch als Ort der Differenz zwischen Neostrukturalismus und Hermeneutik," from the same volume. We also wish to thank the following publishers and individuals: J. C. B. Mohr (Paul Siebeck) for permission to reprint in translation Hans-Georg Gadamer's "Destruktion und Dekonstruktion," from the second volume of his *Gesammelte Werke* (Tübingen: J. C. B. Mohr [Paul Siebeck], 1986), pp. 361–72, and also for permission to reprint a half dozen footnotes Gadamer added to "Text und Interpretation" when it appeared also in that volume, *GW* 2, 330–60; *Revue internationale de philosophie* for permission to reprint in translation Jacques Derrida's "Bonnes volontés de puissance (Une réponse à Hans-Georg Gadamer)," from that journal (*38ème année,* No. 151, 1984, pp. 341–43); *Philosophy and Literature* and editor Dennis Dutton for permission to reprint our translation of Jacques Derrida's "Interpreting Signatures (Nietzsche/Heidegger): Two Questions," from that journal (vol. 10, no. 2, October 1986, pp. 246–62); State University of New York Press and Dennis J. Schmidt for permission to reprint with alterations Schmidt's translation of Gadamer's "Text und Interpretation," from *Hermeneutics and Modern Philosophy,* edited by Brice R. Wachterhauser (Albany: State University of New York Press, 1986, pp. 377–96); University of Notre Dame Press for permission to reprint in abridged form Fred Dallmayr's essay, "Hermeneutics and Deconstruction: Gadamer and Derrida in Dialogue" from *Critical Encounters: Between Philosophy and Politics* (Notre Dame, Indiana: University of Notre Dame Press, 1987, pp. 130–58); *Allgemeine Zeitschrift für Philosophie* and Professor Josef Simon for permission to publish a translation of his "Der gute Wille zum Verstehen und der Wille zur Macht: Bemerkungen zu einer 'unwahrscheinlichen Debatte,' " from vol. 12, no. 3, 1987, pp. 80–90, of that journal; Ferdinand Schöningh Verlag for permission to publish a translation of Gadamer's "Frühromantik, Hermeneutik, Dekonstruktivismus," from *Die Aktualität der Frühro-mantik* (Paderborn: Ferdinand Schöningh, 1987), pp. 251–60.

We would like to extend a special note of thanks to Fred Dallmayr and Hans-Georg Gadamer for permission to translate and publish Gadamer's "Letter to Dallmayr"; to Hans-Georg Gadamer for permission to republish in translation the other texts by him in this volume; and to Jacques Derrida for providing us with the original text of "Interpreting Signatures": "Interpréter les signatures (Nietzsche/Heidegger): Deux questions," for his permission to reprint this essay in translation, and for his friendly correspondence with us.

Bernd Magnus first called our attention to *Text und Interpretation* while we were attending a National Endowment for the Humanities Summer Seminar under his direction in 1985. For his help in getting this project underway, as well as for his ongoing support and encouragement, we are particularly grateful. Others also provided us with indispensable assistance at various stages of this project: Philippe Forget, Fred Dallmayr, Don Marshall, Ernst Behler, Josef Simon, and Manfred Frank. Our thanks go out to them as well as those colleagues who helped us over difficult spots in the translations: Dennis Schmidt, Bernd Magnus, Fred Dallmayr, Suzanne Robbins and Ron Winter. We would like to thank Geoff Waite for forwarding to us his translation of Gadamer's "Destruktion und Dekonstruktion." Both of us gratefully acknowledge a stipend from Internationes, in Bonn, Germany, to underwrite our translations from the German. Richard Palmer thanks the administration and trustees of MacMurray College for a sabbatical leave to pursue writing in the area of hermeneutics and to work on this volume, and Ron Daniels of the library staff for technical help. Finally, we both heartily thank all our contributors for their essays and cooperation in this project.

Introduction

Diane Michelfelder and Richard Palmer

"Hermeneutics" and "deconstruction": two terms that name two bodies of thought, two sets of texts, which today bear the signatures "Gadamer" and "Derrida." Two terms, moreover, that name what are often taken to be clashing, even mutually exclusive standpoints—two radically different interpretations of interpretation, of writing, even of language itself.

In seeking to find a source for the divergence of these two powerful currents of contemporary European thought, one immediately runs up against the body of thought and texts bearing the signature of Heidegger. Following Heidegger's lead, both Gadamer and Derrida deny the possibility of a transcendental, language-free standpoint for human understanding. And both, like Heidegger, regard our relationship to language as a primary philosophical issue, seeing language as the scene of our finitude, the place where we encounter the limits of our subjectivity. But their developments of Heidegger's insights into language are not at all alike. For Gadamer, language is living language—the medium of dialogue. When in *Truth and Method* Gadamer holds up the Platonic dialogue as the model for philosophical conversation, he makes it clear that the success of dialogue depends on the continuing willingness of its participants—right from the point where one of them asks a question that can no longer be repressed—to "give in" to language, to be carried along by the conversation for the purpose of letting meaning emerge in an "event" of mutual understanding. While Derrida would agree that the meanings generated by language always exceed our intentions, he proceeds from a view of language where language is presumed to be always already writing, where the spoken word is seen as an already disrupted sign, infiltrated by absence. So he remains continually on the alert as to how otherness lurks within meaning, and how, for a particular concept at issue, there may be no possibility of deciding, from among its competing meanings, one that is true or authentic.[1]

Heidegger's recognition of the priority of language, then, gets developed in two quite different directions in the texts of Gadamer and Derrida. In Gadamer, this development leads toward a stress on the unity of and in meaning, toward (so it seems) a strengthening of tradition and an emphasizing of the authority and truth of texts. In Derrida, on the other hand, it leads toward underscoring the irreducible equivocation and undecidability of meaning, even apparently toward questioning the concept of meaning itself.

On this basis, hermeneutics and deconstruction seem to offer us extremely different views of language. This is a major reason why they have been thought to be in opposition to each other. But despite their differences, they also have a common ground that needs to be kept in mind. Both Gadamer's philosophical hermeneutics and Derridean deconstruction present a significant challenge to the metaphysics of modernity, whose assumptions continue to dominate not only a good deal of thinking within philosophy but also within other interpretive disciplines, including literary criticism, theology, and the social sciences. And, however far apart their views of language may appear to be, both find a common ground in this challenge itself, in questioning the metaphysical assumption that language is at our disposal. We are not the ones "in charge" of language, Gadamer and Derrida both claim. It is, they insist, the other way around.[2]

Just how really incompatible, then, are hermeneutics and deconstruction? Their undeniable common ground seems to point not to a total absence of any communication between them but instead to the presence of lines of communication that are elusive, puzzling, and difficult to grasp. What do these lines of communication look like? Or, to put it another way: Just how "hermeneutical" is deconstruction? And, likewise, just how "deconstructive" is hermeneutics?

In light of these questions, the meeting between Hans-Georg Gadamer and Jacques Derrida in April 1981 at the Goethe Institute in Paris takes on special significance. This meeting, on the occasion of a symposium on "Text and Interpretation" organized by Sorbonne professor Philippe Forget, was their first in a public, academic setting.[3] But the deeper significance of this "improbable debate," as Forget later called it,[4] lay in the opportunity it offered for each thinker to engage the other in dialogue and to debate face-to-face. In short, this symposium provided a genuine chance to have what Germans call an *Auseinandersetzung:* a confrontation of positions, out of which one could gain not only a greater understanding of each individual standpoint but also of the relationship between them.[5]

But did such a confrontation really take place? The outward signs of the meeting, at least, would seem to suggest that it did. Formal papers were presented by both Gadamer and Derrida; and, at the round table discussion the morning after Gadamer's talk, Derrida addressed three questions to Gadamer in response to his talk and Gadamer offered a reply in turn. Subsequently, in 1984, Derrida's response and Gadamer's reply were published in French in the *Revue internationale de philosophie,* along with a shorter version of Gadamer's paper[6]; and in the same year the complete texts of the entire exchange also came out in German in *Text und Interpretation,* edited by Philippe Forget. One part of our purpose in putting together this volume is to make the complete texts of this exchange available in English. These texts have been assembled as Part I of this book, beginning with Gadamer's paper, "Text and Interpretation."

I

Gadamer's presentation starts out with a brief backwards glance at the development of hermeneutics, but then quickly turns to address what he identifies as the "genuine challenge" of contemporary French thinking—above all, the challenge represented by Derrida. Gadamer specifically singles out Derrida's claim that it is Nietzsche, not Heidegger, who has gone further in freeing philosophy from the grasp of metaphysical concepts of being and truth, and also from a logocentric concept of interpretation as the process of making present a meaning contained within the text. Without hesitating here Gadamer takes up Derrida's challenge. He places himself squarely in opposition to Derrida's reading of Heidegger, supporting Heidegger's own interpretation of Nietzsche as a metaphysical thinker, even while criticizing the later Heidegger for turning to poetical language as a means of getting beyond the limits of metaphysics. Despite Gadamer's unwillingness to follow this movement of Heidegger's thought and language into what he will later call an "impassable" region, he will still here make the claim that Heidegger can be defended as a more "radical" thinker than Nietzsche.

As he takes up Derrida's challenge in "Text and Interpretation," Gadamer likewise accepts the typical structure of academic debate. Siding with Heidegger while at the same time defending his own project of philosophical hermeneutics against Derrida's interpretation, Gadamer risks opening himself up to the force of Derrida's questions, to the possibility that Derrida might vehemently dispute with him in order to defend his own views. Gadamer's remarks in the paper lead us to anticipate the confrontation of positions that seemed to be promised by the very event of this meeting. And, given how on other occasions—in *Spurs,* for instance—Derrida has taken the opportunity to bring out the alignment, the deep connection, existing between the hermeneutical search for meaning and the project of metaphysics, it would not have been surprising had this meeting unfolded into a debate, a genuine encounter between these two thinkers.

But this was not how it went. Derrida responded to Gadamer's presentation with several questions that, at least on the surface, appear to have been misdirected. Paying no attention to Gadamer's claim that it is a mistake to place hermeneutics under the category of metaphysics just because it refers to a meaning presented by the text, Derrida focuses his questions on something Gadamer covers almost in passing, what he takes to be the obvious and necessary precondition for any understanding to be achieved in dialogue, namely, the willingness of each partner in a conversation to be open to what the other has to say. This

Derrida identifies with the Kantian idea of the good will. Gadamer can only react to Derrida's questions by voicing his doubts as to whether he has really been understood, claiming that his concept of good will as a prerequisite for dialogue does not go back to Kant but rather to Plato's *eumeneis elenchoi*. Nothing at all about philosophical hermeneutics, he maintains, depends on Kantian good will.

Likewise, Derrida's own presentation at the colloquium—"Interpreting Signatures (Nietzsche/Heidegger): Two Questions"—does not seem directed toward developing a dialogue between himself and Gadamer. Derrida argues that Heidegger's attempt to understand who Nietzsche is from the perspective of his thought rather than his life—an effort motivated by the good will to save Nietzsche from a psycho-biographical misreading[7]—is itself organized around a misreading of Nietzsche that attributes to him the unity of a proper name, and takes his thought of the eternal recurrence to be about the totality of being. In putting forward this argument, Derrida would seem to be simply assembling more evidence in support of his own view of the relation between Heidegger and Nietzsche. One of the questions that Derrida asks quite rhetorically toward the end of his paper—"Is it perhaps hasty to make Nietzsche out to be a metaphysician, albeit the last one?"—certainly points us in this direction. While Gadamer takes account of the challenge of Derrida, at no point in his formal paper does Derrida even bring up Gadamer's name.

All of this raises the question of just how accurate it is to speak of a "Gadamer-Derrida encounter," as we have done in the subtitle of this volume. Philippe Forget would come to wonder afterwards if, in this "improbable debate," as he called it, an encounter had indeed taken place. And even Derrida prefaces his three questions to Gadamer by registering his doubts as to whether "anything was taking place here other than improbable debates, counter-questions, and inquiries into unfindable objects of thought."[8]

Just what are we to conclude, then, on the basis of all this? Should we conclude that because a "genuine debate" did not unfold, the whole encounter was of no value and the meeting between Gadamer and Derrida was unsuccessful? Does this imply that between hermeneutics and deconstruction there is an unbridgeable gap?

With these questions, we have touched on a second aspect to our purpose in putting together this book: to present Gadamer's own reactions to his meeting with Derrida, reactions that in some sense represent a continuation of this exchange—albeit with an element of absence and deferral. Included in Part II of this volume are three essays written by Gadamer since the encounter dealing with the issues that divide and hold together hermeneutics and deconstruction. In the first of these, "Letter to Dallmayr," Gadamer candidly discusses his reactions to the Paris meeting, while continuing to defend the idea that philosophical hermeneutics is independent of any "philosophy of presence." This defense takes place as a direct reply to Fred Dallmayr's extensive review and critique of the encounter as presented in *Text und Interpretation,* which we have also included here in a shortened version. It is developed further in two other essays: "*Destruktion* and Deconstruction" and "Hermeneutics and Logocentrism." These, along with the "Letter to Dallmayr," are appearing here for the first time in English.

II

Dallmayr titles his review essay "Hermeneutics and Deconstruction: Gadamer and Derrida in Dialogue," yet he does not believe a dialogue took place in the Paris encounter. What occurred there, he writes, was "disjointed"—in fact, a "non-dialogue." So Dallmayr undertakes a "reconstruction" in his essay, in order to "approximate" more closely a genuine confrontation. In drawing on Gadamer's *Truth and Method* and Derrida's Nietzsche-interpretation to bring this reconstruction about, Dallmayr uncovers several layers of oppositions and points of conflict between deconstruction and hermeneutics: differences over concepts of interpretation, over the relation of aesthetic play and meaning, and finally over "practical-political" issues. Commenting on these differences, Dallmayr criticizes Gadamer for failing to fully disconnect hermeneutics from subjectivism but commends him for making a connection between hermeneutics and dialogue, taken as "existential encounter involving mutual testing and risk-taking." In Derrida, Dallmayr welcomes a more thoroughgoing critique of subjectivism. He is bothered, though, by the consequences of Derrida's emphasis on difference and undecidability: his inclination to avoid the risks of dialogue, to "circumvent and elude" interaction with other points of view, and also his indifference to ethics, his "neglect" of the dimension of human activity in which judgment and decision-making are essential.

In his letter responding to Dallmayr, Gadamer readily accepts Dallmayr's characterization of the Paris meeting as a "non-dialogue." His hopes for a conversation between "two totally independent developers" of Heidegger's philosophical thinking, he indicates here, were largely disappointed. But what sort of conversation did Gadamer anticipate? The idea of conversation held by Gadamer in the texts included in this section reflects the model of dialogue as he had set it out earlier in *Truth and Method;* it is according to this model that he gauges the success of his conversation with Derrida. In that work, he took the phenomenon of conversation to be not simply an exchange of remarks but a process of two people understanding each other" (*WM* 363/347) that turns out simultaneously to be a process of the "coming-into-language of the thing itself" (360/341). Language itself is the key for Gadamer to this process of understanding. In back of his remark to Dallmayr that "the word is what one person speaks and another understands" stands the idea that language is "the universal medium in which understanding itself is realized" (366/350). He attributes to language the power to bridge the distance between those who are attempting to speak to each other and the ability to help them reach an agreement about the central issue or "object" [*Sache*] of the conversation.

More precisely, Gadamer's claim that the "emergence of the question" offers up to us "the being of what is asked about" (*WM* 345/326) indicates that the linguistic process of conversation would not be able to advance its course without questioning, and without determining a direction for this questioning. On the basis of this picture of what a dialogue is, Gadamer is indeed hard pressed to identify what took place between Derrida and himself as being a genuine conversation, one where the logic of question and answer leads to a new, more truthful awareness of the issue at stake. Although many questions were put forward during the discussion, it is very difficult to single out an issue that is held in common, oriented toward bringing out a more essential determination of the being of a *Sache*. The questions that Gadamer raised about the nature of linguisticality and interpretation are not followed up by Derrida. But this is not the only noticeable lack in their exchange. The absence of a critical preliminary condition for dialogue to occur—a common language—also stands out. In *Truth and Method* Gadamer asserts that without this common language, partners in a conversation would talk at cross purposes and fail to make any headway toward mutual understanding (*WM* 360/341). His remark in *"Destruktion* and Deconstruction"—that when a dialogue starts out in two different languages, there comes a time when those speaking have to switch to one language for the conversation to advance—echoes this point. But Gadamer and Derrida, in their exchange, would both stick to their own language. One would also find it difficult to point to a philosophical language that the two share. Certainly Gadamer is right in stating, in his response to Dallmayr, that a common ground between them cannot be found in Nietzsche's language. Nor can it be found in the language of the later Heidegger, about whose poetic character, as mentioned earlier, Gadamer expresses strong reservations.

But even though Gadamer runs into difficulties in trying to fit his encounter with Derrida to the model of dialogue as he has already conceived it to be, he continues to put his trust in this model as the form to which any philosophical discussion must adapt. Behind Gadamer's statement that "Whoever wants me to take deconstruction to heart . . . stands at the beginning of a conversation, not its end" is the thought that for any conversation between hermeneutics and deconstruction to take place, those who are involved will have to view themselves as conversational *partners,* engaged in a joint search for meaning and truth.

With this in mind, it becomes possible to read Gadamer's subsequent responses to his meeting with Derrida as an effort to work out a common ground, some points of affinity on the basis of which such a conversation might yet take place. He will discover this common ground not in Heidegger's language but in the fact that he and Derrida are, as he puts it at the beginning of his "Letter to Dallmayr," two persons seeking to develop and carry forward aspects of Heidegger's thought. Gadamer attempts to make this common ground more explicit in "*Destruktion* and Deconstruction," where he places the Heideggerian method of *Destruktion*—the "de-structuring" of the language of metaphysics—in the context of an effort to step back from Hegelian dialectic. In making this move Gadamer is able to locate a dimension common to his hermeneutical project and the projects of both Heidegger and Derrida. Much as Heidegger's philological *Destruktion*—which retrieved the origins of metaphysical concepts in living language—can be seen as countering the dialectical development of concepts, so Derrida's deconstruction can be understood as a "step back" from the emphasis on the unity of meaning central to Hegelian dialectic. Now Gadamer mentions in both the "Letter to Dallmayr" and "Hermeneutics and Logocentrism" that he can readily accept the description of his project as being a "dialectical hermeneutics." But such a dialectical hermeneutics, he argues, shares with Derridean deconstruction and Heideggerian *Destruktion* a desire to resist Hegelian dialectic and to "open up a dimension of communicative understanding which goes beyond linguistically fixed assertions."

Thus, Gadamer finds hermeneutics and deconstruction, in their desire to overcome the metaphysical ideal of the exact determinability and repeatability of meaning, do share interests and have a common concern. This desire, one could say, is a type of being faithful, where the object of faith is the mysterious character of the word. In singling out this faithfulness, Gadamer discovers what he takes to be the common ground between himself and Derrida. In fact, this is a point about which he is quite convinced. In "*Destruktion* and Deconstruction" he writes: "Obviously the principle of deconstruction involves something quite similar to what I am doing." And it is not only with regard to Hegel where Gadamer claims that he and Derrida see eye to eye. One of the most striking aspects about these texts is the frequency with which Gadamer aligns himself with Derrida, emphasizing their similar positions. In the "Letter to Dallmayr," Gadamer claims that he recognizes the internal connection between speaking and writing, the independence of textual meaning from authorial intention, and the penetration of self-understanding by otherness—or rather, that he *too* accepts these views, just as Derrida does. Likewise, in "Hermeneutics and Logocentrism," he insists on the existence of difference, deferral, and distance within thought—on the existence, in other words, of *différance. Selbstverständnis*, Gadamer writes, reflects *différance;* the continuity of self-understanding includes discontinuity, a "constant being-other."

This is not to say that in these texts Gadamer glosses over the differences between hermeneutics and deconstruction. Just as he finds fault with Heidegger's path away from dialectic for having led into "impassable regions" by taking an overly poeticized approach to language, he objects to Derrida for having gone to the other extreme right from the start of his path away from dialectic, for approaching language by way of Husserl and thus, in his understanding of language, privileging the concept of the sign rather than the living word of conversation. Derrida's move of taking the concept of the sign as his starting point, which led to his reading Heidegger through Husserl, had "fateful consequences," Gadamer claims, for his understanding of hermeneutics. To really find *différance* in language, Gadamer seems to be saying here, one needs to go back to the spoken word. In this sense, Gadamer sees philosophical hermeneutics as out-deconstructing deconstruction.

But ultimately, one could say, it is not just these differences which get in the way of a confrontation between Gadamer and Derrida. Rather, Gadamer seems to be suggesting that since they both have a starting point in Heidegger and even have mutual goals because of that starting point (see LD 93 and HL 125), they should be partners in a conversation rather than fierce opponents. With this assumption the otherness, the strangeness, the rough edges of the "challenge" of Derrida are made smooth and a confrontation or debate made more difficult. It is almost as though the "French challenge" represented by Derrida had already been inscribed within the history of German philosophy.

III

It would seem, then, that the mutual ties to Heidegger and mutual goals of deconstruction and hermeneutics offer to Gadamer a common ground for conversation, not for confrontational debate but a conversation in which a mutual testing of complementary ideas—the testing that Dallmayr mentions in his essay—could occur. In theory, Gadamer appears to be saying in the texts presented here, there is nothing to prevent such a conversation from taking place. The failure of a conversation to materialize in Paris would consequently be attributable to Derrida's having seized upon the concept of the sign as the gateway to an understanding of language. Were it not for this move, Gadamer presumes, Derrida would most likely not have come to see dialogue as necessarily tied to logocentrism, dependent on a "Platonic-static sense of one ideal meaning," and thus, mediation and agreement would be just around the corner.

But is this the only source of Derrida's apparent reluctance to engage in dialogue, to participate in the process of question and answer? Certainly Derrida does not discount the importance of questioning in philosophy. He characterizes those who currently participate in philosophical discourse by their relationship to questioning; they are, he writes, members of "a community of the question about the possibility of the question" (*ED* 118/80)—the question of the possibility of surpassing the metaphysics of presence. As Derrida points out, being concerned with this question is a matter of being read into a conversation so that one is "overtaken by the dialogue of the question about itself and by itself" (*ED* 119/80); philosophy does not raise this question because it has decided to, or (as he has said in another place) as a result of the "internal maturation" of its history (*M* 162/134). Just at the point where Gadamer finds it impossible to follow Heidegger's way, Derrida gives Heidegger credit, credit for undertaking an *Abbau* or dismantling on such a grand scale so as to encompass all of Western metaphysics, and for understanding the unique difficulty of this dismantling, of thinking the "beyond" of the metaphysical tradition, of thinking that which is neither present nor absent and so open to assimilation under the category of presence.[9] The question at stake is precisely, as Derrida indicates in "Ousia and Grammé," "a question of something entirely other" (*M* 42/38). The *Sache* of philosophical thinking for Derrida is not something that language can put into words. So Gadamer's model of conversation, where questions are directed toward bringing *something* to language (HL 122), could not be Derrida's.

When looked at from this perspective, the questions that propel Derrida's step back from dialectic and those that motivate Gadamer's appear to have two quite different aims. The latter seeks to break up the fixed, determinable meaning of metaphysical concepts by returning these concepts to speech. The former would aim at a more thoroughgoing dissemination, at disrupting the determinateness of meaning as part of the project of uncovering what is entirely other than meaning and truth. Thus, Derrida would agree with Gadamer that hermeneutics and deconstruction do not represent opposing positions, not because they have so much in common but because their paths unfold on different planes. One cannot really discuss deconstruction and hermeneutics in the same breath or speak of their common "ground." There cannot really be a "ground" for deconstruction if it is not a set of ideas forming a philosophical position to begin with.[10]

So for Derrida hermeneutics and deconstruction do not haunt each other so much as seemingly stand in a relationship of alterity, of non-oppositional difference. And yet perhaps their relationship from Derrida's viewpoint is even more complicated. If they stood in a relationship of radical difference, one could not choose between them as though choosing between alternatives. But what is more, as Derrida has indicated in a number of places, one cannot choose between them at all.[11] For that which evades metaphysics must somehow be inscribed within metaphysics, implicit within it in some way—and this calls for a type of hermeneutic retrieval, which would remain within the tradition in its attempt to undo it. In this sense, hermeneutics would in fact be unavoidable, but not, Derrida would say, unavoidable from the inside, from within his own deconstructive project. This despite the fact that Derrida once called this hermeneutics a form of deconstruction.[12] Such deconstruction, which he linked to Heidegger but which he could just as easily have associated with Gadamer, is not the same as the attempt to dislocate oneself completely from the metaphysical tradition. And if one is not to choose between them, then one must practice both, speaking more than one language at once.

Hence, another way of looking at Derrida's apparent refusal to confront Gadamer would be to see in it an exploration of a way of speaking that would neither be an attempt to strengthen the position of the other or to dogmatically assert one's own position and thus forego dialogue in favor of talking to oneself. A way of speaking with the other that would affirm both the *Destruktion* of metaphysical concepts, and the thinking that seeks to break completely from these concepts. Derrida's non-engagement with Gadamer would thus be a refusal to affirm not dialogue itself but rather what Gadamer perceives as the necessary condition of dialogue: speaking only a single language. To speak more than one language would involve a type of negotiation. Derrida has admitted to having a preference for "negotiation" rather than "dialogue," but at the same time has stated "there is no negotiation without dialogue."[13]

IV

The texts in the final part will provide commentaries on the problematical phenomenon we have called "the Gadamer-Derrida encounter." All were either written or translated especially for this volume. Some will focus on the Paris encounter, some on Gadamer's subsequent essays.[14] Some will defend Gadamer's hermeneutics against the challenge of deconstruction, others will defend deconstruction against the challenge of hermeneutics. Clearly, too, this encounter had a political dimension; it did not take place, for example, on neutral territory. Some of the commentaries will address the political issues raised by the encounter, blaming now deconstruction, now hermeneutics, for lack of political awareness, while others will examine more closely the styles and formal aspects of hermeneutics and deconstruction. Finally, the closing essay will examine the two styles in the light of some recent works of Derrida.

In "Argument(s)," the initial essay in this section, Philippe Forget focuses on the lines of reasoning involved in the debate he had arranged. He takes a particular interest in Gadamer's attempt to put this debate on the ground of a nonethical, hermeneutical good will, and thus to establish a consensus between himself and Derrida. This move prompts Forget to wonder whether it is possible for hermeneutics to take a critical approach to its own prejudices.

To answer this question, Forget sets up another encounter, one that takes place between texts: one passage from *Truth and Method* and another from Derrida's essay, "Préjugés." Forget finds Gadamer's argument in *Truth and Method* in support of a "rehabilitation" of prejudice to be itself riddled with prejudices: that authority is receptive to truth, that dialogue is universal, that the Enlightenment was thoroughly opposed to recognizing prejudice as a positive feature of understanding, and that there is even such a singular event as the

"Enlightenment." In the final section of his essay, Forget turns to look at Gadamer as an interpreter of Celan. Against the logic of Gadamer's reading, which finds closure in Celan's poetic language, Forget proposes another reading that would not cover up the "abyss" of meaning found in language. Cautioning the reader against assimilating Gadamer's concept of polysemy to Derridean dissemination, Forget indirectly questions Gadamer's argument that hermeneutics and deconstruction step back from Hegel in comparable ways.

Manfred Frank's "Limits of the Human Control of Language: Dialogue as the Place of Difference between Hermeneutics and Neostructuralism" was one of the other papers presented at the original colloquium in Paris in 1981. Three themes figure in Frank's essay: language, dialogue, and individuality. Both hermeneutics and French "neostructuralism" emphasize the priority of language structures over specific uses. But, Frank insists, linguistics (from which deconstruction draws conceptual models) treats language quite differently from dialogical hermeneutics, and he finds Derrida's debts to Saussure and Husserl also limit his view of language. It is this view that Gadamer follows in reproaching Derrida at the close of "Hermeneutics and Logocentrism" for "an ontologically unclarified dependence on the semantic starting point" in his concept of language and also in "*Destruktion* and Deconstruction" where he again reproaches Derrida for taking too narrow a view of language. For Frank, dialogue becomes "the place of difference" between Gadamer's hermeneutics and Derrida's deconstructive approach. But Frank has another concern: individuality. He faults both hermeneutics and "neostructuralism"[15] (which includes both Foucault and Derrida) for bypassing the importance of individuality in interpretation. Taking his lead from Schleiermacher,[16] Frank argues that in their perhaps necessary denial of subjectivity (in the name of language, or structures, or convention, or tradition), neither hermeneutics nor deconstruction come to grips with the claims of individuality.[17] Precisely because hermeneutics and deconstruction have in common the denial of subjectivity and an affirmation of the priority of language, they also have in common the neglect of individuality.

Joseph Simon's "Good Will to Understand and the Will to Power: Remarks on an 'Improbable Debate' " takes up Gadamer's question from "Text and Interpretation" as to whether language is a bridge or a barrier, but not for the purpose of resolving it one way or the other. Simon detects in the very way this question is put a major assumption behind Gadamer's emphasis on dialogue: that what the other seeks is to be understood. From this perspective "good will" turns out to be the will to overcome one's own narrowness in order to understand the other. For instance, in his response to Derrida, Gadamer asserts that even Derrida (and even Nietzsche) wanted to be "understood."[18] Otherwise, Gadamer asks, why write at all? Why wish not to be understood? Simon's analysis makes it quite clear why Derrida draws back from Gadamer's eagerness for conversation. It would appear that the considerations of good will in dialogue, especially when Gadamer makes them thematic, do not provide a common ground. Continuing to seek a common ground, Gadamer in his essays in this volume turns to the issue of Heidegger's interpretation of Nietzsche and takes issue with what he takes to be the "position" of Derrida.[19] Yet Simon shows why even this move will fail, because Derrida's strategy is to be always and only a counterposition and never a position.

In a second section of his essay Simon groups Habermas and Gadamer together, for both rely on the "communicative situation" and the rational good will of the other. Both have responded to the French "challenge." Both find their positions radically in question, according to Simon, and their thesis of "good will" finds itself, according to Simon, "either trapped in an antinomy or interpreted as just another, individual, will."

James Risser in his "The Two Faces of Socrates: Gadamer/Derrida" finds common ground between the two thinkers in the fact that the work of both is focused on text and interpretation, and in the fact that both are in quest of liberation through forms of Socratic vigilance: one form is the radical probing of Derrida, the other the unending "conversation that we are" in Gadamer. Both are radically antifoundationalist thinkers. Gadamer's hermeneutics does not seek origins, for "in genuine conversation there is no last word just as there is no first word"; his is a hermeneutics of creative repetition. Thus, both thinkers practice, in different forms, a "vigilance against the pretension of knowing": Gadamer in his "hermeneutics of finitude" and Derrida in his emphasis on irony. They exemplify, according to Risser, two sides of Socrates.

Risser also remarks on the political implications of the Gadamerian form of dialogue in this form of vigilance, which, according to Risser, represents "preparation for a form of community." In the "conversation that we are," the other can be right. This is the condition for democracy, in which difference does not give way to difference but seeks unity in understanding. Thus Risser finds in Gadamer's emphasis on conversation something in harmony with the "ideal of democracy," a participation in something that "posits the goal of human solidarity."[20]

Yet precisely such Gadamerian assumptions are put in question by deconstruction. Thus, can a dialogue between Gadamer and Derrida be imagined? This is the question Charles Shepherdson puts to himself in "Imagine Understanding. . . ." Could these two "arguments" bearing the signatures of Gadamer and Derrida address each other or focus on a common problem? What are the barriers, the problems of translation, to be surmounted in order for Gadamer to deal with what he himself calls the "challenge" of contemporary French thought? Shepherdson finds in the two thinkers two quite different conceptions of dialogue, one oriented to the mode of exegesis and comparison of viewpoints, and the other to the tension between hermeneutic understanding and that which "asserts itself against all reasoning." Gadamer's encounter with the French challenge teaches him the limits of his own interpretation of Heidegger and his own roots in the romantic tradition, and thus is a deeply meaningful experience. Yet for Shepherdson, the idea of a hermeneutical critique of deconstruction or a deconstructive reading of hermeneutics remains questionable and would only "betray the very thinking that one would have imagined oneself to have been following." Thus, Shepherdson remains satisfied to explore in a sensitive way what it might mean for each to understand and speak to the other.

If Shepherdson is concerned with Gadamer's problems in understanding Derrida, G. B. Madison in his "Gadamer/Derrida: The Hermeneutics of Irony and Power," raises the question of Derrida's understanding of Gadamer. Madison finds "thoroughly bizarre" Derrida's apparent view (on the basis of the term "good will") that Gadamer is trapped in the metaphysics of subjectivity and philosophies of will. In fact, says Madison, "it is difficult to make any sense of Derrida's question," so he concludes that Derrida is resorting to a strategy of irony and will to overpower Gadamer through deliberate misunderstanding: "In the final analysis, what Derrida is attempting to do by means of his irony, parodying, performative utterances is perhaps to teach Gadamer a lesson. . . ." As for genuine conversation on the "power" and "power plays" in language, Derrida cannot allow himself to risk "alienating that specialized audience . . . of his particular brand of ultra-ironic discourse." Derrida's vested interests make a genuine dialogue improbable at best.

Derrida's disruptive response is also the focus of Herman Rapaport's "All Ears: Derrida's Response to Gadamer." It seems clear to Rapaport that Derrida is purposely subverting Gadamerian innocence. But while Madison's analysis faults Derrida's irony for undermining dialogue, Rapaport blames Gadamer for not being sensitive to Derrida's "ear-splitting" discourse and instead urging that "everyone hears with the same ears." Gadamer's emphasis on "the experience we all recognize" looks to Rapaport very much like "an interpretive gesture wherein differences are made to adapt to norms of social consensus." Thus, Derrida's strategy is an interruption of rapport, according to Rapaport. Rapaport also finds political implications in Gadamer's thought quite the opposite of Risser's references to the ideal of democracy. Rather he notes that Gadamer in his *Philosophical Apprenticeships* repudiates Nazi "nonsense" in the thirties, thus turning a deaf ear to fascism. He asks: "What are the consequences of this ethical refusal to listen?" What happens, he asks, in situations where "good will" cannot function as a ground for listening?

Donald G. Marshall in "Dialogue and *Écriture*" places the debate over writing in the context of the tension between "literacy and orality." In this context, Marshall finds Gadamer's emphasis on dialogue to be in harmony with Hebrew tradition and such Jewish thinkers as Martin Buber and Emmanuel Levinas. While it may be true that "Reb Derissa" practices a kind of hermeneutics that reflects a Talmudic heritage,[21] Gadamer's turn to dialogue and engagement does find reverberations in Jewish and Christian theology in the twentieth century. Thus, while Rapaport goes so far as to imply Gadamer's unknowing complicity in the holocaust, Marshall argues that Gadamer has a greater affinity than Derrida with Buber and Levinas. In light of Derrida's special relationship with Levinas and with Levinas' concept of the Other, and objections that Gadamer fails to do justice to the other, interesting questions arise that go beyond the intention of Marshall's essay.[22]

Turning away from the advocacy of one side or the other, Richard Shusterman takes a mediating approach in his "The Gadamer-Derrida Encounter: A Pragmatist Perspective." The two thinkers actually have a great deal in common, he asserts, and what is needed is the mediation of American pragmatism. Shusterman argues that "Gadamer's non-foundational, linguisticized, but tradition-respective hermeneutics nicely dovetails with Quine's conservative 'maxim of minimal mutilation' to our inherited web of belief, and with Nelson Goodman's emphasis on tradition's antecedent practice and entrenchment for the projectability and inductive fruitfulness of categorial predicates." On the other hand, "Derrida's non-foundational hermeneutic scepticism and critique of meaning is remarkably parallelled by Quine's and Donald Davidson's arguments against synonymy and for the indeterminacy of translation and interpretation." Furthermore, both Gadamer and Derrida "have been explicitly appropriated and deployed by more radical pragmatists like Richard Rorty and Joseph Margolis" whose work signals an impending rapprochement between the continental and Anglo-American traditions. Instead of faulting Derrida for misunderstanding Gadamer, Shusterman argues that pragmatism can provide "a mode of mediation" for all three of the questions Derrida raises with Gadamer in his response, namely, "the context of interpretation, consensual continuity versus rupture as the basis or precondition of interpretation, and the nature or possibility of perfect dialogical understanding." Thus, pragmatism, according to Shusterman, has something to offer both sides. But the reverse is also the case. Says Shusterman: "The importance of the Gadamer-Derrida encounter transcends the arena of continental philosophy; its issues and disseminations are pregnant with significance for Anglo-American philosophy as well." So it is in the context of a possibility for cross-fertilization and dialogue that Shusterman addresses himself to the three questions raised by Derrida in his response to Gadamer. In relation to each question, he finds that pragmatism can mediate creatively between hermeneutics and deconstruction.

When one takes Gadamer's three later papers responding to Derrida as essentially continuations of the encounter, one can speak of two major focii. The first is centered around Derrida's response to Gadamer's paper and takes up such issues as good will, psychoanalysis, and the possibility of dialogue. The second focus shifts away from issues surrounding good will to the question of Derrida's interpretation of Heidegger, and especially his reading of Heidegger's

Nietzsche-interpretation. With this change of focus, interesting new issues arise to which our next papers address themselves. For instance, to quote David Farrell Krell's " 'Ashes, ashes, we all fall . . .': Encountering Nietzsche," the first of these commentaries, "Why, when Gadamer encounters Derrida, and Derrida Gadamer, are both encountering Heidegger—encountering Heidegger encountering Nietzsche?"

Of course, Derrida in encountering Heidegger questions Heidegger's interpretation of Nietzsche while Gadamer, encountering Heidegger, becomes, as he admits, the "willing victim" of that thinker's powerful interpretation of Nietzsche. Krell, however, wonders about both of their readings of Heidegger's *Nietzsche*. Krell (editor and major translator of Heidegger's *Nietzsche* into English) suggests that both Derrida and Gadamer do not do justice to the deep ambivalence of Heidegger's reading of Nietzsche. Krell asks: "Would it not be better for all concerned to be less convinced both by and about Heidegger's *Nietzsche*?" In fact, says Krell, Heidegger himself was not so very convinced. He hedges his interpretations in *Nietzsche* with the following bit of hermeneutical caution: "We must guard against the presumption that we now belong among those who really understand. . ." (*N* 2 181). Krell ends his essay with a bit of irony: "The supreme *hermeneutician* of the twentieth century"—is Derrida. "The most romantic and adventurous of readers and most flexible of conceptual thinkers, the most open to conversation and debate, the one who shifts the instant his position becomes too rigid—in short, the most *French* of contemporary thinkers"—is Gadamer. Thus, while Marshall had found Gadamer more loyal to Jewish tradition than Derrida, now Krell finds him more French! Is Gadamer at once more Jewish and more French than Derrida? Obviously not; but both Marshall's surprising assertion and Krell's playful reversal of roles give one a clear sense of the play of interpretation.

Robert Bernasconi in "Seeing Double: *Destruktion* and Deconstruction," also offers us a careful examination of Gadamer's reading of Derrida's reading of Heidegger's reading of Nietzsche. Bernasconi takes up the question of whether Derrida's term "deconstruction" is properly understood to be the same as Heidegger's *Destruktion*. Gadamer, in "*Destruktion* and Deconstruction," ventures to suggest that Derrida has misinterpreted this Heideggerian term to have a negative tone it does not possess in Heidegger. Has Derrida misread Heidegger, or has Gadamer misread Derrida? It would seem, and does seem to Bernasconi, that Gadamer was misinterpreting Derrida's use of the term. But Bernasconi also asks: Was even Gadamer correct in his interpretation of Heidegger's use of the term? How does Gadamer "see" Derrida, and how does Derrida "see" Gadamer? Bernasconi suggests that perhaps Gadamer is urging a "single reading" hermeneutics and Derrida a "double reading" hermeneutics. In doing so, he turns to a careful examination of the specific hermeneutical strategies that mark the two thinkers. At the end of his essay, Bernasconi suggests that what starts out as a relationship of opposition actually becomes a relationship of alterity, of two "different strands of contemporary thinking."

In "Interruptions," John Sallis interrupts all this more conventional argumentation with a Derridean approach—a "writerly presentation" that would be very difficult to read orally. One would need two voices, perhaps, interrupting and interpreting each other. Going back to Derrida's *Speech and Phenomena,* Sallis proposes a Derridean critique of dialogue. Dialogue, for Derrida, involves a prior stage of difference within the moment of utterance. Thus, Sallis questions whether Gadamer's model of dialogue is really a sufficient model. For Derrida, the "archaic operation of difference within the dialogue of the soul within itself" is found *before* all dialogue with the other and "otherness is always already operative in what one would otherwise have called monologue." By taking his cue from Derrida's Husserl-interpretation, Sallis addresses himself to the Platonic basis of Gadamer's claims about dialogue. Sallis argues that something more than "good will" is in play when Socrates interacts with his various interlocutors.

John Caputo's lively essay, "Gadamer's Closet Essentialism: A Derridean Critique," presents Gadamer as a "closet essentialist" pretending to follow in the path of Heidegger's historical, existential, finite hermeneutics. Caputo detects two contradictory longings in Gadamer's hermeneutics: one for "deep truths" that rise above all time, the other for a mode of interpretation rooted in our existential, historical, finite existence. Caputo finds this a curious combination of Hegel, German Romanticism, Platonism, and Heideggerian existentialism that only plunges us into the metaphysics from which Heidegger was trying to free us. For Caputo, the difference between Gadamer and Derrida is basically "a conflict between right wing and left wing Heideggerianism."

In putting the issue in terms of "left wing" and "right wing" Heideggerianism, Caputo turns to explore certain political consequences of Gadamer's interpretation of Heidegger in contrast to Derrida's. Even in the ostensibly antifoundationist position of Gadamer Caputo finds a kind of traditionalism. Following Margolis, he asserts that Gadamer is "in headlong retreat from the radicalization of *Wesen* [essence] which was underway in Heidegger." While breaking with Hegelian teleology, Gadamer still seeks a "deep truth" in texts. From a deconstructionist standpoint, Gadamer's use of Heidegger, then, is "half-hearted, indeed reactionary," and actually resists the momentum of Heidegger's critique of metaphysics. But Derrida has "stepped back" out of "the epochs of presence, of the meaning and truth of Being," and thus more faithfully followed the later Heidegger in his radical scepticism about these notions. Derrida, says Caputo, simply does not think there is a "deep ontology inscribed in the *Muttersprache* . . . which usually ends up saying that father knows best." With these associations, Caputo is able to find in Gadamer a political tendency to lean to the right, even while seeing himself as faithfully following the most radical thinker in the century.

Neal Oxenhandler in "The Man with Shoes of Wind: The Derrida-Gadamer Encounter" offers a short meditation on why Derrida seems not to have taken time to enter into a serious dialogue with a thinker of the stature of Gadamer. Rather, Derrida "stands outside of Gadamer's position and subjects it to the cutting edge of irony." Oxenhandler suggests several areas the two thinkers have in common as well as areas of difference. For both thinkers the literary tradition is important and both are interpreters of works of art. For both, the concept of play is important. But for Gadamer "the play of the work, in manifesting a way of being, conveys 'truth,' " whereas for Derrida there is "no closure beyond the ceaseless play of dissemination." A professor of French literature, Oxenhandler finds in Derrida the voices of Mallarmé, Proust, Beckett, and others. And when Derrida visits with him at Dartmouth College, he even ventures to suggest to Derrida that he had become, like Rimbaud, a man with shoes of wind. Derrida could only agree.

The final essay, Gabe Eisenstein's "Dead Ends and the Life of Language: The Privilege of Sharing," opens up new dimensions of contrast between hermeneutics and deconstruction. So rather than bringing a sense of closure, Eisenstein's essay points us beyond the present discussion to other possibilities. Relying on such later texts as "D'un ton apocalyptique adopté naguère en philosophie" (ATRAP) and *Altérités* (A), Eisenstein chooses to put the contrast between Gadamer and Derrida not in terms of hermeneutics versus deconstruction but in terms of two "paradigms": the dialogical paradigm of Gadamer and an "apocalyptic" paradigm of Derrida. In the apocalyptic paradigm, Eisenstein says, "we [as interpreters] inevitably assume, in our best attempts at thinking and speaking clearly, the position of a mystagogue: we speak in such a way as to take up a privileged position with regard to a certain universe of discourse— discourse governed by the *absence* of some fundamental sense-giving experience possessed or intimated by the speaker alone." It is from this privileged position that Derrida, as interpreter, can utter the prophetic command "Come!" yet in a way that is "without message and without destination, without sender or decidable addressee" (ATRAP 94).

Such a model of interpretation stands in radical contrast to Gadamer's paradigm of dialogical understanding as a way to overcome otherness and reach agreement in understanding. Gadamer's dialogical model of interpretation is based on good faith, honesty, and openness to the other. On the other hand, Derrida's prophetic and apocalyptic use of language is "protreptic," according to Eisenstein; it assumes authority to speak. One might also use the word "hortatory": it is the stance of assumed authority philosophers frequently adopt, especially Heideggerians. Interestingly, Eisenstein tells us that what speaks in the apocalyptic dimension is an "absolutely authoritative voice," a narrative voice speaking out of a "radical *alterity*" that "brings into view the limitations that would be overcome in the drama of autonomy" and also marks out the privileges to be enjoyed. Such speaking is "a blow, a transforming gesture rooted in the radical *incommensurability* of differing standpoints." The autonomy of this voice is such that it stands outside and above the other, "irreducibly unequal" to the other. Such a voice and such a model are not unprecedented in the history of hermeneutics, specifically in Hebrew models and also the neoorthodox theology of Karl Barth. Obviously, the articulation of this paradigm as the Derridean standpoint vis-à-vis Gadamer goes beyond anything presently associated with "deconstruction" and perhaps provides the appropriately tantalizing note to be sounded in the final essay of our commentaries.

In closing, we may say that although the encounter between Gadamer and Derrida was short, it was and remains significant. Its importance lies not just in what was said and what happened there but also in what was not said and what did not happen. Both the said and unsaid in this "improbable encounter"—and the range of issues generated by it—provide us with exceptional tools for dealing with the complexities involved in thinking through hermeneutics, deconstruction, and the slippery relationship between them.

I

The Gadamer-Derrida
Encounter: Paris, 1981

Hans-Georg Gadamer

1. Text and Interpretation

A New Translation by Dennis J. Schmidt and Richard Palmer*

The problems with which hermeneutics deals were initially defined within individual areas of study, especially theology and jurisprudence, and ultimately also the historical disciplines. But it was a deep insight of German Romanticism that understanding and interpretation not only come into play in what Dilthey later called "expressions of life fixed in writing," but they have to do with the general relationship of human beings to each other and to the world. In the German language, this insight has also left an imprint upon words that are derived from the word for understanding: *Verstehen*. For instance, the word *Verständnis* means comprehension, insight, appreciation. Thus, in the German language, *Verstehen* also means "to have appreciation for something," to comprehend it [*für etwas Verständnis haben*].[1] The ability to understand is a fundamental endowment of man, one that sustains his communal life with others and, above all, one that takes place by way of language and the partnership of conversation. In this respect, the universal claim of hermeneutics is beyond all doubt. On the other hand, however, the linguisticality of the event of agreement in understanding [*Verständigungsgeschehen*], which is in play between people, signifies nothing less than an insurmountable barrier, the metaphysical significance of which was also evaluated positively for the first time by German romanticism. It is formulated in the sentence: *Individuum est ineffabile*. This sentence

---

Translators' note: A previous translation of this essay by Dennis J. Schmidt appeared in *Hermeneutics and Modern Philosophy*, ed. Brice Wachterhauser (*HMP* 377–96). It was based on a prepublication manuscript. Professor Gadamer added some thirteen pages of text at the end of the earlier essay for its publication in *Text und Interpretation* (*TI* 24–55) and then in his *Gesammelte Werke* (*GW* 2 330–60). The present translation is based on the complete text of this essay as it appears in both *TI* and *GW* 2.

points to a limit of ancient ontology (at any rate, it cannot be documented in the medieval period). However, for the romantic consciousness it meant that language never touches upon the last, insurmountable secret of the individual person. This expresses the feeling for life that characterized the romantic age in a particularly telling manner, and it points to an inherent law of linguistic expression, which not only sets the limits of linguistic expression but also determines its significance for the formation of the common sense that unites people.

I believe that it is helpful to recall these historical antecedents of our present formulation of the question. The consciousness of method found in the historical sciences, which flourished as a result of romanticism, and the influence exerted by the successful model of the natural sciences led philosophical reflection to restrict the universality of the hermeneutical experience to its scientific form. The full extent of the fundamental hermeneutical experience is to be found neither in Wilhelm Dilthey, who attempted to ground the social sciences in their historicality by way of the conscious continuation of the ideas of Friedrich Schleiermacher and his romantic compatriots, nor in the neo-Kantians, who worked toward an epistemological justification of the human studies within the framework of a transcendental critique of culture and values. This lack of any view encompassing the full extent of hermeneutic experience might even have been more pronounced in the homeland of Kant and transcendental idealism than in countries where literature plays a more determinative role in public life. In the end, however, philosophical reflection everywhere went in a similar direction.

Thus, I took as my own point of departure the critique of the idealism and methodologism in our era dominated by epistemology; and in my critique Heidegger's extension of the concept of understanding to an existential, that is to a fundamental categorical determination of human existence, was of particular importance for me. That was the impetus that induced me to go critically beyond the discussion of method and to expand the formulation of the hermeneutic question so that it not only took science into account, but the experience of art and of history as well. With a critical and polemical intent in his analysis of understanding, Heidegger followed the example of former discussions of the hermeneutic circle, maintaining it in its positivity and conceptualizing it in his analysis of Dasein. What one should not forget, however, is that circularity is dealt with here not as a metaphysical metaphor, but rather as the structure of a logical concept drawn from the theory of scientific proof, where it is the doctrine of the "vicious circle." The hermeneutic circle says that in the domain of understanding there can be absolutely no derivation of one from the other, so that here the logical fallacy of circularity does not represent a mistake in procedure, but rather the most appropriate description of the structure of understanding. Thus, Dilthey introduced the discussion of the hermeneutical circle as a means of separating himself from the post-Schleiermacherian scientific epoch. If, along with this, one bears in mind the true extent to which everyday speech accords with the concept of understanding, then one sees that the discussion of the hermeneutic circle is in fact directed toward the structure of Being-in-the-world itself; that is, toward overcoming of the subject-object bifurcation, which was the primary thrust of Heidegger's transcendental analysis of Dasein. Just as one who uses a tool does not treat that tool as an object, but works with it, so too the understanding in which Dasein understands itself in its Being and in its world is not a way of comporting itself toward definite objects of knowledge, but is rather the carrying out of Being-in-the-world itself. With this, the hermeneutical doctrine of method inherited from Dilthey was transformed into a hermeneutics of facticity that was guided by Heidegger's inquiry into Being and that included the retrospective questioning of historicism and of Dilthey.

As is well known, the later Heidegger completely abandoned the concept of hermeneutics because he realized that it would never enable him to break out of the sphere of transcendental reflection. His philosophizing, which in the 'Kehre' attempted to accomplish this withdrawal from the concept of the transcendental, increasingly encountered such difficulties with language that many readers of Heidegger came to believe that there was more poetry than philosophical thought to be found in his work. I believe of course that this view is a mistake.[2] Therefore, one of my own interests was to look for ways in which Heidegger's discussion of that Being, which is not the Being of beings, can be legitimated. That effort led me once again to intense work on the history of classical hermeneutics, and it compelled me to show the new insights that were brought to light by the critique of this history. It seems to me that my own contribution is the discovery that no conceptual language, not even what Heidegger called the 'language of metaphysics', represents an unbreakable constraint upon thought if only the thinker allows himself to trust language; that is, if he engages in dialogue with other thinkers and other ways of thinking. Thus, in full accord with Heidegger's critique of the concept of subject, whose hidden ground he revealed as substance, I tried to conceive the original phenomenon of language in dialogue. This effort entailed a hermeneutical reorientation of dialectic, which had been developed by German Idealism as the speculative method, toward the art of the living dialogue in which the Socratic-Platonic movement of thought took place. This reorientation of dialectic was not intended to lead to a merely negative dialectic even though it was always conscious of the fundamental incompletability of the Greek dialectic. Rather, it represented a correction of the ideal of method that characterized modern dialectic as fulfilling itself in the idealism of the Absolute. This same interest led me to search for the hermeneutical structure in the experience of art and of history itself, which the so-called social sciences have as their 'objects,' rather than initially in the experience that is treated by science. No matter how much the work of art may appear to be an historical given, and thus a possible object of scientific research, it is always the case that it says something to us, and it does so in such a way that its statement can never finally be exhausted in a concept. Likewise, in the experience of history we find that the ideal of the objectivity of historical research is only one side of the issue, in fact a secondary side, because the special feature of historical experience is that we stand in the midst of an event without knowing what is happening to us before we grasp what has happened in looking backwards. Accordingly, history must be written anew by every new present.

Ultimately, the same basic experience holds true for philosophy and its history. Plato, who wrote only dialogues and never dogmatic texts, is not alone in teaching us this lesson. For, in what Hegel calls the speculative element in philosophy (which was at the basis of his own observations of the history of philosophy), we are constantly confronted with a challenge to bring into view this same element in the dialectical method. Thus, I tried to hold fast to the inexhaustibility of the experience of meaning by developing the implications for hermeneutics of the Heideggerian insight into the central significance of finitude.

In this context, the encounter with the French philosophical scene represents a genuine challenge for me. In particular, Derrida has argued against the later Heidegger that Heidegger himself has not really broken through the logocentrism of metaphysics. Derrida's contention is that insofar as Heidegger asks about the essence of truth or the meaning of Being, he still speaks the language of metaphysics that looks upon meaning as something out there that is to be discovered [*vorhandenen und aufzufindenen*]. This being so, Nietzsche is said to be more radical. His concept of interpretation does not entail the discovery of a preexisting meaning, but the positing of meaning in the service of the 'Will to Power'. Only then is the logocentrism of metaphysics really broken. This development and continuation of Heidegger's insights, which understands itself as their radicalization, must, in order to be consistent, discard Heidegger's own presentation and critique of Nietzsche. In this view, Nietzsche is not regarded as the extreme case of the forgetfulness of Being that culminates in the concepts of value and will, but as representing the true overcoming of metaphysics, the very metaphysics within with Heidegger remains trapped when he asks about Being, or the meaning of Being, as if it were a Logos to be discovered. Thus, it was not enough that the later Heidegger developed his special quasipoetical language in order to escape the language of metaphysics, a language that with each new essay by Heidegger seemed to be a new language and was always one that required that each reader be constantly engaged as his or her own translator of this language. To be sure, the extent to which one can succeed in finding the language that fulfills this task is problematic, but the task is posed: it is that of 'understanding'. Since my confrontation with the French continuation of Heideggerian thought, I have become aware that my efforts to 'translate' Heidegger testify to my own limits and especially indicate how deeply rooted I am in the romantic tradition of the humanities and its humanistic heritage. But it is precisely this very tradition of 'historicism,' which has sustained and carried me along, against which I have sought to take a critical stand. In a letter that has since been published,[3] Leo Strauss got to the heart of the matter in saying that for Heidegger it is Nietzsche, while for me it is Dilthey, who forms the starting point for critique. It could be said that the distinctive feature of Heidegger's radicality is that his own critique of the Husserlian brand of neo-Kantianism put him in the position of recognizing in Nietzsche the extreme culmination of that which he called the history of the forgetfulness of Being. But this critical observation is immanent and is one that rather than being inferior to Nietzsche's thought goes beyond him. I find that the French followers of Nietzsche have not grasped the significance of the seductive in Nietzsche's thought. Only in this way, it seems to me, could they come to believe that the experience of Being that Heidegger tried to uncover behind metaphysics is exceeded in radicality by Nietzsche's extremism. In truth, however, a deep ambiguity characterizes Heidegger's image of Nietzsche, in that he follows Nietzsche into the most extreme positions and precisely at that point he finds the excesses [*Un-wesen*] of metaphysics at work insofar as in the valuing and revaluing of all values Being itself really becomes a value-concept in the service of the 'Will to Power'. Heidegger's attempt to think Being goes far beyond such dissolving of metaphysics into values-thinking: or better yet, he goes back behind metaphysics itself without being satisfied, as Nietzsche was, with the extreme of its self-dissolution. Such retrospective questioning does not do away with the concept of Logos and its metaphysical implications, rather it recognizes the one-sidedness and concedes its superficiality. In this regard it is of decisive importance that 'Being' does not unfold totally in its self-manifestation, but rather withholds itself and withdraws with the same primordiality with which it manifests itself. This is the deep insight that was first maintained by Schelling in opposition to Hegel's logical idealism. Heidegger takes up this question once again while applying to it a conceptual power that Schelling lacked.

Thus, my own efforts were directed toward not forgetting the limit that is implicit in every hermeneutical experience of meaning. When I wrote the sentence "Being which can be understood is language,"[4] what was implied thereby was that that which is can never be completely understood. This is implied insofar as everything that goes under the name of language always refers beyond that which achieves the status of a proposition. That which is to be understood is that which comes into language, but of course it is always that which is taken as something, taken as true [*wahr-genommen*]. This is the hermeneutical dimension in which Being "manifests itself." In this sense, I retained the expression the "hermeneutics of facticity," an expression that signifies a transformation of the meaning of hermeneutics. Of course, in my attempt to describe the problems, I took as my guide the experience of meaning that takes shape in language in order to bring to light the limits that are posited for it. The Being-toward-the text from which I took my orientation is certainly no match for the radicality of the limit experience found in Being-toward-death, and just as little does the never fully answerable question of the meaning of art, or the meaning of history as that which happens to us, signify a phenomenon that is as primordial as the question put to human Dasein of its own finitude. I can, therefore, understand why the later Heidegger (and Derrida would presumably agree with him on this point) was of the opinion that I never really abandoned the sphere of phenomenological immanence to which Husserl consistently held fast and which formed the basis of my early training in neo-Kantianism. I can also understand why one could believe that it is possible to recognize methodological 'immanence' in my holding fast to the hermeneutical circle; and in fact it does seem to me that the desire to break out of the circle cannot be fulfilled, indeed such a demand is truly absurd. For after all, this immanence is nothing other than what it was for Schleiermacher and his successor Dilthey, that is, a description of what understanding is. But since Herder, we recognize 'understanding' to be more than merely a procedure to uncover a given meaning. In view of the scope of understanding, the circularity that moves between the one who understands and that which he understands can lay claim to genuine universality, and it is precisely on this point that I believe that I have followed Heidegger's critique of the phenomenological concept of immanence, a critique that is directed against Husserl's notion of an ultimate transcendental justification.[5] The dialogical character of language, which I tried to work out, leaves behind it any starting point in the subjectivity of the subject, and especially in the meaning-directed intentions of the speaker. What we find happening in speaking is not a mere reification of intended meaning, but an endeavor that continually modifies itself, or better: a continually recurring temptation to engage oneself in something or to become involved with someone. But that means to expose oneself and to risk oneself. Genuinely speaking one's mind has little to do with a mere explication and assertion of our prejudices; rather, it risks our prejudices—it exposes oneself to one's own doubt as well as to the rejoinder of the other. Who has not had the experience—especially before the other whom we want to persuade—of how the reasons that one had for one's own view, and even the reasons that speak against one's own view rush into words. The mere presence of the other before whom we stand helps us to break up our own bias and narrowness, even before he opens his mouth to make a reply. That which becomes a dialogical experience for us here is not limited to the sphere of arguments and counterarguments the exchange and unification of which may be the end meaning of every confrontation. Rather, as the experiences that have been described indicate, there is something else in this experience, namely, a potentiality for being other [*Andersseins*] that lies beyond every coming to agreement about what is common. This is the limit that Hegel did not transgress. To be sure, he did recognize the speculative principle that holds sway in 'Logos', and he even introduced proofs of this principle in dramatically concrete ways: he unfolded the structure of self-consciousness and of "self-knowledge in the Being of the other" as the dialectic of recognition and sharpened this into a life and death struggle. In a similar fashion, Nietzsche's penetrating psychological insights brought into view the 'Will to Power' as the substrate even in all devotion and self-sacrifice: "There is the will to power even in the slave." However, for me, Heidegger remains definitive when he finds the logocentricism of Greek ontology in the self-centeredness of this tension between self-abandonment and self-insistence to be continued in the sphere of arguments and counter-arguments, and in the factual confrontation wherein it is embedded.

A limitation of the Greek models of thought can be detected here, one that was persuasively pointed out by the Old Testament, Saint Paul, Luther, and their modern reinterpreters. It is a dimension of dialogue that still does not come into conceptual consciousness even with the celebrated discovery of Socratic dialogue as the basic form of thought. This fits in quite well with the fact that a writer with the poetic imagination and linguistic powers of Plato knew to portray the charismatic figure of a Socrates so that the erotic tension that vibrates about the person is really brought into view. But because Plato's presentation of Socrates shows that when leading the conversation Socrates always insisted upon demanding an account from the other and upon leading others back to themselves by convicting them of their pretended wisdom, it is presupposed that the Logos is common to all and does not belong to Socrates alone. Yet, as we already indicated, the true depth of the dialogical principle first enters philosophical consciousness in the twilight of metaphysics, in the epoch of German romanticism, and then is rehabilitated in our century in opposition to the subjective bias that characterized idealism. This is the point from which I proceeded in asking two further questions: First, How do the communality of meaning [*Gemeinsamkeit des Sinnes*], which is built up in conversation, and the impenetrability of the otherness of the other mediate each other? Second, What, in the final analysis, is linguisticality? Is it a bridge or a barrier? Is it a bridge built of things that are the same for each self over which one communicates with the other over the flowing stream of otherness? Or is it a barrier that limits our self-abandonment and that cuts us off from the possibility of ever completely expressing ourselves and communicating with others?

In the framework of this general formulation of the question, the concept of the text presents a special sort of challenge. This is something that unites and perhaps even divides me from my French colleagues. However that may be, this was my motivation in confronting the theme "Text and Interpretation" once again. How does the text stand in relation to language? What is communication [*Verständigung*] between speakers? And why is it that something like texts can be given to us in common? What does it mean that in this process of communication with one another something emerges that, like texts, is one and the same thing for us? How has the concept of the text been able to undergo such a universal extension? It is obvious to anyone who watches the philosophical tendencies of our century that more is at stake in this theme than reflections upon the methodology of the philological sciences. Text is more than a title for the subject matter of literary research. Interpretation is more than the technique of scientifically interpreting texts. In the twentieth century, both of these concepts have acquired a new importance in our view of knowledge and the world.

Of course, this shift is connected with the role that the phenomenon of language has come to occupy in our thought. But such a statement is tautological. That language has acquired a central position in philosophical thought is, on its part, related to the turn that philosophy took in the course of the last decades. That the ideal of scientific knowledge which modern science follows came out of the model of nature as mathematically ordered (a model that was first developed by Galileo in his mechanics) meant that the linguistic interpretation of the world, that is, the experience of the world that is linguistically sedimented in the lived-world, no longer formed the point of departure and the point of reference for the formulation of questions or the desire for knowledge; rather, it meant that the essence of science was constituted by that which could be accounted for or analyzed by rational laws. In this way, natural language lost its unquestioned primacy, even if it did retain its own manner of seeing and speaking. A logical consequence of the implications of this modern mathematized natural science was that in modern logic and the theory of science the model of language was replaced by the model of univocal notation. Thus, it is in the context of certain limited experiences, which restrict the claim to universality of the scientific access to the world, that meanwhile natural language as a universal has recaptured the center of philosophy.

Of course, this does not signify a mere return to the experiences of the lived-world and their linguistic sedimentation, which we know as the dominant theme of Greek metaphysics, the logical analysis of which led to Aristotelian logic and to *grammatica speculativa*. Rather, it is no longer the logical achievement of language that is being considered, but language as language and as the schematization of our access to the world. In this way, the original perspectives are displaced. Within the German tradition, this move is represented by a return to romantic ideas—of Friedrich Schlegel, Alexander von Humboldt, and others. Neither in the neo-Kantians nor in the first phenomenologists do we find the problem of language considered at all. Only in a second generation did the midworld [*Zwischenwelt*] of language become a theme; thus, we find it in Ernst Cassirer and especially in Martin Heidegger, as well as in the interesting contributions of Hans Lipps. In the British tradition, something similar is to be found in the developments that Ludwig Wittgenstein made from his starting point in Bertrand Russell. Here, the issue is not really one of a philosophy of language that is constructed upon the basis of comparative linguistics, or of the ideal of constructing a language that takes its place in a universal theory of signs; rather, the issue is the enigmatic nexus between thinking and speaking.

Thus, on the one hand, we have sign theory and linguistics, which have led to new knowledge about the way in which linguistic systems function and are constructed; and, on the other hand, we have the theory of knowledge, which realized that it is language that mediates any access to the world. And both of these, working together, have caused us to see the starting point for philosophical justification of scientific access to the world in a new light. The assumption in this starting point is that the subject takes hold of empirical reality with methodological self-certainty by means of its rational mathematical construction, and that it then expresses this reality in propositional statements. In this way the subject fulfills its true epistemological task, and this fulfillment climaxes in the mathematical language with which natural science defines itself as universally valid. The midworld [*Zwischenwelt*] of language is left out of consideration here in principle. Insofar as it once again comes into view as such, it demonstrates against mathematical language the primary mediatedness of all access to the world, and more than this, it demonstrates the inviolability of the linguistic schema of the world. The almost mythical status of self-consciousness—which was adopted in its apodictic self-certainty and elevated to the status of origin and justification of all validity, and the ideal of an ultimate grounding [*Letztbegründung*] in general, over which apriorism and empiricism fight—loses its credibility in the face of the priority of the domain of language, a domain that we cannot undermine and in which all consciousness and all knowledge articulates itself. From Nietzsche we learned to doubt the grounding of truth in the self-certainty of self-consciousness. Through Freud we became acquainted with the astonishing scientific discoveries that resulted from taking these doubts seriously. And in Heidegger's fundamental critique of the concept of consciousness we have seen the conceptual prejudice that stems from Greek Logos-philosophy and that, in the modern turn, put the concept of the subject in the center. All of this lent a certain primacy to the 'linguisticality' of our experience of the world. Over against the illusion of self-consciousness as well as the naïveté of a positive concept of facts, the midworld of language has proven itself to be the true dimension of that which is given.

In light of all this, one can understand the rise of the concept of interpretation. It is a word that originally arose out of the mediating relationship, the function of the intermediary between speakers of different languages; that is, it originally concerned the translator and was then transferred to the deciphering of texts that are difficult to understand. And in the moment when the midworld of language presented itself to philosophical consciousness in its predetermined meaning, interpretation had to take a key position in philosophy. The career of the word began with Nietzsche and became a challenge to all positivism. Does the given exist from whose secure starting point knowledge can search for the universal, the law, the rule, and so find its fulfillment? Is the given not in fact the result of an interpretation? It is interpretation that performs the never fully complete mediation between man and world, and to this extent the fact that we understand something as something is the sole actual immediacy and givenness. The faith in certain agreed-upon theses, or *Protokollsätze*, as the foundation of all knowledge did not last long even in the Vienna Circle.[6] Even in the domain of the natural sciences, the grounding of scientific knowledge cannot avoid the hermeneutical consequences of the fact that the so-called "given" cannot be separated from interpretation.[7]

Only in the light of interpretation does something become a fact, and only within processes of interpretation is an observation expressible. Heidegger's critique of the phenomenological concept of consciousness, and—similarly in Scheler—of the concept of pure perception as dogmatic, revealed itself as even more radical. Thus, the hermeneutical understanding of something as something was discovered even in the so-called perception itself. In the final analysis, however, this means that for Heidegger interpretation is not an additional or appended procedure of knowing but constitutes the original structure of "Being-in-the-world."

But does this mean that interpretation is an insertion [*Einlegen*] of meaning and not a discovery [*Finden*] of meaning? This question, posed by Nietzsche, is obviously a question that decides the rank and extent of hermeneutics as well as the objections of its opponents. In any case, the point that must be firmly adhered to is that only on the basis of the concept of interpretation does the concept of the text come to constitute a central concept in the structure of linguisticality; indeed, what characterized the concept of text is that it presents itself only in connection with interpretation and from the point of view of interpretation, as the authentic given that is to be understood. This is true even in the dialogical process of coming to an understanding insofar as one lets the disputed statements be repeated and thereby pursues the intention to a binding formulation, an event that generally results in a transcript or protocol. In a similar manner, the interpreter of a text asks what is really in the text. This too can lead to a biased and prejudicial response to the extent that everyone who asks a question tries to find a direct confirmation of his/her own assumptions in the answer. But in such an appeal to that which is in the text, the text itself still remains the first point of relation over and against the questionability, arbitrariness, or at least multiplicity of the possibilities of interpretation directed towards it.

This is confirmed by the history of the word. The concept of "text" has entered into modern speech essentially from two fields. On the one hand, there is the text of scripture, whose interpretation was carried out in sermons and church doctrine; in this case, the text represents the basis of all exegesis, which in turn presupposes the truths of faith. The other natural use of the word "text" is found in connection with music. Here it is the text for song, for the musical interpretation of words, and here too such a text is not so much a pregiven as it is a residue of the performance of the song. Both of these natural ways of using the word "text" point back to the linguistic usage of the Roman jurists of late antiquity who, by the Justinian codification of the laws, used this text to overcome the disputability of its interpretation and application. From here the word found a wider extension so that it covered all that which resists integration in experience and represents the return to the supposed given that would provide a better orientation for understanding.

The metaphorical talk of the book of nature rests upon the same foundations.[8] It is a book the text of which was written by the hand of God and that the researcher is called upon to decipher, namely, to render readable and comprehensible by way of his interpretation. Thus, we find the hermeneutical relationship involved in our concept of text whenever we encounter resistance to our primordial assumption of the meaningfulness of the given. The intimacy with which text and interpretation are interwoven is thoroughly apparent insofar as even the tradition of a text is not always reliable as a basis for an interpretation. Indeed, it is often interpretation that first leads to the critical restoration of the text. There is therefore a methodological gain to be realized in making this inner relation of interpretation and text clear.

The methodological gain resulting from this observation made about language is that here "text" must be understood as a hermeneutical concept. This implies that the text is not regarded from the perspective of grammar and linguistics, and as divorced from any content that it might have; that is, that it is not to be viewed as an end product the production of which is the object of an analysis whose intent is to explain the mechanism that allows language as such to function at all. From the hermeneutical standpoint—which is the standpoint of every reader—the text is a mere intermediate product [*Zwischenprodukt*], a phase in the event of understanding that, as such, certainly includes a definite abstraction, namely, the isolation and reification involved in this very phase. But this abstraction moves in precisely the reverse direction from the one upon which linguists rely. The linguist does not want to enter into the discussion of the topic that is spoken of in the text; rather, he wants to shed light upon the functioning of language as such, whatever the text may say. He does not make that which is communicated in the text his theme, but instead asks how it is possible to communicate anything at all by whatever means of punctuation and symbolization that occur.

For the hermeneutical approach, on the other hand, comprehending what is said is the sole concern. For this, the functioning of language is merely a precondition. So also a first precondition is that an expression be acoustically intelligible, or that a printed text be decipherable, so that the comprehension of what is spoken, or written, is at least possible. The text must be readable.

Once again linguistic usage offers us an important clue. We speak of the readability of a text in a rather pretentious sense when we merely wish to express a minimum qualification for evaluating a style or judging a translation. Naturally, this is a figurative way of speaking. But, as is often the case with such speech, it makes things thoroughly clear: the negative correspondence here is unreadability, and this always means that as a written expression the text did not fulfill its task of being understood without any difficulties. We find further confirmation here that we always already look ahead to an understanding of that which is said in the text. It is only from this point that we grant and qualify a text as readable.

From philological work this is well-known as the task of restoring a readable text. However, it is clear that this task is always posed in such a way that it takes as its starting point a certain understanding of the text. Only where the text is already deciphered and the deciphered does not allow itself to be unhesitatingly transformed into understandability, are questions raised about what is really in the text and whether or not the traditional reading, that is, the commonly accepted reading, is correct. The treatment of the text by the philologist who produces a readable text corresponds completely to what happens in direct, yet not only acoustical, auditory transmission. We say therefore that one has heard when one can understand. And correspondingly, uncertainty about a specific reading of a text resembles the uncertainty connected with one's grasp of an oral message. In both cases a feedback [*Rückkoppelung*] comes into play. Preunderstanding, anticipation of meaning, and thereby a great many circumstances that do not appear in the text as such, play a role in the reading of the text [*Auffassung des Textes*]. This becomes completely clear when it is a matter of translation from foreign languages. Here the mastery of a foreign language is a mere precondition. If the "text" can be spoken of at all in such cases, then it is because it not only has to be understood but also carried over into another language. In this manner it becomes a "text"; for that which is said is not simply understood, rather it becomes an object—the point is to reproduce that which was intended rather than the multiplicity of possible intentions. There is still another indirect hermeneutical relation here: every translation, even the so-called literal reproduction, is a sort of interpretation.

In sum, what linguistics makes its theme, insofar as it leaves out of account the matter of reaching agreement in understanding of content, represents for understanding itself only an extreme case of a possible way of viewing. In opposition to this view in linguistics, I believe that what makes understanding possible is precisely the forgetfulness of language, a forgetting of the formal elements in which the discourse or the text is encased. Only where the process of understanding is disrupted, that is, where understanding will not succeed, are questions asked about the wording of the text, and only then can the reconstruction of the text become a task in its own right. In everyday speech, we differentiate between the wording of the text and the text itself, but it is not accidental that both of these designations can always also act as a substitute for the other. In Greek, too, language and writing are both contained in the concept of *"grammatikè."* Indeed the extension of the concept of the text to include oral discourse is hermeneutically well grounded. For in every case, whether of a spoken or written text, the understanding of the text remains dependent upon communicative conditions that, as such, reach beyond the merely codified meaning-content of what is said. One can almost say that if one needs to reach back to the wording of the text, that is, to the text as such, then this must always be motivated by something unusual having arisen in the situation of understanding.

This can be seen in the current use of the word "text" just as clearly as it can be demonstrated in the history of the word "text". Doubtless, there is a sort of vanishing point [*Schwundstufe*] of texts that we could hardly ever call a text, such as one's own notes that provided a support for one's recollections. Here the question of the text is posed only when memory fails and the notes appear alien and incomprehensible, and it is necessary to refer back to the signs and writing; that is, it is necessry to refer back to the notes as text. Generally, however, notes are not a text, because they appear as the mere trace of memory, a trace which is swallowed up in the return of what was intended by the entry.

But there is another extreme form of understanding that, in general, does not provoke a discussion of the text. Here I am referring to something like scientific communication, which presupposes definite conditions of understanding from the outset. The reason for this is to be found in the type of address it is. It is directed toward the specialist. As was true in the case of notes, which are only for myself, so too is scientific communication, even when it is published, not for everyone. It only tries to be understandable for one who is well acquainted with the level and language of research. When this condition is fulfilled, the partner will not generally return to the text qua text. He or she does that only when the information expressed seems to be implausible and he or she must ask whether or not there is a misunderstanding somewhere. The situation is, of course, different from that of the historian of science for whom the same scientific documents really are texts precisely because they require interpretation, in that the interpreter is not the intended reader, so the distance that exists between him and the original reader must be bridged. Indeed, the concept of the "original reader" is extremely vague, as I have emphasized elsewhere.⁹ But perhaps in the course of further research it will gain more exact definition. For the same reasons, one does not generally speak of a personal letter as a text when one is its recipient. Then one enters smoothly into the written situation of a conversation, as it were, so long as no special disruption of understanding makes it necessary to refer back to the exact text. Thus, for a written conversation basically the same fundamental condition obtains as for an oral exchange. Both partners must have the good will to try to understand one another. Thus, the

question becomes one of how far this situation can be extended and its implications applied. What if no particular addressee or group is intended, but rather a
nameless reader—or perhaps an outsider—wants to understand a text? The writing of a letter is an alternative form of attempting a conversation, and as in the
case of immediate linguistic contact or in all smoothly functioning exchanges,
only a disruption in communication provides a motive for reaching back to the
text as the "given."

In any case, like one who is in a conversation, the writer tries to impart what
he or she means, and that includes the other with whom one shared presuppositions and upon whose understanding one relies. The other takes what is said as
it is intended, that is, he or she understands because he or she fills out and
concretizes what is said and because he or she does not take what is said in its
abstract, literal meaning. That is also the reason one cannot say certain things in
letters that one can say in the immediacy of conversation, even when one sends
them to a partner with whom one is very close. There is too much that is
omitted in a letter that, in the immediacy of conversation, carries the proper
understanding; and furthermore, in conversation one always has the opportunity
to clarify or defend what was meant on the basis of some response. That is
recognized especially in Socratic dialogue and the Platonic critique of writing.
The *logoi* [sayings] which present themselves cut loose from any specific situation of communication [*Verständigungssituation*]—and this is collectively true of
written words—risk misuse and misunderstanding because they dispense with
the obvious corrections resident within living conversation.

Here we find a consequence suggested that is essential for hermeneutical
theory. If every printed text is cut off from the communicative situation, then
this implies something for the intention of writing itself. Because as a writer one
knows all of the problems of putting words in print, one is always steered by the
picture [*Vorblick*] one has of the recipient with whom one wants to reach an
equivalent understanding. While in living conversation one tries to reach understanding through the give-and-take of discussion, which means that one searches
for those words—and accompanies them with intonation and gesture—that one
expects will get through to the other, in writing the openness that is implied in
seeking the words cannot be communicated because the text is printed. Therefore a "virtual" horizon of interpretation and understanding must be opened in
writing the text itself, one that the reader must fill out. Writing is more than a
repetition in print of something spoken. To be sure, everything that is fixed in
writing refers back to what was originally said, but it must equally as much look
forward; for all that is said is always already directed toward understanding and
includes the other in itself.

Thus, we speak of the text of a transcript because, from the start, it was
intended as a document, and that means that what is fixed in it is to be referred
to. Precisely for this reason, a transcript requires the special mark and signature

of the partner. The same is true of the closing of contracts in business a~
politics.

With this we come to a comprehensive concept that lies at the basis of ~
constitution of "texts" and simultaneously makes clear the embeddedness of t~
"text" in the hermeneutical context: every return to the "text"—whether
concerns a printed text or merely the repetition of what is expressed
conversation—refers to that which was originally announced or pronounced and
that should be maintained as constituting a meaningful identity. What prescribes
to all reifications in writing their task is precisely that this thing being announced should be understood. The printed text should fix the original announcement [*Kundgabe*] in such a way that its sense is unequivocally
understandable. Here the task of the writer corresponds to that of the reader,
addressee, interpreter; that is, to achieve such an understanding and to let the
printed text speak once again. To this extent, reading and understanding mean
that what is announced is led back to its original authenticity. The task of
interpretation always poses itself when the meaning content of the printed word
is disputable and it is a matter of attaining the correct understanding of what is
being announced. However, this "thing that is being conveyed" [*"Kunde"*] is
not what the speaker or writer originally said, but rather what he would have
wanted to say to me if I had been his original interlocutor. It is well-known that
in the interpretation of "commands" or "orders" [*"Befehlen"*] as a hermeneutical problem, such orders are to be followed "according to their general sense"
[*"Sinngemäß"*] and not in their literal meaning. Accordingly, we must say that a
text is not simply a given object but a phase in the execution of the communicative event [*Verständigungsgeschehen*].

This general state of affairs is particularly well illustrated by judicial codification and correspondingly in judicial hermeneutics. With good reason judicial
hermeneutics functions as a sort of model: here the transference into written
form and the continual reference to the text are in special proximity. From the
outset that which is established as law serves to settle or avoid disputes. This is
always what motivates both the seekers (the parties to a dispute) as well as the
finders and speakers of justice (the judges) in their return to the text. The
formulation of laws, of legal contracts or legal decisions, is thus especially
exacting, and the fact that it is makes it all the more so. Here a verdict or an
agreement is to be formulated so that its judicial sense emerges from the texts
univocally and so that misuse or distortion is avoided. "Documentation" demands that an authentic interpretation must succeed, even if the authors themselves, the legislator or a party to a contract, are not available. This implies that
from the outset the written formulation must take into account the interpretive
free space that arises for the "reader" of the text who has to employ this space.
Here—whether by proclamation or codification—the effort is always to avoid
strife, to exclude misunderstandings and misuse, and to make univocal under-

standing possible. In contrast to the public proclamation of a law or the actual closing of a contract, putting the law or contract into print is only an effort to secure an additional guarantee. This implies, however, that here too there remains a free space of meaningful concretization, a concretization that has to carry out the interpretation for the purpose of practical application.

The claim to validity in the laying down of law, whether codified or not, rests on the fact that it is like a text. Therefore, law, like the statute, constantly requires interpretation for practical application, and conversely this means that interpretation has already entered into every practical application. Legal decisions, precedents, or the prevailing administration of the law therefore always have a creative legal function. To this extent, the judicial example shows with exemplary clarity just how much every construction of a text is related in advance to interpretation, that is, to its correct, analogous application. I would maintain that the hermeneutical problem is basically the same for oral and written discourse. One thinks, for example, of taking testimony from witnesses. In order to guarantee their neutrality, witnesses are not supposed to be initiated into the larger context of the investigation and the rigors of the process of making a judgment. So the question that is put to them is something they encounter as having the abstractedness of a "text," and the answer that they have to give is equally abstract. This means that it is like a written utterance. The discontentedness of a witness with the written transcript of his testimony bears this out. He or she certainly cannot dispute his/her language, but he/she does not want to let it stand in such isolation and would prefer right away to interpret it himself, or herself. It seems to the witness that the duty of the court stenographer in making the transcript is to render an account such that, when the transcript is read back, every possible justice is done to the intended meaning of the speaker. Conversely, this example of the testimony of a witness shows how the procedure of writing, namely, the written component in proceedings feeds back into the way in which the conversation is handled. The witness, whose assertions are already placed in an isolated context, is, so to speak, already isolated because the results of the investigation will be put into written form. A similar state of affairs obviously holds true in cases where one has given a promise, an order, or a question in writing: this situation also contains an isolation from the original communicative situation and must express the original living sense in the style of something fixed in writing. What remains clear in all these instances is a relating back to the original communicative situation.

One way this relating back to the original communicative situation can also be facilitated is through the adding of punctuation, which points to the proper understanding that was found meanwhile in the record. Thus, the question mark, for example, is such an indication of how the recorded sentence really must be articulated. The very appropriate Spanish custom of putting a question between two question marks makes this basic intent clear in a persuasive manner: one already knows at the beginning of the sentence how one has to articulate the relevant phrases. On the other hand, the dispensibility of such punctuation aids, which were not to be found at all in many ancient cultures, confirms how understanding is, nevertheless, possible solely through the fixed givenness of the text. The mere sequence of written symbols without punctuation represents communicative abstraction in an extreme form.[10]

Now I should remark that there are doubtless many forms of linguistic communicative behavior that cannot possibly be subjected to this kind of finality. These are texts to such a degree that they are still regarded as self-evidently texts even when they are encountered totally apart from a person being addressed—as is the case, for instance, in literary representation. But even within the communicative event itself, we find texts that offer resistance and opposition to textualization. In order to throw into relief what it means for a text to fulfill its authentic being [*Bestimmung*] as text, and to do so in terms of textual forms, I would like first to distinguish three forms of opposition to textuality. These will form a backdrop that will enable the eminent mode of textualizing [*Textierung*] to become accessible to our view—and in the form of texts [*in Textgestalt*]. I shall call these three oppositional forms "antitexts" [*Antitexte*], "pseudotexts" [*Pseudotexte*], and "pretexts" [*Prätexte*].

By 'antitexts' I have in mind forms of discourse that oppose or resist textualization because in them the dominant factor is the situation of interactive speaking in which they take place. In this category falls every kind of joke. For, the fact that we do not mean something seriously but rather expect that it will be taken as a joke surely stations this form in the process and event of communication. It is in this event and not in the text itself that we find the signal that this is a joke—in the tone of voice, the accompanying gesture, the social situation itself, or whatever. Furthermore, a joking remark clearly belongs to the moment and thus really cannot be repeated.

Basically, the same applies to another quite classical form of mutual agreement, namely, irony. For the use of irony presupposes a common set of prior cultural understandings [*gemeinsame Vorverständigung*]. When one is able to say the opposite of what one means and still be sure that what one really means is understood, this clearly shows one is operating in a functioning communicative situation [*Verständigungsituation*]. The extent to which such "dissembling" or "pretending" ["*Verstellung,*" dissimulation, sham] (which really is none) is possible in the modality of writing depends on the degree of communicative preunderstanding and of reigning agreement [*der kommunikativen Vorverständigung und des Beherrschenden Einverständnisses*]. We know that the use of irony existed, for example, in very early aristocratic society and made a smooth transition into writing there. In this context we may mention the use of classical citations [popular in antiquity], often in a bowdlerized form. Here, too, the use of this form had the aim of societal solidarity. In this case, there was the proud rule of certain presuppositions with regard to culture, and thus they served and validated the interests of the aristocratic class. However, in cases where the relations among these preconditions for mutual understanding are not so clear, the transition into the fixity of written form becomes problematical. Just for this reason, interpreting the use of irony often poses an extraordinarily difficult hermeneutical task, and even the hypothesis that one is dealing with irony may be hard to defend. It has been said, and probably not unjustly, that to interpret something as irony often is nothing but a gesture of despair on the part of the interpreter. On the other hand, in our everyday life, if we use irony and are not understood, this registers a clear breakdown in mutual understanding [*Einverständnis*]. All this makes it quite clear that for a joke or irony to be possible at all, one must presuppose the existence of a *supporting mutual understanding* [*ein tragendes Einverständnis*]. Of course, one might argue that we could build up mutual understanding among people by having everyone recast ironic expressions into straightforward formulations that could not be misunderstood. Even if that were actually possible, such straightforward and unambiguous meaning will fall far short of the communicative meaning ironic discourse possesses.

The second type of text-opposed texts or "countertexts" I have labelled "pseudotexts." I refer here to the linguistic usage in speaking, and also in writing, of elements that really do not actually transmit the sense but rather are fillers [*Füllmaterial*] that provide something like rhetorical bridges over the flow of speaking. One could define the role of rhetoric in our speech by saying it is that which is other than the factual matter of our propositions [*Äußerungen*, expressions] and that it is the meaning-content that is conveyed in the text. It is that which possesses the purely operational and ritual function of exchange through speaking, whether in oral or written form. It is that component or portion of language which is devoid of meaning that I label "pseudotext." Every translator knows this phenomenon when, in transferring a text from one language into another, he or she has to recognize what is self-evidently filler material in the text and deal with it in an appropriate way. Sometimes the translator assumes there must be some authentic meaning in this filler material and by carrying over this dead wood into the target language actually destroys the authentic flow of what is being transmitted in the text. This is a difficulty that confronts every translator. It is not to be denied that the translator can often find equivalent expressions for such filler material, but the true task of translating means translating only what is meaning-bearing in the text. Meaningful translation must recognize and purge such filler materials. However, glancing ahead, I should emphasize the following point: this does not apply at all to any text with true literary quality, those that I call a "texts in the eminent sense" [*eminente Texte*]. Precisely on this difference rests the limit of translatability with regard to literary texts, an untranslatability that shows itself in the most varied nuances of meaning.

The third form of text-opposing or counter-texts are "pretexts." I mean by pretexts all communicative expressions or texts the understanding of which is not completed when one grasps the meaning that is intended in them. Rather, in them something masked or disguised comes to expression. Pretexts are texts that we interpret on the basis of something that is precisely what they do not mean. What they mean is merely pretence, an excuse, behind which is concealed the "meaning" [»*Sinn*«]. The interpretive task is posed, then, in terms of seeing through the wall of pretence and mediating what is truly coming to expression in the text.

Belonging to this type are ideologically slanted texts that are designed to shape public opinion. The very concept of ideology wants to suggest that what is involved in media that shape public opinion is not real distribution of information but a hidden guiding interest for which the distributed information serves only as an excuse, a pretext. Therefore the critique of ideology strives to go back behind the thing said and to trace the interests that are masked in it; for instance, the special interest of the bourgeois class in the context of capitalistic conflicts of interests. Even so, it is interesting to note that the attitude of the "critique of ideology" [*Ideologiekritik*] can itself be criticized as ideological, in that it represents antibourgeois interests, or whatever interests they may be, while at the same time masking its own tendentiousness as critique. One could view as the general motivation of this effort to get back to the hidden, underlying interests a concern about the breakdown of consensus, something Habermas calls "distortion of communication" [*Kommunikationsverzerrung*]. Distorted communication manifests itself both as a disruption of possible agreement in understanding and possible consensus, and thus motivates us to search for the true meaning behind the distortions. This turns out to be something like a decoding process.

The role that dreams have played in modern depth psychology represents yet another example of interpretation as going back behind a wall of pretext. It is certainly a fact that the experiences in our dream life are inconsistent. In them the logic of ordinary experience is for the most part put out of play. Of course, that does not exclude the possibility that out of the surprise-logic of dream life there can also arise an immediately attractive meaning that is comparable to the un-logic of fairy tales. In fact, narrative literature has taken as one of its possessions the genre of dreams and of fairy tales, as we find, for example, in the German Romantic. But in this case it is an aesthetic quality that narrative literature enjoys in the play of dream fantasy and which naturally can be interpreted in a literary and aesthetic way. In contrast, the same phenomenon of the dream can become the object of a totally different kind of interpretation if one seeks to go behind the fragments of dream recollection in order to reveal a true meaning, a meaning which has only disguised itself in the dream fantasies and which is capable of being decoded. It is this that constitutes the tremendous significance

of dream recollection in psychoanalytic treatment. With the help of dream interpretation, the analysis is able to set in motion an associative conversation that
removes mental blocks and ultimately frees patients of their neuroses. As is
well-known, this process of so-called analysis goes through many complicated
stages in reconstructing the original dream text and its meaning. Certainly this
meaning is something quite other than that which the dreamer "intended" or
even that which the two dream interpreters had read out at the beginning, a
meaning which now, through its clarification, has resolved the unsettling element in the dream experience. Rather, what motivates the interpreters here to go
back behind what is consciously "meant" [*das »Gemeinte«*], behind the wall of
pretext [*Vorwand,* also excuse] is the fact that the occurrence [*Geschehen*] of
consensual understanding on which mutual agreement rests has been totally
disturbed, put out of order [*die totale Gestörtheit des auf Einverständnis beru-
henden Verständigungsgeschehens*], which is what we call "neurosis."

The same general interpretive structure is also found in the well-known psychopathology of daily life, which is an area quite separate from concern with
specific neurotic disturbances. In psychopathology, actions that go wrong
[*Fehlhandlungen*] are rendered suddenly quite intelligible by recourse to unconscious feelings and impulses. Here again the motivation for going back to the
unconscious is the incoherence, the incomprehensibility, of the action in question [the *Fehlhandlung*]. Through the light that is shed on it the puzzling action
is rendered comprehensible and its irritating quality removed.

The relation between text and interpretation, which I have taken as the theme
of this essay, in these instances takes a special form, a form which Ricoeur has
called the "hermeneutics of suspicion." However, I believe it is a mistake to
privilege these forms of distorted intelligibility, of neurotic derangement, as the
normal case in textual interpretation.[11]

The point I have been trying to make, or prepare for, in everything I have said
so far is that the connection between text and interpretation is fundamentally
changed when one deals with what is called the "literary text." But before
finally turning to this kind of text, let us sum up. In all the cases we have
discussed, we saw the motivation for interpretation emerge and we saw that
something in the communicative process was constituted as a text, but the interpretation, like the so-called text itself, was subordinated and ordered to the
process of reaching agreement in understanding [*das Geschehen der Verständigung*]. This corresponds perfectly, of course, to the literal meaning of the term
interpres, which refers to someone who speaks between and therefore has first
of all the primordial function of the interpreter, someone who stands between
speakers of various languages and through intermediary speaking brings the
separated persons together. In the same way as an interpreter overcomes the
barrier of a foreign language, so also within one's own language, when disturbances of agreement in understanding arise, something like this translation pro-

cedure is required, whereby the identity of the proposition being asserted is found by going back to the communicative event, and this means by potentially dealing with it as a text.

In this form of interpretation, whatever is alienating in a text, whatever makes the text unintelligible, is to be overcome and thereby cancelled out by the interpreter. The interpreter steps in and speaks only when the text (the discourse) is not able to do what it is supposed to do, namely be heard and understood on its own. The interpreter has no other function than to disappear completely into the achievement of full harmony in understanding [*Verständigung*]. The discourse of the interpreter is therefore not itself a text; rather it *serves* a text. This does not mean, however, that the contribution of the interpreter to the manner in which the text is heard is completely swallowed up. It is just not thematic, not something objective as text; rather, it has entered into the text. In general, this is the way the relation of text and interpretation is usually characterized. Interestingly enough, this is the point at which a hermeneutically structural moment pushes itself into bold relief. For this stepping between and speaking [*Dazwischenreden*] has itself the structure of dialogue. The linguistic interpreter, who is mediating between two parties, cannot avoid experiencing his/her own distance between the two positions as a kind of superiority over the partiality of each side. His/her help in reaching agreement in understanding is therefore not limited to the purely linguistic level; rather it always gets into mediating the matter itself, seeking to bring about a settlement of the claims and the limits of both parties. The one who was merely an "interlocutor" [*Der »Dazwischenredende«*] becomes a "go-between" [*»Unterhändler«*, negotiator, intermediary]. Now it seems to me that the relationship between text and reader is a similar one. When the interpreter overcomes what is alienating in the text and thereby helps the reader to an understanding of the text, his/her own stepping back is not a disappearance in any negative sense; rather, it is an entering into the communication in such a way that the tension between the horizon of the text and the horizon of the reader is dissolved. I have called this a "fusion of horizons" [*Horizontverschmelzung*]. The separated horizons, like the different standpoints, merge with each other. And the process of understanding a text tends to captivate and take reader up into that which the text says, and in this fusion the text too drops away.

But then there is literature! That is to say, texts that do not disappear in our act of understanding them but stand there confronting our understanding with normative claims and which continually stand before every new way the text can speak. What is it that distinguishes these texts from all others? What does it betoken for the mediating discourse of the interpreter that a text can be "there" in this way?[12]

My thesis is this: These texts are only authentically there when they come back into themselves. Then they are *texts* in the original and authentic sense.

The words of such texts are authentically there only in coming back to themselves. They fulfill the true meaning of the text out of themselves. They speak. Literary texts are such texts that in reading them aloud one must also listen to them, if only with the inner ear. When such texts are recited, one not only listens but inwardly speaks with them. They attain their true existence only when one has learned them "by heart." Then they live. They live in the remembrances of the great bards, the chanting choruses [*Choreuten*], the lyric singers. As if written in the soul, they are on their way to scripturality [*Schriftlichkeit*]. Thus, it is not surprising at all that in cultures that read, such distinguished texts are called "literature."

A literary text is not just the rendering of spoken language into a fixed form. Indeed, a literary text does not refer back to an already spoken word at all. This fact has hermeneutic consequences. Interpretation in this case is no longer merely a means of getting back to an original expression of something [*ursprüngliche Äußerung*]. Rather, the literary text is text in the most special sense, text in the highest degree, precisely because it does not point back to some primordial or originary act of linguistic utterance but rather in its own right prescribes all repetitions and acts of speaking. No speaking can ever completely fulfill the prescription given in the poetic text. The poetic text exercises a normative function that does not refer back either to an original utterance nor to the intention of the speaker but is something that seems to originate in itself, so that in the fortune and felicity of its success, a poem surprises and overwhelms even the poet.

Thus, it is far from accidental that the word "literature" has acquired a sense of positive valuation, so that when something belongs to the category of literature this represents a special distinction. A text of this kind represents not just the rendering of oral discourse into a fixed form; rather, it possesses its own authenticity in itself. When we look at the basic nature of discourse, we find that what constitutes it is that the listener needs both to follow it from beginning to end and at the same time to be focussed on what the discourse is conveying to him or her. But in literature we find that *language itself* comes to appearance in a very special way.

This self-presentation of the word is not easy to grasp correctly. Words in literary texts obviously still maintain their discursive meaning and carry the sense of a discourse that means something. The quality of a literary text is necessarily such that it leaves untouched this primacy of the content belonging to all discourse; in fact, the primacy of the discursive meaning so increases that the relation of its assertions to actuality is suspended. This does not mean, however, that one should overemphasize how a text is said [*das Wie des Gesagtseins*, the how of its being said]. For then we will end up speaking not of the art of the words but of artistry, not of a certain tone that prescribes how a song is to be sung but rather about matters of poetising imitation. That is to say, we would be speaking not of style whose incomparability we may rightly admire but rather of manner, whose presence now is disturbingly noticeable. Nevertheless it is true that a literary text demands to become present in its linguistic appearance and not just to carry out its function of conveying a message. It must not only be read, it must also be listened to—even if only mostly with our inner ear.

Thus, it is in the literary text that the word first attains its full self-presence [*Selbstpräsenz*]. Not only does the word make what is said present; it also makes itself present in its radiant actuality as sound. Just as style constitutes a very effective factor in a good text and yet such a text does not put itself forward as a piece of stylistic decoration [*als ein Stilkunststück*], so too is the actuality of words and of discourse as sound always indissolubly bound up with the transmission of meaning. Nevertheless, there is a profound difference between the functioning of words in ordinary discourse and in literature. On the one hand, in discourse as such we are continually running ahead in thought searching for the meaning, so that we let the appearance of the words fall away as we listen and read for the meaning being conveyed; on the other hand, with a literary text the self-manifestation of each and every word has a meaning in its sonority, and the melody of the sound is also used by the discourse to augment what is said through the words. In a literary work, a peculiar tension is generated between the directedness to meaning inherent in discourse and the self-presentation inherent in its appearance. Every part of speech, every member, every individual word that submits to the unity of meaning in the sentence, represents in itself also a kind of unity of meaning insofar as through its meaning something meant is evoked. So far as the word issues forth from the play within its own unity and does not function merely as a means of conveying the meaning of the discourse as a whole [*Redesinn*], to that extent the multiplicity of meaning within the word's own naming power is allowed to unfold. Thus, we refer to connotations that also speak along with a word when, in a literary text, the word shines forth in its full meaning [*in seiner Bedeutung erscheint*].

But the individual word as carrier of its own meaning and as co-carrier of the meaning of the discourse [*Redesinn*] is still only an abstract moment in the discourse. Everything must be seen in the larger whole of *syntax*. Of course, in a literary text this is a syntax that is not unconditionally and not only the customary grammar. Just as the speaker enjoys certain syntactic freedoms that the hearer is able to accommodate because he/she is also taking in all the modulations and gesticulations of the speaker, so also the poetic text—with all the nuances which it shows—has its own freedoms. These nuances are so subordinated to the actuality of sound that they help the whole of the text to a greatly strengthened power of meaning. Indeed, even in the realm of ordinary prose we know that a discourse is not the same thing as a written document [*eine Rede keine »Schreibe« ist*], and an address [*Vortrag*] is not the same thing as a lecture [*Vorlesung*]—that is to say, it is not a "paper." This applies even more strongly in the case of literature in the eminent sense of the term. It overcomes not just the abstractness of being written in such a way that the text becomes readable, that is to say, intelligible in its meaning. Rather, a literary text possesses its own status. Its linguistic presence as text is such as to demand repetition of the words in the original power of their sound—not in such a way as to reach back to some original speaking of them, however, but rather looking forward toward a new, ideal speaking. The web of connections between meanings is never exhausted in the relations that exist between the main meanings of the words. In fact, precisely the accompanying play of relations of meaning that is not bound up with discursive meaning-teleology gives the literary sentence its volume. Certainly, these relations of meaning would never come to appearance at all if the whole of the discourse did not, so to speak, "hold onto itself" [*an sich hielte*], inviting the reader or hearer to tarry, and impelling the reader or hearer to listen and listen. This process of becoming a listener nevertheless remains, of course, like every listening, a listening to something, something that is grasped as the pattern or totality of meaning of a discourse [*die Sinngestalt einer Rede*].

It is very difficult to assign cause and effect here. That is to say: Is it this enhancement in volume that suspends a text's referential and message-conveying function and makes it a literary text? Or is it the reverse: that the suspension of the positing of reality that characterizes a text as poetry, and this means as the self-manifestation of language, lets the fullness of meaning first emerge in its total volume? Manifestly the two factors are inseparable, and in the continuum between artistic prose and pure poetry the place the text occupies will depend in each individual case on how strong a role is played by manifestation of language in the totality of the meaning.

How complex the role orderly sequence in discourse is for achieving unity and how important is the placement of its building blocks—that is, the words— becomes clear in extreme cases—for example, when a word in its polyvalence suddenly pops up and asserts itself as an autonomous carrier of meaning. Something like this we call a "play on words" [*Wortspiel*]. For instance, it is not to be denied that often a play on words is used only as a kind of discursive decoration [*Redeschmuck*]—an ornament that allows the spirit of the speaker to radiate forth, while it remains fully subordinated to the intentional meaning of the discourse. However, the play on words can elevate itself to a kind of autonomy [*Selbständigkeit*] and declare its independence. The result is that what the discourse as a whole is supposed to mean suddenly becomes ambiguous, and the clarity of its intention is lost. Behind the unity of the manifestation of the word in sound there suddenly shines forth the hidden unity of variegated and even opposing meanings. In this context, we recall that Hegel has spoken of the dialectical instinct of language, and Heraclitus found in the play of words one of the best tools for illustrating his basic insight that opposed things in truth are one and the same. But that is a philosophical manner of speaking. Here, too, it is a matter of breakdowns [*Brechungen*] in the natural tendencies of meaning in discourse, which are productive for philosophical thinking precisely because language in this way is compelled to give up its immediate signifying of objects and to help bring to appearance mental mirrorings, mirrorings of thought [*gedanklichen Spiegelungen*]. The multiplicity of meanings found in word-plays represents the densest form in which speculative thinking comes to appearance, a thinking that explains judgments that oppose each other. Dialectic is the representation of the speculative, as Hegel says.

For the literary text it is a different matter, however, for precisely the following reason: The function of word-play is just not compatible with the many riches and dimensions [*vielsagenden Vielstelligkeit*] of the poetic word. In a literary text, the accompanying meanings that go along with a main meaning certainly are what give the language its literary volume, but they are able to do this by virtue of the fact that they are subordinated to the unity of meaning of the discourse and the other meanings are only suggested. Plays on words, however, are not simply plays on the polyvalence of words out of which poetic discourse is shaped; rather, in them independent meanings are played off against each other. Thus, play on words shatters the unity of discourse and demands to be understood in a higher relation of reflective meanings. Just for this reason, if someone persists in the use of word-play and witticisms, we become irritated because it disrupts the unity of the discourse. Certainly in a song or a lyric poem, indeed everywhere that the melodic figuration of the language predominates, the insertion of a play on words would scarcely enhance the effect. Naturally it is somewhat different in the case of dramatic speaking, where the interaction is there to govern the scene. One thinks, for instance, of stichomythia, or of the self-destruction of the hero that is already announced as a play on words in the hero's own name.[13] And again it is quite different where the poetic discourse takes the shape neither of the flow of narrative, nor the stream of song, nor dramatic presentation, but rather consciously engages in the play of reflection, to which obviously belongs the shattering of one's discursive expectations. Thus, in a very reflective lyric, the play on words can take on a productive function. One thinks, for instance, of the hermetic lyrics of Paul Celan. Yet one also must ask oneself here if the path of placing such a reflexive burden on the words does not in the end just become no longer passable. It is quite clear that Mallarmé, for instance, tried out word-plays in some of his prose pieces, like *Igitur,* but when he came to the full body of sound in poetic forms, he hardly plays with words. The verses of his *Salut* are certainly many-layered and fulfill expectations of meaning on such various levels as a drinker's toast and a balance sheet of life, wavering between the foam of champagne in the glass and the trail left in the waves by the ship of life. But both dimensions of meaning can be carried out as the same melodious gesture of language and in the same unity of discourse.*

This also holds good for *metaphor*. In a poem, metaphor is so bound up with the play of sounds, word meanings, and the meaning of the discourse that it does not really stand out as metaphor. For in a poem the prose of ordinary discourse is not found at all. Even in prose poetry [*dichterische Prosa*] metaphor scarcely has a place. Metaphor disappears when intellectual insight which it serves is awakened. Actually, rhetoric is the realm where metaphor holds sway. In rhetoric one enjoys metaphor as metaphor. In poetry, a theory of metaphor as little deserves a place of honor as a theory of word-play.

This brief digression teaches us how multileveled and differentiated the interplay of sound and meaning is in discourse and in writing, when it comes to literature. In fact, one begins to wonder how the mediating discourse of the interpreter could be taken over into the act of interpreting the poetic text at all. The answer to this question can only be approached in a very radical way. For in contrast to all other texts, the literary text is not interrupted by the dialogical and intermediary speaking of the interpreter; rather it is simply accompanied by the interpreter's constant co-speaking. This allows the structure of temporality

---

*GW 2 355 offers the following footnote, superseding Forget's footnote in *TI*: "The sonnet of Mallarmé, of which I offer an artless German paraphrase [represented here in English translation] runs as follows:

Rien, cette écume, vierge vers	Nothing, this foam, innocent verse
A ne désigner que la coupe;	Points only to the edge of the cup;
Telle loin se noie une troupe	In the farther distance splash a troop
De sirènes mainte á l'envers.	Of sirens, mostly turned away.
Nous naviguons, ö mes divers	We travel thence, my so unlike
Amis, moi déjà sur la poupe	Friends—I already at the stern
Vous l'avant fasteaux qui coupe	You at the proud bow, which cuts
Le flot de foudres et d'hivers;	The flux of lightning and storms [not winter?]
Une ivresse belle m'engage	A fine intoxication lets me
Sans craindre mëme son tangage	Without even fearing its oscillation
De porter debout ce salut	Offer, standing, this salute
Solitude, récif, étoile	Solitude, cliff, star
A n'importe ce qui valut	May be whatever it may be
Le blanc souci de notre toile.	Wherever the care of the white sail leads us.

Philippe Forget, the editor of *Text und Interpretation* (Munich, 1984), cites page 50 of Uwe Japp, *Hermeneutik* (Munich, 1977), pages 80ff. There three levels are distinguished (borrowing from Rastier): there "saturated analysis" [»gesättigte Analyse«] is carried to absurd extremes, *salut* is no longer understood as *greeting* but as *rescue* (*récif* !! [cliff, reef]) and the white care [*blanc souci*] is paper, something not to be encountered at all in the text, even not in the self-related *vierge vers* [virginal verse]. This is indeed method without truth.

[*Zeitlichkeit*], which belongs to all discourse, to be annulled. Indeed, the categories of time that we use in connection with discourse and works of art in language constitute a peculiar difficulty when it comes to literary texts. One speaks of presence in relation to literary texts and even of the self-presentation of the poetic word as I myself did above. But I must emphasize: One draws a false conclusion if one thinks one can understand such presence with the language of metaphysics as presence-at-hand [*des Vorhandenen*], or with the concept of objectifiability. That is not the presentness which belongs to the literary work, indeed, it does not belong to any text at all. Language and writing exist always in their referential function [*Verweisung*]. They *are* not, but rather they *mean,* and that applies also then even when the thing meant is nowhere else than in the appearing word. Poetic speaking comes to pass only in the act of speaking [*Vollzug des Sprechens*] or reading itself, and of course this entails that it is not there without being understood.

The temporal structure of speaking and of reading represents a largely unexplored problem. That one cannot apply the simple schema of succession here becomes immediately clear when one sees that such a schema really describes the process of spelling but not that of reading. Someone wanting to read by spelling things out is not reading. In general the same principles apply to silent reading and to reading aloud. To read aloud well to another means to so mediate the interplay of meaning and sound that it seems to occur for itself and to come forth anew. When one reads aloud one reads to someone, and that means one turns and addresses him or her. And the reader belongs to the text. Reading out loud, like lecturing, remains "dialogical" [*Vorsprechen wie Vorlesen bleibt* »*dialogisch*«]. Even the simple act of reading in which one reads something to oneself is dialogical, in that in it one must bring the sound and the meaning as much as possible into harmony.

The art of recitation is not fundamentally any different. It only demands special technique because the audience is an anonymous mixture of people and yet it is necessary that the poetic text be taken up and realized in each individual listener. We are all familiar with a practice we call "reciting" [*Aufsagen*] that actually corresponds to spelling out what we read. Again, this is not really speaking but merely arranging a series of fragments of meaning one after another. In German, this happens when children learn lines of poetry by heart and recite them to the joy of the parents. In contrast, a person truly skilled in recitation, or a great artist, will render a linguistic gestalt fully present, like the actor who must play his role as if the words had been newly found at that very moment. This cannot be a mere series of pieces of discourse; rather it must be a whole, made up of meaning and sound, which "stands" in itself. For this reason, the ideal speaker will make not him- or herself but only the text present, which must reach in its full power even a blind person who cannot see his gestures. Goethe once said, "There is no higher and purer pleasure than with closed eyes to have someone recite to you—not declaim—in a naturally right voice a piece of Shakespeare."[14] There is some question, however, whether this kind of recitation is possible for every type of poetic text. Are there perhaps some where it is not possible at all? What about meditative poetry? Even in the history of lyric poetry this problem arises. Choral lyrics, and in general everything musical that invites one to sing with the singer, are completely different from the kind of tone one finds in the elegy. Reading meditative poetry seems possible only as a solitary process.

In any case, one sees that the schema of serial succession is totally out of place here. It is instructive to recall what in Latin class was called "construing," an art one learned in connection with parsing Latin prose: The student must look for the verb and then the subject, and from there articulate the whole collection of words until elements that at the outset seemed disparate suddenly come together into a meaning. Aristotle once described the freezing of a liquid when it is shaken as a *schlagartigen Umschlag,* a sudden reversal that comes like a blow from without. It is like this with the blow-like suddenness of understanding, as the disordered fragments of the sentence, the words, suddenly crystallize into the unity of a meaning of the whole sentence. Listening and reading apparently both possess the time structure of understanding, whose circular character counts among the earliest insights of rhetoric and hermeneutics.

This general structure holds for all listening and all reading. In the case of literary texts the situation [*Sachlage*] is far more complex. There we do not just have to do with the gleaning of a piece of information transmitted by a text. In reading a literary text one does not just hurry impatiently and unswervingly to the end-meaning, the grasping of which signals that one has gotten the message. Certainly it is true that there is something like a sudden instant of understanding here in which the unity of the whole formulation is illuminated. We find this phenomenon both in relation to the poetic text as well as the artistic image. Relations of meaning are recognized—even if vague and fragmentary. In both of these cases the operation of copying the real is suspended. The text with its charge of meaning [*Sinnbezug*] constitutes the only present. When we utter or read literary texts, we are thrown back on the meaning and sound relations that articulate the framework of the whole, not just once but each time. We leaf back through the text, begin anew, read anew, discover new dimensions of meaning. What stands at the end is not the secure consciousness of having understood the matter so that now one can leave the text behind, but rather just the opposite. One goes ever deeper into the text the more the charges of meaning and sound in it enter into consciousness. We do not leave the text behind us but allow ourselves to enter into it. We then are in the text like everyone who speaks is in the words he says and does not hold them at a distance as if they were tools that one uses and puts away. For this reason, to talk in terms of "applying" words is incorrect in a rather curious way. It does not come to grips with actual speaking but deals with speaking more as if speaking were like using the lexicon of a foreign language. One must set fundamental limits on all discourse about rules and prescriptions when one is dealing with actual speaking. This applies with a vengeance to the literary text. The literary text is not "right" because it says what anyone and everyone would have said but it has a new, unique kind of rightness that distinguishes it as a work of art. Every word "sits" there in such a way that it appears almost without possibility of substitution, and in a certain way it really can have no substitute.

It was Wilhelm Dilthey who, in a later development of Romantic idealism really pointed the way for us in this matter. In trying to defend himself against the prevailing monopoly of causal thinking, he spoke of a *matrix of effects—Wirkungszusammenhang*—instead of simple cause and effect, that is of a set of connections existing among the effects themselves, leaving fully aside the fact that they each had their causes. For this purpose he introduced the later highly respected concept of "structure," and showed how the understanding of structures necessarily has a circular form. Taking his lead from musical listening— for which absolute music with its extreme lack of conceptual content [*Begriffslosigkeit*] provides a prime example because it positively excludes all theory of representation—he spoke of a concentration into a middle point and he made the temporal structure of understanding a theme. This has a parallel in aesthetics where, whether of a literary text or a picture, one speaks of "form" or "structure" [*Gebilde*, something shaped into a certain form or structure; cf. *Wahrheit und Methode*, "*Verwandlung ins Gebilde*," "transformation into structure"]. The general meaning of "*Gebilde*" suggests something not understood from the vantage point of a preplanned finished state one knows in advance but rather something that has developed into its own pattern from within and thus is perhaps to be grasped in further formations [*Bildung*]. To understand this idea is, in itself, clearly an important task. The task is to build up and establish what a *Gebilde* [shaped form, structure] is; to construe something that is not "constructed"—and that means that all efforts at construction are withdrawn. With regard to literary texts, while it is true that the unity of understanding and reading is only accomplished in a reading that understands and at that moment leaves behind the linguistic appearance of the text, it is also true that something else speaks in the literary text that makes present the changing relationships of sound and meaning. It is the temporal structure of this movement [*die Zeitstruktur der Bewegtheit*], which we call "whiling" [*Verweilen*, tarrying, lingering], that occupies this presence and into which all mediatory discourse of interpretation must enter. Without the readiness of the person receiving and assimilating [*des Aufnehmenden*] to be "all ears" [*ganz Ohr zu sein*], no poetical text will speak.

In closing, perhaps a famous example may serve as illustration. It is the final line of a poem by Mörike, *Auf eine Lampe—On a Lamp*. [15] The line reads: "*Was aber schön ist, selig scheint es in ihm selbst."* ["What is beautiful, however, shines blissfully in itself."]

This particular line was the focus of a discussion between Emil Staiger and Martin Heidegger. I am interested in it here, however, only as an exemplary case. In this verse, one encounters two apparently trivial and commonplace words: *"scheint es."* This can be understood in the sense of *"anscheinend"* [apparently], *dokei* [Greek: it appears], *"videtur"* [Latin], *"il semble"* [French], "it seems," *"pare"* [Italian], and so forth. This prosaic understanding of the phrase makes sense and for this reason has found its defenders. But one also notices that it does not obey the law of verse [*Gesetz des Verses*]. This will allow us to show why *"scheint es"* here means "it shines," or *"splender"* [Latin, radiates]. In this case, a hermeneutical principle can be applied: In cases of conflict [*bei Anstöße*] the larger context should decide the issue. Every double possibility of understanding, however, is an offense [*Anstoß*]. Here it is decisively evident that the word beautiful in the line is applied to a lamp. That is what the poem as a whole is asserting and is a message that should be understood throughout the poem. A lamp that does not light up any more because it has become an old-fashioned and bygone thing hanging in a *"Lustgemach"* [pleasure room] ("Who notices it now?"), here gains its own brightness because it is a work of art. There is little doubt that *das Scheinen* here was said of the lamp, a lamp which shines even when no one is using it.

In a very scholarly contribution to this whole discussion Leo Spitzer described in great detail the literary genre of such thing-poems and he presented in a very persuasive way their place in literary history. Heidegger, for his part, has correctly explored the conceptual connection between *"schön"* and *"scheinen,"* which is reminiscent of Hegel's famous phrase about the "sensory appearing/shining forth of the Idea"—*sinnlichen Scheinen der Idee.* But there are other grounds immanent in the text, also. It is precisely the way the sound and meaning of the words work together that provide us with a clear further point that is decisive. The "s"-sounds in this final line form a firm web [»*was aber schön ist, selig scheint es in ihm selbst*«] and together with the metric modulation of the line (a metric accent falls on *schön, selig, scheint, in,* and *selbst*) this constitutes a melodic unity of phrase that leaves absolutely no place for a reflexive irruption such as *"scheint es"* in its prosaic sense would be. For in general we speak prose all the time, as Molière's Monsieur Jourdain learns to his surprise. In fact, precisely this has led contemporary poetry to extremely hermetic styles in order not to let prose break in. Here, in Mörike's poem, such a wavering in the direction of prose is never far away. Several times the language of this poem actually gets close to prose (»*wer achtet sein?*«). Given the place of this line in the whole, namely that it is the conclusion of the poem, it has a specially gnomic weight. In fact, the poem illustrates through its own assertion why the gold of this line is not of the order of some kind of note of instruction, like a banknote, or a piece of information, but itself has its own value. This shining is not only understood but it radiates out over the whole of the appearing [*Erscheinung*] of this lamp that hangs unnoticed in a forgotten pleasure room. And it never shines more than in these verses. The inner ear hears the correspondences between "*schön*" and "*selig*" and "*scheinen*" and "*selbst*"; moreover, the "*selbst*" with which the rhythm ends and falls silent, lets the silent motion resound within our inner ear. It allows to appear to our inner eye the quiet self-streaming-away of the light [*Sich-Verströmen des Lichtes*], which we name "shining" [*scheinen*]. Thus, our understanding understands not only what is said about the beautiful and what is expressed there about the autonomy of the work of art, which does not depend on any context of use; our ear hears, and our understanding takes in, the shining of the beautiful [*den Schein des Schönen*] as its true nature. The interpreter, who gives his reasons, disappears—and the text speaks.

Jacques Derrida

2. *Three Questions to Hans-Georg Gadamer**
Translated by Diane Michelfelder and Richard Palmer

During the lecture and ensuing discussion yesterday evening, I began to ask myself if anything was taking place here other than improbable debates, counter-questioning, and inquiries into unfindable objects of thought—to recall some of the formulations we heard. I am still asking myself this question.

We are gathered together here around Professor Gadamer. It is to him, then, that I wish to address these words, paying him the homage of a few questions.

The first question concerns what he said to us last evening about "good will," about an appeal to good will, and to the absolute commitment to the desire for consensus in understanding. How could anyone not be tempted to acknowledge how extremely evident this axiom is? For this is not just one of the axioms of ethics. It is the point where ethics begins for any community of speakers, even regulating the phenomena of disagreement and misunderstanding. It confers "dignity" in the Kantian sense on the good will, to know that which in a moral being lies beyond all market value, every negotiable price, and every hypothetical imperative. So this axiom would be unconditional—and would stand beyond any kind of evaluation whatsoever and beyond all value, if a value implies a scale and a comparison.

My first question, then, would be the following: Doesn't this unconditional axiom nevertheless presuppose that the *will* is the form of that unconditionality, its last resort, its ultimate determination? What is the will if, as Kant says, nothing is absolutely good except the good will? Would not this determination belong to what Heidegger has rightly called "the determination of the being of

---

*This text originally appeared in French under the title, "Bonnes Volontés de Puissance (Une Réponse à Hans-Georg Gadamer)," ["Good Will to Power (A Response to Hans-Georg Gadamer)"], and in German as "Guter Wille zur Macht (I): Drei Fragen an Hans-Georg Gadamer" ["Good Will to Power (I): Three Questions to Hans-Georg Gadamer"]. For our title here, we have chosen the subtitle from the German edition.—Trans.

beings as will, or willing subjectivity?" Does not this way of speaking, in its very necessity, belong to a particular epoch, namely, that of a metaphysics of the will?

A second question—still in relation to last evening's lecture: What to do about good will—the condition for consensus even in disagreement—if one wants to integrate a psychoanalytic hermeneutics into a general hermeneutics? This is just what Professor Gadamer was proposing to do last evening. But what would good will mean in psychoanalysis? Or even just in a discourse that follows the lines of psychoanalysis? Would it be enough, as Professor Gadamer seems to think, simply to enlarge the context of interpretation? Or, on the contrary—as I am inclined to look at it—would this not involve a breach, an overall re-structuring of the context, even of the very concept of context? Here I am not referring to any specific psychoanalytic doctrine but only to a question traversed by the possibility of psychoanalysis, to an interpretation worked on by psychoanalysis. Such interpretation would perhaps be closer to the interpretive style of Nietzsche than to that other hermeneutical tradition extending from Schleiermacher to Gadamer with all the internal differences that one may wish to distinguish (such as were singled out last night).

Professor Gadamer describes this context of interpretation to us as the context of what he terms *"un vécu,"* a "lived experience" [*Lebenszusammenhang*] in living dialogue; that is, in the living experience of living dialogue. This was one of the most important and decisive points in all that he said to us about context-related coherence—systematic or not, for not every coherence necessarily takes systematic form. For me, it was equally one of the most problematical. And this applies also to everything he told us concerning the definition of a text, be it literary, poetic, or ironic. Here I am also reminded of the final question posed by one of the participants in the discussion. It had to do with the closure of a corpus [*la clôture d'un corpus*]. What is the relevant context in this regard? And what, strictly speaking, would be an "enlargement of a context?" Would it be a continual expansion, or a discontinuous re-structuring?

A third question also has to do with the underlying structure of good will. Whether or not psychoanalytic afterthoughts are brought into the picture, one can still raise questions about that axiomatic precondition of interpretive discourse which Professor Gadamer calls *"Verstehen,"* "understanding the other," and "understanding one another." Whether one speaks of consensus or of misunderstanding (as in Schleiermacher), one needs to ask whether the precondition for *Verstehen,* far from being the continuity of *rapport* (as it was described yesterday evening), is not rather the interruption of *rapport*, a certain *rapport* of interruption, the suspending of all mediation?

Finally, Professor Gadamer has insistently referred to "that experience [*Erfahrung*] that we all recognize," to a description of experience that is not in itself to be taken metaphysically. But usually—and maybe even always—metaphysics presents itself as the description of experience as such, of presentation as such. Furthermore, I am not convinced that we ever really do have this experience that Professor Gadamer describes, of knowing in a dialogue that one has been perfectly understood or experiencing the success of confirmation.

In the tangle of this web of questions and remarks, which I abandon here in their elliptical and improvised form, can one not glimpse a quite different way of thinking about texts?

Hans-Georg Gadamer

3. *Reply to Jacques Derrida**
Translated by Diane Michelfelder and Richard Palmer

Mr. Derrida's questions prove irrefutably that my remarks on text and interpretation, to the extent they had Derrida's well-known position in mind, did not accomplish their objective. I am finding it difficult to understand these questions that have been addressed to me. But I will make an effort, as anyone would do who wants to understand another person or be understood by the other. I absolutely cannot see that this effort would have anything to do with "the epoch of metaphysics"—or, for that matter, with the Kantian concept of good will. I stated quite clearly what I mean by good will: for me, it signifies what Plato called "ευμενεις ελενχοι." That is to say, one does not go about identifying the weaknesses of what another person says in order to prove that one is always right, but one seeks instead as far as possible to strengthen the other's viewpoint so that what the other person has to say becomes illuminating. Such an attitude seems essential to me for any understanding at all to come about. This is nothing more than an observation. It has nothing to do with an "appeal," and nothing at all to do with ethics. Even immoral beings try to understand one another. I cannot believe that Derrida would actually disagree with me about this. Whoever opens his mouth wants to be understood; otherwise, one would neither speak nor write. And finally, I have an exceptionally good piece of evidence for this: Derrida directs questions to me and therefore he must assume that I am willing to understand them. Certainly this is completely unrelated to Kant's "good will," but it does have a good deal to do with the difference between dialectic and sophistics.

Now I also do not believe I have been understood if one attributes to me a desire to integrate a psychoanalytic hermeneutics—that is, the process by which

*This reply was published in the German edition under a title formulated by its editor, Philippe Forget, "Und dennoch: Macht des Guten Willens." We have chosen a simpler title.—Trans.

an analyst helps a patient to understand him or herself and to get over his or her complexes—into a general hermeneutics, and to extend the classical-naive forms of understanding over into psychoanalysis. My aim was quite the reverse: to show that psychoanalytic interpretation goes in a totally different direction. Psychoanalytic interpretation does not seek to understand what someone wants to say, but instead what that person doesn't want to say or even admit to him or herself.

I, too, see this as a breach, a *rupture,* and not another method for understanding the same thing. It would never occur to me to deny that one could approach the task of understanding utterances with an intention totally different from that which would lead to mutual understanding. My question was straightforward: When and why does one bring about such a breach? I wanted to point out this breach because I know that Ricoeur, for example, rejects the idea of a radical break when he places the hermeneutics of suspicion and the hermeneutics of intention side by side as two different methods for understanding the same thing.

But I am not under any illusion that Derrida, even though I agree with him on this point about a "breach," is really in agreement with me. Surely he would say that this breach must always be made, because a continuous understanding of another person simply does not exist. As far as he is concerned, the concept of truth which is implied in harmonious agreement and which defines the "true" opinion of what something means, is itself a naive notion that ever since Nietzsche, we can no longer accept.

No doubt it is for this reason that Derrida finds my speaking about a lived context [*Lebenszusammenhang*] and the fundamental place of living dialogue especially problematical. It is in this form of exchange—of word and word, question and answer—that a genuine mutual understanding [ὁμολογια] can be produced. This is the way, Plato emphasized constantly, by means of which one is able to eliminate the false agreements, misunderstandings and misinterpretations that cling to words taken by themselves. Indeed, much more than a linguistic system as a system of signs is constituted through συνθεκε[*Syntheke*], or agreed-upon conventions. This is especially true of the communicative sharing in which what Derrida himself calls "collocution" takes place (see *VP* 40ff.).

So it seems to me entirely justifiable to start with the process in which mutual agreement is shaped and reshaped in order to describe the functioning of language and of its possible written forms. Surely this is not at all a kind of metaphysics, but the presupposition that any partner in a dialogue must assume, including Derrida, if he wants to pose questions to me. Is he really disappointed that we cannot understand each other? Indeed not, for in his view this would be a relapse into metaphysics. He will, in fact, be pleased, because he takes this private experience of disillusionment to confirm his own metaphysics. But I cannot see here how he can be right only with respect to himself, be in agreement only with himself. Of course I understand very well why he invokes Nietzsche here. It is precisely because both of them are mistaken about themselves. Actually both speak and write in order to be understood.

Now certainly I would not want to say that the solidarities that bind human beings together and make them partners in a dialogue always are sufficient to enable them to achieve understanding and total mutual agreement. Just between two people this would require a never-ending dialogue. And the same would apply with regard to the inner dialogue the soul has with itself. Of course we encounter limits again and again; we speak past each other and are even at cross-purposes with ourselves. But in my opinion we could not do this at all if we had not traveled a long way together, perhaps without even acknowledging it to ourselves. All human solidarity, all social stability, presupposes this.

But doubtless Derrida thinks—and I am hoping he will excuse me if I try to understand him—that matters are different when it comes to texts. To him, any word appearing in written form is always already a breach. This applies especially in the case of a literary text, indeed, with regard to every linguistic work of art, in that it demands of us that we break with the customary course of our experience and its horizons of expectation. To put it as Heidegger does: A work of art thrusts itself upon us, it deals us a blow [*Stoss*]. In no way does it signify the reassuring confirmation of mutual agreement. All the same, we ought to be able to understand ourselves on the basis of it. The experience of limits that we encounter in our life with others—is it not this alone that conditions our experience and is presupposed in all the common interests bearing us along? Perhaps the experience of a text always includes such a moment of encountering limits; but precisely for this reason it also includes all that binds us together. In the text I presented yesterday I tried to show that a literary text—a linguistic work of art—not only strikes us and deals us a blow but also is supposed to be accepted, albeit with an assent that is the beginning of a long and often repeated effort at understanding. Every reading that seeks understanding is only a step on a path that never ends. Whoever takes up this path knows that he or she will never be completely done with the text: one accepts the blow, the thrust [*er nimmt den Stoß an*], that the text delivers. The fact that a poetic text can so touch someone that one ends up "entering" into it and recognizing oneself in it, assumes neither harmonious agreement nor self-confirmation. One must lose oneself in order to find oneself. I believe I am not very far from Derrida when I stress that one never knows in advance what one will find oneself to be.

Jacques Derrida

4. *Interpreting Signatures (Nietzsche/Heidegger): Two Questions*

Translated by Diane Michelfelder and Richard Palmer

The first question concerns the *name* Nietzsche, the second has to do with the concept of totality.

I

Let us begin with chapters 2 and 3 of Heidegger's *Nietzsche*—dealing with "The Eternal Recurrence of the Same" and "The Will to Power as Knowledge," respectively. We will be turning especially to the subsection on chaos ("The Concept of Chaos," *N* 1:562–70/3:77–83) and to "The Alleged Biologism of Nietzsche" (*N* 1:517–27/3:39–47). In view of the fact that the same interpretation is regularly at work throughout, the risks involved in choosing this strategy are, I hope, quite limited. In each instance, a single system of reading is powerfully concentrated and gathered together. It is directed at gathering together the unity and the uniqueness of Nietzsche's thinking, which, as a fulfilled unity, is itself in a fair way to being the culmination of occidental metaphysics. Nietzsche would be precisely at the crest, or ridge, atop the peak of this fulfillment. And thus, he would be looking at both sides, down both slopes.

What about this unity—this doubled unity? What is its connection to the name—or rather, the signature—of Nietzsche? Does Heidegger take any account of this question—which others might call biographical, autobiographical, or autographical—of the singularity of a signature ostensibly the proper name of Nietzsche? To put the matter another way, if one can glimpse behind Heidegger's reading of Nietzsche the foundations of a general reading of Western metaphysics, then the question arises: To what extent does this interpretation of metaphysics in its totality and as a whole contain an interpretive decision about the unity or singularity of thinking? And to what extent does this interpretive decision also presuppose a decision about the "biographical," about the proper name, the autobiographical, and about signature—about the politics of signature?[1]

Heidegger's position on this subject I will indicate first of all with a summarizing and simplifying statement, which one could, I hope, demonstrate is not wrong: there is a unity in Nietzschean thought even if it is not that of a system in the classical sense. This unity is also its uniqueness, its singularity. A thesis explicitly advanced by Heidegger is that every great thinker has only one thought. This uniqueness was neither constituted nor threatened, neither gathered together nor brought about, through a name or proper name—nor by the life of Nietzsche, either normal or insane. This unique unity is something it draws from the unity of Western metaphysics which is gathered together there at its crest, which one could also compare to the simple unity of a line created by a fold. The result of all this is that biography, autobiography, the scene or the powers of the proper name, of proper names, signatures, and so on, are again accorded minority status, are again given the inessential place they have always occupied in the history of metaphysics. This points to the necessity and place of a questioning which I can only sketch here.

Such would be a simplified version of the question. Now let us read Heidegger a little more closely and seek to confirm the strongest coherence of his interpretation or, beyond its coherence, his deepest thought. As a provisional concession to the classical norms of reading, let us take this book at its beginning, or even before its beginning at the beginning of the preface. Naturally, this preface was, like so many others, written later. As we know, the book goes back to a series of lectures given between 1936 and 1940, and to some treatises written between 1940 and 1946. One should take most careful note of these dates if one is to bring this interpretation, as a whole and in detail, into connection with the historico-political and institutional field of its presentation. The preface, however, dates from 1961. The intention of the two pages in this case, as almost always, is to justify the publication of this collection by reference to the essential unity of its totality: "This publication, rethought (*nachgedacht*) as a whole (*als Ganzes*) should provide a glimpse of the path of thought which I followed between 1930 and the *Letter on Humanism* (1947)." The unity of this publication and of this teaching is, then, also the unity of the path of thought of Heidegger at a decisive moment and traced through a period of over fifteen years. But at the same time this also means that the unity of his interpretation of Nietzsche, the unity of Western metaphysics to which this interpretation is referred, and the unity of the Heideggerian path of thought are here inseparable. One cannot think the one without the other.

Now what are the first words of this preface? What does one find in that first phrase? To be elliptical, let us say one finds *two things,* and both of them have a literal connection with the *name* of Nietzsche.

First, the name is placed in quotation marks.

Now what happens when a proper name is put between quotation marks? Heidegger never asks himself. Still, his whole undertaking, although entitled "Nietzsche," has perhaps put all its powers together in such a way as to nullify the urgency and necessity of this question.

Second, let me read you the first sentence of the preface in the French translation by Klossowski: " 'Nietzsche'—the name of the thinker here names the *cause* of his thinking [*intitule ici la cause de sa pensée*]."[2] Heidegger's next paragraph explains and, up to a point, justifies Klossowski's translation of a certain German word [*Sache*] by "cause." For in Heidegger's next paragraph we read: "A case, the legal case, is, in itself, *ex-pli-cation*—or in German, *Aus-einander-setzung*—one party taking a position in relation to another. To let our thought be penetrated by this "cause"—to prepare it for this—that is the content of the present publication."[3]

Now to someone who simply opens up this book without knowing the German text, such an approach could seem both odd and at the same time consonant with the latest modernity, not to say the latest style: the *name* of the thinker would thus be the *cause* of his thought! The thinking, then, would be the *effect* caused by his proper name! And here is a book on the name Nietzsche and on the connections between his name and his thought. Taking into account the fact that in this French edition, through a strange typographical error, the name Nietzsche is cut in two (Niet-zsche), who knows what heights this new reader, in the freshness of his too great or too limited perspective, could attain in his analysis of the schism of the proper name, an analysis which, through a parcelling out of the signifier or the semantic elements, could make a connection between the Slavic (Polish) origin of the name, on the one hand, and what Nietzsche himself said about the negativity of his own name and the destructive power of his thought, on the other. And if this analysis were carried to delirious extremes, it would then connect this negative element, *Niet-* (and why not? why stop half-way?) with the only two cities in which he said in 1887 he could think or wanted to think: Venice and Nice (specifically, in a letter to Peter Gast dated September 15, which Heidegger cites near the beginning of the book and chapter on *The Will to Power as Art* [*N* 1:22/1:14]). These two cities remain the only cure for Nietzsche, the only possible escape. Ah, says our ingenuous and zealous reader, "I see, I see! *il veut Nice, il Venise, il veut Nietzsche, il veut et il ne veut pas,*[4] there you have the two places, the two said places, the toponyms of his *Will to Power!*" But unfortunately this sequence can only work in French and the delirium must come to a halt the moment one notices that Venice in German is *Venedig* and Nice in German is *Nizza*. As Nietzsche says, cited by Heidegger: *"Somit läuft es auf Venedig und Nizza hinaus . . . ."*—"Therefore it has turned out to be a matter of Venice and Nice. . ." (*N* 1:22/1:14).

But then, pursuing his reading, our French reader still asks: What does it mean, "Nietzsche, the name of the thinker names the cause of his thinking?" Even within the confines of the French translation the content of the next paragraph is enlightening for it clearly says, Do not take the word *cause* in its opposition to *effect* as material, efficient, formal, or final cause of his thought but understand it as the Latin *causa:* legal debate, litigation, opposition of two parties. Still, this perspective too can exercise a kind of modish temptation for the French reader of today: the name Nietzsche as contentiousness of thinking, as stake in a game, war, or legal battle—that scarcely sounds classical any more. Such, taking this new, fresh start, would be an initial reading. But if he consults the original text, the reader discovers something else, quite different from *cause* either in the derivative sense *or* the usual sense of the word: " 'Nietzsche,' the name of the thinker stands as the title for *die Sache seines Denkens,"* the *subject-matter* [*Sache*] of his thought, for *what* he thinks.

The German word that one usually translates into French as *cause* [English: "cause"] is *Ursache* [the cause or reason for something]. Because the two words are alike, Klossowski felt justified in translating *Sache* as "cause." But normally *Sache* designates the "thing"—not the sense object or even the thing at hand but the thing in question, the affair, which eventually can lead to litigation. In this sense, the Latin *causa,* cause in the sense of litigation or a trial, is a good translation. It poses not only the thing in question but also the question of the thing [*Die Frage nach dem Ding*], which is dealt with elsewhere, namely in Heidegger's great meditation by that title and above all in reference to the relation to all semantic determinations of cause. Indeed, the translation of *Sache* by the French word *cause* [instead of *chose,* thing] can find, as we have said, support in the course of the text itself. For Heidegger continues, *"Die Sache der Streitfall, ist in sich selbst Auseinandersetzung"*—"the matter, the point of dispute, is in itself a placing in opposition, a confrontation."

But when he says that the name of the thinker stands as title "for the *Sache* of his thinking," he certainly does not intend to make the name the cause of an effect that would be the thinking. The genitive "of" here designates the *Sache* [matter] *as* his thinking. Everything will confirm this once one considers the proper name not as that of an individual or of a signatory; it is the name of a thought, of a thought whose unity gives in return sense and reference to the proper name. "Nietzsche" is nothing other than the name of this thinking. The syntax of the genitive misleads us in the other direction, if one may put it that way, for the name is not before the thought, it is the thing that is thought; it is produced and determined by it. Only in thinking this thought will one think the possessive, the genitive, and the proper name. One will learn *who Nietzsche is* and what his name says only from his thinking—not from card files packed with more or less refined biographical facts.

At this point two paths present themselves. One would consist in taking a new approach to the problematic of the name, at the risk of seeing the name dismembered and multiplied in masks and similitudes. We know what Nietzsche risked in this respect. The name would be constituted on the far side of the "life" of the thinker, from the vantage point of the future of the world, from an affirmation of the "eternal recurrence."[5]

The other path would be to determine the essentiality of the name from the "subject matter of thought," of thought itself defined as the content of theses, and to let fall into inessentiality the particular proper name, which has become the index of the "biography" or a "psychology" of an individual. In legitimately scorning biographism, psychologism, or psychoanalysis, one instead embraces reductionist empiricisms that in turn only cover up what is given as thinking. This is what Heidegger does, for the best reasons in the world. But in doing this does he not thereby fall back on a gesture of classical metaphysics, indeed at the very moment in which he is appealing for something other than metaphysics—that is, at the moment when he situates Nietzsche on the crest of that metaphysics? This classical gesture also reappears in his dissociating the matter of life or of proper name from the matter of thought. Hence, the beginning of Heidegger's lecture course: In a very conventional fashion he dissociates his summary and "official" biography of Nietzsche, on the one hand, from the grand questions that stretch the great philosopher to the limit of his powers, on the other. Such is the form of this first lecture, which conforms to the old pedagogical model: very quickly one runs through the "life of the author" in its most conventional features, then turns to the thought, that which Heidegger calls "the authentic philosophy of Nietzsche." This philosophy, Heidegger notes, "does not arrive at a definitive elaboration nor is it ever published as a work."

Then, criticizing the edition of the complete works, Heidegger notes some of its limitations. It adhered to the principle of integrality [*Vollständigkeit,* completeness] that pushed everything, and which resurrected nineteenth century models, to the point of that biologism and psychologism that are like a monstrous perversion of our age. Heidegger criticizes that editorial enthusiasm that "proceeds in the manner of biological and psychological elucidation," which "traces minutely all the data" of the life of the author, including the opinions of contemporaries. It is an "excrescence" [*Ausgeburt,* monstrosity, product], a "monstrous product of the addiction of our time to the psycho-biological [*der psychologish-biologischen Sucht unserer Zeit*]." Says Heidegger, "Only the proper preparation of an authentic edition of the *Works* (1881–1889), if that task is ever accomplished in the future, will bring access to the 'works of Nietzsche,' properly speaking." Furthermore, Heidegger adds, "This will never be genuinely accomplished if in the questioning we do not grasp Nietzsche as the end of Western metaphysics and press over to the quite different question of the truth of Being" (*N* 1:18–19/1:10). To pose the question of the truth of Being beyond ontology, and to determine the place of Nietzsche as the end of Western metaphysics—these are the prerequisite conditions if one wishes eventually to gain access to the "biography" of Nietzsche, to the name, and above all to the textual corpus of Nietzsche—if one wishes, in other words, to know "who Nietzsche was."

Prior to all other questions, we need to be attentive to the fundamental necessity for such a schema as Heidegger puts forward, and also attentive to everything in a certain historical and political situation that could justify it. The psychological and biological eagerness in the *style* he so often practices circles around and thereby misses the *content* of a thought—its necessity and its internal specificity. A well-known schema. Besides, at the time he was teaching his "Nietzsche," Heidegger had begun to put some distance between himself and Nazism. Without saying anything in his lecture itself that was directed against the government and the use it was making of Nietzsche (on so much prudence and silence one can certainly put an interpretation—but elsewhere), Heidegger is in the process of overtly criticizing the edition that the government is in the process of supporting. Heidegger appears at first to have been associated with it, then he backed out; the issue had to do with instituting, in cooperation with Nietzsche's sister, falsifications in that edition: "For knowledge of Nietzsche's biography," Heidegger continues, "the presentation by his sister, Elisabeth Förster-Nietzsche, *The Life of Friedrich Nietzsche* (published between 1895 and 1904), remains always important. As with all biographical works, however, use of this publication requires great caution. We will refrain from further suggestions and from discussion of the enormous and varied secondary literature surrounding Nietzsche, since none of it can aid the endeavor of this lecture course. Whoever does not have the courage and perseverance of thought required to get involved in reading Nietzsche's own writings has no need to read anything *about* him either" (*N* 1:19/1:10–11).

Here and elsewhere one of the targets of Heidegger is what he calls "philosophy of life." The object of Heidegger's attack here was not only Nazism, but also a classical university tradition as well, which made of Nietzsche a "philosopher-poet," a life-philosopher without conceptual rigor whom one could denounce "from the height of German chairs of philosophy." But in either case one praises or condemns that "philosophy of life" which Heidegger from *Being and Time* onward had combatted as an absurdity.

This critique of psycho-biologism underlies also his critique of Nietzsche's "alleged biologism" ("Nietzsches angeblicher Biologismus," *N* 1:517–27/3:39–48). It answers the question of the name of Nietzsche, the question "What is that we call Nietzsche?" There, once again, in response to the question, "Who is Nietzsche?", right at the opening of the third chapter, "The Will to Power as Knowledge," in the first subsection (again the first words), which has the title "Nietzsche as Thinker of the Fulfillment of Metaphysics":

> Who Nietzsche *is* and above all who he *will be* we shall know as soon as we are able to think the thought that he gave shape to in the phrase "the will to power." We shall never experience who Nietzsche is through a historical report about his life history, nor through a presentation of the contents of his writings. Neither do we, nor should we, want to know who Nietzsche is, if we have in mind only the personality, the historical figure, and the psychological object and its products. But wait . . . . (*N* 1:473/3:3).

At this point, Heidegger brings forward an objection he will soon reject. Before going into this, however, I should like to offer a cautionary remark against oversimplifying the question I am directing to Heidegger's procedure. Doubtless there is an effort by Heidegger to reduce the name of Nietzsche or the "Who is Nietzsche" question to the unity of Western metaphysics, even to the uniqueness of a limit situation on the crest of that metaphysics. Nevertheless, the question "Who is X?" was a rare question when applied to a thinker; it is so still if one does not understand it in a biographically trivial way—as the man and the work, the man behind the work, the life of Descartes or Hegel associated with a kind of doxography. But to ask in another sense "Who is Nietzsche?"—to make his name the title of a book on his thought—that is something not so conventional.

Here is the objection Heidegger raises in a *pro forma* way just after he has rejected psychobiography: "But just a minute! Has not Nietzsche himself as a last act completed a work for publication entitled *Ecce Homo: How One Becomes What One Is?* Does not *Ecce Homo* speak as Nietzsche's last will and testament, to the effect that one must deal with this man, and let it be said of him what the excerpts of that writing suggest: 'Why I am so wise? Why I am so intelligent? Why I write such good books? Why I am a destiny?' Does this not point to an apex in unrestrained self-presentation and measureless self-mirroring?" Heidegger answers: *Ecce Homo* is not an autobiography, and if anything culminates in it, it would be the final moment of the West, in the history of the era of modernity. Without a doubt things get knotted together right in this place. One can admit, easily enough, that *Ecce Homo* is not Nietzsche's autobiographical history. But when Heidegger simply lets stand the conventional concept of autobiography instead of reshaping it, and only opposes to it the destiny of the West whose "carrier" Nietzsche would be, then one has to ask: Does Heidegger himself escape a fairly traditional opposition between biographical factuality—psycho-biographical, historical—and an essential thinking on the order of a historical decision? One can also ask what interest is served by this Heideggerian discourse being carried out along these lines.

By means of this strategy, Heidegger intends to rescue Nietzsche from his own singular fate. This fate has remained ambiguous. It has provoked odd uses of his thinking, uses which turned against what Heidegger calls Nietzsche's "innermost will." Thus, it is a matter of gaining access to this innermost will and to oppose it to the duplicity of the empirical figure of Nietzsche as well as to the ambiguity of its subsequent effects—its immediate after-effects, for Heidegger believed that the future will work to restore that innermost will. After saying this in order to rescue Nietzsche from ambiguity, Heidegger directs this whole interpretation of Nietzsche's essential and singular thinking to the following argument: this thinking has not really gone beyond the end of metaphysics; it is still itself a great metaphysics and even if it points to such an overcoming, it is just barely, just enough to remain on the sharpest crest of the boundary. Or, in other words, to remain in complete ambiguity.

This, then, is essential ambiguity! Not just Nietzsche's, as Heidegger sees it, but also Heidegger's own ambivalence with regard to Nietzsche. It remains constant. In saving Nietzsche, Heidegger loses him too; he wants at the same time to save him and let go of him. At the very moment of affirming the uniqueness of Nietzsche's thinking, he does everything he can to show that it repeats the mightiest (and therefore the most general) schema of metaphysics. When he is pretending to rescue Nietzsche from this or that distortion—that of the Nazis, for example—he does so with categories that can themselves serve to distort—namely, with that opposition between essential and inessential thinkers, authentic thinkers and inauthentic ones, and with the definition of an essential thinker as someone selected, chosen, marked out or, I would even say, "signed" [*gezeichnet*]. Signed—by what? By whom? By nobody—by the history of the truth of Being. Nietzsche was sufficiently chosen for that, and yet he was condemned by this same destiny to bring metaphysics to its completion, and without reaching a decision which he alone had prepared, even without recognizing the scope of that decision: "between the hegemony of *beings* and the lordship of *Being*" ["*Zwischen der Vormacht des Seienden und der Herrschaft des Seins*"]. For all these points I refer you to the first pages of the chapter, "The Will to Power as Knowledge," whose first section carries the heading, "Nietzsche as Thinker of the Consummation of Metaphysics" (*N* 1:473ff./3:3ff.).

It was doubtless necessary to set up this interpretation-schema of Nietzsche's *biographein* in order to penetrate to an interpretation of his "alleged biologism." There too it is a matter of rescuing—in a most ambiguous way—the uniqueness of a thinking from the ambiguity of a life and work. The marking out of the boundaries of the biographical and of the proper name opens up the general space in whose interior the interpretation of the biological occurs.

Before the first words I quoted moments ago from the preface there is an exergue.[6] It is taken from the *Gay Science* and its first word is "life." "Life" stands at the extreme outset of Heidegger's book—even before its beginning, before any decision between biography and biology. Here, strangely enough, Heidegger is not satisfied with breaking off the passage before its end. He also skips over a few words and replaces them with ellipses: "Life . . . more mysterious since the day the great liberator came over me—the thought that life should be an experiment of knowers." Among the words he skips over are the words "true" and "desirable," both of which pertain to life. Here is the fragment from Nietzsche in its—if one may speak this way—integral character.

> *In media vita!* No! [These four words—the title, in short—and above all, these two exclamation points, are omitted by Heidegger—this time without ellipses. JD] Life has not disappointed me! On the contrary, I find it truer, more desirable and mysterious every year—ever since the day when the great liberator came over me: the idea that life might be an experiment of knowers—and not a duty, not a calamity, not trickery! And knowledge itself: let it be something else for others; for example, a bed to rest on, or the way to such a bed, or a diversion, or a form of leisure—for me it is a world of dangers and victories in which heroic feelings, too, find places to dance and play. *"Life as a means to knowledge"*—with this principle in one's heart one can live not only boldly but even gaily, and laugh gaily, too! And who knows how to laugh anyway and live well if he does not first know a good deal about war and victory? (*Gay Science,* § 324)

These are fundamentally secretive assertions, very difficult to interpret, just like the title *In media vita!* That makes life out to be a medium—as much in the sense of a mean between two extremes as in the sense of an elementary milieu in which the experiment of knowledge finds its place. In situating itself within life, this experiment uses life as a means, steers it from the inside, and—with this power to steer the living—comes to be beyond and outside of life, on the side of its end and its death, and so on. One can see why Heidegger took this passage as an exergue. He appears to be making a biological reading of Nietzsche more difficult in advance, whether one understands this reading in the sense of a subordination under the model of biology or as a celebration of life as the ultimate aim—even to the determination of life as the Being of beings, or being as a whole.

This choice of an exergue is sufficient evidence that the question about life and the "alleged biologism" stand at the active center of Heidegger's *Nietzsche.* And yet the paradoxical character of this passage (*In media vita!*) could also thwart Heidegger's hermeneutical strategy. Life does have a beyond, but it does not allow itself to be made into something secondary. As itself and in itself it unfolds the movement of truth or knowledge. It is in itself as its own beyond.

Not to mention the stresses and the joys, the laughter and the war, the question marks and exclamation points—those things that Heidegger, considering how he effaces or conceals them, obviously does not want to hear spoken of here. . . .

I would like to point out a second thing about this exergue—or rather, once again, a first thing, something completely first—pre-first. I said "life" was the first word of the citation. Strictly speaking, it is the first word in the quotation from Nietzsche. Before this quotation Heidegger adds a short sentence which—strangely enough—presents the exergue itself: "Nietzsche himself names the experience that determines his thinking: '. . .' ". Hence, it is Nietzsche himself who *names* what determines his thinking, the patient experience of his thinking. And, if the name of the thinker designates the matter of his thinking, as Heidegger wants to show immediately afterwards, then the exergue as a whole means: Nietzsche names himself, he names himself from that out of which one must be able to name him. He will give himself a name from out of the experience of his thinking, and from it he receives his name. And so the thinking, so named, must rightly be understood from within this autonomous circle. But is it correct to say, as Heidegger so positively claims, that this thinking is one?—that Nietzsche then has only one name? Does he name himself only once? For Heidegger, his naming takes place only once, even if the place of this event retains the appearance of a borderline, from which one can get a look at both sides at once, at the summit of Western metaphysics, which is gathered together under this name.

But who ever has said that a person bears a single name? Certainly not Nietzsche. And likewise, who has said or decided that there is something like a Western metaphysics, something which would be capable of being gathered up under this name and this name only? What is it—the oneness of a name, the assembled unity of Western metaphysics? Is it anything more or less than the desire (a word effaced in Heidegger's Nietzsche citation) for a proper name, for a single, unique name and a thinkable genealogy? Next to Kierkegaard, was not Nietzsche one of the few great thinkers who multiplied his names and played with signatures, identities, and masks? Who named himself more than once, with several names? And what if that would be the heart of the matter, the *causa,* the *Streitfall* [point of dispute] of his thinking?

As we have just now seen, Heidegger wants to save Nietzsche at any cost, to save him from ambiguity by a gesture which is itself ambivalent. And what if it would be this rescue which must be called into question in the name or names of Nietzsche?

When reading Heidegger's lectures on Nietzsche it is possibly less a matter of suspecting the content of an interpretation than of an assumption or axiomatic structure. Perhaps the axiomatic structure of metaphysics, inasmuch as *metaphysics itself* desires, or dreams, or imagines its own unity. A strange circle—an axiomatic structure that consequently demands an interpretation, one, gathered up, around a thinking unifying a unique text and, ultimately, the unique name for Being, for the experience of Being. With the value of the *name* this unity and this oneness mutually guard themselves against the dangers of dissemination. Here, perhaps—to take the words from Heidegger's preface—lies the *Streitfall* or the *Auseinandersetzung* between the Nietzsches and Martin Heidegger, between the Nietzsches and so-called [*ladite*] Western metaphysics. Since Aristotle, and at least up until Bergson, "it" (metaphysics) has constantly repeated and assumed that to think and to say must mean to think and say something that would be a *one,* one *matter.* And that not thinking-saying some one matter or principle is not thinking-saying at all, but a loss of the *logos.* Here is perhaps what the Nietzsches have put in question: the *legein* of this *logos,* the *gathering* of this logic.

This plurality starts to look like the family names of wanderers and tightrope walkers. It leads one away to the feast. Nietzsche and Heidegger speak of this feast with added emphasis. I leave it to you to consider this difference:

> The error will be recognized only when a confrontation with Nietzsche is at the same time conjoined to a confrontation in the realm of the grounding question of philosophy. At the outset, however, we ought to introduce some words of Nietzsche's that stem from the time of his work on "will to power": "for many, abstract thinking is toil; for me, on good days, it is feast and frenzy" (XIV, § 24).
>
> Abstract thinking a feast? The highest form of human existence? Indeed. But at the same time we must observe how Nietzsche views the essence of the feast, in such a way that he can think of it only on the basis of his fundamental conception of all being, will to power. "The feast implies: pride, exuberance, frivolity; mockery of all earnestness and respectability; a divine affirmation of oneself, out of animal plenitude and perfection—all obvious states to which the Christian may not honestly say Yes. *The feast is paganism par excellence*" (*Will to Power,* § 916). For that reason, we might add, the feast of thinking never takes place in Christianity. That is to say, there is no Christian philosophy. There is no true philosophy that could be determined anywhere else than from within itself. For the same reason there is no pagan philosophy, inasmuch as anything "pagan" is always still something Christian—the counter-Christian. The Greek poets and thinkers can hardly be designated as "pagan." Feasts require long and painstaking preparation. This semester we want to prepare ourselves for the feast, even if we do not make it as far as the celebration, even if we only catch a glimpse of the preliminary festivities at the feast of thinking—experiencing what meditative thought is and what it means to be at home in genuine questioning (*N* 1:14–15/1:5–6).

What happens in the course of the feast to the *legein* of this *logos,* which demands of the thinking-saying of the essential thinker that it be a thinking-saying of the one and the unique? The Nietzsches' feast risks tearing it into pieces or dispersing it in its masks. Certainly it would protect it from any kind of biologism, but this would be because the "logism" in it would lose its hold from the start. And another style of autobiography would come into being, bursting open (in every sense of the expression *faire sauter*) the unity of the name and the signature, disturbing both biologism and its critique, so far as it operates, in Heidegger, in the name of "essential thinking."

These are the preliminary remarks that I wanted to suggest for a future [*ultérieure*] reading of Heidegger's Nietzsche—for this ambiguous life-saving act, in the course of which one stretches out the net for the tightrope walker, the one who runs the greatest risk overhead on the narrow rope, only insofar as one has made sure that he—unmasked and protected by the unity of his name, which in turn will be sealed by the unity of metaphysics—will not be taking any risks. In other words: he was dead before he landed in the net.

Certainly none of that will have taken place in *Zarathustra*—nor in Basel, Venice, or Nice—but in Freiburg im Breisgau, between 1936 and 1940, during the preparation for a feast, preparation for a "being at home in genuine questioning" (*N* 1:15/1:6.).

II

Since I have been speaking for far too long (and I hope you will excuse me), I will be even more schematic in linking up a second question to the one we have just discussed. All this will be barely even preliminary, and, as I indicated at the beginning, will have to do with the concept of totality. One knows that the reference to the "totality of beings" in Heidegger's interpretation of Nietzsche, as well as in Western metaphysics itself, plays a structuring role. In order to speed things up, I am first of all going to mention two quotations. Heidegger takes the first one from the notes for *The Will to Power:* "Our whole world is the *ashes* of countless *living* creatures: and even if the animate seems so miniscule in comparison to the whole, it is nonetheless the case that *everything* has already been transposed into life and so departs from it." After this quotation Heidegger continues: "Apparently opposed to this is a thought expressed in *The Gay Science,* number 109: 'Let us guard against saying that death is the opposite of life; the living creature is simply a kind of dead creature, and a very rare kind.' "

The first thought points to a paradox in totality as a value. It shows itself disrespectfully in the face of the assurance of all that one generally thinks under the category of totality. But let us not forget that Heidegger defines metaphysics as the thinking of beings as a whole such that the question of the Being of beings is excluded; and on the basis of this definition he often makes Nietzsche out to be the last metaphysician. Without getting tangled up in the complexity of this whole question, one can already surmise just by reading this one passage that Nietzsche by no means trusts any thought of totality. He who says, "Even if the animate seems so miniscule in comparison to the whole, it is nonetheless the case that *everything* has already been transposed into life and so departs from it," expresses a thought about life and death that by no means subordinates itself to an unequivocal meaning of totality, of the relation between a whole and a non-whole. The idea of the eternal recurrence, obviously pervading this statement, is not a thought about totality. But Heidegger presents it *as* a thought about totality. It is one of the most insistent and most decisive themes of his reading. For instance, he writes at the end of the entire interpretation, which began with the two quotations that I recited:

> For one thing, we have circumscribed the field in which the thought of return belongs and which the thought as such concerns: we have surveyed this field of being as a whole and determined it as the interlacing unity of the animate and the lifeless. For another, we have shown how in its foundations being as a whole—as the unity of animate and inanimate—is structured and articulated: it is constituted by the character of force and the finitude of the whole (at one with infinity) that is implied in the character of force—which is to say, the immeasurability of the "phenomenal effects" (*N* 1:355/2:96–97).

We must remember that Heidegger takes the will to power to be the principle of the knowledge of the eternal recurrence of the same. It is the *Verfassung* [composition] of beings (their *quid,* their *quidditas,* their *essentia*); the eternal recurrence is the modality (the *quomodo, die Weise* [the manner of being]) of beings as a whole (*N* 1:425/2:162). In order to analyze Nietzsche's metaphysical *Grundstellung* [fundamental position], Heidegger must examine the accepted answer to the question about beings as a whole. The answer, he finds, is a two-fold one: the totality of beings is will to power and it is eternal recurrence. Whether or not these two answers are compatible, complementary, or combinable is basically less determinable from their content than their mutual relation. In point of fact, they are responses to two questions that throughout metaphysics form a pair (Being as *quidditas* or *essentia;* Being as manner of existing). As Heidegger sees it, because we did not know to identify this "metaphysical" pair of questions, we have erred up to now before the enigma of this two-fold answer. But you can very well see that in each of these two questions the question of beings as a totality remains implied. This question about beings as a whole is one that Nietzsche, as the metaphysician he is (according to Heidegger), would stubbornly seek to answer.

And now my question: If in the first of the two statements Heidegger cites (". . . even if the animate seems so miniscule in comparison to the whole, it is nonetheless the case that *everything* has already been transposed into life and so departs from it") the thought of the eternal recurrence does not coincide either with the thought of totality or any opposition of whole and part, is it perhaps hasty to make Nietzsche out to be a metaphysician, albeit the last one? At least if a metaphysician is, as Heidegger sees it, a thinker who adheres to the thought of beings as a whole. It just may possibly be that Nietzsche is not at all a thinker of beings, if indeed an essential connection exists between beings as such and totality.

Is it not also worth noting that it is life-death that deprives the value of totality of any privileged status? Is it not to be thought—following a very Nietzschean gesture, for we could well have other indications—that the living (the-living-the-dead) is not an existent being, does not fall within an ontological determination? Indeed, one time Nietzsche proposed to think the word "being" starting from life and not the other way around.

A second preliminary remark: Heidegger has put these two quotations together on the ground of their apparent contradiction. He notes that they appear to "stand opposed" [*entgegenstehen*] to one another. Even if what we have here is an hypothesis or a feigned objection, it seems to me that its very principle is thwarted in Nietzsche's sentence. There, opposition or contradiction no longer constitutes a law dictating prohibitions to thought. And that without dialectic. Life and death (life-death), from which we think everything else—are not the whole. Neither are they opposites. "Let us guard against saying that death is the opposite of life; the living creature is simply a kind of dead creature, and a very rare kind." In one blow Nietzsche thwarts all that governs the thought or even the anticipation of totality, namely, the relationship of genus and species. Here we are dealing with a unique inclusion—without any possible totalization—of the "whole" in the "part," with a metonymizing free from limits or positive devices. Let us defend ourselves against all our defenses—Nietzsche seems to be saying, at the beginning of a long aphorism (*Gay Science,* § 109), which, one more time, Heidegger does not quote in its entirety. This is yet another metonymical violence that is involved in his interpretation, it seems to me. But I do not want to impose upon your time; somewhere else, some other time, perhaps I will come back to these matters. Here I simply wanted to take the risk of sketching out two questions.

II

Gadamer Responds to the Encounter

Fred R. Dallmayr

Prelude
*Hermeneutics and Deconstruction: Gadamer and Derrida in Dialogue**

Issues of interpretation are presently at the forefront in the humanities and also in the social sciences. Eclipsed by post-empiricist and Continental philosophical arguments, positivist modes of social inquiry have given way to—or at least made room for—novel approaches stressing intersubjective understanding [*Verstehen*], textual analysis, and cultural exegesis. A common denominator in these approaches is frequently said to be the focus on "meaning" or significance—a meaning generated by actions or events and recovered or decoded through hermeneutical efforts. Yet, contrary to initial expectations, the recent hermeneutical "turn" has not produced a paradigmatic consolidation. On closer inspection or in actual practice, interpretation emerged as a far from straightforward or unilinear enterprise; once the correlation and mutual implication of interpreter and texts (including social events) was fully taken into account, the status of significance quickly appeared dubious. What surfaced at this point was not so much an external boundary of hermeneutics as rather an in-

---

*This essay was originally presented as a scholarly paper in Paris at the World Congress of the International Political Science Association held July 15–20, 1985. It was included in his recent volume *Critical Encounters: Between Philosophy and Politics* (Notre Dame: Notre Dame University Press, 1987) and is republished here by permission of author and publisher. In order to conserve space in the present volume, we have (with Professor Dallmayr's permission) omitted his preliminary summary of the encounter (Part I) and also a few sentences from the remainder of the essay.—Editors' note.

ternal ambivalence or rift. For, does the notion of meaning not inevitably presuppose a dimension of non-meaning—just as intentional acts intimate a
non-intentional foil? Over two hundred years ago, Vico's *New Science* alluded to
this dilemma in these terms: "Just as rational metaphysics teaches that man
becomes all things by understanding them [*homo intelligendo fit omnia*], imagi-
native metaphysics shows that man becomes all things by *not* understanding
them [*homo non intelligendo fit omnia*]; and perhaps the latter proposition is
truer than the former, for when man understands he extends his mind and takes
in the things, but when he does not understand he makes the things out of
himself and becomes them by transforming himself into them."[1]

In the contemporary setting, the fissures of interpretation or of interpretive
perspectives were for some time kept in abeyance (partly due to a shared anti-
positivist stance). To the extent that dilemmas were articulated, the emphasis
was placed on external limits or boundaries of hermeneutics supposedly erected
by empirical science or the structures of power.[2]

More recently, however, attention has begun to shift to more intrinsic dilemmas or conflicts. The main conflict in this area is highlighted by the labels of
"hermeneutics" and "deconstruction" or by the opposition (to speak loosely)
between the German and the French schools of interpretation—the former represented chiefly by Gadamer and the latter by Jacques Derrida. In large measure,
it is true, "opposition" has tended to amount to little more than coexistence
without contact or mutual engagement.

In April of 1981, an important event took place in Paris, namely, a tentative
exchange of views between the leading spokesmen of the two camps—an exchange whose German version was recently published under the title *Text und
Interpretation*. Even in this case, one must admit, the exchange took the form
more of an alternation of statements than of a genuine dialogue. Over long
stretches, the linking ingredient in the opposing statements was Heidegger or
Heidegger's mode of exegesis, a fact not entirely surprising given the Heideggerian affinities of both spokesmen—affinities, to be sure, pointing in radically
different directions. While Gadamer's *Truth and Method* may be said to integrate the tradition of *Geisteswissenschaften* with existential analysis (as outlined
in *Being and Time*), Derrida pursues themes in Heidegger's later work where
notions like "meaning" or "being" are already problematical (though hardly
abandoned).

The conflict of interpretations is not simply an academic debate. Behind
seemingly esoteric questions of textual reading and exegesis, broader issues of a
practical-political sort can be seen to surface. As it appears to me and as I intend
to argue, one of the central issues raised by the Gadamer-Derrida exchange
concerns the political communication and interaction appropriate to our "global
city" or to the emerging cosmopolis. This implication, I acknowledge, is not
immediately evident and requires some careful preparation. In the following

pages, I shall approach this goal in several successive steps. The initial section [omitted in this volume] will review the main themes of the Gadamer-Derrida exchange of 1981, leaving intact the somewhat disjointed and non-dialogical character of the exchange. The next section will reconstruct and flesh out the same encounter in the direction of a more cohesive dialogue or confrontation by relying on additional texts published by the two spokesmen. The aim of the final section will be to explore the broader implications, including the practical-political dimension, of the exchange—an endeavor placing its accent in large measure on the relationship between hermeneutical "good will" and decon-structive 'Will to Power' or, more generally, between political education [*Bildung*] and aesthetics.

* * * * *

The exchange between Gadamer and Derrida clearly touched on crucial questions regarding interpretation and intersubjective communication. But it did so in a somewhat oblique and elusive fashion. Frequently, the two spokesmen seemed more intent on reiterating firmly held positions than on exposing them to mutual testing and scrutiny. Occasionally, as in the case of "rupture," the issues underlying the exchange were nearly joined (or capable of being joined)— only to be abandoned or set aside in favor of more marginal concerns. To some extent, the joining of issues was complicated by a partial overlap or convergence of perspectives, an overlap due (as indicated) mainly to shared Heideggerian leanings. Among the two protagonists, Gadamer was certainly more ready and eager to engage in conversation or a genuine interplay of question and response; however, this willingness was counterbalanced by a certain oscillation of views, especially by the juxtaposition of intentional hermeneutics—inspired by the tradition of *Geisteswissenschaften*—and existential ontology. In the following, I intend to flesh out the contours of the respective arguments by drawing on relevant additional sources—in an effort to approximate the exchange more closely to a dialogical interaction. In Gadamer's case, I shall rely chiefly on his magisterial *Truth and Method* (containing a kind of *summa* of his teachings); in the case of Derrida, the primary focus will be on his interpretations of Nietzsche (and Heidegger).

Although immensely impressive in both its scope and structure, Gadamer's *Truth and Method* manifests the same kind of ambivalence: while seeking to articulate a "philosophical" or "ontological" type of hermeneutics, that work gives ample room to such concepts as "hermeneutical consciousness" and intentional "meaning"—thus, paying tribute to the traditional philosophy of reflection (that is, to the legacy of modern metaphysics). Gadamer's ontological ambitions emerge powerfully in the first part of the work, which is dedicated to the critique of modern aesthetics and especially of the linkage of art with subjective taste, a treatment inaugurated by Kant and continued by romanticism. As presented by Kant, he observes, taste is a purely "subjective principle to which common sense is reduced; abstracting from the content of objects judged to be beautiful, taste merely claims that they are accompanied a priori by a feeling of pleasure in the subject" (*WM* 39/40). As employed and modified by romanticism, the Kantian concept of taste was entirely divorced from ethical and ontological considerations and anchored in subjective feeling styled as "aesthetic consciousness." From the vantage point of this feeling, Gadamer continues, "the connection of the work of art with its world is no longer of any importance; on the contrary, aesthetic consciousness becomes itself the experiencing center from which everything termed art is assessed" (80–81/76). Regarding criteria of aesthetic beauty, the romantics and their epigones ascribed such standards at best to the special competence of the artist seen as creative "genius." In application to the multitude of readers or interpreters, on the other hand, aesthetic consciousness gave way to an anarchy of private whims and arbitrary preferences—to what Gadamer calls "an untenable hermeneutic nihilism." In terms of this outlook, he writes, "every encounter with a work of art has the rank and legitimacy of a new production . . . . If Valéry occasionally drew such conclusions for his work in order to avoid the myth of the unconscious productivity of genius, he actually (in my view) became only more deeply entangled in this myth: for now he transfers to reader and interpreter the power of absolute creation which he himself no longer desires to exert." In the end, "absolute discontinuity, that is, the disintegration of the unity of the aesthetic object into a multiplicity of experiences, is the necessary consequence of an aesthetics of feeling" and subjectivity (90/85).

Against the subjectivism of modern aesthetics, *Truth and Method* marshals an ontological conception of art revolving around the pivotal notion of "play"—a notion, to be sure, purged of romantic or subjectivist connotations. "What matters here," Gadamer asserts, "is the need to free this concept from the subjective meaning it has for Kant and Schiller and which dominates the whole of modern aesthetics and philosophical anthropology. If, in connection with the experience of art, we speak of 'play', this refers neither to the behavior nor to the feeling-state of the artist or the consumer of art, nor to the freedom of a subjectivity expressed in play, but rather to the mode of being of the art-work itself." Basically, play "fulfills its 'purpose' only if the player loses himself in the play." Contrary to the romantic tradition, an ontological approach to art thus shifts the accent from feeling to the play of the art-work itself. What must be "maintained against the levelling effect of aesthetic consciousness," Gadamer states, in a passage clearly reminiscent of Heidegger's "art-work" lectures, "is that works of art are not objects standing over against an isolated subject; rather art-works have their true being in the fact that they generate a transformative experience. The 'subject' of the experience of art, that which remains and endures, is not the subjectivity of the experiencing individual, but the art-work itself. This is precisely the significance of the mode of being of play: for play has its own essence, independent of the consciousness of players" (*WM* 97–98/ 91–92).[3]

Truth and Method is emphatic in downgrading the role of subjects or intentional agents in the domains of art and play. "The subject of play," we read, "are not the players; instead, through players the play merely reaches presentation [*Darstellung*]." In a sense, the dynamics or movement of a play operates "without a substrate": what matters alone is "the game that is played, irrespective of whether there are subjects at play." In Gadamer's perspective, ordinary language provides support for this construal of "play" by using the term frequently in a "medial" or intransitive sense (as when we say that a film is "playing" at a theater): "As far as language is concerned, the actual subject of play is obviously not the subjectivity of an individual who among other activities also plays, but rather the play itself. But we are so used to relating a phenomenon like playing to subjectivity and its modes of behavior that we miss these clues supplied by language." An important corollary of the primacy of play is the risk involved for players or participants: by engaging in play their original identities are liable to be jeopardized. In participating in a play and its various possibilities or moves, Gadamer writes, "we may become so engrossed in them that they, as it were, outplay and prevail against us. The attraction that the game has for the player lies precisely in this risk." Actually, in his view, the hazard or "overplaying" element involved in play is so pronounced that activity begins to shade over into passivity, playing into being played: "From this vantage point we can indicate a general characteristic of the way in which the nature of play is reflected in playful behavior: *all playing is a being-played*. The attraction or fascination that a game exerts consists precisely in the fact that the play tends to master the players." Differently phrased, playing is a peculiarly purposeless or nonintentional kind of activity, an activity at rest (or carrying its purpose) within itself: The action or agency of a play is located not "in the player, but in the game itself; the game is what holds the player in its spell, draws him into play, and keeps him there" (*WM* 98–99/92–93; 101–102/95–96).

From the perspective of players, engagement in play involves a transformation or change of status—a change particularly evident in artistic plays amenable to performance or presentation: "I call this change in which human play finds its genuine completion as art, 'transformation into structured form or work' [*Gebilde*]; only through this change does play acquire its ideality so that it can be intended and understood as play." According to *Truth and Method*, change in this sense does not mean an incremental, continuous development, but rather a complete reversal or rupture. In Gadamer's words, the implications for the definition of art "emerge when one takes the sense of transformation seriously: Transformation is not ordinary change, not even a change of particularly large proportions." Ordinary change denotes that what is changed "also remains the same and is held on to." By contrast, transformation means "that something turns suddenly and as a whole into something else; that this other transformed thing that it has become is its true being, in comparison with which its earlier mode is nothing." Thus, there cannot be a "transition of gradual change leading from one to the other" since the two modes imply a "mutual denial." The effects of transformative rupture are manifest on a number of levels, especially the level of intentional agents—including artists, performers, and interpreters. In relation to all of them, Gadamer affirms, art-work seen as play possesses "an absolute autonomy." What is put aside and counts no longer is "first of all the players, with the poet or composer being considered as one of the players." Properly construed, play is transformative to such an extent "that the identity of the players remains for no one the same." On another level, the rupture affects empirical reality or the world of everyday life: "What exists no longer is above all the world in which we live as our own. Transformation into structure is not simply transposition into another (ordinary) world"; rather, a new and transfigured world arises in the play. Finally and most importantly, art involves a kind of ontological "sea-change," a shift from contingent phenomena to true being or the truth of being: "Transformation at this point is transformation into truth. It is not enchantment in the sense of a bewitchment that waits for the redeeming word to return things to their previous state; rather, it is itself redemption and restoration to true being. In the presentation of play 'what is' comes to the fore" (*WM* 105–7/99–101).[4]

As sketched so far, Gadamer's outlook in *Truth and Method* carries a distinctly post-Cartesian and post-idealist (perhaps even post-metaphysical) cast; yet, references to rupture or reversal are offset or counterbalanced by repeated endorsements of a subjective-intentional hermeneutics. Pondering the transformative effects of art and aesthetic experience, Gadamer quickly retreats to the vantage points of finite individual existence. Even if aesthetics should erect limits to self-consciousness, he notes, "we do not have a standpoint which would allow us to see these limits and conditions in themselves, and us as limited or conditioned from the outside. Even what transcends our understanding is experienced by us as *our* limit and thus belongs to the continuity of self-understanding in which human existence moves." What play and playfulness, therefore, involve is not so much a transgression of understanding as rather a distinctive challenge: the challenge "of preserving—despite this discontinuity of aesthetics and aesthetic experience—the hermeneutic continuity which constitutes our being" (91/86). In the end, art-works are explicitly integrated in, and subordinated to, a quasi-idealist hermeneutics of understanding and self-consciousness—notwithstanding the discussed "ontological" reformulation of aesthetics. "Actually," Gadamer affirms, "hermeneutics should be understood in so comprehensive a sense as to embrace the whole sphere of art and its range of questions. Like any other text a work of art, not only literature, needs to be understood—and this understanding must be nurtured and trained. With this, hermeneutical consciousness acquires a comprehensive scope that surpasses even aesthetic consciousness: *aesthetics must be absorbed into hermeneutics.*" To facilitate this absorption, to be sure, hermeneutics itself needs to be reinterpreted in a manner which "does justice to the experience of art." Accordingly, understanding has to be seen as part of the "event or happening of meaning" [*Sinngeschehen*] in which "the significance of all statements—those of art and of tradition in general—is formed and completed" (*WM* 157/146).[5]

Read in conjunction with the Gadamer-Derrida exchange, the preceding comments are prone to highlight a profound antagonism: If there is a central focus or target of Derridean deconstruction it is the notion of an unfolding meaning or continuity of understanding. This target furnishes the critical impulse in all of Derrida's writings; it looms particularly large in his assessments of Nietzsche. His *Spurs,* subtitled *Nietzsche's Styles,* is a concerted attack on the search for continuous meaning or what Derrida calls (somewhat elliptically) "onto-hermeneutics." Over long stretches, the monograph offers a discussion of "woman" or womanhood—mainly because woman is seen as the basic confounder and antagonist of cumulative meaning and stable identity. Woman, Derrida writes, is "perhaps not a distinct thing, not the determinable identity of a figure or appearance . . . . Perhaps—as a non-identity, non-figure, a simulacrum—woman is the very *abyss* of distance, the distancing of distance, the thrust of spacing, distance itself or *as such* (if one could still say such a thing which is no longer possible)" (*Spurs* 49). Contrary to an essentialist ontology and to a hermeneutics wedded to stable meanings, there is for Derrida "no such thing as the essence of woman because woman differentiates, and differentiates herself from herself. Out of endless, bottomless depths, she engulfs and distorts all vestiges of essentiality, of identity, and of propriety or property. And philosophical discourse, blinded, founders on these shoals and is hurled down these depthless depths to its ruin" (51). Despite his occasional diatribes against women and his apparent "anti-feminism," then, Nietzsche himself in that study approximates this vertiginous quality of womanhood. By placing traditional essences or meaning-structures "between the tender-hooks of quotation marks," we read, "Nietzsche's writing is at best an 'inscription' of truth. And such an inscription, even if we do not venture to call it the feminine itself, is indeed the feminine 'operation' " (57).[6]

Apart from contrasting essence with non-identity, *Spurs* also links "woman"—and Nietzsche—with artistry or aesthetics. In Derrida's presentation, woman cannot be subsumed under the rubrics of linear-cognitive "truth," rubrics celebrated by traditional philosophy (or metaphysics). "There is no such thing as the truth about woman," he writes; "but this is so because that abyssal divergence of truth or that non-truth *is* 'truth': woman is but one name for that untruth of truth" (*Spurs* 51). At the same time, however, woman is not just the negation of truth or the identity of non-truth, for "she knows that such a reversal would only deprive her of her powers of simulation" and would "force her just as surely as ever into the same old apparatus" (61). Instead, woman places truth in quotation marks or under "veils" of modesty, with which she toys playfully: not believing in truth she still "plays with it as she would with a new concept or doctrine, gleefully anticipating her laughter" (61). According to *Spurs*, woman occupies basically three positions vis-à-vis truth or cognitive meaning. In the first, she is identified with untruth and denounced as a "potentate of falsehood—in the name of truth and dogmatic metaphysics"; in the second case, she is placed on a pedestal and idealized as truth or as a "potentate of truth," again by "credulous" philosophers. Only in the third case does woman escape this dichotomy and come into her own: "Beyond the double negation she is recognized and affirmed as an affirmative power, a dissimulatress, an artist, a dionysiac" (97). Actually, woman is able to exert this playful potency in the first two instances as well: "Seen as a model for truth she can display the gifts of her seductive power, which rules over dogmatism and disorients and routs those credulous men, the philosophers. And to the extent that she does not believe in truth (but still finds it in her interest) she is again a model, only this time a good model—or rather a bad model, because she plays at dissimulation, at ornamentation, deceit, artifice, at an artist's philosophy, manifesting her affirmative power" (67). The same playful delight or artistry—the study claims—can also be found in Nietzsche, as is shown in his (alleged) preference for "style" or multiple "styles" over stable meaning: "With its spur (or pointed thrust) style can also protect against the terrifying, blinding or mortal danger of whatever *presents* itself or is obstinately encountered: presence, content, the thing itself, meaning, or truth" (39).[7]

In emphasizing playfulness and artistry, Derrida in a sense complements Gadamer's discussion of "play"—but with a radical difference: instead of integrating play into the understanding of meaning, or aesthetics into hermeneutics, *Spurs* presents art as the rock or riff (another sense of the French *éperon*) on which intentional hermeneutics founders. As portrayed in that text, woman—according to one passage—"describes a margin where the control over meaning or code is without recourse" and which "erects a limit to the relevance of hermeneutical or systematic inquiries" (99). Assimilating—perhaps too abruptly—existential or ontological hermeneutics with the cognitive aspirations or traditional logic (or metaphysics), Derrida finds in woman the antidote to univocal meaning and intelligible continuity. "From the moment," he writes, "the question of woman suspends the decidable opposition between the true and non-true; from the moment it installs the epochal regime of quotation marks for all the concepts belonging to the system of philosophical decidability—from that moment the hermeneutical project postulating a true sense of the text is disqualified. Reading at this point is freed from the horizon of the meaning or truth of being, liberated from the values of the product's production or the present's presence. Whereupon the question of style is immediately unleashed as a question of writing." As he adds, the "spurring-operation" of this question of style—in Nietzsche's case the operation of the "grand style" manifest in the will to power—"is more powerful than any content, thesis or meaning" (107).[8]

These strictures against the "hermeneutical project" are said to apply also to Heidegger's textual exegesis, especially to his attempt to find *a* meaning or *the* meaning of Nietzsche's writings—an endeavor which, in Derrida's words, "remains throughout the near totality of its trajectory in the hermeneutical space of the question of the truth (of being)" (*Spurs* 115). Once, however, the undecidability of truth and non-truth, and also of identity and otherness, property and non-property, is taken into account, Heidegger's exegesis is bound to be disoriented. "On such a track," he notes, "we might perhaps flush out again Heidegger's reading of 'Nietzsche', and abscond with it outside the hermeneutical circle and everything it reflects, towards a field of enormous dimensions, a field immeasurable except perhaps by the steps of a dove" (123). According to Derrida, the impossibility of finding a single, comprehensive meaning in Nietzsche is not due to a shortcoming of Heidegger or any other interpreter: not even Nietzsche may have possessed the key to his opus. "Could Nietzsche," he asks, referring to a particular fragment, "have disposed of some more or less secret code which, for him or some unknown accomplice of his, would have made sense of this statement? We shall never know; at least it is possible that we will never know and that possibility (of ignorance) must somehow be taken into account." This inability is "imprinted on the remains of this non-fragment as a trace, withdrawing it from any assured horizon of a hermeneutical query" (127). The fragment in question—a scribbled note saying "I have forgotten my umbrella"—thus assumes a prototypical status for exegesis: "If Nietzsche had indeed meant to say or express something, might it not be just that limit of the will to mean—which, as effect of a necessarily differential will to power, is forever divided, folded, and multiplied? To whatever lengths one might carry a conscientious interpretation, the hypothesis that the totality of Nietzsche's text, in some monstrous way, might well be of the type 'I have forgotten my umbrella' cannot be excluded" (133).

* * * * *

In light of the preceding amplifications, the broader parameters of the discussed exchange should have emerged into sharper relief. What surely has surfaced is the multidimensionality of the issues at stake. On a first level—perhaps the most prominent one—the exchange revolves around a conflict of interpretations or conceptions of interpretation, conjuring up a powerful array of dichotomies or oppositions: understanding versus non-understanding, immanence versus otherness, continuity versus rupture, truth versus non-truth. On another level—not sharply segregated from the first—the issues have to do with modes of inquiry and categories of human behavior, giving rise to another set of antinomies: intentional activity versus non-intentional playfulness, ethics versus art, practical hermeneutics versus aesthetics. Behind these levels, as I shall argue, yet another cluster of questions lies in wait: one dealing with the status of political interaction and communication in our time. Viewed in a gross and overly simplified manner, the two spokesmen might each be assigned to one side of the polar oppositions: with Gadamer representing understanding, immanence, continuity, and truth, and Derrida non-understanding, rupture, and artistry. However, both thinkers are too adroit and subtle to fit neatly into these rubrics—although a certain overall tendency can hardly be denied, namely, the tendency in one case to return to traditional metaphysics and, in the other, to leap briskly beyond it. My ambition here is not to award a palm to the winning side of the debate (if there were such a winning side); more modestly, I seek to cut a path through the thicket of arguments that defies easy solution. Fortunately, my venture is facilitated by the life-work of the thinker to whom both spokesmen, from diverse angles, pay tribute.

Focusing first on Gadamer's comments, one can hardly fail to appreciate the intensity of his hermeneutical élan and commitment to transpersonal understanding—a commitment, I believe, embodying the best features of the great tradition of humanistic learning and education. Equally attractive, to me, is his close association of hermeneutics and dialogue—with dialogue signifying not a sequence of soliloquies but an existential encounter involving mutual testing and risk-taking. Despite these and many similar virtues, however, I am troubled by Gadamer's persistent oscillation or a certain half-heartedness of his "ontological turn"—an oscillation that has been noted repeatedly above, and that only needs to be recalled here briefly. A central ambivalence concerns the relation between the "universality" or "universal claim" of hermeneutics and the notion of hermeneutical "limits"—two views Gadamer seems to endorse simultaneously (but without clarifying their compatibility). Can one plausibly argue that "the universal claim of hermeneutics is undeniable" and that the hermeneutical circle in particular enjoys "true universality," and yet add almost instantly: "For my part I was always careful not to forget the limits implicit in the hermeneutical experience of meaning. When I wrote that 'intelligible being is language' I meant to say that being can never be completely understood." A related quandary has to do with the status of traditional philosophical (or metaphysical) discourse, a quandary highlighted by the issue of "logocentrism." Is it possible to criticize the "logocentrism of Greek ontology" from the vantage point of biblical and theological sources, and yet extol the merits of Plato's *eumeneis elenchoi* and affirm that, on the model of Platonic dialogues, "the exchange of speech and counterspeech, question and answer, can produce genuine consensus"? A more specific issue in the same context is the status of

German idealism and particularly of Hegelian dialectics—a dialectics which, on the one hand, is closely assimilated to hermeneutical interaction and, on the other, castigated for skirting the domain of otherness ("the boundary which he did not transgress").[9]

Both in the Paris exchange and in *Truth and Method,* a crucial ambivalence concerns the role of "rupture" or transformative change, and the relationship between continuity and discontinuity. In formulating an "ontological" conception of art, *Truth and Method*—as indicated—places heavy stress on the rupturing or transformative quality of art-works, a quality radically different from merely incremental, continuous change. In contrast to a "gradual transition" leading from one point to the next, the transformation occurring in art-works is said to imply "that something turns suddenly and as a whole into something else." Relying on Heideggerian teachings, Gadamer also refers to the rupturing "push" [*Stoss*] involved in the experience of art-works, a push that disrupts or disorients "complacent meaning expectations." With regard to subjective agents (artists and interpreters alike), the rupturing effect is claimed to be such that "the identity of the players remains for no one the same." As also noted, however, comments of this kind do not prevent Gadamer in the end from reaffirming the ineluctable primacy of understanding or "hermeneutical consciousness": even what transcends or outstrips our immediate grasp belongs, in his view, to "the continuity of self-understanding in which human existence moves" or that "hermeneutic continuity which constitutes our being." What remains unresolved at this point—or unevenly resolved by fiat—is a question Gadamer articulates in "Text and Interpretation," namely, the question, "How the unity of meaning established in dialogue and the impenetrability of otherness can be reconciled or mediated—that is, what language [*Sprachlichkeit*] ultimately signifies: bridge or barrier?"

The question clearly affects the status and range of hermeneutics. Perhaps Heidegger was not ill-advised when, following *Being and Time,* he became apprehensive of, and even turned his back on, hermeneutics, since—as Gadamer states—"he realized its inability to help him break through the parameters of transcendental reflection" or through the "sphere of phenomenological immanence." Needless to say, hermeneutics cannot simply be vindicated hermeneutically; nor can the scope and possible limits of hermeneutics be assessed through a recourse to self-understanding. In *Truth and Method* Gadamer asserts that we do not have a "standpoint" that would "allow us to see" what limits or conditions us. However, in portraying the rupturing effect of art and the dislocation of identity, does he not himself implicitly invoke such a standpoint?—which, I would add, is nothing but the standpoint of philosophy or, better still, the vantage point of that post-philosophical (or post-metaphysical) reflection that Heidegger calls "poetic" or "recollective" thinking [*Andenken*]. The dimension of such thinking is actually not alien to *Truth and Method.* "The question of philosophy," it observes at one point, "asks what is the 'being' of self-understanding? With this question it transcends in principle the horizon of this self-understanding." The question, Gadamer adds, is raised with particular intensity in Heideggerian philosophy: "In uncovering time as its own hidden ground, this philosophy does not preach blind commitment out of nihilistic despair; rather, it opens itself to a hitherto concealed experience transgressing subjectivity or subjective reflection, an experience that Heidegger calls 'Being' " (*WM* 95/89).

In comparison with Gadamer's magnum opus, Derrida is much more resolute in seeking to transgress phenomenological "immanence" and the boundaries of transcendental reflection. Aiming his critique beyond Gadamer at the legacy of Cartesian metaphysics, his writings confront subjectivity or subjective complacency at every step with the challenge of non-understanding, rupture, and non-identity. Following Heidegger's lead but attempting to outdistance him, "deconstruction" pinpoints the limits of an intentional or existential hermeneutics—limits not externally imposed but endemic to the endeavor of understanding itself. While admiring the intellectual and stylistic zest of Derrida's work, however, I am troubled by a certain aloofness or non-engagement characterizing his thought (at least over long stretches)—more pointedly put: by a potential indifference or apathy resulting from the celebration of "difference." In part, this concern is prompted by the occasional exuberance of his deconstructive zeal: his tendency not so much to engage traditional philosophy or divergent views as to circumvent and elude them. On this score, it would be easy to quote Derrida against Derrida. As he stated in one of his earlier writings: "The step 'beyond or outside philosophy' is much more difficult to conceive than is commonly imagined by those who pretend to have made it long ago with cavalier ease, and who in general remain tied to metaphysics together with the entire body of discourse they claim to have severed from it" (*ED* 416/284). Echoes of these sentiments can still be found, intermittently, in *Spurs*. "Heidegger," we read there, "warns us against an aestheticising confusionism which, as blind to art as it is to philosophy, would—in its precipitate interpretation of Nietzsche's propositions regarding the beginning era of the philosopher-artist—have us conclude that conceptual rigor is now less intractable and that it will henceforth be admissible to say anything in militating for the cause of irrelevance" (73–75).

Taking one's cues from these statements, one cannot help feeling uneasy about some of Derrida's recent arguments—especially his treatment of key metaphysical categories like truth, being, or totality. In this respect, incidentally, he seems often less than generous in acknowledging Heideggerian motifs; for, is it really necessary to instruct the latter about the complexity or ambivalence of these categories? Was it not Heidegger who (in "The Essence of Truth" and elsewhere) first enlightened us about the correlation of truth and non-truth, being and non-being, concealment and unconcealment—a correlation that did not lead him to abandon these terms but to reformulate them (as in the case of "truth")? In portraying both "woman" and Nietzsche's position, Derrida sometimes pretends to be entirely beyond such categories. "There is no such thing as a woman or a truth in itself about woman in itself," we read in *Spurs* (101). "For the same reason there is also no such thing as the truth of Nietzsche or of Nietzsche's text" (103). Commenting on Nietzsche's phrase "these are only—*my* truths" he adds: "The very fact that '*my* truths' is so underlined, that they are multiple, variegated, contradictory even, can only imply that these are not *truths*. There is then no such thing as a truth in itself, but only a surfeit of it; even about myself, truth is plural" (103). However, to say that truth is plural is clearly not the same as to claim that there are no truths or no such thing as truth—because even a multiple, variegated truth still invokes the category of truth. Moreover, does not Derrida himself aim to disclose the truth about woman and about Nietzsche—to be sure, the truth in all its complexity and multiplicity? Equally difficult as the surrender of truth seems to me the escape from "being." Juxtaposing Heidegger's notion of "propriation" [*Ereignis*] and the category of being, Derrida affirms: "Because it is finally undecidable, propriation is more powerful than the question *ti esti,* more powerful than the veil of truth or the meaning of being." And he instantly continues: "Propriation is all the more powerful since it is its process that organizes both the totality of language's operation and symbolic exchange in general" (11). But the phrase "propriation is" already enlists in its service the entire question of "*ti esti*" and thus the problematic of (the meaning of) being.[10]

A central target in both *Spurs* and the Paris exchange is the category of "unity" or "totality" as applied to Nietzsche's thought. Countering Heidegger's interpretation, Derrida insists on the variegated and refracted character of Nietzsche's writings, a character that cannot be assembled into a unified or holistic synthesis of meaning. As a first reaction one probably might want to question the holistic compactness of Heidegger's approach. As is well-known, his exegesis originated in a series of lectures held, and essays written, during an extremely turbulent decade in German history (1936–1946) and in explicit response to this turbulence—a fact Derrida acknowledges when he notes that "these dates are of utmost importance if one wishes to relate this exegesis, in whole or in part, to its historical-political context" (IS 59). On closer inspection, the different parts of Heidegger's analysis actually reveal distinct shifts in focus and emphasis (shifts particularly evident between the first and second volumes of the German edition).[11] At the same time, Derrida's own reading is not free of unifying or holistic elements. In presenting woman's (and Nietzsche's) relations to truth, *Spurs* assembles these relations into a threefold matrix or "finite number of typical and matrical propositions" (95; woman as truth, as non-truth, and as artist)—an arrangement that may be less than a code but still forms an intelligible combination. More important here is the status of unity or totality itself. In shunning unitary meaning, Derrida asserts, Nietzsche's work also "unhinges what governs the thought or simple anticipation of wholeness, namely, the species-genus relationship. What prevails, rather, is a singular inclusion of 'whole' in the 'part', and this without any totalization" (IS 71). As a critical stratagem this point is elusive. For, did Heidegger not expressly exempt "being" from the species-genus nexus? Moreover, does the postulated inclusion of the "whole" in the "part" not presuppose a notion, however inchoate, of the whole?[12]

Regarding Derrida's own reading of Nietzsche, I would add, the source of the claimed multiplicity deserves further investigation. In some passages, this source seems to be the thinker himself. To repeat a previous citation: "Who has decided that one carries only one name? Surely not Nietzsche . . . . Next to Kierkegaard, was Nietzsche not one of the few who multiplied his names and played with signatures, identities, and masks—who named himself several times and with different names?" (IS 67). In this passage, Nietzsche appears as the master-artist who playfully toyed with identities and ingeniously concealed himself behind a multitude of masks and disguises. But where, in this case, is the supposed exit from metaphysics? Far from evading its stranglehold, Nietzsche on this reading seems firmly entrenched in Cartesian-Kantian subjectivity or, in Gadamer's terms, in "aesthetic consciousness." The impression is reinforced by the stress on non-dialogue and non-communication—which seems to ensconce the thinker even more safely in the bulwark of self-identity (if not solipsism). Derrida, to be sure, is not satisfied with this reading and strenuously seeks to avoid its consequences. "Not that we need to side passively with heterogeneity or parody," he writes in *Spurs*. "Nor should one conclude from all this that the unavailability of a unique and ungraftable master-meaning is actually due to Nietzsche's infinite mastery, to his impregnable power, his impeccable manipulation of some trap, or to a sort of infinite calculus like that of Leibniz' God— only this time to a calculus of the undecidable so as to foil the grasp of hermeneutics. In seeking to elude the latter absolutely, one would just as surely fall back into its trap, by turning parody or simulacrum into an instrument of mastery in the service of truth" (99; see also QS 186).

As a result, the source of multiplicity must be found elsewhere. In this respect, I find instructive and inspiring Gadamer's comments on aesthetics and especially on the transformative quality of art and play. As previously noted, play in his portrayal involves not merely a sequence of intentional activities but rather a kind of reversal of intentionality or counter-intentionality: in his words, "all playing is a being-played." Equally attractive in my view is his stress on the experiential dimension of play and genuine dialogue: the aspect of exposure, vulnerability, and risk. "Being played" in his assessment denotes not merely a passive endurance or external happening but rather a human "pathos": the labor or travail undergone in the process of transformation. Such labor, moreover, is rarely smooth and painless; for, how could we really be dislodged or "decentered" from our customary identity or way of life without discomfort or pain? On this score, Gadamer's position bears some affinity with Nietzsche's Zarathustra who at one point proclaimed himself the teacher or advocate "of life, of suffering, and of the circle." Derrida is not entirely a stranger to this perspective. "The festival of Nietzsche," he says in the Paris exchange, "implies the risk for the thinker to be torn to pieces and to be dispersed into his masks" (IS 68). But how can such a dispersal happen on the level of "styles" alone—the level of a formal-literary "spurring-operation" divorced from "any content, any thesis, any meaning?" How can we be torn away from our moorings through "mere" words or an infinite "play of signifiers"—a play which does not penetrate to and transform us in our substance or "being?" (See IS 68–69).[13]

At this point, the normative or ethical dimension of play and dialogue also comes into view—the relevance of what Gadamer calls "good will." In denying a master key to Nietzsche's self-understanding, Derrida states in *Spurs*: "No, somewhere parody always presupposes a naiveté, backed up by the unconscious, a vertiginous non-mastery, a loss of consciousness. An absolutely calculated parody would be either a confession or a table of law" (101). But how is such naiveté, such a loss of mastery possible without a curtailment of self-centeredness, that is, without an overcoming of all those selfish impulses and desires that block the road to innocence? In participating in play or dialogue, do agents not have to curb or put aside their private vendettas and animosities? And is this overcoming or curbing not the gist of ethics seen as striving for "goodness?" In alerting us to the role of "good will" Gadamer (I think) is again not far from the spirit of Nietzsche and his notion of "overcoming." On the other hand, in stressing only "styles" and artistry Derrida tends to slight or disregard Nietzsche's ethical fervor, his search for ever new "values"—although this search aimed at nobility above and beyond conventional "goodness." "The noble man wants to create something new or a new virtue, while the good want the old and its preservation," Zarathustra affirms, adding: "But this is not the danger of the noble man that he might become one of the good, but that he might turn into a churl, a mocker, a destroyer."[14] The same fervor also pervades the "three metamorphoses" or the ascending sequence of camel, lion, and child—although Nietzsche himself tended to prefer mostly the roaring of the lion, a roar calling for the coming of the child. To quote Zarathustra again: "Why must the preying lion still become a child? The child is innocence and forgetting, a new beginning, a game [*Spiel*], a self-propelled wheel, a first movement, a sacred 'Yes'."[15]

The neglect (if not disparagement) of the ethical dimension is particularly evident in Derrida's stress on non-judgment or "undecidability." In seeking to evade metaphysics, *Spurs* presents all traditional categories as basically exchangeable or undecidable—including truth and non-truth, meaning and non-meaning, being and nothingness (and, by implication, good and evil). The question of woman at one point is said to "abstract truth from itself," suspending it "in indecision, in the *epoché*" (59); according to a later passage, the same question is claimed to "suspend the decidable opposition of true and non-true, inaugurating the epochal regime of quotation marks" (107). Still later, *Spurs* speaks of the "undecidable oscillation" in women between "giving oneself" and "giving oneself for," and also of the "undecidable equivalence" of "gift-poison" [or gift-*Gift*] (121). Turning to Heidegger's notion of "propriation," Derrida discovers a more profound, quasi-ontological undecidability. Although propriation, he writes, "is as if magnetized by a valuation or ineradicable preference for the proper or property, it all the more surely leads to property's abyssal structure," a structure where "property is literally sunk" by "passing into otherness" (117). This abyssal structure is finally presented as the vortex in which being and non-being become interchangeable and where all distinctions or decidable issues vanish into nothingness: "Once the question of production or the question of the *event* (which is one meaning of *Ereignis*) has been up-rooted from ontology," we read, "property or propriation is named exactly as that which is proper to nothing and no one; it (propriation) no longer decides of the appropriation of the truth of being, but rather casts into its bottomless abyss truth as well as non-truth, concealment and unconcealment, enlightenment and dissimulation. The history of being becomes a history in which no being, nothing, happens (except *Ereignis'* unfathomable process)" (119).[16]

It is (at the latest) at this juncture that Derrida's key notion of "difference" shades over into a celebration of indifference, non-engagement, and indecision. Coupled with the emphasis on discontinuity and fragmentation, this indifference begins to approximate closely Gadamer's "aesthetic consciousness" (if not the "aestheticizing confusionism" castigated by Derrida elsewhere). In Gadamer's words: "Absolute discontinuity, that is, the disintegration of the unity of the aesthetic object into a multiplicity of experiences, is the necessary consequence of an aesthetics of feeling." Gadamer at this point invokes Kierkegaard's decisionism—the Danish thinker's powerful "Either-Or"—as an antidote to aesthetic indifference. "As it seems to me," he writes, "Kierkegaard has demonstrated the untenability of this position, by recognizing the destructive consequences of subjectivism and by describing—prior to anyone else—the self-destruction of aesthetic immediacy. His theory of the aesthetic stage of existence is developed from the standpoint of the moralist, one who has realized the desperate and untenable state of an existence lived in pure immediacy and discontinuity. Hence, his critique of aesthetic consciousness is of fundamental importance because he shows the inner contradictions of aesthetic existence, contradictions that force it to go beyond itself" (*WM* 91/85). What emerges behind Kierkegaard's "Either-Or" is the question of the relationship between ethics and aesthetics—including an aesthetics reformulated along Gadamerian or Heideggerian lines. As it seems to me, aesthetics—especially a non-subjectivist aesthetics—can by no means be divorced from ethics, to the extent that the latter signifies the overcoming of subjective self-centeredness. Not that aesthetics can in any way be derived from ethics: as non-intentionality, play or art cannot be deliberately produced or fabricated. Rather, the two appear mutually (but non-causally) implicated: to guard its naiveté, art presupposes ethics; but the latter, in turn, can only arise through "recollection" of playful innocence.[17]

This leads me finally to the practical-political connotations of the reviewed exchange. In this domain, Gadamer is known for his long-standing insistence on the linkage between hermeneutics and *"praxis"* (although, in his treatment, the latter term shares some of the ambivalence of hermeneutical inquiry). His Paris comments presented the "capacity for understanding" as a "basic human endowment which sustains social life," while the possibility of consensus was described as prerequisite of "all human solidarity and the viability of society." Seen from this perspective, social and political interaction clearly requires ethical engagement or the reciprocal display of "good will"—though an engagement which, in its more intense or accomplished modes, makes room for non-intentional playfulness. This combination or sequence seems to me to be the gist of *"Bildung"* or of public education and culture. Again, Gadamer deserves praise for having rescued this notion from its contemporary oblivion or efface-ment. "Viewed as elevation to a universal or common vista," he writes in *Truth and Method*, *"Bildung* constitutes a general human task. The task requires sac-rifice of (mere) particularity for the sake of something common or universal—where sacrifice of particularity means, in negative terms, the curbing of desire and hence, freedom from the object of desire and freedom for its objectivity" (10/13).[18] Construed as educational process or the formation of public "charac-ter," incidentally, *Bildung* is by no means synonymous with the imposition of an abstract-universal scheme or an external pedagogical system; rather, like Gada-merian dialogue, it involves mutual exposure and risk-taking—and above all, participation in the labor or travail of individual and communal transformation. Needless to say, such participation is a far cry from the non-engagement and neutral indifference prevalent in liberal societies (a stance present implicitly or as a tendency in Derrida's occasional aestheticism).

Projected onto a broader scale, the hermeneutics-deconstruction theme has repercussions for cross-cultural political relations, that is, for the emergence of the "global city." On this level, the central issue concerns the appropriate char-acter of political communication and interaction. Rooted in the venerable tradi-tion of humanistic learning and *Geisteswissenschaften*, Gadamer's hermeneutics encourages us to venture forth and seek to comprehend alien cultures and life-worlds; however, the question remains whether, in this venture, cultural differ-ences are not simply assimilated or absorbed into the understanding mind (which is basically a Western mind). On the other hand, by stressing rupture and radical otherness Derrida seeks to uproot and dislodge the inquirer's comfortable self-identity; yet, his insistence on incommensurability and non-understanding tends to encourage reciprocal cultural disengagement and hence non-learning. In *Truth and Method,* Gadamer at one point expresses the central maxim of philosophical heremeneutics: "To recognize oneself (or one's own) in the other and find a home abroad—this is the basic movement of spirit whose being consists in this return to itself from otherness" (11/15). But clearly this maxim engenders, and needs to be complemented by, another maxim, namely, the challenge to recognize otherness or the alien in oneself (or one's own). Much, perhaps everything, will depend on our ability to find a mode of interaction balancing hermeneutics and counter-hermeneutics, cumulative self-understanding and self-abandonment, identity and transformation. As it seems to me, some incipient steps along this road have been made by Heidegger in his "Dialogue on Language" (subtitled "Between a Japanese and an Inquirer"). Referring to the "hermeneutical circle" as a relation of calling and being called, message and addressee, the inquirer states: "The messenger must come from the message; but he must also already have moved toward it." Whereupon the Japanese: "Did you not say earlier that this circle is inevitable and that, instead of trying to avoid it as an alleged logical contradiction, we must follow it?" And the reply: "Yes. But this necessary acceptance of the hermeneutical circle does not mean that the hermeneutic relation is properly experienced through a conceptual formulation of the accepted circle" (*US* 150/51).[19]

Hans-Georg Gadamer

*1. Letter to Dallmayr**

Translated by Richard Palmer and Diane Michelfelder

My encounter with Derrida in Paris three years ago, which I had looked forward to as a conversation between two totally independent developers of Heideggerian initiatives in thought, involved special difficulties. First of all, there was the language barrier. This is always a great difficulty when thinking or poetizing strives to leave traditional forms behind, trying to draw out of one's own mother tongue new ways of thinking. Of course, in the wake of Heidegger this is especially so, and it apparently also holds once again in the case of the Paris encounter. The German publication of the encounter, which appeared in 1984 under the title *Text und Interpretation,* suffers precisely from the fact that the French contributions appear in German. In German, Derrida's style of deconstruction loses some of its suppleness. (On the other hand, my academic philosophizing would probably lose some of its earnestness when rendered into French.)

Nor did the artistry of Nietzsche's language help to provide us with a common ground. For it is precisely the case that one can read Nietzsche in fundamentally different ways. One reader may see a shifting play of masks in his attempts and enticements as portending the end not only of metaphysics but of philosophy itself.[1] And this cuts the ground out from under all efforts at a unitary understanding of Nietzsche. Thus, Derrida rejects the effort of Heidegger's Nietzsche-interpretation from the ground up. He sees in it the logocentric bias of metaphysics, from which Heidegger's thinking had futilely tried to escape. Certainly, I myself became a willing victim of the violent power of Heidegger's dialogues with philosophical or poetic texts, a violence that is also

---

*This letter was received by Professor Fred Dallmayr of Notre Dame University, Notre Dame, Indiana, in response to a manuscript version of his essay, "Hermeneutics and Deconstruction: Gadamer and Derrida in Dialogue." It is published here with the kind permission of Professor Gadamer and Professor Dallmayr.

present in his Nietzsche-interpretation. I found Heidegger's bringing together in thought of the will to power and the eternal recurrence to be fully persuasive and irrefutable. Along with Heidegger, I see metaphysics in Nietzsche in the process of self-disintegration, so to speak, and thereby in search of a bridge into a new language, into another thinking (which perhaps does not even exist).

Perhaps Derrida could have written this last sentence? Especially the part in parentheses at the end—wouldn't he only need to translate it into French? It looks as if, at least between Heidegger and Derrida, the intrinsic ambivalence or multivocity of Nietzsche does offer something like a common ground. In light of this, it is I myself who, in taking up and continuing hermeneutics as philosophy, would appear at best as the lost sheep in the dried up pastures of metaphysics.

Of course, this self-characterization does not fully please me. Have I really gone astray even though I intended to follow Heidegger when he spoke about the overcoming of or recovering from metaphysics? Certainly it is true that I have held fast to hermeneutics—which he placed at the center of his ontology of Dasein—against his own later decision in this regard. But in so doing, I did not by any means intend at the same time to hold fast to his transcendentally conceived fundamental ontology. Rather, it is precisely the new trajectories in thought opened by the *later* Heidegger—drawing into the hermeneutical dimension the themes of the artwork, the thing, and language—that have guided my way, or better confirmed my own path of thought. In following this path, I cannot see that I have somehow fallen into that very metaphysics or ontotheology whose overcoming and recovering from was Heidegger's task of thinking. In his view, metaphysics is certainly a "logocentrism" whose question about the "whatness of beings" obscures the question of the "there" of Being. Heidegger's fruitless effort to retrieve the question of the "There"—the question of being—from the αληθεια [*alētheia*] of the Presocratics confirms, in my view, the fact that Greek thought was already on the path of metaphysics. It was finally to reach its fulfillment as onto-theo-logy, in which the question of Being is indissolubly linked with the question of the highest being.[2] Clearly that is the kind of metaphysics whose ontotheological form was appropriated by Christian theology and dominated the years to come, so that eventually in the age of science the question of Being became unintelligible. This is what Heidegger ultimately had in mind in his analysis of presence-at-hand. It is also what one is accustomed to think of in Christian metaphysics as the relationship of the *intellectus infinitus* to the order of created being. And this is presumably what Derrida means when he speaks of the metaphysics of presence, whose force obviously also still dominates Husserl's analyses of time.

Actually, in *Being and Time* Heidegger had already gone beyond such a concept of being. We can clearly see this in his analysis of the hermeneutical structure of "*Existenz.*"[3] So, when I go on to put the notion of dialogue as a mode of being truly "on the way to language" in the place of Heidegger's 'existential structure' of speech [*Rede*], and when I place in the foreground the light that one can bring to another and which constitutes (I would claim) "the authenticity of Being-with," I am holding very systematically to the starting point of *Being and Time*—that is, Dasein understanding itself in its being. But this self-understanding [*Selbstverständnis*] is, in all its forms, the extreme opposite of self-consciousness [*Selbstbewußtsein*] and self-possession [*Selbstbesitz*]. Rather, it is an understanding that always places itself in question, which is not only grounded on the "mine-ness" of my being [*die Jemeinigkeit*] that is revealed in the possibility of death, but at the same time encompasses all recognition of oneself in the other, which first opens up in dialogue. The fact that conversation takes place wherever, whenever, and with whomever something comes to language—whether this is another person or a thing, a word, or a flame-signal (Gottfried Benn)—constitutes the universality of the hermeneutical experience. The fact that this experience contains its own limits within itself is in no way inconsistent with its universality. Quite the contrary. The universality of the hermeneutical experience fits perfectly well with the factual limitedness of all human experience and with the limits governing our linguistic communication and possibility for expression.

So I think I am completely consistent in asserting that the conversation that we are is one that never ends. No word is the last word, just as there is no first word. Every word is itself always an answer and gives rise always to a new question. Thus, I don't see why Dallmayr is offended by this point. Certainly it should be completely clear that I cannot agree here with Derrida, who would relate the hermeneutical experience, especially in live conversation or dialogue, to the metaphysics of presence. Heidegger has critically and insightfully spoken of the "superficiality of the Greeks" with respect to their ocularity, their *eidos*-oriented thinking, their leveling of the *logos* into logic of referential thought [*Logik der Apophansis*]. One could call this logocentrism and thereby feel united with Kierkegaard, Luther, and the Old Testament, in view of the fact that the Judeo-Christian experience of faith is based on hearing and listening to the voice of God. But then to go on to speak about his criticism of logocentrism as itself a logocentrism represents, in my view, a misunderstanding of the mysterious character of the word. The word is what one person speaks and another understands. How does presence play a role in this? Who listens at all to his or her own voice? And who understands what he or she merely hears? Here, it seems to me that Derrida, in his quite accurate criticism of Husserl's *Logical Investigations* and of his concept of *Kundgabe*[4]—developed in his fine book *Speech and Phenomenon* (*VP*)—lets himself be led into making a false imputation. And this has fateful consequences for his approach to Heidegger and to hermeneutics.

Certainly, I too see the inner closeness of speaking and writing that lies in the capability of language to be written. I, too, regard every utterance as "on the way to writing," as I called a short essay I wrote in 1983.[5] But what is writing if it is not intended to be read? Certainly I share with Derrida the conviction that a text is no longer dependent on an author and his/her intention. When I read something, I do not seek to hear in myself the familiar sounds of the voice of the other. On the contrary, we all have had the experience of being alienated from a familiar text by hearing the voice of its author reading it aloud. Even so, I only read a text with understanding when the letters are not just deciphered but when the text begins to speak, and that means when it is read with appropriate modulations, articulations, and emphases. The art of writing—and I really do not need to tell this to a writer of Derrida's rank—consists in the fact that the writer so controls the world of signs making up the text that the return of the text into spoken language succeeds. In modern times, this means mostly soundless speaking, but even now it consists in the wonderful interplay of sound and meaning that distinguishes well-written books—and poetry even more so—as "literature." I really would like to know what understanding—and by implication, reading with understanding—has to do with metaphysics.

I too affirm that understanding is always understanding-differently [*Andersverstehen*]. What is pushed aside or dislocated when my word reaches another person, and especially when a text reaches its reader, can never be fixed in a rigid identity. Where understanding takes place, there is not just an identity. Rather, to *understand* means that one is capable of stepping into the place of the other in order to say what one has there understood and what one has to say in response. That does not at all mean to repeat something after the other. Rather, in its literal sense, understanding means to stand for the other and represent a matter "before the court" or before whomever.

Now Derrida will certainly object that I do not take Nietzsche seriously enough: that is to say, the end of metaphysics, that break which, since Nietzsche, makes all identity and continuity with oneself and with the other illusory. He takes these to be logocentric illusions from which even Heidegger did not escape, as his Nietzsche-interpretation shows. Ultimately, for Derrida, all this remains Hegel, and that means precisely: metaphysics. Now it is certainly true that it was Hegel's claim to have reconciled dialectically the breach of otherness, and indeed every kind of otherness, gaining self-knowledge through the being of the other [*Selbsterkenntnis im Anderssein*]. But just this—this ultimate fulfillment of metaphysics—has supposedly become obsolete since Nietzsche. All talk of the continuity of meaning is to be considered a relic of metaphysics.

Here, on the issue of continuity, Dallmayr is inclined to agree with the hermeneutical perspective against Derrida. Yet, it is certainly characteristic of the difficulty he finds in my position that he approves more of my analysis of the experience of art and especially of my use of the term "*Verwandlung ins Gebilde*" [transformation into structured form] than of my hermeneutical efforts to integrate the experience of art into the continuity of one's own self-understanding. The half-heartedness he ascribes to my "ontological turn" consists, in his view, in my persistent relapse into the classical-romantic "mental" idea of understanding. The philosophical expression of this, however, would be the complete transparency of the self. Precisely such self-identity is for him actually an illusion.

The basis of this disagreement, it seems to me, is a misconception of what self-understanding is. "Self-understanding" is perhaps a misleading term that I have used and in which I found a natural connection with modern protestant theology and also with Heidegger's own linguistic tradition. However that may be, this word actually does not refer at all to the unshakable certainty of self-consciousness. Rather, *Selbstverständnis* has a pietistic undertone suggesting precisely that one cannot succeed in understanding oneself and that this foundering of one's self-understanding and self-certainty should lead one to the path of faith. *Mutatis mutandis* this applies to the hermeneutical usage of this same term. For who we are is something unfulfillable, an ever new undertaking and an ever new defeat. Anyone who wishes to understand his or her being is confronted by the simple unintelligibility of death. But again I would like to ask: is this really "the way of metaphysics?" Is this logocentrism?

Here we come up against the central problem resonating in all hermeneutic endeavors and which also forms the basis, I think, of Derrida's qualms about my venture in thought: Is there not in hermeneutics—for all its efforts to recognize otherness as otherness, the other as other, the work of art as a blow [*Stoß*], the breach as breach, the unintelligible as unintelligible—too much conceded to reciprocal understanding and mutual agreement? This objection is one that Habermas had earlier raised against me when he argued that distorted understanding makes what I call mutual agreement mere appearance and even a form of manipulation. His objection, of course, was pointed in another, politically motivated, direction and not toward the question of the metaphysics of presence. But the issue remains the same. One can learn from Levinas how serious this objection is, even for those who favor no specifically political option but only seek to give a thoughtful account that tries to say what *is*. Of course, I am quite conscious that in this regard a constant temptation arises to sidestep the "either-or" that has been placed before us as beings acting and living with each other.

My allusion to Kierkegaard at this point is not accidental. I must admit that one of the early influences on my thinking was Kierkegaard's radical confrontation of the ethical and aesthetic stages of existence. This, in fact, is the basis for my hermeneutical option for continuity, designated by the figure of William, the assessor in *Either/Or*. In him ethical continuity stands over against aesthetic immediacy and the self-criticism of the conscience-bearing will is opposed to aesthetic enjoyment. When I first read *Either/Or* as a nineteen-year-old, I certainly did not realize that even within this opposition there lurks the infinite "mediation" of Hegelian reflection. But I was to have a whole lifetime to learn this.

So I can understand how one might want to call my hermeneutical venture a dialectical hermeneutics. It is true that not only Plato but also Hegel offer me constant help in thinking—especially Hegel, since I seek to resist his "infinite mediation." Thus, one may also catch a scent of the metaphysics of presence in my own work, because I continue to speak the language of metaphysics—and is that not the language of dialectic? It seems to me this is the point Derrida criticizes in Heidegger when he says that Heidegger falls back into the language of metaphysics. And does not Heidegger himself say that we are always in danger of falling back into the language of metaphysics? Certainly he has said this about my development of his "hermeneutical" initiative.

In response to this I would ask: What is "the language of metaphysics" really supposed to mean? Is there actually any such thing? What I gained from the powerful impetus of the young Heidegger consists in the following: after years of naive, uncritical use of the conceptual tradition of neo-Kantianism—above all Hegel's *Logic,* which like a rich quarry furnished material for Friedrich Trendelenburg, Hermann Cohen, Paul Gerhard Natorp, Ernst Cassirer, and Nicolai Hartmann—I learned from Heidegger what *"Begrifflichkeit"* [conceptuality, thinking in concepts] is and what it means for thinking. Above all, I learned to see how much self-alienation lurked in the conceptual tradition of modern thought. So as I encountered Heidegger, I immediately felt pursued by the pathos of *Destruktion.*[6] This feeling corresponded to a certain craving, an inner demand that constantly ran through my first ventures in thinking, above all in relation to the poetic word. Moving beyond this, I have sought to consolidate my project through extensive philological studies in the history of concepts. However, I have not been able to follow Heidegger, or anybody else, when they speak of the "language of metaphysics," the "right language of philosophy," or the like. Language, for me, is always simply that which we speak with others and to others. If we are speaking in another language than our own, it is again something that is spoken with others and in which I have to listen to others. Everybody has experienced how difficult it is to have a conversation with someone when each one speaks his/her own language and both only to some degree understand the language of the other.

In talking about the language of philosophy, one can only have in mind the concepts that play a role in it. It is true, of course, that in science, concepts such as signs or symbols are arbitrarily chosen and defined. Their function is purely communicative: to insure that experience is designated in the most univocal way possible and thereby becomes controllable. This is experience of the sort that allows univocal identification and thus univocal symbolization. The artificiality of this conceptual symbolism used in the empirical sciences seems to me to find its most extreme expression when this procedure is applied to concrete, complex unities of experience [*Erfahrungsbestände*], ones that cannot be artificially produced in a natural-scientific experiment. This is especially true for the social sciences, where a nd of *lingua internazionale* dominates. Even Max Weber's encyclopedic clear-sightedness, for instance, was paired with a genuine excess of definition-making. One can see that when it is simply a matter of ordering unities of experience, this concern with definitions makes good sense. But when it comes to philosophy, such a passion for constructing definitions gives one away as a dilettante. Philosophy must give ear to an older wisdom that speaks in living language. Plato in a less romantic image said this was like the good cook who knows how to carve the flesh of wild game by so putting the knife into the joints that he does not saw through the bones (*Phaedrus*).

Philosophy, in the Western sense of the term, developed in Greece, and this means that it has developed its "concepts" from the Greek language. Language, however, is always the language of conversation. Who can fail to recognize that the language we humans speak has always pre-formed our thinking? Aristotle's lexicon of concepts in Book V (Delta) of the *Metaphysics* is an excellent illustration of how concepts can be further developed out of linguistic usage. In putting forward his analysis of various word-meanings [in Greek, *posachos legetai*], Aristotle clearly aims to further the elaboration of concepts that will be essential for his thought. All the while, however, he firmly upholds this analysis in relation to the actual spoken usage of words. Thus, his lexicon of concepts is like a living commentary on the fundamental concepts of his thinking. The alienation experienced by Greek conceptuality in its transposition into Latin and then in its insertion into modern languages renders Aristotle's commentary speechless. Thus, this alienation confronts us with a task: the task of a *Destruktion*. In Heidegger, the word "*Destruktion*" never means destruction but rather dismantling [*Abbau*]. Its purpose is to take concepts that have become rigid and lifeless and fill them again with meaning. Such an activity does not serve the purpose of pointing back to a mysterious origin, an *arché,* or the like. That is a fatal misunderstanding, which gets used as an objection above all against the later Heidegger. However, this is not the place to discuss the special achievement represented by Heidegger's *Destruktion* of the concept of the subject and its roots in the Greek concept of substance and the Greek understanding of being as presence-at-hand, nor why Heidegger through this *Destruktion* of a metaphysical conceptuality blazed a trail to a better understanding of today's experience of being and *Existenz*.

The slogan of *Destruktion* can be taken up with very different intentions and very different purposes. *Destruktion* is always a process of criticism directed at concepts that no longer speak to us. Thus, Heidegger's *Destruktion* of the concept of the subject had the specific purpose of pointing back to the Greek ὑποκειμενον [*hupokeimenon*]. This was in no way just an effort to correct the usage of a word. It seems to me a misunderstanding of the nature of philosophical concepts to think that a thematic usage of a well-defined word, whether in philosophical discussion or fixed in a philosophical text, somehow places hobbles on our thinking. Even now, I can recall the tone of my academic teachers when, with downright holy feeling in their voices, they assured me that to confuse "transcendent" with "transcendental" immediately betrayed one as a philosophical dilettante! Kant had once and for all put an end to the possibility of interchanging these two words. Today, I would venture to say that in this case Kant himself was a philosophical dillettante. Obviously, he often used the word transcendental to mean transcendent, just like anybody else at that time. Much the same applies in Greek with regard to the concept of *phronesis*. Its Aristotelian conceptual sharpening stands in opposition to the general free usage of the word, to which Aristotle himself also adhered. For this reason I think it is wrong to try to draw conclusions about the chronology of Aristotle's works on the basis of the use of a word, as I once argued against Werner Jaeger.

And I believe one ought to grant me the same privilege. When I speak of *Bewußtsein* [consciousness]—for example, of *wirkungsgeschichtliches Bewußtsein* [effective-historical consciousness]—it is not to espouse Aristotle or Hegel. What counts is knowing that consciousness is not a *res,* a thing. This does not require a purification of linguistic usage in relation to "mental" concepts. Likewise, Wittgenstein's famous criticism of "mental" concepts has its argumentative function, directed towards the pragmatics of language and the undoing of the dogmas of psychology. But this too does not prescribe a purified language. The context justifies the usage.

The goal of *Destruktion* is to let the concept speak again in its interwovenness in living language. This is a hermeneutical task. It has nothing to do with obscure talk of origins and of the original. Heidegger has taught us, for example, to recognize in *ousia*—the presentness of presence—the Greek *oikos,* and so to grasp in a new way the meaning of the Greek thinking of Being. But this is not a turning back to a mysterious origin, even if Heidegger himself speaks of the "voice of Being." In any case, while turning back out of scholastic alienation, Heidegger actually achieved a self-discovery through this insight into Greek thinking, leading him to sound the theme of *Being and Time,* which, when carried to its ultimate consequences for the temporality of being, he later called *"Ereignis."* All this was achieved on the path of the *Destruktion* of a tradition-hardened conceptuality. But what motivated Heidegger to burst this hardened conceptuality, what special need caused him to undertake this *Destruktion,* is another question. It is well known that he was agitated by doubts about Christian theology, doubts shared to some extent by Franz Overbeck. Indeed, Heidegger learned from Luther that with every return to Aristotle one must also abjure Aristotle.

Granted, it was a risky venture when Heidegger chose to entrust the ways of his own thinking to the poetic power of Hölderlin's language. Metaphors like "the voice of Being" could be misinterpreted as sentimental nullity and emptiness. All the same, I do not have to defend Heidegger here but rather myself. It is true that I, for my part, turned to the openness of Plato's dialectic and that I followed Hegel a few steps in his speculative renewal and recovery of Aristotle, but I don't see that this implies a relapse into the logocentrism of Greek metaphysics. Even Plato—indeed even Parmenides (as Heidegger admitted only very late)—paid obeisance to the *logoi,* although aware of their undeniable weakness. Yet Plato never succumbed to them fully. Rather, his ceaseless dialectical and dialogical labors retained something of the great secret of conversation, whose continuation not only transforms us but always throws us back on ourselves and joins us to each other. Plato's poetic power was such that it was able to do what he himself also did—bring each reader to a constantly new present. Which also means that he himself engaged in that *Destruktion* of rigidified words—and even, in many of his myths, the deconstruction [*Dekonstruktion*] of no longer binding ideas—which sets thinking free.

In saying this, I certainly do not deny that the unaltering pathos of the *logoi* compelled Plato as well down the path of logical-dialectical argumentation and thus cleared the way for the history of Western rationality. It is our historical fate as children of the West that we are compelled to speak the language of concepts. Even Heidegger, in spite of his poetizing efforts, saw poetry and thinking, with Hölderlin, as "*auf getrenntesten Bergen*" [on the most widely separated mountains]. But we should not forget that this separation has made science possible and has called philosophy to its task of working with concepts, as dubious as this philosophical enterprise may appear in an age of science. I really do not see how—for Nietzsche, or for Derrida himself—deconstruction can mean the repudiation of this history.

Hans-Georg Gadamer

2. Destruktion *and* *Deconstruction**

Translated by Geoff Waite and Richard Palmer

When Heidegger took the topic of understanding and elevated it from a methodology for the human sciences into an *"Existentiale"* and the foundation for an ontology of Dasein, this meant that the hermeneutical dimension no longer represented merely a higher level of a phenomenological research into intentionality, a research ultimately grounded in processes of bodily perception. Rather, it brought onto European soil and into the whole direction on phenomenology a major breakthrough, a breakthrough which, at almost exactly the same time, was gaining currency in Anglo-Saxon logic as the "linguistic turn." This was of special importance because in the original development of phenomenological research by Husserl and Scheler, language had remained completely overshadowed by other factors, in spite of the strength of the turn to the world of "lived experience."

In phenomenology, then, the same abysmal forgetfulness of language, so characteristic of transcendental idealism, was repeated, thus appearing to confirm, albeit belatedly, Herder's ill-fated criticism of the Kantian transcendental turn. Even in Hegelian dialectic and logic, language occupied no special place of honor. To be sure, Hegel occasionally alluded to the "logical instinct" of language, whose speculative anticipation of the Absolute posed for Hegel the task of his brilliant work on logic. And in fact, after Kant's intricately rococo Germanizing of the terminology of scholastic metaphysics the significance of

*This paper was presented in Rome in 1985 and later published in the second volume of Gadamer's collected works under the title "Destruktion und Deconstruction" (*GW 2* 361–72). Since the essay is in part an effort to show that Heidegger's use of the term *Destruktion* does not mean "destruction" at all but something quite different, we have left the term untranslated in the title and throughout this volume.—Editors' note.

Hegel's contribution to philosophical language is unmistakable. His great linguistic and conceptual energy remind one of Aristotle, and indeed Hegel comes closest to Aristotle's great example to the extent that he was able to recuperate the spirit of his mother tongue in the language of concepts. Of course, just this circumstance set up in front of Hegel's writings a barrier of untranslatability that was simply insurmountable for more than a century, and even to this day remains a most difficult obstacle. Even so, language, as such, was never made a central theme in Hegel's thought.

With Heidegger a similar and even stronger explosion of primal, originary linguistic power occurred in the realm of thinking. But accompanying this breakthrough came Heidegger's conscious reversion to the originality of Greek philosophical discourse. With the sheer palpable power of a vitality rooted in the indigenous soil of the life-world, "language" thus became a force which burst powerfully through the highly refined descriptive art of Husserlian phenomenology. At that point it was inescapable that language itself would become the object of philosophical self-reflection. Already in 1920, as I myself can testify, a young thinker—Heidegger, to be exact—began to lecture from a German university podium on what it might mean to say "*es weltet*": it "worlds." This was an unprecedented break with the solid and dignified, but at the same time scholasticized, language of metaphysics that had become completely alienated from its own origins.

What Heidegger was doing signaled a profound linguistic event in its own right, and at the same time the achievement of a deeper understanding of language in general. At that time, what the tradition of German idealism in von Humboldt, the Grimm brothers, Schleiermacher, the Schlegels, and finally Dilthey, had contributed with regard to the phenomenon of language—and that also had given unexpected impetus to the new linguistic science, above all comparative linguistics—still remained within the conceptual limits of *Identitätsphilosophie,* the philosophy of identity. The identity of the subjective and objective, of thinking and being, of nature and Spirit, were maintained right up into Cassirer's philosophy of symbolic forms, among which language was preeminent. This tradition reached its highest peak, of course, in the synthetic achievement of the Hegelian dialectic: here, throughout all the oppositions and differentiations, identity was reconstructed and the originally Aristotelian conception of *noesis noēseoos* [sic] reached its purest elaboration. The final paragraph of Hegel's *Encyclopedia of the Philosophic Sciences* has given this conception its most challenging formulation. As if the whole long history of the spirit [*Geist*] was really working toward a single goal, which Hegel expressed by borrowing from a famous verse of Virgil: "*Tantae molis erat se ipsam cognoscere mentem*"—"Such was the cost in heavy labor of coming to know one's own mind."[1]

Actually, a perennial challenge to the new postmetaphysical thinking in our

century resides in the fact that Hegel's dialectical mediation had already accomplished the overcoming of modern subjectivism. We need look no further than
the Hegelian notion of objective spirit for eloquent witness to this. Even the
religiously motivated critique that Kierkegaard's "either/or" directed at the
"this, but also that" of Hegel's dialectical self-supersession of all propositions
could be incorporated by Hegel's dialectic into a totalizing mediation. Indeed,
even Heidegger's critique of the concept of consciousness, which, through a
radical ontological *Destruktion* showed that idealism of consciousness in its
totality was really an alienated form of Greek thinking, and which boldly confronted the overly formal, neo-Kantian element in Husserl's phenomenology,
was not a complete breakthrough. For what he called the "fundamental ontology
of Dasein" could not—despite all the temporal analyses of how Dasein is constituted as *Sorge* ["Care"]—overcome its own self-reference and hence a fundamental positing of self-consciousness. For this reason, fundamental ontology
was not able fully to break away from immanent consciousness of the Husserlian
type.

Heidegger himself very soon acknowledged this problem, and so made his
own the hazardously radical thought experiments with Nietzsche, without, however, finding any paths other than *Holzwege,* the kind of circuitous dead-ends
cut by loggers on wooded hillsides. And these paths, after the *Kehre,* or turn of
the way of Heidegger's thinking toward Being, led into impassable regions.
Could it be that only the language of metaphysics sustains this paralyzing spell
of transcendental idealism? In turning away from the foundationalist thinking of
metaphysics, Heidegger drew the extremest possible consequences from his
critique of the ontological groundlessness of consciousness and self-
consciousness: he turned away altogether from the conceptual attempt of metaphysics to ground itself. Yet, both his "turn" and this "turning away"
remained locked in a permanent wrestling match with metaphysics. Not only
did Heidegger, in order to prepare for the overcoming of metaphysics, propose
to go beyond modern subjectivism through the *Destruktion* or de-structuring of
its unproven concepts, but also—on the positive side—to recover the primordial
Greek experience of Being by lighting up the idea of Being lying behind the rise
and dominance of Western metaphysics. In actuality, though, Heidegger's step
back from Aristotle's concept of Being as *physis* to the experience of Being in its
Presocratic beginnings remained an adventurous journey into error. Granted, the
distant goal, however vague, was always before his eyes: to think anew the
beginning, the primal, the originary. But to come closer to the beginning always
means to become aware, in retracing the path from whence one came, of other
open possibilities.

Whoever stands at the very beginning must choose his path. If one gets back
to the beginning, one becomes aware of the fact that from that starting point one
could have gone other ways—perhaps just as Eastern thought has taken other

ways. Perhaps the direction taken by Eastern thought (like that taken by the West) did not arise from a free choice. Rather, it may be due to the circumstance that no grammatical construction of subject and predicate was present to steer Eastern thought into the metaphysics of substance and accident. So it is not surprising that one can find in Heidegger's journey back to the beginning something of a fascination with Eastern thought, and he even sought to take a few steps down that path with the help of Japanese and Chinese visitors—in vain. Languages—especially the basic structure common to all the languages in one's culture—are not easily circumventable. Indeed, even when tracing one's own ancestry one can never reach back to its beginning. It always slips away into uncertainty, as it does for the wanderer on the coast in the famous depiction of stepping back in time that Thomas Mann gives us in *The Magic Mountain,* where each final promontory of land yields to yet another in an endless progression. Similarly, Heidegger hoped to find in Anaximander, then in Heraclitus, then in Parmenides, then again in Heraclitus, in the originary experience of Being, testimony to the mutual interweaving of concealment and disclosure. In Anaximander he believed he found presence itself and the tarrying of its essence, in Parmenides the untrembling heart of *Aletheia,* or truth as unconcealment, and in Heraclitus the *physis* that loves to conceal itself. But in the end, although all this was valid enough for the kind of indicative linguistic gesture that would point off into timelessness, it was not really valid for the speaking— that is to say, the kind of self-interpretation—one encounters in the early Greek texts. In the name, in the naming power of words and their labyrinthian paths to error, Heidegger found precious veins of gold, in which he could only recognize again and again his own vision of Being: that "Being" is not to be construed as the Being of beings. But, over and over again, each of these texts turned out not to be the final promontory on the way to a free and unobstructed view of Being.

So it was almost predetermined, so to speak, that on this path of mining the primal rock of words Heidegger would finally encounter Nietzsche, whose extremism had already ventured the self-destruction of all metaphysics, all truth, and all knowledge of truth. Of course, Nietzsche's own conceptual artistry could not satisfy Heidegger, however much he welcomed Nietzsche's breaking of the spell of dialectic—"Hegel's veil and those of other veil-makers [*Schleier-macher*]"—and however much he wanted to corroborate Nietzsche's vision of philosophy in the tragic age of Greece, as still something other than the metaphysics of a true world behind our world of appearances. Yet, all these things really only meant for Heidegger becoming a fellow traveller with Nietzsche for a short stretch of his own way. "So many centuries—and no new God"—this was the motto for Heidegger's reception of Nietzsche.

But what did Heidegger know of a new God? Did he dimly imagine God and lack only the language to evoke Him? Was he too bewitched by the language of metaphysics? In spite of all its preconceptual inescapability, language is not simply the Babylonian captivity of the human mind. Nor does the tower of Babel story from our Biblical heritage mean only that human hubris has led to the multiplicity of languages and linguistic families. Rather, this story also encompasses in its meaning the strangeness that arises between one human being and another, always creating new confusion. But precisely in this fact lies the possibility of overcoming confusion. For language is conversation. One must look for the word that can reach another person. And it is possible for one to find it; one can even learn the language of the other person. One can cross over into the language of the other in order to reach the other. All this is possible for language as language.

To be sure, the "binding element" in conversation, in the sense of that which produces itself in the form of the self-generating language of mutual comprehension, is by its very nature necessarily surrounded by *Gerede,* or idle chatter, and thus by the mere appearance of speaking. Jacques Lacan was right when he said that the word not directed to another person is such an empty word. Just this suggests the primacy that must be accorded to the kind of conversation that evolves as question and answer and builds up a common language. A familiar experience among two people who do not speak each other's language yet can halfway understand the language of the other person is that one discovers that one cannot hold a conversation on this basis at all. In effect, a slow motion duel takes place until one of the two languages is spoken by both people, however badly one of the partners may speak it. Anyone can experience this, and it suggests something quite important. For in fact not only do conversational partners speaking different languages experience this, but also partners speaking the same native language, making mutual adjustments as they talk. It is only the answer, actual or potential, that transforms a word into a word.

All rhetoric, too, falls within the scope of this experience. Because it does not permit a constant exchange of question and answer, speaking and responding, rhetoric always contains bursts of empty words that we recognize as fluff or as a mere "manner of speaking." Likewise, the same thing goes on in the actual event of understanding as we listen or are in the process of reading. The fulfillment of meaning in these cases, as Husserl in particular has shown, is interspersed with empty intentions.

At this point we must think further about whether that phrase, "the language of metaphysics," really has a meaning. Certainly what it can mean is not the language in which metaphysics was first developed, namely, the philosopher's language of the Greeks. Rather, what it does mean is that certain conceptual formulations, derived from the original language of metaphysics, have impressed themselves into the living languages of present-day speech communities. In scientific and philosophical discourse we call this the role of terminology. In the mathematics-based natural sciences—above all the experimental sciences—the introduction of terms is purely a matter of convention, serving to designate states of affairs available to all and which do not involve any genuine relation of meaning between these terms introduced into international use and the peculiarities of national language; for instance, in thinking of a "volt," is there anyone who also thinks of Alessandro Volta, the great scientist?

When it comes to philosophy, though, things are quite different. In philosophy there are no generally accessible, that is to say, verifiable realms of experience designated by prearranged terminology. The concept-words coined in the realm of philosophy are, rather, always articulated by means of the spoken language in which they emerge. Of course, here, as in science, concept formation also means that among the many rays of possible meaning a given word has acquired, its definition moves toward a more exactly determined meaning. But in philosophy such concept-words are never completely separable from the semantic field in which they possess their full meaning. Indeed, the complete separation of a word from its context and its enclosure (what Aristotle calls "*horismos,*" boundary) within a precise content not only makes it into a concept but also necessarily threatens its use with an emptying out of meaning. Thus, the formation of such a basic metaphysical concept as *ousia,* or substance, is never fully accessible so long as the sense of the Greek word is not present with it in the full breadth of its meaning. In this regard, it enhances our understanding of the Greek concept of Being to know that the primary meaning of the word *ousia* in Greek referred to agricultural property, and that the meaning of this concept as the presence of what is present originates from this.

This example teaches us that there is no "language of metaphysics." There is only a metaphysically thought-out coinage of concepts that have been lifted from living speech. Such coinage of concepts can, as in the case of Aristotelian logic and ontology, establish a fixed conceptual tradition and consequently lead to an alienation from the living language. In the case of *ousia,* such alienation set in early with Hellenistic pedagogy and was continued as this pedagogy was carried over into Latin. Subsequently, with the translating of the Latin into the national languages of the present to form a contemporary pedagogical language, the concept of *ousia* has increasingly lost its original sense as grounded in the experience of being. Thus, the task of a *Destruktion* of the conceptuality of metaphysics was posed. This is the only tenable sense of talk about the "language of metaphysics": this phrase simply refers to the conceptuality that has been built up in the history of metaphysics.

Early on, Heidegger was to put forward as a rallying cry the task of a *Destruktion* of the alienated conceptuality of metaphysics: the ongoing task of contemporary thinking.[2] With unbelievable freshness, he was able to trace in thinking the concepts of the tradition back to the Greek language, back to the natural sense of words and the hidden wisdom of language they contain, and in so doing, to give new life to Greek thought and its power to address us today. Such was Heidegger's genius. He had a penchant for restoring to words their hidden, no longer intended sense, and then from this so-called etymology to draw fundamental consequences for thinking. It is significant in this regard that the later Heidegger speaks of "*Urworten,*" or "primal words," words in which what he regards as the Greek experience of the world is brought to language far more palpably than in the doctrines and propositions of the early Greek texts.

But Heidegger was certainly not the first to realize the scholasticized language of metaphysics had become alienated from its subject-matter. Since Fichte and above all since Hegel, one finds German idealism already striving by means of the dialectical movement of thought to dissolve and melt down the Greek ontology of substance and its conceptuality. Precursors of this striving existed even among those who employed scholastic Latin, especially in cases where, alongside their scholastic treatises, the living word of vernacular preaching marched in parallel, as in Meister Eckart or Nicolaus Cusanus, but also later in the speculations of Jacob Boehme. Admittedly, these were marginal figures in the metaphysical tradition. When Fichte put the word "*Tathandlung*" [action, deed] in place of "*Tatsache*" [fact], he anticipated in a basic way the provocative coinages and definitions of Heidegger, who loved to stand the meaning of a word practically on its head. This shows, for example, in his understanding of *Entfernung,* or distancing, as *Näherung,* or bringing near,[3] or understanding sentences like "*Was heißt Denken?*" ["What does thinking mean?"] as meaning "What commands us to think?" Or, "*Nichts ist ohne Grund*" ["Nothing is without reason"] as asserting that *nothing* itself is groundless. All of these interpretations are clearly acts of violence committed by a swimmer who struggled to swim against the current.

Those who thought within the tradition of German idealism, however, on the whole sought to modify the form of traditional metaphysical conceptuality not so much through recovering words and forcing the meaning of words as rather through the sharpening of propositions to the point of opposition or contradiction. Dialectic has for ages meant the sharpening of immanent oppositions to such a point; and if the defense of two contradictory propositions does not just produce a negative result but instead aims precisely towards a unity of the opposing factors, then the most extreme possibility of metaphysical thinking is reached. Thinking, now moving into primordial Greek concepts, becomes capable of grasping the Absolute. But life is freedom and spirit. The strict, inner consistency of such a dialectic—a dialectic that Hegel saw as fulfilling the ideal of philosophical proof—did in fact enable him to go beyond the subjectivity of the subject and to think mind as objective, as we mentioned earlier. Ontologically, however, this movement culminated, once again, in the absolute presence of spirit present to itself, as the end of the *Encyclopedia* attests. It was for this reason that Heidegger remained in a constant and tense confrontation with the seductive appeal of dialectic, which instead of working towards the *Destruktion* of Greek concepts continued to develop the dialectical concepts of spirit and freedom—while at the same time domesticating its own thinking.

We cannot analyze here how Heidegger in his later thinking actually held to his fundamental project by maintaining, in a sublimated form, the deconstructive [*destruktive*] achievement present in its beginnings. The sibylline style of his later writings testifies to this. He was fully aware of just how "needful" language is—both his and ours. But it seems to me that, along with Heidegger's own efforts to leave behind "the language of metaphysics" with the help of Hölderlin's poetical language, two other paths exist and have in fact been taken in efforts to overcome the ontological self-domestication belonging to dialectic and move into the open. One is the path from dialectic back to dialogue, back to conversation. This the way I myself have attempted to travel in my philosophical hermeneutics. The other is the way shown primarily by Derrida, the path of deconstruction. On this path, the awakening of a meaning hidden in the life and liveliness of conversation is not an issue. Rather, it is in an ontological concept of *écriture*—not idle chatter nor even true conversation but the background network of meaning-relations lying at the basis of all speech—that the very integrity of sense as such is to be dissolved, thereby accomplishing the authentic shattering of metaphysics.

In the space of this tension [between philosophical hermeneutics and deconstruction] a most curious shift of emphasis arises. From the perspective of hermeneutic philosophy, Heidegger's doctrine of the overcoming of metaphysics, with its culmination in the total forgetfulness of Being in our technological era, skips over the continued resistance and persistence of certain flexible unities in the life we all share, unities which perdure in the large and small forms of our fellow-human being-with-each-other. Deconstruction, on the other hand, takes the opposite perspective. To it, Heidegger lacks ultimate radicality in continuing to seek the meaning of Being and thereby clinging to a question which, one can show, can have no meaningful answer corresponding to it. To the question of the meaning of Being Derrida counterposes the notion of "*différance*" and sees in Nietzsche a more radical figure in contrast to the metaphysically tempered claim of Heideggerian thinking. He views Heidegger as still aligned with logocentrism, against which he poses as a counterthesis what he calls "*écriture*": a term signifying a meaning always dispersed and deferred and shattering all totalizing unity. Manifestly, Nietzsche here represents the critical point.

Thus, if one wants to contrast and weigh the outlooks that the two paths leading back from dialectic that we have just described open up, the case of Nietzsche stands out: it allows us to discuss what possibilities there are for a thinking that can no longer continue as a metaphysics.

When I give the name "dialectic" to the point of departure from which

Heidegger seeks his own way back, it is not just for the obvious reason that Hegel created his secular synthesis of the heritage of metaphysics by means of a speculative dialectic that claimed to gather into itself the entire truth of its Greek beginnings. Rather, it is above all because, unlike Marburg Neokantianism and Husserl's Neokantian reshaping of phenomenology, Heidegger himself refused to remain within a tradition of modifying and perpetuating the heritage of metaphysics. What he strove to accomplish in the "overcoming of metaphysics" was not exhausted in a mere gesture of protest, as was the case with the left Hegelians and men like Kierkegaard and Nietzsche. Rather, he attacked his task as being a matter of hard conceptual labor, which one should learn from the study of Aristotle. Thus, the term dialectic, as I am using it here, refers to the whole wide-ranging totality of the Western tradition of metaphysics—just as much to what Hegel called "the logical" as to the "*logos*" in Greek thinking, which had already shaped the first steps in Western philosophy. It is in this sense of the term that Heidegger's quest to ask anew the question of Being, or better, to pose it for the first time in a non-metaphysical sense, the quest he called "the step back," was a way *back from* dialectic.

Likewise, the hermeneutic turn toward "conversation" that I have pursued not only seeks in some sense to go back before the dialectic of German idealism, namely, to Platonic dialectic, but it also aims even farther back before this Socratic-dialogical turn to its presupposition: the *anamnēsis* sought for and awakened in *logoi*. The "recollection" that I have in mind is derived from myth and yet is in the highest degree rational. It is not only that of the individual soul but always that of "the spirit that would like to unite us"—we who are a conversation.[4]

To be in a conversation, however, means to be beyond oneself, to think with the other and to come back to oneself as if to another. When Heidegger thinks the metaphysical concept of *Wesen* or essence no longer as the property of presence in present objects but understands the noun *Wesen* as a verb, he injects it with temporality. *Wesen*, or essence, is now understood as *Anwesen*, as actively being present, in a way grammatically counterposed to the common German expression *Verwesen*, to decay or decompose. This means, however, that Heidegger—in his essay on Anaximander, for example[5]—imputes another meaning to the original Greek experience of time, namely, a sense of dwelling, abiding, or tarrying, such as is captured in the common expression, "a space of time." In this way, he is in fact able to make his way back behind metaphysics and the whole horizon of metaphysics when it is seeking to interrogate Being. Heidegger himself reminds us that when Sartre quotes Heidegger's sentence "*Das Wesen des Daseins ist seine Existenz.*" ["The essence of Dasein is its *Existenz*, or existential possibility"], he is misusing it if he is not aware that the term "*Wesen*" is enclosed in quotation marks.[6] At stake here is decidedly not any concept of "*Essenz*," or "essence," that somehow as essence, is to precede existence or existent things. Nor at stake is some concern with the Sartrean inversion of this relation, so that existence is said to precede essence. In my opinion, when Heidegger inquires about "the meaning of Being," he is not thinking the term "meaning" in the way that metaphysics with its concept of essence does, but rather in the sense of a question that does not await a specific answer, but instead points in a certain direction for inquiry.

As I once said, "Sense is sense of a direction"—"*Sinn ist Richtungssinn.*"[7] One time, Heidegger even introduced an orthographical archaism in spelling the term "*Sein*" as "*Seyn*" in order to underscore its character as a verb. Similarly, my philosophical hermeneutics should be seen as an effort to shake off the burden of an inherited ontology of static substance, in that I started out from conversation and the common language sought and shaped in it, in which the logic of question and answer turns out to be determinative. Such logic opens up a dimension of communicative understanding that goes beyond linguistically fixed assertions, and so also beyond any all-encompassing synthesis, in the sense of in the monologue-like self-understanding of dialectic. Now admittedly, the dialectic of German idealism never completely denied its derivation from the speculative foundational structure of language, as I have explained in the third part of *Truth and Method* (*WM* 432ff./414ff.). But when Hegel put dialectic in the context of science and method, he actually covered up its ancestry, its origin in language.

Thus, philosophical hermeneutics pays particular attention to the relation of the speculative, dual unity playing between the said and the unsaid. This dual unity truly precedes any subsequent dialectical sharpening of a proposition to the point of contradiction and its supersession in a new proposition. It seems very misleading to me for someone to say that just because I emphasize the role of tradition in all our posing of questions and also in the indication of answers, I am asserting a super-subject and thus (as Manfred Frank and Philippe Forget go on to maintain) reducing the hermeneutical experience to an empty word. There is no support in *Truth and Method* for this kind of construction. When I speak there of tradition and of conversation with tradition, I am in no way putting forward a collective subject. Rather, "tradition" is simply the collective name for each individual text (text in the widest sense, which would include a picture, an architectural work, even a natural event). Certainly the platonic form of Socratic dialogue, led by one partner and followed by the other willingly or unwillingly, is a special kind of conversation, but still it remains the pattern for all conversational process insofar as in it not the words but the mind or spirit of the other is refuted. The Socratic dialogue is no spectacular play of dressing up and unmasking for the purpose of knowing better what we already know. Rather, it is the true carrying out of *anamnēsis*. What is accomplished in conversation is a summoning back in thought [*denkende Erinnerung*] that is possible only for the soul fallen into the finitude of bodily existence. This is the very meaning of the speculative unity that is achieved in the "virtuality" of the word:[8] that it is not an individual word nor is it a formulated proposition, but rather it points beyond all possible assertions.

Clearly, the dimension in which our questioning is moving here has nothing to do with a code, and the business of deciphering one. It is certainly correct that a certain decoding process underlies all writing and reading of texts, but this represents merely a precondition for hermeneutic attention to what is said in the words. In this regard, I am fully in agreement with the critique of structuralism. But it seems to me that I go beyond Derrida's deconstruction, since a word exists only in conversation and never exists there as an isolated word but as the totality of a way of accounting by means of speaking and answering.

Obviously the principle of deconstruction involves something quite similar to what I am doing, since in carrying out what he calls *écriture,* Derrida, too, is endeavoring to supersede any metaphysical realm of meaning which governs words and their meanings. Furthermore, the achievement of this *écriture* is not an essential Being but a contour or furrow, a trace that points. So Derrida speaks out against a metaphysical concept of *logos* and against the logocentrism that is inscribed even in Heidegger's question about Being as a question about the *meaning* of Being. But this is an odd Heidegger, a Heidegger interpreted back through Husserl; as if all speaking consisted merely of propositional judgments. In this sense, it is certainly true that the tireless constitution of meaning, to which phenomenological research is dedicated and which operates in the act of thinking as the fulfillment of an intention of consciousness *does* mean "presence." It is the declarative voice (*voix*) assigned to the presence of what is thought in thinking. Even in Husserl's efforts to build a respected philosophy, however, it is precisely the experience of time and time-consciousness that forms the prior basis of all "presence" and even the constitution of supratemporal validity. It is, of course, correct that the problem of time held Husserl's thought in an unbreakable spell because he himself held on firmly to the Greek concept of Being—a spell Augustine had already broken with the riddle he presented to himself about the being of time: that, to put it in Hegelian terms, the "now" both is and at the same time is not.

Like Heidegger, Derrida immerses himself in the mysterious multiplicity lodged in a word and in the diversity of its meanings, in the indeterminate potential of its differentiations of meaning. The fact, though, that Heidegger questions from the proposition and assertion back to the openness of Being that first makes words and propositions possible at all allows him, at the same time, to gain an advantage for understanding the whole dimension of assertions, antitheses and contradictions. In the same way, Derrida appears to be on the track of those traces that are to be found only in the act of reading. He has, in particular, sought to recover the analysis of time in Aristotle: that "time" appears in Being as deferred difference, or what Derrida calls "*la différance.*" But because he reads Heidegger through Husserl, he takes Heidegger's borrowing of Husserlian concepts, which is clearly noticeable in the transcendental self-description present in *Being and Time,* as evidence of Heidegger's logocentrism. Likewise, he deems as "phonocentrism" the fact that I take not only conversation but also the poem and its appearance in the inner ear as the true reality of language. As if voice, or discourse, could ever attain presence simply in the act of its performance, even for the most strenuous reflective consciousness of the speaker, and were not rather itself an act of disappearance. This is no cheap argument about reflection but a reminder of what happens to every speaking and thinking person: precisely because one is "thinking," one is not aware of oneself.

So we may take Derrida's critique of Heidegger's Nietzsche-interpretation—an interpretation of Nietzsche that in fact I myself find persuasive—as an illustration of the unsettled problematic before which we find ourselves. On the one side stands the bewildering richness of facets and the endless play of masks in which Nietzsche's bold experiments in thinking appear to disperse themselves into an ungraspable multiplicity. On the other side, there is the question one may put to Nietzsche of what all the play in this enterprise might mean. It is not as if Nietzsche himself ever had the unity of this dispersal clearly before him and had a conceptual grasp of the inner connection between the basic principle of will to power and the noontime message of the eternal return of the same. If I understand Heidegger correctly, this is precisely what Nietzsche has not done, so these metaphors of his last visions look like mirroring facets with no underlying unity. In any case, such a unity, Heidegger would say, represents the unified ultimate position in which the question concerning being itself forgets itself and loses itself. This is what the technological era signifies, the era in which nihilism in fact brings about an endless return of the same.

To think this through, to take up Nietzsche in a thoughtful way, does not seem to me to be some kind of falling back into metaphysics and the ontological concept of "essence" in which it culminates. If it were such a relapse, Heidegger's own ways of thinking, in pursuit of an "essence" with a completely different, temporal, structure, would not always lose themselves in impassable regions—let alone be the conversation that may be enriching itself in our own day with great new partners drawn from a heritage extending across our planet. This conversation should seek its partner everywhere, just because this partner is other, and especially if the other is completely different. Whoever wants me to take deconstruction to heart and insists on difference stands at the beginning of a conversation, not at its end.

Hans-Georg Gadamer

3. *Hermeneutics and Logocentrism**

Translated by Richard Palmer and Diane Michelfelder

To speak about deconstruction and *Destruktion,* about the relationship of Derrida and de Man to hermeneutics as I have developed it into a philosophical theory, is not that simple. I have known Paul de Man for a longer time, ever since his teaching days in Zurich, when he was quite well disposed towards hermeneutics. Since then, we have met each other socially a number of times, but meanwhile he has clearly affiliated himself with the poststructuralist turn of Derrida and so changed his view of hermeneutics. I myself have followed the course of Derrida's work for some years. Within the whole French scene, it was clearly he with whom I shared the most starting points. He too came from Heidegger. Also, unlike almost everyone else who undertook to understand Heidegger, he began not just with Heidegger alone but with Aristotle. Surely this is a basic precondition without which no dialogue at all about Heidegger can be taken seriously. Thus, over the years, beginning with *Speech and Phenomena* (1967; *VP*) and *"Ousia* and *Grammē"* (1968; *M* 31–78/31–67), I have sought to work my way into the world of Derrida's thinking.

*This essay originally served as the concluding address at a colloquium on the contemporary relevance of early Romanticism held in August 1986 at the Reimer Stiftung in Bad Homburg, Germany. The papers from that colloquium were subsequently published as *Die Aktualität der Frühromantik,* edited by Ernst Behler and Jochen Hörisch (Paderborn: Ferdinand Schöningh, 1987). In that volume Gadamer's contribution (pp. 251–60) carried the title "Frühromantik, Hermeneutik, Dekonstruktivismus." The unpublished manuscript which was given to us by Professor Gadamer for translation, however, simply carried the caption, "Abschließender Beitrag zum Frühromantik-Kolloquium"—a title it also carried in the galley proofs kindly forwarded to us by Professor Behler for comparison to our manuscript. At the time of conveying the manuscript to us, Professor Gadamer suggested the title "Hermeneutik und Logozentrismus," which we have used in this volume.—Eds.

Any common starting point invariably has its point of conflict. Between Derrida and myself this lies with Heidegger's interpretation of Nietzsche. This is obviously the point at which Derrida intends to free himself from Heidegger's influence, which he had experienced early on through Jean Beaufret and which, in some sense, he generally sought to hold onto in marking himself off from Husserl. Precisely when it comes to interpreting Nietzsche, I am convinced that Heidegger—this great master of powerful interpretations—has put forward an extraordinarily penetrating and fitting interpretation. So in Derrida's eyes I have supported the worst, so to speak, in Heidegger.

In Derrida's writings, this worst thing is called "logocentrism." This very word, which he applies to Heidegger, strikes one as peculiar. Certainly it has to be granted that even in *Being and Time* Heidegger was unambiguously critical of propositional logic and its ontological equivalent. There the key word was "presence at hand" [*Vorhandenheit*], a term that has never seemed fully satisfactory to me because Heidegger used it to unite such heterogeneous things, such as the ancient Greek concept of being as presence—which is accessible through theory—as well as the modern concept of objectivity, which is defined by method. Later on, especially in the essay, "The Age of the World Picture," Heidegger refined this point even further. Now it is clear enough that what the Greeks brought together in their understanding of being was something quite different from the determinability of facts. This insight, in fact, has constantly guided my own Greek studies. Really, then, there is an open question here—but, in any case, neither Heidegger nor the hermeneutical turn in phenomenology can be accused of logocentrism, in the sense found in Derrida's critique of Husserl.

Now Derrida does in fact draw support for this accusation chiefly from his critical reading of Husserl. In his analysis of time consciousness, Husserl characterized presence [*présence*] with the greatest explicitness, and in the first of the *Logical Investigations* fully established a unity between expression [*Ausdruck*] and meaning [*Bedeutung*]. An expression is not a meaningless indicator; rather, it has an ideal meaning. In every case, though, a sign is a sign for something absent, and the past "now" of retention fundamentally refutes the identity of the "now" of the present. This is certainly enough to convince one that any sign, even one that is "ideal" and so should be taken as a word, must therefore be interpreted. But does language let itself be grasped on the basis of its elements, such as word and meaning? And does time let itself be understood on the basis of the now that is past and the now of the present? Where is the multiplicity of meaning really located? Isn't it to be found in the constitution of sense that takes place in the concrete give and take of language, and not in the factuality of the signs themselves?

Heidegger's interpretation of the concept of metaphysics and his call for the overcoming [*Überwindung*] of metaphysics, or the recovery [*Verwindung*] from metaphysics, are certainly not easily equatable to my own efforts. Heidegger had definitely convinced us young people that the question about the highest being and the question about being as such were inseparable in Aristotle, and therefore that metaphysics is onto-theology. From here, though, I soon became entangled in difficulties. Because I had become a classical philologist, Heidegger's Plato-interpretation could not convince me. Can Plato be regarded simply as a necessary stage on the way towards Aristotelian onto-theology? Can the concept of metaphysics be applied to Plato at all? It would make more sense to describe Plato's position with respect to nature [*Physis*] as "metamathematics" than as metaphysics. This would take into account the Pythagorean element that endures in Plato and permits him to speak only in mythical terms about the origin of the universe and the composition of nature. So authentic reality, for Plato, is the "rational," which appears in symmetry and in numerical relations, and above all in music and in the stars.

Now in a broader sense not only Plato but also Aristotle could be interpreted in terms of logocentrism, as Derrida has interpreted them, and the temporal character of presence could be attributed to their implicit ontology. But it is difficult to understand how the criticism that Heidegger directs against the temporality of Greek ontology should permit the term "logocentrism" to be applied to his own thinking. From the very beginning, Heidegger—as a person of the modern, post-Enlightenment era—sought to understand himself on the basis of his will to Christian belief. Aristotelian metaphysics, in its understanding of being and even in its Thomistically-sanctioned theological interpretation, was not acceptable to Heidegger. This religious impulse led him from the start to criticize the Greek concept of being from the standpoint of temporality. One piece of evidence for this is the following: In the lecture course Heidegger gave in 1921–1922 under the title "Phenomenology of Religion," he took half a semester to speak, as he was known to do, on all possible conceptions—both correct and incorrect—of phenomenology. Not a single word about religion. Then the students complained to the Dean that they had registered for the course as theological students. In response, Heidegger rearranged the course after Christmas and began anew with an exegesis of the Letter to the Thessalonians. In this Letter, the oldest document of the New Testament that we possess, Paul is writing from Athens to the first community of believers in Thessaloniki after its foundation to say that it ought not to be incessantly asking when the Redeemer will return. He will come like the thief in the night. Today we have no difficulty recognizing here a preliminary glimpse of Heidegger's later critique of "calculative" thinking, a critique running consistently throughout his work. So the whole analysis of Dasein in *Being and Time* is centered on the futurity of Dasein. Futurity, not presence, characterizes the being of Dasein. This comes out clearly not only in *Being and Time* but also in the many preliminary studies that have meanwhile come to light.

One of these studies—prepared for publication as a book and forming one of the most significant volumes of the new, monumental edition of Heidegger's works—is the text of a course of lectures given in 1921–1922 called "Introduction to Aristotle." Naturally, in this course Heidegger never got around to Aristotle at all. We can immediately recognize the Kierkegaard-stage in Heidegger from this text. By this I mean Heidegger's direct effort to repeat in a philosophical sense what Kierkegaard had done as a religious writer and as an accuser of the Christian church of his time. Kierkegaard had insisted that Christ's death on the Cross should not be taken as an event lying far back in the past, some forty generations ago. Rather, if we want to follow the message of the gospels, we must be contemporaneous with this event. Heidegger quite clearly incorporated this idea into his own conception of philosophy. Here too one must free oneself from understanding only "at a distance." Heidegger's struggle against the *logos* in the sense of logic can be seen here very clearly. Even though Kierkegaard could only speak the language of Hegelian dialectic, the moment of decision he so strikingly speaks of is not the "now" of the Aristotelian-Augustinian-Husserlian analysis of time. Now certainly something like distance [*Abstand*] can also be found in the essence of the *logos*. Aristotle correctly pointed out in the *Politics* that a sense of time is situated there, a desistance [*Abstandnahme*] from an immediate reaction to what is present. But when he went on from this point to say that a sense for the contributory and thus for the just and unjust is also situated in the *logos,* an understanding of time is implied that decisively points beyond that sense of *logos* which in the *Physics* leads to the rigid consequences of the physical analysis of time.

Thus, by basing myself on Aristotle's practical philosophy, I could further develop the stimulus that I received initially from Kierkegaard and later from Heidegger, to the point of seeing the essence of language in conversation. Insofar as this view of language goes beyond Heidegger's analysis of Dasein's "very ownness" [*"Jemeinigkeit"*] and its fallenness [*Verfallenheit*] into the world, it represents a more important experience: namely, dialogue. For no subjective consciousness, neither that of a speaker nor of whomever is addressed, already knows enough to fully encompass what comes to light in dialogue.

This recollection should make clear what a challenge it meant for me when Derrida attacked hermeneutics in *Speech and Phenomena* for being not only logocentric but, even worse, for being "phonocentric." Of course I have to wonder where in the hermeneutical approach the ontology of presence is supposed to be found. The doctrine of the unity of expression and meaning, which aroused Derrida's critique, lies long behind us—and indeed it already lay behind Husserl in 1910. Who listens to the sound of a word, once it is understood? Who listens to one's own voice while speaking? Whoever does this will become mired in the middle of a word, and whoever focuses on a speaker's voice will no longer understand what is meant. It is a false logocentrism or metaphysics of presence that Derrida's starting point in sign theory misrepresents in *Speech and Phenomena*. Conversation defines itself precisely by the fact that the essence of understanding and agreement are not found in the *"vouloir-dire"* or intended meaning, through which the word supposedly finds its being, but rather in what aims at being said beyond all words sought after or found. Derrida is right to insist on this essential "difference" [*"Differenz"*], and I myself recognize it fully. But in my view, it does not require any return to *"écriture,"* to writing. For me, *"lecture,"* or reading, where writing is at least "on the way to language," is ambiguous enough.

Here the German word *"Verstehen"* can be very helpful. Admittedly, given its place in German intellectual history, finding a parallel to it in other languages is no easy task. What is the literal meaning of *Verstehen*? It means "to stand in for someone." In its original sense, this word is applied to someone who stands in for another before a judge: a lawyer. He understands his party well enough so that, as we would say today, he is able to "hold a brief" for him. He acts on behalf of his client and stands in for him. He does not just repeat what has been told or dictated to him in advance; rather, he speaks for whom he represents. But this means that he speaks from himself as another and is turned toward others. Obviously, this implies *différance*. Already in 1960, I myself wrote in *Truth and Method:* "Whoever understands must understand *differently* if he wants to understand at all." If Derrida is going to insist that signs are ambiguous and for this reason wants to allow *écriture* to somehow speak like an inner voice, he should not forget that writing is intended to be read. What is involved here is not the ambiguity of a typeface or of a stock of physical marks, but rather an ambiguity as to what these designate when they are actualized by someone reading them. One cannot read what is written without understanding it—that is, without expressing it and thereby making an intonation and modulation that anticipates the sense of the whole. Only then can writing return to speaking (which in no way has to be a "reading out loud"). In any case, the actualizing of writing, like the actualizing of spoken words, always already demands interpretation in the sense of thoughtful understanding. In light of this situation, it looks to me like a sheer misunderstanding for Derrida to see the metaphysics of presence here at work. His starting point in the Platonic-static sense of an ideal meaning has, it seems, led him into this misunderstanding. But the art of nailing someone down to something he or she said is not hermeneutics. Rather, hermeneutics is the art of grasping what someone has really wanted to say.

The dialogical turn in hermeneutics, of course, puts me in the neighborhood of the early Romantics. Naturally I have been aware of this connection, and there are occasional references to it in my writings. However, I have been interested to learn that Friedrich Schlegel had anticipated this perspective in more ways than I had found. For instance, there is yet another word whose meaning as it has unfolded historically in the German language reflects one of Derrida's

leading themes, that of *différance*. I have in mind the term *"Selbstverständnis,"*
"self-understanding." This is a relatively new word whose slow emergence in
the theology of the 1920s was certainly assisted by the philosophical contribution of Heidegger, given how its construction reflects the notion of "moving
forward." When I ask myself what self-understanding means, immediately old
layers of the religious use of language come to the fore, ones that emerge in
Schlegel but which certainly go back to Pietism. The statement "I don't understand myself" expresses a primal religious experience within Christianity. Indeed, human life is a matter of the continuity of one's self-understanding, but
this continuity consists in constantly putting oneself into question and a constant
being-other [*ein beständiges Anderssein*]. Just for this reason, one can never
achieve self-consciousness in the sense of a full self-identification. (It appears to
me that the project of philosophical analysis that Dieter Henrich and his students have undertaken in Heidelberg is closely related to this point in demonstrating that even in Kant there is much more involved here than mere
identification.)

Now Derrida would object by saying that understanding always turns into
appropriation and so involves a covering-up of otherness. Levinas, too, values
this argument highly, so it is definitely an observation that one cannot dismiss.
Yet it seems to me that to make an assumption that such identification occurs
within understanding is to disclose a position that is idealistic and logocentric,
one we had already left behind after World War I in our revisions and criticisms
of idealism that the translations of Kierkegaard by the Swabian minister Sch-
rempf helped to promote. Theologians like Karl Barth and Rudolf Bultmann, the
Jewish critique of idealism by Franz Rosenzsweig and Martin Buber, as well as
Catholic writers like Theodor Haecker and Ferdinand Ebner served to determine
the climate in which our own thinking moved at the time. When I speak in my
own work of the necessity for the horizon of one person and the horizon of
another to merge into one for any understanding between them to take place, I
am not referring to an abiding and identifiable "one" [*Eines*], but just to what
takes place in conversation as it goes along.

In this regard, I see my position corroborated by the thoroughly enlightening
contribution to this colloquium by Rudiger Bubner on the relation of Schlegelian
irony to Hegel's dialectic.[1] It made clear to me once again that Kierkegaard's
turn to Socrates is not so completely misguided as we classical philologists are
accustomed to consider it. Of course, romantic irony had nothing to do with the
social and pedagogical thrust of Socratic irony. Nevertheless, in Socrates we
find an idea from which one must start out and from which I too have started out
as I sought to reach an understanding of and with Derrida. One must seek to
understand the other, and that means that one has to believe that one could be in
the wrong. In regard to Derrida, I have adhered to this view to the point where,
beyond the boundary of our ways of bringing things out, our common starting

points and common goals became more and more clear to me. As philologists
we are all familiar with how one can really defend the evidence one has accumulated only when all efforts to doubt it have failed. This is a part of the moral
aspect of the so-called objectivity of research. As a virtue, this is a nonnego-
tiable moral achievement, surpassing a mere exclusion of subjective elements
for the purpose of insuring the objectivity of scholarly knowledge with the
help of an appropriate method. Just like Derrida's "deconstruction," self-
understanding—to which understanding contributes—goes completely beyond
the position of Husserl's first *Logical Investigation* and the so-called Platonism
of phenomenology.

The correspondences between early Romanticism and my own philosophical
development in the twentieth century are neither supported nor represented
solely by my reappropriation of the thinking of that late-born Romantic, Søren
Kierkegaard, during the epoch before and immediately after World War I. A
number of other persuasive correspondences also exist, chief among which is
the parallel between the dominant place attained by Fichte in the Romantic
period and by Heidegger in our century. Manfred Frank has described with a
great deal of subtlety Fichte's "positing theory" [*Setzungtheorie*] and its offen-
siveness to the historical consciousness of early Romanticism.[2] I see it in exactly
the same way, although I must also insist that during this time we were acquainted with a scaled-down Fichte, since the second part of the *Elements of a
Unified Doctrine of Knowledge (Grundlage der gesamten Wissenschaftslehre)*
was little known, as were also the clues in the early Fichte to the later Fichte.
Hegel's schema of subjective, objective, and absolute idealism is an ingenious
construction. Fichte's absolute idealism was [in his early period] already self-
evident. And this suggests that the turn that emerges so clearly in Fichte's late
"*Wissenschaftslehren*" [*doctrines or sciences of knowledge*] cannot be conceived as a kind of "reversal" ["*Kehre*"], but rather as a working out of motifs
contained within his "science of knowledge" from the beginning.

Hence, the self-understanding of thinkers such as Fichte and Heidegger bears
a striking similarity. Fichte has said also that his early *Elements* was the real
foundation for everything that came later. Likewise, from his later works until
his death, Heidegger maintained the same thing about *Being and Time,* in spite
of the talk about a "reversal." In his case, it was Protestant theology that sought
to cling to the call for authenticity and the pathos of *Being and Time* against
Heidegger's later view in this regard. Indeed, this belongs to the nature of the
history of the reception of a work [*Wirkungsgeschichte*]. In a similar manner
Romanticism simultaneously constructed its own critical opposition when it took
the first part of the *Elements* as the whole thing. Thus, I find Frank's presentation completely persuasive. Of course, in making these comparisons, I do not
want to claim that Heidegger's later development links up to his initial starting
points and his position in *Being and Time* in exactly the same sense in which the

late Fichte connects up to the earlier Fichte. Still, it seems to me one can see here deep-seated correspondences and motifs.

So it appears to me completely justifiable to seek to express the turn of thought in our century by means of concepts shaped by German idealism, as I have done in my own works. Thus, I basically have no objection when my contribution is called a "dialectical hermeneutics." In fact, I have for example spoken in dialectical terms of "effective historical consciousness" ["*wirkungsgeschichtliches Bewusstsein*"] when I said that it is actually more being than consciousness.

The discussion I became involved in with Heidegger in this regard focused on his concept of the language of metaphysics, into which one supposedly falls again and again. I maintained that this is a poor, inexact expression. There is no language of metaphysics. There is always only one's own language, where concepts shaped within the metaphysical tradition live on in a variety of transformations and a manifold of layers. Thus, German idealism has continued to speak, to a certain extent, a latinized Greek conceptual language. At the same time, German idealists, primarily on the basis of the Lutheran Bible and the language of mysticism, have introduced major innovations into philosophical language. What is the language of metaphysics really supposed to be? Is it really a language? There is no problem in understanding what it means for a concept to bear a metaphysical determination. Here it seems completely crucial to me that the profound message of *Destruktion* that the young Heidegger brought to us never—at least for those who at the time really had an ear for the German language—had the negative tone of destruction that clings to the foreign usage of this word by the British, the French, and others. *Destruktion* is for us a dismantling [*Abbau*], a dismantling of what has been covered up. When we mean "destruction," we do not say "*Destruktion*" but "*Zerstörung.*" So Heidegger introduced the word *Destruktion* in the 1920s. I assume Derrida was not really familiar with its usage and thus chose what, to my feeling for language, is a peculiar and redundant verbal construction [namely, "deconstruction"] because he was unable to hear anything but *Zerstörung* in *Destruktion*.

Now words themselves are not so important. But the matter at stake [*die Sache*] is important. It has to do with making concepts and their expressions speak once more, with taking them out of the merely functional context in which they are employed as overdetermined terms, and bringing them back to their original role within language. That was Heidegger's great service: the *Destruktion* of the academic language of metaphysics. He has shown that Greek conceptual determinations were words in living language containing—for all their conceptual precision—a multiplicity or, to put it as would modern poetic theory, a "multivocity" of semantic elements, which still go on speaking together in the background. Thus, in his famous lexicon of concepts, Aristotle not only captured conceptual distinctions but also brought out connections among concepts; as, for example, in a note—doubtless important for Heidegger—that *ousia* means, first of all, things that are present: the farm, the property that the farmer cultivates, which belongs to him and to which he belongs. For Aristotle, all this is always contained in the meaning of *ousia*. Likewise, our word *"Anwesen"* or "real estate" obviously accommodates the temporally-related senses of *"Anwesenheit"* or "presence" thematized by Heidegger. The fact that *Anwesen* as the German equivalent of *ousia* is at home in the same region of meanings (including real estate) clarifies the nature of Heidegger's insight into the temporal character of being. So, through Heidegger's interpretation, Aristotle became a very concrete Aristotle. This has misled us for a long time into thinking that what Heidegger had in mind was really a critique of metaphysics. And certainly he did not have in mind something like what is conveyed by the term *Präsenz* [presence]. *Being and Time* makes this point completely clear, for in that work *Vorhandenheit,* the objective presence of something at hand, is treated as a mode stemming from a still more primordial understanding of the *"Da"* [the "there"] of being.

Thus, the new turn of events in phenomenology involved not only a thematizing of the conceptuality in which thinking expresses itself, but it also brought to life the relationship between concepts and conceptual expressions and so between thinking and language. As I see it, if one takes phenomenology seriously as a way of research, one has to recognize that Heidegger's transformation of Husserlian phenomenology—which certainly would not have been possible without the influence of Dilthey and Kierkegaard—moved language to the center of philosophical questioning on the Continent, approximately at the same time as the "linguistic turn" was taking place in Anglo-American philosophy. This is not to erase the differences between these two events. The Anglo-American tradition proceeds—and Derrida follows it in this regard—from the concept of the sign which, in its ambiguity, that way of looking at things takes to be the ur-phenomenon. This holds for Husserl as well. There were good reasons why Derrida could productively direct criticism toward Husserl's theory of signs. On the other hand, the hermeneutical turn in phenomenology opens itself up, above all, to that which is mediated through language, and just for this reason I have elevated the conversational character of language to the foreground. In a conversation, it is *something* that comes to language, not one or the other speaker.

Here the closeness of the hermeneutic turn in phenomenology to early Romanticism suggests itself. Such closeness has not surprised me. Indeed I myself have occasionally been able to relate in a positive way back to Schleiermacher as well as Schlegel. But as I participated in the present discussion, I saw that the agreements go much further. For instance, I learned from the lecture by Alexander von Bormann that the critical analysis of consciousness and awareness in the Romantic era had already been developed in a temporally-related course with the interpretation of *"nous"* as being like lightning.[3] On a large piece of bark above the door of Heidegger's hut in the Black Forest stood the words of Heraclitus: "Lightning steers all things." This too is to be understood temporally. In a flash of lightning everything is clear and bright, for an instant—then it sinks into the depths of the night. The fact that Heraclitus and Plato had something similar in mind with their use of *"nous"*—awareness and being alive—can thus be convincingly shown in a number of different ways.

Furthermore, on one issue that has for a long time especially occupied my attention—the issue of *"intentio auctoris"* or the intention of the author—I clearly am in much greater proximity to Schlegel than I had previously realized.[4] This connection has primarily to do with the emphasis Schlegel puts on the concept of the work. On this point, I have long had to defend myself vehemently against the spirit of the times, which wants to set aside the hermeneutical sense of the concept of the work. Here a feeling for the history of concepts can be helpful. "Work" [*Werk*] does not mean anything different from the Greek word *"ergon"*. It is characterized—just like *"ergon"*—by the fact that it is detached both from the producer and the activity of production. This points to an ancient Platonic problem: The design of a particular thing does not depend on who makes it but on who is to use it. This applies to all work, particularly to works of art. Of course, a work of art, unlike an object of handicraft, is not made for a designated use but rather is suspended from use and consequently from misuse. It stands, so to speak, only for itself and in itself. Now this is decisive for dealing with the question at hand concerning the intention of the author. When it comes to a work of art, it could be said that the intention has, so to speak, "gone into" the work, and can no longer be sought behind it or before it. This sharply limits the value of all biographical insights related to a work of art, as well as those associated with the history of its origins. Works of art are detached from their origins and, just because of this, begin to speak—perhaps surprising even their creators.

Here the reception-aesthetics of Hans-Robert Jauss comes into play.[5] Jauss does not want to go along with my critique of aesthetic consciousness, because he thinks that he has located in the reader, the appreciator, the recipient, the true ground that immunizes him against the aesthetics of genius. Nevertheless, the work stands in itself. I have sought to show that when it comes to poetry and other literary arts, neither the word nor the sentence nor, as one would say today, the discourse refers back to the intention of the author. Things are rather the other way around. Every reader sees himself subjected to the command [*Diktat*] of the poem and the text. That poetry is called a *"Diktat"* seems to me to point to the phenomenological upheaval generated when a work, in its own intention, in what it really says, has something to say to us. The work stands there. Certainly it also possesses a history of its reception, but we do not need to know every use and misuse it has been through.

It has also become very clear to me how my own defense of what Hegel called "bad infinity" rests on the intentions of Fichte and Schlegel. Just as conversation gets its illumination from out of the conversational situation, so too such a situative moment holds for all thinking. This has been greatly heightened in Hegel through his stylizing of the dialectical movement of contradiction into the appearance of a method, which exerts a good deal of false coercion. Yet it remains correct that every assertion must be understood as the answer to a question if it is to be understood at all. The same goes for an assertion made by a work of art.

In conclusion, let me try to shed some light on the relationship between my own endeavor and that of Derrida, and on our mutual relationship to the hermeneutical turn in phenomenology. When Derrida goes back to the concept of *écriture* in order to get hold of the true nature of the sign, I can very well understand that he wants to do justice to the multivocity of language while striving at the same time to overcome the trivial fixation of words and meanings on the basis of discursive sense and intention. But I have my doubts as to whether he begins thereby at the truly decisive point. He seems to me much too dependent here on the concept of the sign, which represents the unquestioned starting point in Edmund Husserl, Ferdinand de Saussure, C. S. Peirce, Charles Morris, and others, as well as, of course, in the whole tradition of semantics and semiotics. I well understand this effort to go behind, by means of the concept of *écriture,* all bogus univocity and all false multiplicity of interpretations. In the tradition, this means getting back to the *"verbum interius,"* the word that has not yet been splintered into various languages and expressions.

To me, however, it seems necessary to separate the concept of the word from its grammatical sense, as I myself have sought to do. The word is that which says something, above the distinctions of grammatical parts such as sentences, words, syllables, and so forth. It seems perfectly reasonable to me that precisely on the basis of the concept of *écriture* one is thrown back to this broader sense of what a word is. Writing, in all its spirituality, is only there when it is read. So words are what they are only as spoken discourse. At just this juncture the hermeneutic turn, which consists in going beyond the present, becomes unavoidable. This turn urges on us the point that clearly no oral reading or voicing is able to fulfill the intended sense and sound of a poetic text. I am speaking here about an inner ear, to which a kind of inner intonation corresponds, neither of which is totally absorbed by the contingency of any particular appearance. I recognize another aspect of this in what Derrida calls the "silent voice." These are all aspects of the same phenomenologically basic datum through which words become words that speak. This is manifested in our experience in a familiar way. Whoever reads a text or repeats words without understanding them—no matter how much expression, articulation, and intonation goes into such speaking—will pass right by the sense of the words and their meaning will not be conveyed. No one can grasp the application of speech or the deciphering of writing who does not come to the words themselves with understanding; for example, in reading aloud with understanding. So to *écriture* there corresponds *lecture,* reading. Both belong together, but neither of the two is ever fulfilled in the sense of a simple self-identity. Both are only what they are when they stand in "difference" ["*Differenz*"], and when they stand back from unmediated identity.

This leads us back necessarily to the concept of the work and to its ownmost hermeneutical autonomy and substantiality. Here one may recall Hegel. The only form in which what is common to us all—what otherwise only actualizes itself in the continuous give and take of conversation—is always already there is the work of art, which imposes itself on us like a command. Hegel recognized the work of art as a form of "absolute" spirit; and in fact what presents itself in art is not conditioned by what one or another person thinks about it, nor even by what went on in the mind of its creator. It belongs to the essential nature of the communicative power of the artwork, that only in it is constituted what is common to us all.[6] So I think that in a certain sense Derrida has pursued a path extending from Heidegger's thought very much like my own. But it seems to me that his path is marked by an ontologically unclarified dependence on the semantic starting point involved in his view of language. The unavoidability of the hermeneutic standpoint is the theme of my confrontation with Derrida. This standpoint really has nothing to do with the establishment of the correct meanings of words, as if meanings were firm or possessed a firmness that could be grasped. Difference exists within identity. Otherwise, identity would not be identity. Thought contains deferral and distance. Otherwise, thought would not be thought.

Commentaries

Philippe Forget

1. Argument(s)

Translated by Diane Michelfelder

In the course of organizing a meeting in April 1981 between Gadamer and Derrida—these figureheads of two conflicting currents in Western philosophical thinking—I did not intend to force an encounter between them. At most, I was hoping that this event (if indeed there was one, and nothing is less certain) would make a contribution towards forming the conditions under which these two currents of thought would confront each other head-on rather than mutually avoiding each other—in other words, that they would agree to subsume denial [*déni*] within the challenge [*défi*]. As it turned out, the encounter would uphold denial, at the challenge's expense. Still, though, we do not need to see this as a failure. By means of the strategies that the "encounter" imposed on this denial in using it, it thereby became more open to interpretation. The initial publication resulting from this encounter [*TI*] vouches for this. Indeed, the echo it aroused, of which this present publication will no doubt constitute a major part, confirms it, as do also some recent publications by Gadamer—and here, one can't help but observe (without intending to be biased) how these texts make a fairly insistent fuss about Derrida and so feed the ongoing discussion with new *arguments*.

"*Arguments*"—apart from a set of parentheses—that word will be the title of this particular essay.

Taken in the singular, the French word *argument* means a brief statement of theses to be developed. It is also precisely what is at issue here.

In the plural, *arguments* signifies—not only in French—the presentation of lines of reasoning, of more or less logical sequences of ideas, seeking to justify a point of view or a theoretical position. And, following its usage in the text emphasized here, it is never just a matter of exposing arguments here and there, but also of arguing from these arguments, which are really always arguments from other arguments, drawn along by a logic of *debate*. So it is also specifically this debate that will be in question here—this debate or, taking into account the meaning argument can have in the language in which this text appears—this quarrel. For one to be persuaded that there is a quarrel here, a brief review of the forms of address Derrida and Gadamer use in their "exchange" recorded in *Text und Interpretation* will suffice.[1]

Here I am alluding to two short texts appearing in the present publication (pp. 52–57). I will refer to them again, particularly in connection with the discussion centering around "(the) psychoanalysis." But I do not intend now to reproduce my introduction to *Text und Interpretation* ["Leitfäden einer unwahrscheinlichen Debatte"—"Clues to an Improbable Encounter"] (*TI* 7–23). That preview-text (even if it did already sketch out several arguments), does not correspond to all the aspects of the title named here. Consequently, I felt it necessary to refer often to previously published texts, some also included in this volume. On the other hand, some other references—the most insistent among them—point towards much older texts, which demand to be reread in the light of this encounter. Still, in order to respect the dimensions of my earlier German introduction, some choices were necessary. So I will say nothing about the text in this exchange that Derrida devotes to Heidegger's Nietzsche.[2] Here in this essay I will be following another thread.

In order to spell out the general perspective of "Argument(s)" more clearly, I will begin by referring to a passage from "*Destruktion* and Deconstruction," where Gadamer is replying to Manfred Frank's critique of the validity of the perspective of the *Horizontverschmelzung* or "fusion of horizons."[3] Gadamer questions Frank's critique as follows:

> It seems very misleading to me for someone to say that just because I emphasize the role of tradition in all our posing of questions and also in the indication of answers, I am asserting a super-subject and thus (as Manfred Frank and Philippe Forget go on to maintain) reducing the hermeneutical experience to an empty word. There is no support in *Truth and Method* for this kind of construction. When I speak there of tradition and of conversation with the tradition, I am in no way putting forward a collective subject. Rather, "tradition" is simply the collective name for each individual text ("text" in the widest sense, which would include a picture, an architectural work, even a natural event). (DD 111[16])

Here one can observe that Gadamer dismisses more than defuses an objection. Certainly, the reference to Lacan is not the best angle from which to approach Gadamer's thought critically with regard to tradition and dialogue. Obviously [Lacan's] "empty speech" forms a system with full speech (*la parole pleine*), and so with an entire lexicon and postwar philosophical range of concepts (German as well as French), such as Heidegger's ideas of authenticity and truth as *alētheia*, that come very close to Lacan's idea of full speech. To critique

Gadamer starting from such notions therefore amounts to situating him in a space still homogeneous with his line of thinking. For Lacan, just as for Gadamer, all speech calls for a response: "I shall show that there is no speech without a reply, even if it is met only with silence, provided that it has an auditor: this is the heart of its function in analysis" (*E* 247). It is easy to see how such a remark inscribes itself within the perspective of a "dialogue," even when the one in question is the unique dialogue belonging to psychoanalysis. In any case, it is clear how empty speech, like full speech, is tied to a response. But whereas the effect of full speech is to "reorder past contingencies by conferring on them the sense of necessities to come, such as they are constituted by the little freedom through which the subject makes them present" (256), the empty word is one "where the subject seems to talk in vain about someone who, even if he were his spitting image, can never become one with the assumption of his desire" (254). More than to "emptiness" (and all the misunderstandings to which this idea can give rise), "empty speech" refers to conflict and division [*clivage*], a division that troubles and fissures the homogeneity of speech. Hence, one might say that "empty speech" calls for a response perhaps even more than "full speech," because it is from this response that "consciousness" will restore, be it as a phantasm, the homogeneity of its discourse. Thus, the call for a response, a dialogue, would be the repressive signifier [*signifiant dénégateur*] of the unity of discourse and consciousness, and empty speech would be the speech whose business it is to avoid the repression constitutive of discourse.

For reasons already given, one does not have to stick to this terminology. The real problem lies in knowing whether one can sustain such a critical discourse concerning Gadamer's hermeneutics. Going back to the argument alleging that *Truth and Method* is not vulnerable to such a critique, I will make a further effort to show how, starting from the values of prejudice and authority as they are set out in that work, the notion of truth dominating Gadamer's text (truth as *adaequatio*) does indeed justify such a critique. This would make the reference to Lacan superfluous.

I. The Choice of a Ground

For any confrontation to take place or merely to be able to take place, one needs at the very least to have at one's disposal a fairly well-defined and common ground. It is important to be careful about calling this a "consensus." It exists only to allow questions to be raised about the respective positions involved, or about one position from the critical purview of the other. This is to say that one can never simply choose a ground. It can only be constituted by the intersection traced by divergent approaches to the "same" (but is it the same?) problematic. And my preliminary critical remark concerning the eventual "fissure" of hermeneutical discourse points toward a problematic that seems to pull together the necessary conditions. One could put it like this: for both deconstruction and hermeneutics (in its reflection on tradition), self-consciousness does not constitute the ground on which either one sets itself up or takes its position [*se pose ou se poste*]. For Derrida, self-consciousness would be the illusion of hearing oneself speak, of hearing one's own voice while it is speaking. For Gadamer, even though he does not abandon the idea of self-consciousness or certain of its predicates, the illusion would consist in thinking that self-consciousness can escape being formed in advance by tradition.

Now even if this constitutes a kind of minimum common ground, it is not, as one can already see, "neutral" territory. It is determined from one side to the other by multiple and for the most part widely diverging prejudices, including a connection having to do with articulated prejudices and the unconscious, an inevitable motif in such a terrain. Derrida must put these to the test in critical discourse itself, because he cannot have any preliminary theorization of such "forces"[4] such as is shown programmatically in Gadamer by a principle of selection permitting one to distinguish productive from destructive prejudices.

A common ground, but not a neutral one. That is to say, one of the protagonists must receive the other. The very form of an encounter—perhaps itself determined by a more profound necessity[5]—would have demanded that Gadamer receive Derrida in Paris and kick things off with his lecture dedicated to "Text and Interpretation," thereby giving himself the advantage of situating the discussion around topics he had chosen. With each of my guests therefore becoming the host of the other and the other of a host, according to the double meaning that this word has in French, the debate could get under way.[6]

II. Understanding—On the Good Will

In presenting his argument, Gadamer put the debate under the sign of the "good will" in the sense of the Platonic *eumeneis elenchoi*, that is to say, not the desire to prove that one is right by flushing out the weaknesses of what the other has to say, but rather the disposition to strengthen the other's point of view by going along with his most insightful thought. For Gadamer, such an idea has no essential ties to ethics or any sort of voluntarism. It is just a simple observation, set off in the final analysis from that "hermeneutical experience" behind which Derrida glimpses an entire metaphysical machinery. (One could note here how Gadamer's repeated reference to "that experience that we all recognize" is always used as a counterargument, implicit or not, but without satisfying the cognitive conditions that would turn it into an argument—a symptom of how the "hermeneutical experience" is invested in Gadamer's discourse as a truth that would always already be grounded on yet another truth.)[7]

The choice of this "attack" clearly appears in his strategy: the "good will" presupposes agreement on the conditions of understanding; so if Derrida agreed to meet with Gadamer, it would be (so Gadamer thinks) in order to try to understand him rather than to evade him by some means or another (and there are more radical ways of evading someone than bypassing him or her). Gadamer also sees his own point of view strengthened by the wave of questions Derrida puts to him: anyone who addresses questions to another must surely suppose that the other is disposed to receive them as questions and respond to them. And one might even add the following: On this basis, Gadamer has the right to confirm some sort of consensus between Derrida and himself, since even if they otherwise accept the idea that no preliminary consensus can be found between their respective positions, an agreement on the lack of a consensus clearly implies a consensus of some kind.

Certainly, there is no doubt about this. But such a "consensus" determines nothing of what follows from it. For their positions are acquired this side of the very idea of consensus. Also, it is not out of the question that Derrida, not having it within his power (which goes without saying) to stick to the terms of "good will," follows an interpretive practice which is not totally heterogeneous with it. The striking element in how Derrida reads is his attention to small details and the patience with which he "deconstructs" texts from the philosophical tradition, driving their "logic" to the farthest extreme. Hence, the split between Gadamer and Derrida occurs at another level: whereas the former defends a unitary concept of understanding—if not with respect to conscious discourse, then at least to a type of unified coherence homogenous with the structure of hermeneutical "self-consciousness"—Derrida considers such limits as "philosophèmes" or "philosophical units," themselves susceptible to deconstruction to the extent that they "actively" participate in structuring a discourse. This explains why for Derrida the act of reading texts demands structurally that one take into account

> the law of their internal conflicts, of their heterogeneity, of their contradictions, and that one not simply cast an aesthete's glance over the philosophical discourse which carries within it the history of the oppositions in which are displaced, although often under cover, both critical formalism and psychoanalytic hermeneutics.
> Like Nietzsche, reinterpret interpretation.
>
> ("Qual Quelle," *M* 362/305.)

III. Reinterpreting "psychoanalysis" [Réinterpréter 'la' psychanalyse]

Under such conditions, all that remains is to see how hermeneutical "good will" is carried out in practice. The Paris encounter gives us an excuse to do this, specifically in relation to the discussion on pyschoanalysis as a method of reading. When Gadamer brought this matter up in his lecture, Derrida did not fail to question him about it, but at the expense of a misunderstanding. Clearly, Derrida anticipated Gadamer's position in immediately identifying it as a "hermeneutical psychoanalysis." This is why he is astonished that one could at the same time keep up a voluntaristic sort of discourse and likewise claim to be carrying out a psychoanalytic reading, which could only break down the notion of the (good) will. Now, if psychoanalysis, outside of its therapeutic effect, can be, as Lacan says, nothing more than a method "which proceeds to decipher signifiers *without regard for any pre-supposed form of existence of the signified(E* 748, italics added)," it is clear that Gadamerian hermeneutics has to remain entirely impervious to it, a position which, moreover, Gadamer himself affirms elsewhere on more than one occasion. Where, then, does the misunderstanding come from? Is it a question here of just a misunderstanding? The only way to answer these questions is to take a close look at what Gadamer actually has to say and not his alleged or preconceived position.

For this examination, we will adopt an angle that is the reverse of Derrida's. "What would good will mean in psychoanalysis? Or even just in a discourse that follows the lines of psychoanalysis?" These will not be our questions. Instead, we will ask: "How does a discourse which assumes a non-voluntaristic idea of 'good will' as a precondition of understanding understand 'psychoanalysis'?"

The question of psychoanalysis came up in the course of the discussion following Gadamer's lecture, after a series of questions having to do with the criteria for "good" understanding. I felt I had to ask Gadamer how understanding acts in the face of texts such as Georg Trakl's, whose meaning clearly surpasses understanding according to hermeneutical rules. Gadamer responded by saying that one can enlarge the context of understanding by examining all available elements—biography, for example—following the lines of psychoanalysis.

Of course, psychoanalysis is presented here as a continuous whole in step with a hermeneutical reading,[8] and so becomes integrated with the latter in advance as its potential expansion. And if one wants a reference to this particular point in Gadamer's text, one should reread the following passage:

> In fact, narrative literature has taken as one of its possessions the genre of dreams and fairy-tales, as we find, for example, in the German Romantic. But in this case it is an aesthetic quality which narrative literature enjoys in the play of dream fantasy and which naturally can be interpreted in a literary and aesthetic way. *In contrast,* the same phenomenon of the dream can become the object of a *totally different kind of interpretation* if one seeks to go behind the fragments of dream recollection in order to reveal a true meaning, a meaning which has only disguised itself in the dream fantasies and which is capable of being decoded. (39[25], emphasis added)

It is easy to see here how Gadamer completely rules out a psychoanalytic reading from aesthetics and the interpretation of literature, although he describes psychoanalysis (which he takes to be solely a therapy that permits a restoration of the homogeneous relationship between self and other) according to the purposes of classical hermeneutics, namely, knowing how to decipher or decode a meaning assumed and preconceived to be the "authentic" one.

One can see from this that the hermeneutics of good will cannot press psychoanalysis in its logic or its logics. The most striking indication of this is the usage of the singular article (*"la psychanalyse"*), which identifies psychoanalysis in the mirror of a hermeneutical discourse which itself is assumed to be homogeneous. So Derrida's misunderstanding [*Le malentendu de Derrida*] is also a case of having "understood all too well" [*"trop-bien-entendu"*]. The difference is in the "tone." As Derrida sees it, Gadamer introduced psychoanalysis in a positive way in his discourse, although his purpose was negative, and perhaps even repressive [*dénégateur*].

IV. Authority of Prejudice, Prejudice of Authority

At any rate, in this section, we are going to conduct an experiment with the limits of hermeneutical good will. Elsewhere, we saw how an absolute division or rupture, far from preventing one from going along with a thinker (of a text) in his or her most insightful or powerful thought (in its significance), could give it new momentum, not from the circularity of replenishment within a unified and continuous truth, but, alternatively, from the short-circuited "delirium" of grafting something on.[9] Thus, one could say that divergence rests exclusively on the apprehension of unity[10] and cannot be interpreted as some sort of bad will or deconstructive bad faith; that kind of suspicion, supported by Gadamer's reproach to Nietzsche and Derrida for contradicting themselves by writing what they write in order to be understood, puts the debate back on the ethical ground which Gadamer excludes from his concept of good will . . . .[11]

This apprehension of unity (part of the *"Vorgriff der Vollkommenheit"* ["anticipation of perfection"]) poses a question that has in effect already imposed itself from the beginning: the question of prejudices. Does hermeneutical good will have the power it claims of looking back on its constitutive prejudices, those which we are as well as those we have—or to put it another way by rephrasing Heidegger's well-known remark on language—those which have us, in all the senses of the word, as well as those which we have? In apprehending unity, doesn't good will suspend precisely the moment of critique, becoming powerless from then on to put under criticism the prejudices that structure understanding (*krinein*: to make a definitive judgment), even though it will inconsistently assume that a clear line can be drawn between good and bad prejudices, that is to say, between productive prejudices and obstructive ones?

But here let us not rush to be critical. First, let us carefully reread an argument of Gadamer's that is fundamental to the economy of his hermeneutics. Then we will match this text against a remark by Derrida (*"Préjugés,"* Préj) which was still unpublished at the time of the encounter.

The argument I have in mind is a decisive passage from *Truth and Method*. In it Gadamer resolutely opposes the positions of the Enlightenment, so characterized by out-and-out hostility towards prejudice itself. This hostility, rooted in the prejudices of the scientific viewpoint, does not enable the Enlightenment to escape prejudice. On the contrary, it turns prejudice into the unsuspected general condition of its own discourse—the condition, in some sense, of its own possibility. Thus, Gadamer can find in this discourse what he calls an *"Entmachtung der Überlieferung,"* a rendering powerless, a defusing [*desamorçage*], of tradition (*WM* 255/240).

Once assured of this ground, he takes up a different project: the rehabilitation of prejudice and authority, notions that for him are substantially the same (*WM* 263/247). With this move, he puts off the criticism addressed to him by Habermas, who accused him of using the recognition of the prejudicial structure of understanding for the purposes of calling for a rehabilitation of prejudice such as it is.[12] For if the ground indeed fits Gadamer's description of it, then the rehabilitation of the potential value of prejudice (not prejudice itself) would necessarily pass through a phase of reversal. Thus, Gadamer does not make a hasty judgment in an effort to invalidate Habermas's criticism. He merely tables coming to a decision about it, making it necessary to take a fresh look at a number of questions.

Although it is tedious, we must stay vigilant. Any reversal of a proof remains imprisoned in the system within which it works, confirming it instead of shaking its foundations. We can avoid such an experience only be means of a swerve, a leap to the other side, which lets us bypass any reversal and deploy another logic or system. On this basis and hence also from a strategic and methodological perspective, it is appropriate to examine Gadamer's description of prejudice as a constitutive structure of understanding. For there is just no doubt that prejudice is constitutive for thought, which cannot turn its own historicity into an abstraction. This fact leads Gadamer to bestow an ontological dignity on prejudice: "That which presents itself, under the aegis of an absolute self-construction by reason, as a limiting prejudice belongs, in fact, to historical reality itself" (*WM* 261/245–46). "That is why the prejudices of the individual, far more than his judgments, constitute the historical reality of his being" (*WM* 261/245).

Gadamer's move inscribes itself in a context of prejudice (not in the sense of "what must precede judgment" but as "that which includes it a priori"). If one does not yet know how one's argument will unfold, one does know what it is looking for: to rehabilitate authority and tradition (and the authority of tradition) by offering a critique of the way of thinking that proposes "globally" to "overcome" them (*WM* 260/244) through an analytical dissolution of prejudices.

Thus, Gadamer begins by reminding us that if we look at the history of prejudice, we will find it is not solely the negative concept we so often categorize it as whenever we identify a prereflexive judgment with an accepted idea. In juridical terms, a prejudice is a "preliminary verdict before the final judgment," a verdict that can certainly carry some weight when it comes to making the final decision, with which it is structurally homogeneous. Still, the apparent negativity of such a prejudice is not constitutive. It does not affect the structure of prejudice in itself (*WM* 255/240). And out of this idea comes the distinction between "prejudices" and "false judgments," as well as the observation, "*Es gibt préjugés légitimes*"—"There are such things as *préjugés légitimes*" (*ibid*).[13] Without elaborating on all the consequences, let us note that this statement implies a restriction: other prejudices also exist, illegitimate ones, and it is precisely the task of hermeneutical understanding not to allow these to spread (*WM* 261/246). Hence, it likewise implies that prejudices should be dealt with from the basis of a distinction between what is "legitimate" and "illegitimate," and thus ultimately that some law can operate like a sieve to separate one from the other.

Now let us reinsert Gadamer's remark into the flux of the argument. To the Enlightenment, judgments had dignity only insofar as they were based in reason and could be methodologically justified (*WM* 255/240). But Gadamer himself puts forth a similar claim at the beginning of his analysis by saying that a systematic understanding inspects its anticipations by bringing them before consciousness, "just what the historical, hermeneutical consciousness requires in any case" (*WM* 254/239). And a little earlier: "Understanding achieves its full potentiality only when the fore-meanings that it uses are not arbitrary" (*WM* 252/237). True enough, criticism can only hold up here if "anticipations" can in one way or another be assimilated under the category of prejudice. This does, though, seem to be the case. Obviously anticipation is not *a* prejudice—it is not a content of thought but a movement of understanding *in actu*. Even so, the "pre-" [*Vor-*] of "prejudice" [*Vorurteil*] implies the existence of some systematic tie to anticipation. Could one say that prejudice is a judgment *as* an anticipatory idea?

For Gadamer, just as for the Enlightenment, prejudice paradoxically presupposes the possibility of bringing itself to judgment, of bringing itself before itself to judge itself on the basis of an act of discrimination (as Gadamer sees it) that therefore also precedes it: a judgment that would be a pre-prejudgment, wholly heterogeneous to prejudice itself—and have we not, without seeking to do so, defined the place of self-consciousness?

In this context, Gadamer's remarkable analysis of the concealed relation between Schleiermacher's so-called romantic discourse and that of the Enlightenment is instructive. He reveals an objective accord between these two discourses (or opposing prejudices) that discloses itself indirectly in Schleiermacher's working distinction between prejudices caused by a restricted viewpoint, and other "momentary" ones, caused by haste. Only those of the first type, being "lasting" prejudices, have any methodological value (*WM* 262/247). With this classification in mind (one which, one might also observe, could only exist on the basis of a prejudgment about time: that is, that what lasts is a priori more valuable than what is ephemeral[14]), Gadamer lays out the following argument: to speak about prejudices in which we would be "caught up" or even "held captive,"[15] is already to judge or prejudge prejudices from the point of view either of their dissolution [*Auflösung*] or their illumination [*Aufklärung*] (*WM* 263/247). Such talk therefore would apply only to *unberechtige Vorurteile,* illegitimate prejudices. Thus, Schleiermacher perceived only illegitimate prejudices, and so contributed to the fulfillment of the maximalist program of the Enlightenment.

We may, in this context, note two points:

First of all, this same reasoning could basically apply to Gadamer's own discourse, as we earlier pointed out to the reader in connection with the proposition *"es gibt préjugés légitimes."*

Secondly, it was likewise mentioned that "legitimate prejudices" themselves also demand to be brought out by a discriminating act of reason. Thus, it is a mistake for Gadamer to hasten to conclude that Schleiermacher recognizes only illegitimate prejudices. Gadamer identifies these prejudices with the necessity of bringing them to light. But the act of becoming aware of a prejudice does not at all presuppose that the latter is illegitimate—except a priori to tuck Schleiermacher's thought back under rationalistic categories. Such a prejudgment means, if we have been able to follow Gadamer (if we have followed him far enough, but not too far), that a prejudice—to be legitimate—should not be capable of being brought to light. If indeed Gadamer's efforts at rehabilitation lead us to this conclusion, we have to admit that it totally contradicts his methodological presupposition as stated earlier; but still, it seems to be confirmed by the description Gadamer gives of the relationship between prejudice and authority. Is there any way to shed light on this twofold problem?

It is precisely on the basis of this stated identification that Gadamer again brings up the argument about authority. If there are also legitimate prejudices (ones that are *berechtigt,* literally, "authorized"), the problem of authority remains with us (*WM* 263/247). Now we already know the response to this: *"Es gibt préjugés légitimes."* This makes the question of authority insurmountable and superfluous at the same time, as the re-deployment of the argument on this point shows.

Gadamer blames Schleiermacher for not having seen the possible truth-content of prejudices relating to authority (*WM* 262–263/247–48), the notion of truth being substantially the same as that of authority. ("It no longer even occurs to Schleiermacher that among the prejudices in the mind of one whose vision is narrowed by authorities there might be some that are true—yet *this was included in the concept of authority in the first place"* (*WM* 262–63/247, italics added). But it is just as true that Gadamer simplifies or rather homogenizes—by oversystematizing it—the connection between authority and truth. He makes a kind of double bridge between them, without seeing or wanting to see that their connection cannot be simply symmetrical. We cannot assume, presume or preconceive authority as being receptive to the truth. It is truth (without prejudging here all the questions that come up around this concept) which is authoritative, not authority; it is not authority (wherever it comes from—and where does it come from? *d'où qu'elle vienne-d'où vient-elle?*) which produces *sui generis* whatever is taken as true.

Moreover, in connection with this point, Gadamer shows a renewed eagerness to see in the Enlightenment nothing more than the systematic refusal of prejudice. For anyone who has read Moses Mendelssohn's response to this charge, such a construal is not defensible.[16] The following passage, taken from this response, deals precisely with the relation of prejudice to truth, which must control our relation to prejudice itself:

> . . . so the virtue-loving man of the Enlightenment proceeds with caution and care, and sooner would tolerate prejudice *than drive it out with the truth so firmly tangled up with it*. Certainly this has become a maxim for any defense of insincerity or duplicity, and we have it to thank for so many centuries of barbarism and superstition. As often as one wants to seize this offense, it escapes into the realm of the holy. Yet the humanitarian himself in this most enlightened age must still, in spite of this, show consideration for this view. Indeed it is difficult, but not impossible, to find the boundary which here divides proper from improper use.[17]

Here again,[18] we find that Gadamer's systematic employment of the singular article when speaking about "the Enlightenment" corresponds to a gesture of dominance, both dominating and dominated by and for an argument full of prejudices.

When Gadamer goes on to describe authority and its relation to truthful prejudices, we find this feature standing out again. When we place a value on authority—that is, on a person who is authoritative—Gadamer tells us, we do not abdicate our reason, but rather, through an act of "recognition and knowledge" ["*Anerkennung und Erkenntnis,*"] (*WM* 263/248), realize the other's superior judgment. This recognition is not blind. It confirms knowledge; it is an act of reason itself, which understands itself sufficiently to also recognize its own limits (*WM* 264/248). This is why Gadamer can affirm that authority is not bestowed [*verliehen*] on someone, but is in fact acquired [*erworben*], taken up by someone.[19] This affirmation—and here we will not question the validity of its content—clearly functions to prepare an *objectification* of prejudice. This is a necessary preface to the reasoning that will follow and is even homogeneous with it, since the introduction of this description cannot fail to arouse criticism. Gadamer meets this criticism head-on. It might very well be, this objection runs, that the recognition of authority does not depend on an act of reason, on the impression that the reasoning of another makes on oneself, but on a different ground altogether, for example, the unconscious. How then to sort this out? Gadamer's answer demands to be read first of all from the text itself:

> The prejudices that they [the authorities] implant are rendered legitimate by the person himself. Their validity demands that one should be biased in favour of the person who presents them. But this then makes them, in a sense, objective prejudices, for they bring about the *same* bias in favour of something that can come about through other means, e.g. through solid grounds offered by reason. (*WM* 264/249, emphasis added)

One would expect that Gadamer, coming to this point in the argument, would show how to make the necessary division between good and bad prejudices. But no: here we learn that this recognition actually presupposes a prejudice in favor of the person who has authority, and this prejudice makes such a division superfluous. It is exactly on the basis of this prejudice that prejudices become "objective" [*sachlich*], since they involve the same favorable predisposition for something or some matter [*Sache*] which authority defends—a favorable predisposition or prereflective adherence which could also, Gadamer tells us, be adopted in some other way, for example, through solid grounds posed by reason itself.

Indeed, there are solid grounds not to let this claim by without questioning it. Isn't such reasoning completely circular? Doesn't it only confirm its own subject or its own condition, namely, to know the objective power (of the prejudice) of authority? And doesn't it also contradict what Gadamer stated earlier, namely, that recognition is acquired rather than bestowed? Far from being discriminating, the prejudice of authority (the prejudice projected on authority as the prejudice which comes from it) would be posed as absolute, objectal [*objectal*] rather than objective [*objectif*], letting reason be conserved, to become in some sense the prejudice of authority itself. It is this latter identification which finally explains how Gadamer can at the same time be opposed to "the Enlightenment" and repeat, in denying them, the *aporia* concerning the division between good and bad prejudices, and the good use and abuse of prejudice.*

Gadamer's reasoning rests on a particular concept of truth, truth as the adequation of the individual to what is said and what is said to the individual, and so also on a particular concept of coherence. Surely all of this rests on a prejudice transmitted by the authority of the tradition, but that is a different issue,

---

*Cf. the passage cited above from Moses Mendelssohn.

and we are interested here solely in testing the matter at hand. So we can begin by letting a remark of Derrida's resonate here, an observation very closely connected to our subject: "Truth as *adaequatio* is essentially linked to judgment, to the proposition; that is to say it is *founded on* a non-judicative, prejudicative revelation, on another truth" (Préj 96).

Now we can see the *aporia* hampering Gadamer, and better understand why his hermeneutics can only at this point run into criticism (which is a matter of record) over the absence of a reliable principle of selection.[20] But we can also prompt a displacement of this criticism: here it is no longer simply a matter of observing, as many others have done, that Gadamer's hermeneutics does not state a principle of selection, nor even of demanding *how* such a principle could be conceived in a thinking that would overcome hermeneutics but still remain homogenous with it. Instead, here is the question to which we will now seek an answer: Why is it that this hermeneutics finds it necessary to pose the question of a principle of selection and is at the same time unable to respond to it? In dealing with this question we will be able to come up with a general strategy of textual interpretation that can cut across the dogmatic exclusions of "hermeneutical philosophy." This, I propose, could be called "textonomics" [*textonomique*], and its "object" or goal, a "textonomy" [*textonomie*].

As Gadamer describes it, the criterion or principle of selection can only come from the order of reason and consciousness.* In this critique we have outlined the idea that in proving this principle these authorities remain subordinated to an authority of prejudice, which deprives them of all credibility of discrimination. In fact, the authority of reason/consciousness really seems to have in Gadamer only the value of an appeal to legitimacy.[21] At the point of invoking this appeal, Gadamer forgets that prejudice is heterogeneous with reason and consciousness. This means it is also heterogeneous with a theoretical consciousness or a merely methodological one.

To recapitulate: on the one hand, prejudice must be brought in front of consciousness by reason (the solid grounds of reason) or be led to reason by consciousness (be it methodological or historical-hermeneutical). Here we would be within a juridical register, making judgments about good and bad prejudices. On the other hand, authority allows for an economy pertaining to judgment. The prejudice favorable to authority provides *a priori* testimony, one might say, for backing up what the solid grounds of reason could also state in their own way. This judgment of reason and consciousness, this methodological claim, yields to the prejudgment of prejudice as soon as it becomes an issue of describing an actual relation to (good) prejudice through the value of authority, and the necessity of stating the criteriology of the principle of selection is forgotten.

---

*Cf. *supra* the citations from *WM*.

As appearances would lead us to believe, isn't there an incoherent discourse here, a contradiction between theory and practice? If the criteriology can be forgotten, it is at the expense of a new series of (ad)equations posed between authority and tradition, then between tradition and freedom, and finally between freedom and history: "The fact is that tradition is constantly an element of freedom and of history itself" (*WM* 265/250). This freedom is also that which causes us to accept our morals: "They (our morals) are freely taken over" (*WM* 265/249).

For the same reason, the notion of prejudice can be effaced in this context, and so it would no longer be necessary to fall back upon a possible principle of selection concerning it. This claim that we freely accept our morals looks extremely prejudiced when one considers it outside of the circular (and therefore recuperating) structure of Gadamer's argument. Lessing, who passes for an enlightened authority, shows himself to be more attentive to prejudice when he has Nathan say, while telling a story, that we cling to one of three revealed religions (rather than the other two) not through a free act on our part, but rather through the actuality of historical prejudice.[22] Thus, freedom would not come into play until after the fact, in the recognition that other religions also have a value or even a legitimacy equal to that of the religion within which we have been reared. Likewise, our freedom does not play a role in the act of accepting the morals of our society; it figures in later, beyond prejudices—in prejudices which are at the same time given and acquired, undistorted either way—in order to make us recognize their relativity and put us on guard against universalizing them.

The claim to discrimination both given and deferred [*remisée*] by Gadamer's hermeneutics in fact recovers (literally speaking) another issue at stake: that of legitimating a certain practice of interpretation, closed to "its" prejudices (and one will see that they are never only its own), while outwardly fussing about a point of method—a move that furnishes the illusion of being critically concerned with the prejudices that go to make up the practice of hermeneuts: their hermeneutics/the lure of hermeneutics.[23]

One could, on this basis, radically put back into question the claim to universality of such an act or practice, a claim found throughout Gadamer's self-legitimating and badly confused writing. By definition alone, a hermeneutic which is based exclusively on the rehabilitation of its own prejudices and therefore on a series of exclusions (of the "signifier," for example) cannot be universal. It is this argument, it seems to me, to which Gadamer implicitly responds in his "Letter to Dallmayr," basing his own argument on the experience of dialogue:

> The fact that conversation takes place wherever, whenever, and with whomever something comes to language—whether this is another person or a thing, a

word, or a flame-signal (Gottfried Benn)—constitutes the universality of the hermeneutical experience. The fact that this experience contains its own limits within itself is in no way inconsistent with its universality. Quite the contrary. The universality of the hermeneutical experience fits perfectly well with the factual limitedness of all human experience and with the limits governing our linguistic communication and possibility for expression.[24]

But what is Gadamer doing in this "response," if not, through a simple act of inversion, repeating the fundamental prejudice of hermeneutics, namely, the postulate of the universality of dialogue? Certainly, dialogue (or certainly rather the illusion of dialogue) can take place anywhere and everywhere, not only among rational beings, and one can experience in this context the limits of understanding. But if Gadamer starts here from the "particular" experience of limits, and not from the postulate of universality, it is in order to immediately universalize this particular "experience" by establishing a relation of absolute adequation between this experience of limits and the limits of all "human communication," which always amounts to setting up one specific field as a universal absolute, the field of dialogue, of understanding within dialogue, and of a specific interpretation of "communication" that exists only on the basis of a system of exclusion.[25] That the postulate of universality emerges from the description of an "experience," or that experience shall be in harmony with this postulate—such is the logic Gadamer's argument follows. Here is a universality enclosed in itself, since it exists only under the condition of universalizing its own constitutive prejudices. An interpretive practice of this type cannot be active—that is also to say, transforming—because it replenishes itself only from itself, or more exactly from this founding prejudice which is not simply identifiable with the thought that it leads to or lures, since, according to the all-powerful logic of truth as *adaequatio* under which one can subsume Gadamer's thought, that thought itself must assimilate the founding prejudice (to the point of no longer seeing it as a prejudice), which in return would maintain itself (as the founding prejudice) at a distance which thought cannot cross. One could say that it embodies it [*elle l'a incorporé*].

One might ask here if the expression "founding *prejudice*" is not contradictory and if it would not be better to speak of a "founding pre-judgment," since the term prejudice itself presupposes a judgment, which would logically make that judgment the founding element, rather than the prejudice itself. I will continue to use this expression, however, because it seems to me to correspond to the logic of truth as *adaequatio*. If another truth—the absolute point [instance] on which all truth is based (the Platonic Idea, for example, to begin with that which identifies itself with this movement)—is not itself responsible to anything higher, then it would constitute the absolute prejudgment, the prejudice on which truth as adequation is based. It is by virtue of this that truth as *adaequatio* is "essentially linked to judgment." To put it very concisely: *Equating judgment with prejudice is the truth of truth as adaequatio.* An unthinkable equation, for Gadamerian hermeneutics.

Earlier, we saw why hermeneutics had to pose the question of the principle of selection between good and bad prejudices (namely, because it is a philosophy of consciousness). We can now better understand why it cannot give an answer to this question. And we are also now in a position to understand why the interpretive practice issuing from hermeneutics simultaneously affirms and denies its juridical dimension, a dimension both given and deferred in the postulate of the universality of understanding. It is because the very perspective of the question "Can one tell the difference between good and bad prejudices?"—a question that assumes the possibility of a principle of selection—is itself situated outside of judgment and thus implies its impossibility. If such a principle were to exist, if in fact one could respond to this question by coming up with the terms of such a principle, all judgment would be impossible. Or rather, as Derrida puts it: "Judgment would not exist at all. At most, there would be knowing, technique, application of a *code,* appearance of decision, false process, or else story, the narrative simulacrum of the subject of judgment."[26]

V. Gadamer's Reading: Paul Celan

In order both to conclude and not conclude here, it would now be necessary to go systematically back through the examples that Gadamer sets out in "Text and Interpretation"—each of them also *arguments*, illustrations in support of his theses (which thus go to constitute a new movement of dominance). For instance, we would have to analyse the role he assigns to the concept of irony, confined to the field of "anti texts" by being thrown off the field of the text, and oppose to it a concept of irony seen as "the question posed to language by language."[27] It would also be necessary to go back to Gadamer's description of word-play, which clearly has Derrida's writing in mind [*vise*], to show that the very fact of speaking about word-play reintroduces a purpose [*une visée*] for consciousness and for intelligibility that does not get hold of the Derridean "machine," which forbids identifying intentional language-play with the "aleatory encounter, that chance coming together of heterogeneities which begins to suggest a meaning and a temporal context" (*Schib* 70). At the same time, it would be necessary to go back to everything Gadamer says about Derrida's "concepts" in the texts published in this volume, for example, to his reduction of *trace* to the monstrosity of a line (". . . the line [*Linie*], the trace that points," DD 371/112). It would be further necessary to pay closer attention to Gadamer's closing argument that deals with the meaning to give to *scheinen* in the last line of Morike's poem, *"Auf eine Lampe,"* the object of a well-known polemic between Heidegger and Emil Staiger. And, furthermore, it would be necessary to reexamine this matter in its entirety, because perhaps more can be said about it than just to back up Heidegger's interpretation—which is certainly a better argument than Staiger's—for the whole debate is devoted to the selection of a single meaning.

Here, though, I will set these arguments aside, because in the few pages I have left I would not be able to lay them out with any rigor. I will merely develop one of them, also to an insufficient extent. It has for its starting point a brief remark that Gadamer makes about Paul Celan towards the end of "Text and Interpretation," a remark that Gadamer apparently sees as peripheral, since it occurs in a "digression" (*TI* 51/46). Nevertheless, even as the object of a digression, the argumentative chain that it constitutes in the course of his remarks about "wordplay," and the implicit protocol that it constitutes with respect to a particular reading of Mallarmé (another "example" that I can only :ouch on here), makes that remark, and the developments to which it can lead, important enough for me here to let this reference suffice without unduly reducing the perspective of the reading. In order to give these two short sentences better emphasis, I shall set them in the argumentative field in which they occur:

> And again it is quite different where the poetic discourse takes the shape neither of the flow of narrative, nor the stream of song, nor dramatic presentation, but rather consciously engages in the play of reflection, to which obviously belongs the shattering of one's discursive expectations. Thus in a very reflective lyric, the play on words can take on a productive function. *One thinks, for instance, of the hermetic lyrics of Paul Celan. Yet one also must ask oneself here if the path of placing such a reflexive burden on the words does not in the end become no longer passable.* It is quite clear that Mallarmé, for instance, tried out word-plays in some of his prose pieces, like *Igitur,* but when he came to the full body of sound in poetic forms, he hardly plays with words. The verses of his *Salut* are certainly many-layered and fulfill expectations of meaning on such various levels as a drinker's toast and a balance sheet of life, wavering between the foam of champagne in the glass and the trail left in the waves by the ship of life. But both dimensions of meaning can be carried out as the same melodious gesture of language and in the same unity of discourse.(*TI* 49–50/45–46[35]; "emphasis added")

First off, Gadamer labels Celan's poetry as "hermetic," in a move that immediately situates it within a horizon of a meaning to be understood, at the risk of running into the impossibility of such a task. This indeed confirms the sentence following it: such poetry risks leading the reader beyond passable ways, towards a space of noncomprehension where the poetic word would no longer know the possibility of a response, and therefore of a reading. What does Gadamer's commentary say about Celan? What does it make him say, what *must* it make him say so that something more can be said, and does it then do anything other than speak for him? Only by taking the risk of testing Gadamer's interpretation can we respond to these questions.

Here I will stick to just one interpretation of one of Celan's poems, among all the other interpretations proposed in Gadamer's collection *Wer bin ich and wer bist du? (WBI)*—more specifically, to the treatment of a "citation" (the meaning of these quotation marks will appear soon) summoned up to support this interpretation. This "citation" appears in his commentary on the poem *MIT ERDWÄRTS GESUNGENEN MASTEN*, predetermining it and prejudicing it through and through.[28]

> *MIT ERDWÄRTS GESUNGENEN MASTEN*
> *fahren die Himmelwracks.*
>
> *In dieses Holzlied*
> *beisst du dich fest mit den Zahnen.*
>
> *Du bist der liedfeste*
> *Wimpel.*

> WITH MASTS TURNED EARTHWARDS, SINGING OUT
> sail the wrecks of heaven.
>
> Into this woodsong
> You sink your teeth securely.
>
> You are the song-secured
> Flag.

One could look at Gadamer's interpretation of this poem in its entirety as conforming to Aristotle's theses on the function of poetry as establishing harmonious unity or aiming towards such unity and so capable of overcoming the experience of rupture or dissonance. In Gadamer's own words: "As the flag of a sinking ship is still the last thing projecting out of the water, so is the poet with his song as a last thing, a proclamation and a promise of life, a last holding-high of life" (*WBI* 64). From this perspective, the two compound nouns in which the word "song" [*Lied*] appears, so decisive to this interpretation, are interpreted by Gadamer in a "positive" sense. By taking the "woodsong" [*Holzlied*] as a "rescuing plank" [*Rettungsplanke*], the act of planting one's teeth in this woodsong is logically interpreted as belonging to the shipwrecked person who saves his life in gripping onto it [*sich festklammern*]. Using the same logic, Gadamer takes "song-secured" [*liedfest*] as an indication that the "you" of the poem cannot be separated from the mast, so long as he or she holds to it firmly [a possible meaning of *fest*].

To help support this interpretation, Gadamer quotes the "profound words" of Celan from "Meridien": "*Wer auf dem Kopf steht, sieht den Himmel als Abgrund unter sich*" ["He who stands on his head, sees heaven under him as an abyss."] Without any doubt, the quotation clearly shows the world remaining just the way it is, without the experience of a rupture that resists the unity of poetic language. Only the one who has his head beneath him—that is to say the one who, in a certain sense, has "lost his head"—sees the sky turned upside down, *changed into an abyss*, as the threat of perdition and not as what it "is": a horizon of hope, the haven or promise of peace. Within such optics, the question here is indeed one of vision, of an illusion due to the position of this "you" of which Gadamer speaks and, no doubt a little over-hastily, identifies with the poet himself.[29] For Gadamer, it suffices to rectify one's position—to put one's head back in place and thereby to hold on to the preexisting unity of the poem and the world—in order for hope to be reborn in the very place of the shipwreck.

The problem here is that "Meridian" does not really say what Gadamer insists on making it say.[30] The quotation mentioned above does not exist. "Meridien" starts out with a citation from Büchner's "Lenz"—". . . only it was sometimes annoying to him that he could not go about on his head" [". . . *nur war es ihm manchmal unangenehm, dass er nicht auf dem Kopf gehn konnte*"]—which gives a positive sense to the impossible but still desirable experience of walking on one's head—and then goes on: "*Wer auf dem Kopf geht, meine Damen und Herren, wer auf dem Kopf geht, der hat den Himmel als Abgrund unter sich.*" "He who *goes* along on his head, ladies and gentlemen, he who *goes* along on his head, *has* under him the sky as an abyss" (emphasis added). "Meridien" speaks of a man who realizes the desire of "Lenz" and underscores its consequence: He who walks on his head has the sky open up like an abyss below him. The sky is no longer that which holds out hope but a foundation that no longer discloses any transcendence, which escapes itself as such (*Ab-grund*) and on which one can no longer base any hope. To this person a new space, the consequence of a reversal—a space connected with the shipwreck of a promised heaven of intelligibility granted through an axis of transcendence—is "abruptly opened" (*jäh aufgetan*).[31]

Now let us get back to the poem. The masts are "sung,"—but what masts? These masts are wrecked, no longer of useful value. They do sing out, but they are upside-down, no longer a sign of heavenly transcendence, but the very signifier of its wreckage. The word "you," absent from the first line, takes on a growing importance in its return in the last two lines, and the on-going isotopy of *gesungene Masten/Holzlied/liedfester Wimpel*, structured by the presence or the absence of the "you," bestows on the poem an "economy" that extends beyond itself: One can read the first line as a poem, about which the two following lines would serve as commentary, itself submerged as a poem for which the first line would then be the title. We cannot find an alternative between the poem title and the commentary poem. Here there is a double necessity programmed by a *you* that is irreducible to the unique person of the poet or to a humanistic universalization. This necessity goes beyond any horizon of delimitable meaning. The wreckage of heaven as the space of intelligibility is accepted—here lies the meaning of "walking on one's head." The song itself opens up into the abyss.

Let us keep in mind that to Celan the poem or song is on the way toward an "open place" (*un "lieu ouvert"*): "the place where all tropes and metaphors demand to be pushed to the point of absurdity" [*"Und das Gedicht wäre somit der Ort, wo alle Tropen und Metapher ad absurdum geführt werden wollen."*] On this reading, the "woodsong" [*Holzlied*] would become a song which, by analogy to the *Holzweg* [forest path], "would lead nowhere." This is a misleading translation of *"Holzweg,"* however, in the sense that it is always somewhere, at some place of arrival, an ultimate point of reference—but above all, not at hope. In planting one's teeth in a "woodsong" (one is tempted to say: in taking the woodsong by the teeth),[32] one accepts the idea that the poem has no purpose other than itself: the madness of song. To accept this, to actively submit to it and to read according to its law—this is the meaning, also by analogy (to a compound noun like *bibelfest,* meaning "well-versed in the Bible") of being "song-secured." And to be the "song-secured flag" [*"liedfeste Wimpel"*] is to manifest one's belonging to the law of the song, in a new reversal that makes the flag a non-referring signifier to an identifying signified. The infinite-undefined-indefinite space [*L'in (dé) fini*] which this opens up, this "knowledge" that is primarily an acknowledgment of ignorance, is only an illusion when seen (not read) from the standpoint of the song's closure upon an absolute signified, from a need emerging from a false citation.

Indeed, it is closure which Gadamer once more addresses in his comments on Mallarmé's poem "Salut." Here one finds him defending a *delimited* kind of polysemy, whose criteria would again have to be investigated, the least important of which is certainly neither an overly-classical conception of the meaning of the title, nor particularly the reduction of the text ("reef," "star") to a totally classical catalog of motifs and tropes. More important, though, than either of these: the fact that the word *"coupe"* ["cut"] occurs twice at the end of rhyming lines, first as a noun and then as a verb. The poem cuts: saying what it does, doing what it says, and, because of this, is always displaced in relation to what it is supposed "to be." Mallarmé's text cuts through any thematic, closure-seeking reading. For anyone who would like to read further about this, I would suggest the interpretation made by Lucette Finas, in which one will find new reasons to match dissemination against the concept of polysemy just mentioned.[33]

Wouldn't Gadamer say that to read in this way—that is, to read without regard to understanding [*Verständnis*] or good sense [*Verstand*]—would be not to read at all?[34] Such a response would no doubt be able to satisfy a devotee of dialogue—but, after all, is a response really what is at issue here? And is a response required?

Manfred Frank

2. *Limits of the Human Control of Language: Dialogue as the Place of Difference Between Neostructuralism and Hermeneutics**

Translated by Richard Palmer

Aside from a few possible exceptions, there is virtually no dialogue today [1981] between two mighty currents within European philosophy, namely, neostructuralism and hermeneutics. To assert that there is an invincible enmity between them would probably be going too far. For in order to develop hostile feelings against any position, one would at least have to possess a little knowledge. But the process of reciprocal getting to know one another has never really gotten underway. It would perhaps be realistic to observe that both standpoints are suspicious of one another, for suspicion is motivated; but this suspicion rests on presuppositions about the other whose legitimacy has not been demonstrated.

It is certainly quite true that the implicit demand for harmonizing that hovers over dialogical arrangements can become a serious hindrance to working out intellectual and material differences (and differentiations). Nevertheless, who can really say that the dialogue that is not taking place between German hermeneutics and French neostructuralism would have to stand under a mandatory ban against conciliation *if* in fact a conversation had taken place? Of course, there remains one indispensable presupposition (as Schleiermacher's *Dialectic* has

---

*"Die Grenzen der Beherrschbarkeit der Sprache: Das Gespräch als Ort der Differenz von Neostrukturalismus und Hermeneutik," from *TI* 181–213 (translated portions, pp. 181–90, 206–209).

made us aware): disputants must relate themselves to the same issue; otherwise they are not disputing with each other but just expressing a variety of judgments, a variety which, since it refers to different matters, has not yet achieved the clarity and sharpness of opposition. Now in the controversy between neostructuralism and hermeneutics, I maintain that there is a commonality in the matter at hand [*die Sache*]: Both are dealing with philosophy after Hegel, after Nietzsche, and after Heidegger; for neither of them does absolute consciousness offer any possibility of escape from the fact of finitude and the fact of history; in neither of them does one see a transcendental value invoked to justify life: rather, the contours of value-assignment are delineated in the process of an "infinitely perspectival interpretation"; the epistemological subject is no longer the lord of his being but acquires his "self-understanding" in the semiotic context of a world into whose structure a certain interpretation of the meaning of being has entered. Finally, neostructuralism and hermeneutics are both essentially philosophies of language, which guides the "consciousness" of man by virtue of what Jacques Lacan has called the "*défile du signifiant*" ["the marching past of the signifier"]. In Germany, one invokes as essential forerunners in this regard Friedrich Schleiermacher, Alexander von Humboldt, Friedrich Nietzsche, and Martin Heidegger; in the French language standing in the foreground is the implicit theory of language in poetic Symbolism (especially Stephane Mallarmé), and of course the linguistics of Ferdinand de Saussure. We now know, through the critical edition of Saussure's posthumous works, how much Saussure was indebted to the thinking of Humboldt, Schleiermacher, and Hermann Steinthal (partly through the influence of their writings, partly through life-historical contact). Here, the supposed difference between two different traditions, namely, neostructuralism and hermeneutics, is greatly reduced.

Where, then, do the differences lie? Presumably the contributors to this volume [*Text und Interpretation*] have more manifested than explored them. The reader must likewise try, in the conversation over neostructuralism and hermeneutics, to catch the participants in this debate (à propos of Heidegger's interpretation of Nietzsche) in the act, to catch a glimpse in the conversation of what they have for so long successfully refused to say. Before the conversation is conducted and then concluded (but where is the conclusion of a conversation?), before the partners have been able to bring their positions closer to each other, we say every assertion of good will and tolerance, or of the lack of it, is hasty and unfounded.

I have elsewhere already presented my own position with regard to this (non-existing) debate.[1] Perhaps what separates us is at the same time the thing that holds us together: a consciousness of the fundamental non-controllability of a conversation [*der prinzipielle Nicht-Beherrschbarkeit eines Gesprächs*]; of the non-prescribability [*Nicht-Festlegbarkeit*] of the sign, which we exchange with each other; the non-identity of the meanings on which we agree; the fundamentally hypothetical nature of every conceivable consensus.

About these matters, let me venture a few remarks, first historical and then systematic.

Hermeneutics—as "the art of rightly understanding the speech, chiefly in written form, of another"[2]—is something relatively recent in the history of knowledge; it is a Romantic invention. Certainly the problems of textual explication, and efforts at working them out systematically, have existed since antiquity, and the broadening of the scope of hermeneutics to universal dimensions so as to include the whole of the sign-mediating interaction between persons was already achieved during the Enlightenment. So it was not the claims to universality by an understanding oriented to techniques that provoked the Romantic break with the Enlightenment model of interpretation; rather its target was the Enlightenment conception of the nature of language, the language which served as the object of their interpretations. Grossly oversimplifying, one may say that until the mid-eighteenth century exegesis [*Auslegung*] played no role as a specific problem within forms of knowledge related to language because the linguistic form [*Sprachform*] rendered truth present as a logical form,[3] and because the logical form of synthesis in judgment related directly to facts. Thus, rational speech (which by its nature is universal, true, and enlightening) was absorbed into factual speech [*sachhaltigen Rede*] and the problem of reaching agreement in understanding over the specific meaning of a given speech in terms of application, or with regard to the ways and means by which our linguistic world is constructed, simply did not arise. By a preestablished harmony, grammatically correct speech became an immediate and reliable representation of logically and correctly combined "ideas" ["*Vorstellungen*"]. Grammar and reason were taken as universal: thus, every application of their laws only reproduced the essential universality of the code in the concrete instance, as a case is subsumed under a law which it manifests but does not modify. To understand something *as* something under these epistemological premises meant to shed light on the uttered or written word in terms of its rational content; this meant grasping it as that universal which it never stops being even in its historically unique situation of application.

Under the conditions of validity in this universal-grammatical model of representation, hermeneutics, as the art of rightly understanding a spoken or written utterance, was totally or virtually reduced to a "rational" (*raisonnée*) decoding of the language in which a discourse or a text was couched.

All this changed with the Romantic age. Foucault has—although without express reference to hermeneutics and the foundational status that it acquires here—given us insights into the "fundamental event" affecting the paradigms of representation and order during that part of its history. Foucault speaks in *Les mots et les choses* [*The Order of Words*] of a major shock to the classical paradigm in which nothing less than the classical conception of reason itself was shaken: "It took a fundamental event—certainly one of the most radical that ever occurred in Western culture—to bring about the dissolution of the positivity of Classical knowledge, and to constitute another positivity from which, even now, we have doubtless not entirely emerged."[4]

I would characterize the result of this epistemological breach within the model of representation as it was carried over into the model of universalized interpretation as follows (in extremely simplified form): After the breakdown of the axioms of universality in reason, the Romantic theory of language was compelled to explain the trans-individual validity of language in a different way than on the basis that language, because of its natural transparency to reason, must also itself be rational (and universal). The now only relative universality of "language," a universality narrowed down to a "community of thought," now appears only as an idealising abstraction from innumerable (and always historically situated) speech-transactions, which, on their side, are insufficiently described if one does not grasp them as, first, acts of individual construction of a world, and, second, answers to speaking done by others (as a discourse that agrees and carries things further or else contradicts and opposes), that is, as moments of a conversation. Or, to put it another way, language is purely a virtuality, an idealizing within an analytic intention and never more than a mere permanently disputed hypothesis based on the real speaking of individuals and always arising within a situation. Far from determining the reality of the linguistic construction of the world (whose reduction to its pure lawfulness was called "reason"), language is never more than the changeable situation of the conversation of a communicative community consisting of innumerably many individuals individually communicating with each other, a conversation projected upwards to the level of the universal. Conversation, in this model of interpretation, is an individual universal [*einzelnes Allgemeines*]. It is universal [*allgemein*, common to all] because without the super-individual fixing of the sense of expressions agreement in understanding would be excluded in principle; but it is at the same time individual, because the universality of the available sign-syntheses and rules of combination always has to stand the test of the world construction of the individual speaker. Schleiermacher put it as follows:

> Just as . . . the unconveyable feeling necessarily becomes at the same time again exterior and takes on the character of the community, so must the general thoughts we hold in common again take on the character of something singular and individual. Seen first of all from the side of language, this means that language must become individualized. Otherwise, it can only be thought of as a capacity [*Vermögen*] and can never exist in actuality. It is this, too, of course. In its process of becoming individual, language as the highest product of organization depends on the great cosmic conditions for organization in general. Then it descends and its most highly determined form is its individualizing for each individual person in style and usage of language. These we all recognize as true and necessary, so certainly we believe in a higher criticism. (*HuK* 364)

Thus, there is "language" as such only in the concreteness of real conversation; it is in real conversation, once again, that the meanings of signs, with
whose help we reach agreement, are not simply reproductions of a transhistorical code of rationality but the fixed results of a basically unlimited process of
communal but ultimately individual explication of the world [*Welt-Auslegung*].
Thus, interactive speaking confirms the validity of language as a "*fait social*"
[social fact], and places limits on it. We know it confirms it because only
through communicating is there language as a framework of meaning and agreement in understanding common to many persons. But at the same time conversation challenges this framework because we will only designate as a
conversation that which (differently than in bee-language) leaves room for an
answer. One who is free (within certain limits, of course) to answer has at his/
her disposal the commonality [*Gemeinschaftlichkeit*] of a symbolically sealed
agreement in understanding; one's power to interpret this agreement in understanding [*Einverständnis*] in a new and different way breaks the unity of the
social code.

As I see it, the main currents of thought in contemporary linguistics and
philosophy of language represent a gradual displacement of this romantic experience. The famous sentence in which Saussure, concluding his *Cours de linguistic générale,* sums up his "*idée fondamentale*" (and which, as is
well-known, does not originate with him but was inked in from Bally and Seche-
haye), offers an impressive piece of evidence for this: "Linguistics has as its
special and only object language taken in itself and for its own sake."[5] One could
find this formulation trivial, in that it is similar to ones found in Humboldt and
Jakob and Wilhelm Grimm, and also because it revives a kind of topos from
classical science of language, if one were not aware that "language" here is
understood in the spirit of structuralism as "the system of *langue*" (thus: as the
"code," cf. *Cours* 1. c. 31, passim; 423, note 66), as something which in its
abstraction leaves behind the innovative acts that Saussure (like Schleiermacher)
left to be grounded in the individual use of language,[6] as well as the level of
living symbolic interaction.

Let me venture a great simplification in what follows. I want to bring into
view a premise common to several language-theoretical and text-theoretical
models. Operating as a kind of silent minimal consensus, this premise brings
together within the unity of one paradigm a wide range of schools presently
struggling to be separate, all the way from (text) linguistic structuralism, generational grammar, analytic philosophy of language, epistemological archeology,
information and speech-act theory, to parts of Gadamer's "*wirkungsgeschich-
tliche*" [effective-historical] hermeneutics.

All these currents of thought carry out what has been called the "linguistic
turn," thus testifying to their origin in the crisis of philosophy of reflection (or
philosophy of representation). In contrast to the Romantic hermeneutical theory

of language, however, they seek to replace the loss of a world interpreted throughout by the concepts of reason (as it is represented by universal grammar for the purpose of communication) with the model of a linguistic "code" (of grammar, of language game, of language-system, of structure, of an archive, of the taxonomy of illocutionary acts, of consciousness impregnated by tradition, and so on) on the basis of which individual occurrences of situated speech would simply be deduced like special cases of a general rule. The result of this more recent, quasi-rationalistic negation once again of the crisis of classical rationalism is the difficulty which all of the schools we named above have with the problem of ambiguity or semantic innovation, as well as with the transformation of languages and with determining the status of the identity of signs. The minimal consensus of all linguistic theories that work on the basis of the code-model (or a related operations-schema like the model of a "tradition" which also, as a symbolic entity, must have its rules of formation, like a Foucaultian "*archiv*") rests on an interest that can be characterized as scientific: In order scientifically to achieve the capacity to control their object, language, they must unavoidably presuppose that linguistic events follow a certain lawfulness. These laws do not unconditionally have to have the status of being beyond temporality [*Außerzeitlichkeit*], as the seventeenth and eighteenth century wanted (for instance, the law apply to systems of convention or tradition), but they do nevertheless insure that multiple occurrences of such linguistic events can be recognized as realizations of one and the same linguistic (or archaeological, or pragmatic, or whatever) *type*. In the words of John Searle:

> Any linguistic element written or spoken, indeed any rule-governed element in any system of representation at all must be repeatable, otherwise the rules would have no scope of application. To say this is just to say that the logician's type-token distinction must apply generally to all the rule-governed elements of language in order that the rules can be rules. Without this feature of iterability there could not be the possibility of producing an infinite number of sentences with a finite list of elements; and this, as philosophers since Frege have recognized, is one of the crucial features of any language.[7]

This citation formulates the basic assumption of the code-model very precisely; and at the same time it makes it clear that the theoretical decision for control-through-systematizing defines in advance the way of being of the object of linguistic science. Under the presupposition—but also only under this presupposition—that languages are conceived systematically and determine their expressions, it is analytically true that every repetition of a linguistic type (or of a "typized" linguistic act) "involves the notion of the repetition of the same" (Searle 207).

Of course, the choice of a conventionalistic conception of language is only grounded through an epistemological decision; nothing proves that this conclusion *must* be drawn. The experience in conversation of the unity of meaning being displaced and the insight into the undecidability of whether to allocate a token under the heading of a certain type or not permit us to see that the code-model appears to be particularly unsuited to serve as the basis for a theory of conversation. If these scientific premises were valid for conversation, if it were true that in the back and forth of speech and counterspeech the selfhood [*Selbigkeit*] of the linguistic type may not be touched, then all speaking is reduced to the practice of the *parole vide* [empty speech]. In this regard, the conversation of the social technicians, which is called "conversational analysis," may serve as an example.

But what justifies our speaking of "empty speech" [*"leere Rede"*) here? Jacques Lacan introduced this expression in his famous 1953 convention paper on "The Function and Field of Speaking and Language in Psychoanalysis" [*"Fonction et champ de la parole et du langage en psychanalyse"*] and therewith sought to recall the fundamental and yet, in contemporary linguistic science, neglected fact that every speech calls for an answer and without this directedness toward the goal of an answer remains "empty" (*"toute parole appelle réponse," "il n'est pas de parole sans réponse"* ["every instance of speaking calls for a response," "there is no speaking without response"] *Écrits*, p. 247). Empty spots in speaking do not mean that the speaker in fact receives no answer. On the contrary, the silence of a partner can be grasped as a signal of "opposition" [*"Widerstand"*], while his ready response can be an indication that he makes his voice into a thick wall that serves to bounce back to the ear of the speaker not an answer but merely an echo. Empty speaking collects the answer of the other not into a dialectic of authentic conversation with the self but into a dialectic of mirror-like [specular] conversation with the self (as Feuerbach reproached Hegelian dialectic for being) in which both roles are played by one and the same subject.

At first glance, Lacan's critique of empty speech would seem to converge with the deepest impulse of Gadamerian hermeneutics: in any case with what has had the strongest impact on the hermeneutical discussion in the German-speaking world. Both Lacan and Gadamer part company with that naïveté that believes it is able to gain a controlling access to the activity of conversation by recourse to a transhistorical, conversation-independent code, as well as the naïveté that conceives that the individual entering into discourse is the sovereign producer of signs with whose help he or she addresses the other. In truth, the conversation that we "are" rather than "lead" (*WM* 361/345) does not permit us to go behind it; conversation is not the representation of a "truth" subsisting above and beyond itself but the constitution of truth in the very process of fusing two horizons: that of the tradition (speaking in a text or in a live speech) and that precisely (this text, this speech) which appropriates the tradition. In this sense, the narcissism of a self-reflexive, self-understanding epistemological subject is already banished at the outset: self-understanding is always beforehand a being referred to the speech of the other, a speaking which, on its side, does not go away from the conversation unchanged, for it was fused with the alien horizon of its partner. Meaning arises in the reciprocity of an agreement in understanding that cannot be anticipated in advance, which Gadamer has characterized as *"wirkungsgeschichtliches Bewußtsein"* [effective-historical consciousness]. This famous term tells us that all self-understanding of an historical subject develops and evolves in reference to a tradition with which it stands in conversation and through which it attains to its knowledge of itself.

In Gadamer's approach, one recognizes the traces of a conception that was basic to the whole of post-Hegelianism and especially to Heidegger, namely, that our self-consciousness grows up on a ground, which, as its origin, it cannot itself see. Gadamer shares with the philosophy of neostructuralism—with Lacan, for example (but also with Derrida)—this premise: self-consciousness presupposes a stance within a symbolically articulated world, which puts in one's hand the signs with whose help one can identify oneself (it is the same whether one speaks here of "tradition" or of the "symbolic order"). The world, language, or the "context of involvements" ["*Bewandtniszusammenhang*"], defines the place in which a subject gains understanding of itself and of all that is, of things as a whole [*des Seienden im ganzen*]. Now one must see that the priority, or as Gadamer likes to put it, the "unsurpassability" ["*Unüberholbarkeit*"] of tradition over and against the self-understanding of the subject certainly interrupts the reflexivity of the subjective self-relation and clouds but does not call a halt to its transparency: "It remains correct that *all such understanding is in the end self-understanding*" (*WM* 246/231). The circularity of "Fore-having" (of always already dwelling in the disclosedness of a symbolic order/tradition) and of "Fore-seeing" (the progressive exceeding of tradition in the direction of its future being-for-me) determines the "thrown project" ["*geworfenen Entwurf*"]—that Gadamer, following Heidegger, grasps Dasein (human being) as being—to exist in a speculative relationship through which being [*ein Sein*], which is at first out of reach of the existing subject, is constantly conveyed back to itself in forms of being-present-to-itself. In this way, Gadamer's hermeneutics is to be found already in the approach of Hegelian dialectic, whose reflexive and integrating power Gadamer, in his discussion of Schleiermacher, distinguishes from the concept of a mere reconstruction of the originally intended meaning (*WM* 158ff./147ff.): Understanding is *Aufhebung* [supersession]: the transgressive appropriation of the apparently alien.

Gadamerian hermeneutics can, to this extent, be considered a modification (undertaken in the name of the finitude of Dasein) of the model of a "dialectical" (*WM* 366, cf. also 328/350, 310), or as Gadamer also calls it, a "speculative" self-relationship. Thus, the constant ambiguity of Gadamer's style of argumentation in *Truth and Method*: On the one hand, in the name of the finitude of consciousness and its incapacity ever to be transparent to itself ("To be historical means never to be wrapped up in self-knowledge" or, as in the English translation: "To exist historically means that knowledge of oneself can never be complete," *WM* 285/269), the narcissism of a specular and unhistorically conceived self-presence is, as in Lacan, humbled, and the subject is subordinated to the happening of tradition as its historical *a priori*. On the other hand, in order to make "self-understanding" and its reflexivity possible, Gadamer has to think effective-history itself as subjectivity, or he must maintain that tradition only comes to itself in the act of an understanding self-relation, as which, it would be that of an individual subject. Now in the first case, what Gadamer has aptly designated as "the continuum of meaning" ["*Sinnkontinuum*"] (*WM* 351/333) is indistinguishable from that superindividual subject that Hegel conceived as absolute spirit; in the second case, the individual subject becomes the final authority in the formation of meaning, since only in the individual subject can tradition enter as a self-relationship aware of meaning, truth, or consciousness. In neither case, however, does a "fusion of horizons" really take place but rather the subordination of one of the sides of the relationship to the other: either the event of the transmission of tradition is absorbed by the appropriating subject, or the subject is absorbed by the event of the transmission of tradition. Thus, the speculative dialogue of effective-history ultimately becomes a version of the speculative monologue of the dialectic, that is, empty speech. . .[8]

In *Positions* (1972) Jacques Derrida coined the expression—borrowing from [Louis] Hjelmslev—of the infinite or universal text in order to explore the consequences for literary studies of the irreducible nonsimultaneity [*Ungleichzeitigkeit*] of the levels of meaning in a text; that is to say, in order to enter into what Maurice Blanchot had called *L'entretien infini* [*The infinite conversation*]. He asserted:

> What I call *text* is also that which "practically" inscribes and overflows the limits of such a discourse. *There is* such a general text everywhere that (that is, everywhere) this discourse and its order (essence, sense, truth, meaning, consciousness, ideality, etc.) are *overflowed*, that is everywhere that their occurrence is put back in the position of a *mark* in a chain. . . ." (*P* 82/59)

I would like to show that Derrida's idea of a deboundarized [*débordé*] conversation with the text (cf. *P* 82/59) is not in opposition to what we know of Saussure but very close to the thinking of the Geneva linguist. Just as Saussure inquired into the reasons why it was difficult to assign a semantic identity to the linguistic sign differently in hypothetical judgments, so also Derrida seeks an equally radical and illuminating explanation for what he names the "undecidability" of the assignment of meaning.

To the theorists of textual grammar he concedes that the repeatability of the linguistic sign or of whole expressions (this means pragmatically interpreted propositions) is a structural possibility of rule-governed speaking. But, in opposition to the very idea of a nontemporal taxonomy of the text, Derrida questions the justification for concluding that in a functioning grammar every repetition of a sign is necessarily the repetition of a *self-same* [*Selbigen*]. (We recognize in this the basic premise of information theory.)

There is, says Derrida, no preestablished co-presence of author and reader; indeed, strictly speaking, even the author is never co-present with that which he or she writes. For only under the condition that one's individual intention simultaneously breaks away from the meaning of the signs by which one expresses oneself can the signs one brings forward become more than elements of a merely individual message—in other words, types and social facts. The individual steps back in order to make space for the generality [*Allgemeinheit,* universality] of the system. In retaliation, however, this suspension of an individual sense makes the sign free to take on another individual meaning, for, as Saussure says, the chain of signs experiences its ultimate determination always and only in a situation, through the consciousness of an individual (cf. *CFS* 15, 1957, 10; *EC* 111 C277, al. 2022). There it is not just a matter of an individual coloration that the intersubjectively shared meaning leaves intact. The individual element affects the substance of the meaning. For realizing the meaning of an expression means indeed precisely to venture an individual hypothesis from among an (open) group of opposing possibilities (an hypothesis that precisely does not congeal into a merely objective determination of sense). Sense, says Lacan, with a play on words, takes its place (*insiste*) in the chain of expression, but none of the elements of the chain have their existence (*consiste*) in the meaning that it is capable of in precisely this instant: "*c'est dans la chaîne du signifiant que le sense insiste, mais qu'aucun des éléments de la chaîne ne consiste dans la signification dont il est capable au moment même*" (*E* 502). As soon as codified linguistic types are used in a conversation, it must in principle (which does not mean: at every instant) be possible to replace the first or original articulation/interpretation with a second, and thus to free it from subservience to the (still merely virtually existent) conventional or discursive maxims. Derrida speaks of the "re-mark," that is, of the constant possibility for the speaker/author/reader/hearer/interpreter to place a new emphasis on the meaning of a word, a sentence, a text, or a culture.

This possibility follows, again, from the temporality of the text, a temporality that undermines talk about a co-presence of sender and receiver as well as assumptions about the synchrony of *concept* and acoustic/graphic image. Indeed, every form of being-present-with has the structure of a differentiation: something is *with* something (accordingly it is not one with that which it is with), and something is *after* something. The present separates the self and the same from each other—as both the grammar of the use of pronouns and reflection teaches us—in order to unite them again on the other side of a minimal but never insignificant distance. The meaning of a sign or an expression is separated from itself by every new use; it is dis-placed (déplacé). Who can show (and by virtue of what criterion) that *after* passing through the gaps of iteration the meaning consists of the same synthesis with its expressive substratum as at the beginning? *"Le déplacement de sense confirme la loi que j'indique ici: le temps et le lieu de l'autre fois* (the other time) *travaillent et altèrent dèja, at once, aussi sec, la première fois, le premier coup et l'at once."* ["The displacement of sense confirms the law that I indicate here: the time and the place of *l'autre fois* ("the other time") work and change already and at once, *aussi sec* (the first time), the first instance, *and* the "at once."] It is astonishing here how close this is to Saussure, who has noted: *"Ce qui a échappé ici aux philosophes et aux logiciens, c'est que du moment qu'un système des symboles est indépendant des objets désignés, il était sujet à subir, pour sa part, par le fait du temps, de déplacements non calculables pour le logicien"* (EC 2 (Note 10):13). ["What has escaped the philosophers and logicians here is that from the moment a system of symbols is *independent* of the objects designated, it becomes subject to submitting *by the fact of time* to displacements *not calculable by the logician*."]

But there is a further and more disquieting consequence that Derrida recommends the sciences of communication should draw. Not only can the sign which is repeated (within time) not guarantee its identity, he says, but also that sign which was used only once. And this, indeed, because semiological arrangements [*Ordnungen*], traditional connections, discourses, and so on, are only able to lend meaning to their elements through the fact that they distinguish every individual element from all others. But one can say of something which can only mediate its own identity by a detour through all other identities, that it is also separated from itself (it is itself the other). And this, its "self," is already—as we saw—a function of the immense and incalculably open aggregate of all the other applications of signs which I, in the course of a communication process, constitute and from which, differentiating, I separate myself. . . .

If sense and meaningfulness arise in the complex interrelatedness of various pieces of expression, then the identity of a term can only be assured through a condition of closure and the invariability of the system. Indeed, the model which lies at the base of the scientific sciences of communication (above all, linguistics and structural text theory) is not far from the crystal grill [*grille*] in which, by achieving lower and lower temperatures all atoms or molecules are tied down in their places, distinguished from all others as well as united with them. Now, in contrast to the world of these physical elements, the historical-cultural world (in which and with which our conversations deal) cannot be cooled down to an absolute freezing-point. Conversation and literature only flow in a certain warm temperature, like a river: this warmth allows exchange and the new arrangements of signs. Conversations are always transformations of other and earlier conversations, just as signs are always new articulations of other and earlier signs. As Saussure put it:

> *La langue, à quel moment que nous la prenions, si haut que nous remontions, est à n'importe quel moment un héritage du moment précédent. L'acte idéal par lequel, à un instant donné, des noms seraient distribués aux choses, l'acte par lequel un contrat serait passé entre les idées et les signes, entre les signifiés et les signifiants, cet acte reste dans le seul domaine de l'idée. . . . Jamais une société n'a connu la langue que comme un produit plus ou mois perfectionné par les générations précédentes et à prendre tel quel (EC III, C 312, al 1187ff.).*

Language, at whatever moment we would take it, as high as we would ascend, is at every moment a heritage from the preceding moment. The ideal act by which, at a given instant, names are distributed to things, the act by which a contract was reached between ideas and signs, between the signifieds and the signifiers, that act remains only in the domain of ideas. . . . There has never been a society which has not known language as a product more or less perfected by the preceding generations and to be taken as it is.

*   *   *   *   *

Josef Simon

3. *Good Will to Understand and the Will to Power: Remarks on an "Improbable Debate"**

Translated by Richard Palmer

The recent widespread interest in Nietzsche possibly has to do with the fact that he has not yet been understood. This sounds paradoxical. But perhaps his philosophy, precisely that which cannot be understood in the customary philosophical sense and which cannot be reduced to concepts—precisely in its *un*timeliness in this sense—is a symptom of the times. Perhaps it documents a crisis of understanding. We are accustomed to understand and to claim understanding; so much so that, for example, it seems to us a moral obligation that we should work through to an understanding of the events of World War II, so as to prevent "something like that" from ever happening again. We are thereby presupposing that there is something there that is understandable, such that one could say "what" it was and that "something like that" could happen again. One seeks to place oneself before history like a spectator in order to win from it a theory and thereby grasp destiny. In contrast to this, Nietzsche calls himself "a destiny." He does not believe one can or should grasp destiny. Rather, he affirms and loves it. "Amor fati" is his formula for "what is individual in man," and he even says there is "something offensive in being understood."[1] Understanding, for Nietzsche, is the translation of what is alien into one's own self. Understand-

*This essay first appeared as "Der gute Wille zum Verstehen und der Wille zur Macht: Bemerkungen zur einer 'unwahrscheinlichen Debatte' " in the *Allgemeine Zeitschrift für Philosophie,* vol. 12, no. 3(1987): 79–90. The translation has been reviewed and approved for publication by its author. —Editors' note.

ing appropriates. A sign which is understood is passed over in its individuality and changed into a general meaning.

I

In an "improbable debate" with the "French scene," represented above all by Derrida, Hans-Georg Gadamer plays the part of an advocate for tradition. Tradition wishes to find itself again in its history. Naturally it cannot understand "everything," for example, the terrible. Were it to do so without any problem, it would have something in common with it. A hermeneutical distance is required so that it will take on general [*allgemeine*] contours, through which it becomes theoretizable. According to Gadamer, philosophy and its history want "to bring 'the speculative' to presentation," ["*zur Darstellung bringen*"] but Heidegger, however (also according to Gadamer), based on "insight into the central significance of finitude," has taught us that this can only be an "endeavor," a "constant challenge" (*TI* 27/TI24), that is, a matter of "good will," so to speak.

For Gadamer, "the encounter with the French philosophical scene" is also "a genuine challenge." This challenge is expressed in Derrida's understanding of Heidegger, according to which the latter "never really broke with the logocentrism of metaphysics" because he grasped "sense" as something on hand [*vorhandenen*] that could be found out. In Derrida's understanding of him, Nietzsche is here "more radical" than Heidegger.

What Gadamer says he misses in the French followers of Nietzsche, however, is a comprehension of "the true significance of the seductive in Nietzsche's thought." It is only because of this, he says, that they can "think that the experience of Being, which Heidegger is endeavoring to uncover behind metaphysics, is still surpassed in radicality by Nietzsche's extremism." "In truth," Being, in Nietzsche's "valuing and revaluing of all values," itself becomes only "a value-concept [*Wertbegriff*] in the service of the 'Will to Power' " (*TI* 28; 25). For Heidegger, says Gadamer, "what is of decisive importance is that 'Being' does not unfold totally in its self-manifestation, but with the same primordiality with which it manifests itself, it also withholds itself and withdraws." Certainly Gadamer denominates "Being which can be understood" as language. But what is implicit in this statement is "that what *is* can never be completely understood" (TI 28f./25). The hermeneutic circle as "the circularity that moves between the one who understands and that which he understands" (29/26) is, for Gadamer, universal. One might say this circle has its place in the difference between Being and beings which, within a certain approach to understanding, are understood as something. Indeed, as Gadamer understands it, understanding continually struggles against this difference and seeks to overcome it: "What we find happening in speaking is not a mere reification [*Fixierung*] of intended meaning, but an endeavor that continually transforms itself, or better: a continually recurring temptation to engage oneself in something or to become involved with someone" (29/26). But this means: "to expose oneself and to risk oneself." In fact, "the mere presence of the other before whom we stand," helps "to break up our own bias and narrowness, even before he opens his mouth to make a reply." In this there is "a potentiality for being other that lies beyond every coming to agreement about what is common" (30/26).

Socrates, who, according to Nietzsche, was the originator of theoretical thinking, a thinking that views everything in terms of how well it can do in logical confrontation or argument [*logische Auseinandersetzung*], is for Gadamer *the* other par excellence, so to speak, because he "was able to lead others back to themselves by convicting them of their pretended wisdom" (30/27). In doing so, of course, Socrates assumed "that the Logos is common to all and does not belong to Socrates alone." But "the true depth of the dialogical principle," according to Gadamer, "first enters philosophical consciousness in the twilight of metaphysics, in the epoch of German romanticism, and then is reclaimed in our century in opposition to the subjective bias that characterized idealism" (30–31/27. At this point Gadamer tells us he linked up with the discussion by posing two questions: "How do the communality of meaning, which is built up in conversation, and the impenetrability of the otherness of the other mediate each other?" and "What, in the final analysis, is linguisticality [*Sprachlichkeit*]? Is it a bridge or a barrier?" (31/27).

The problem is obvious. It lies in the question of how the "communality of meaning" and the "impenetrability of the otherness of the other" interact and are mediated by each other [*miteinander vermitteln*]. This question about how already presupposes, of course, that they are mediated, and therewith also presupposes that this otherness really is somehow to be understood. The universal and unshaken presupposition of understandability culminates in Gadamer's concept of the text. According to him, the interpreter asks "what is really there?" ["*was eigentlich da steht*"] and the text remains "the firm point of relation over and against the questionability, arbitrariness, or at least multiplicity of the possibilities of interpretation directed towards the text" (34/30).

What "is there" ["*da steht*"] is not something linguistic. "What makes understanding possible," according to Gadamer, is "precisely the forgetfulness of language, a forgetting of the formal elements in which the discourse or the text is encased. Only where the process of understanding is disrupted, that is, where understanding will not succeed, are questions asked about the wording of the text" (37/32). The text is that which, in the process of passing over the *signifiant* or signifier, is to be understood and toward which the one who understands should transgress his/her own narrow horizon; indeed, in "good" will to understand also will to transgress it. The other, who understands the text differently, should, accordingly, be able to help only by virtue of the fact that he/she understands it differently. His/her otherness in this process becomes the means to an ultimately unbiased understanding of what he/she hopes "is really there," just as also in direct encounters between various persons both should have "good will" to "understand one another" (38/33). In conversation one always retains, in contrast to one's encounter with a written text, the opportunity, in case of objection, to clarify or defend what was meant. The individual situation of communication [*Verständigungssituation*] here, is, according to Gadamer, precisely not something that stands in the way of a common understanding that is the same for everyone; rather, it is an opportunity to correct one's own understanding through that which is to be understood. The other person can tell me what he had intended to say, whereas the text remains mutely exposed to whatever interpretation is given at the time, at least so long as it finds no advocate for its meaning in another interpreter, who again will interpret it differently on the basis of his or her understanding.

This picture of understanding that endeavors to reach a commensurate understanding on the basis of "good will" obviously becomes the target of Derrida's critique, following Nietzsche. The instrument of this critique is Nietzsche's concept of "Will to Power." According to Heidegger's understanding, Nietzsche's thought still belongs to metaphysics because it seeks to understand under the rubric of this concept everything that is, and therewith it causes everything to arise in presentness within this understanding. Derrida, on the other hand, interprets the "Will to Power" quite differently, namely, as a counterconcept to the concept of a commensurate and therefore true understanding. If everything is will to power, then all understanding is will to power. It wills to bring itself to bear precisely in its seeking to understand. It wills to annex, to appropriate the other. The ostensible "good will" to reach a commensurate understanding is, in Derrida's view, really only a delusion, eventually a self-delusion.

Understanding is, then, imagining the other into one's own world-picture, reconstructing a world-picture whose coherence has been disturbed by the other. The presupposition of a common understanding is, on this reading, a means of making one's own understanding prevail. Or, borrowing from Nietzsche, one could perhaps better say: finding an understanding that is one's own, an understanding which can possibly be found only in confrontation with a divergent understanding. Therefore, "good will" to understand is seen as actually a "good will to power."

In Nietzsche this can be quite well substantiated. Gadamer's answer is characteristic of his position. He speaks of "finding it difficult to understand" what Derrida, following Nietzsche, objects to in him (*TI* 59/55), including Derrida's skepticism about Gadamer's view that "in dialogue knowing that one has been understood perfectly," or "the success of confirmation" by the other ["*le succès de la confirmation*"] (*TI* 58/*RIP* No. 151: 343) really do take place. Consistent with his position, Gadamer would like to make the effort to understand, "as anyone would do who wants to understand another person or be understood by the other," and he asserts that he "absolutely cannot see that this effort has anything to do with 'the epoch of metaphysics,' or, for that matter, with the Kantian concept of good will" (*TI* 59/55). By the term "good will" Gadamer refers to what Plato calls *"eumeneis elenchoi"*: "That is to say, one does not seek . . . to prove that one is always right, but one seeks instead as far as possible to strengthen the other's viewpoint so that what the other person has to say becomes illuminating." For Gadamer, this has nothing to do with ethics; it is "nothing more than an observation." He "cannot believe that Derrida would actually disagree with me about this." For "whoever opens his mouth wants to be understood; otherwise, one would not speak nor write." And finally he has "an exceptionally good piece of evidence" for his side: Derrida directs questions to him and therewith "he must assume" that Gadamer is "willing to understand them" (*TI* 59/55). Derrida and Nietzsche have, according to Gadamer, "both been unfair to themselves": Actually, "they speak and write in order to be understood" (*TI* 61/57). Gadamer then ventures to interpret Derrida—with the ironic request that Derrida pardon him for trying to understand him—going into the fact that as regards writing things are different and concedes that every reading of writing is "only a step on a path that never ends," and "whoever takes up this path" knows that he or she "will never be completely done with the text" (61/57).

Gadamer here takes the position of Socrates in his famous dialogue with the sophist Gorgias. According to Socrates' own self-characterization here, he is one of those "who would very much like to be refuted" if they are wrong, "and who also gladly refutes anyone if that person is wrong," but certainly "no less gladly finds oneself proven wrong than prove someone else wrong" (*Gorgias* 458a).[2] The "improbable debate" between Gadamer and Derrida took place in a quite similar vein. On the one side, it is a matter of a general truth that both partners aspire to disregard their own individuality; on the other side, one endeavors to maintain oneself against the otherness of the other striving to overcome otherness by pretending that the matter at issue is truth. In the following discussion I shall refer to the former viewpoint as Position and the latter as Counterposition. Counterposition says, just as Position does, that he wills to understand his opponent. But as a consistent position, Counterposition has its weak point in that it concedes that this will is the same as the effort to cancel the other in his otherness, since the other cannot be understood in any other way than from the understander's own standpoint. The attempt to take seriously the other's position, for example in answering to the "subtleties" of his or her expression, is for Derrida, as it was already for Nietzsche, only a more elegant method of taking people in, after which they are supposed ultimately to agree with one's point.

That there remains something that is not to be taken in at all, thus lending to the endeavor to understand a certain infinite dimension, for example in the case of the text, constitutes, in the view of Counterposition, a metaphysical interpretation of the process of understanding and is thus already an interpretation from a certain perspective. That this perspective supposedly has nothing to do with metaphysics but is thought to be simply "a superior bit of evidence" is for Counterposition an example of naïveté, but it is a naïveté that tries to assure its superiority in the fact that it will not allow itself to be interpreted as metaphysical. This naïveté insists on being "simply an observation." But Counterposition is not buying this kind of positivism. He understands Position quite differently from the way it wills itself to be understood. Counterposition wants to expose Position as a position—if necessary against the latter's self-understanding—not to be a position at all. Position alleges an increasing "fusion" of the given "horizons" in the understanding process. It implicitly suggests that understanding as such is a progressive, linear process leading into an open space of intelligibility, so to speak, and that it is not the case that positions simply perish in opposition to other positions and we are always already under the influence of positions which have won out over others. Thus, Position would really have to assume that the strong positions have also been the true ones, because supposedly strength resides in truth—admittedly not yet discovered—or at least in the efforts we make to attain it.

But this presupposition is contested by Counterposition as metaphysical and on this basis criticized as mere positionality. Logically, Counterposition cannot wish to contest Position for the sake of truth. Before discussing the question of what it can mean to contest a position in some way differently than for the sake of truth, we need to sketch the general line of Counterposition's arguments in order to make them "as strong as possible" (conforming with Gadamer's account of dialogical good will in Socrates, above). Counterposition has his particular strength in emphasizing the individuality in *each* position. Individuality is *"ineffabile,"* which means that it cannot be determined discursively; it can only be affirmed. That is, over against all efforts to do justice to it, one really can only insist on it. In any case, justness in understanding is viewed by Counterposition as impossible. If Nietzsche, for instance, "sets forth the doctrine" that everything "is" Will to Power and therewith says something universal, this is in his own eyes an "exoteric" doctrine, a turning outwards against metaphysical doctrines of the ontological sort, a polemic. Heidegger has misunderstood this fact when he represents this as a "doctrine" that Nietzsche understood to be "true," and then on the basis of this judges Nietzsche to be still a part of metaphysics. What Heidegger overlooks is how problematic for Nietzsche any concept of a doctrine is which, as such, teaches the universal. Thus, according to his "esoteric" philosophy, there are "no wills" (*KSA* 12,187; *KG* VIII 5[9]), because there are only individuals, and there is *nothing* universal. In the use of general concepts one is always already following a certain schema of understanding, and this means one incorporates, one assimilates, the other to oneself, even—and in fact, in an especially thorough fashion—in the "finest" forms of understanding.

Seen in this way, the matter of whether one understands or is understood is not at all a question of will, and certainly not of "good will." Heidegger and Gadamer are—in the view of the Counterposition—still too much Platonists to want to follow this and be able to understand it. According to Nietzsche, metaphysics resides in language and not primarily in what one thinks and says in language. For this reason, metaphysics also does not allow itself to be "overcome" ["*überwinden*"] as Heidegger supposes. Indeed, the late Heideggerian expression of "*Verwindung*" ["recuperation from"] registers a certain embarrassment about this problem, and language does not permit anything to be thought and said in it that, as Gadamer alleges, has nothing to do with metaphysics. Nietzsche speaks of a schema that we can name as such but which we are "*not able to throw off*" (*KSA* 12, 194; *KG* VIII 5 [22]). The real injustice toward the other, according to Nietzsche, does not reside in the fact that one does not will to understand him but in the fact that one *must* understand him in the only way one can: one thinks about the other in concepts that occur to oneself and as they become clear to oneself, if one is seeking to be fair to the other. This is something that cannot be otherwise, and Gadamer himself says he "cannot imagine" that Derrida really means what he is saying.

"Good will" to understand the other not only does not help; rather, speaking about it veils the fact that already in using the concept of "will" one is alleging that there is something that really is not there, not "given" [*was es nicht "gibt"*]: a will as something common to all, so that one already knows, without one's own interpretation, what "will" is.

Actually, the "French scene" comes closer to Nietzsche than that position which, influenced by Heidegger's understanding of Nietzsche, hears in the expression "Will to Power" something metaphysical and then wishes to have no part of it. The latter position hears in this term an affront to the "good will" to truth. Such an antithesis, however, is quite alien to Nietzsche's thought. According to Nietzsche, we cannot will truth because even in understanding ourselves to be willing "something" we are already relating to something universal as we are able to think it; let us say, in setting a goal, about which Kant has told us that it is a thinking in which the preconceived concept is thought of as cause. Thus, the good will to understand does indeed have something to do with Kant's concept of "good will": nothing is good, according to Kant, except a "good will," and that is here a will that in an inner understanding with itself binds itself to the categorical imperative of pure reason always to act in accordance with such maxims as allow themselves to be thought of as, at the same time, universal law, whereby in the inner understanding it is quite clear what falls under the concepts of action being applied under the maxims for acting. But in the concrete action itself, as an external expression of a will standing over against others, that which had been taken as understood—as Kant and Hegel had already seen—can immediately become questionable once again. The other does not have to think as I do when I am thinking in my "specifying" concepts, in which I am able to grasp something in terms of genus and species. He can say, for instance, that what I am doing is not at all something of which one may think in pure reason that it would be morally required. He can concede that I have "good will" but at the same time think that I cannot do otherwise than will to preserve my identity as a thinking subject also in the encounter with him. In this way, he would have done justice to me and my good will to understand him, but he would nevertheless feel he had not been understood. He does, however, no longer require me to understand him because in that case he would be demanding the impossible, that is, a surrender of my identity. He does not require it even if it appears possible for me with my good will to surrender my individual identity in order to be absorbed within a common symmetrical, reciprocal understanding. But there remains, on the debit side, the burdensomeness of the other, which, to preserve one's own identity, one seeks to escape, possibly even in the way in which one understands and responds to the other.

The issue in this debate, then, is whether, even with all good will, there can be justice in understanding. In other words, we have to do with a critique of good will from the standpoint of an other who feels misunderstood even within my best will. And therewith it is a matter of philosophical distrust of a philosophy erected on the moral ontology of good will. For this philosophy, the truth is what the understanding, from within itself and under the conditions of possible understanding given within it, understands or even could understand, in which a good will for commensurate understanding is already itself a value, if not ultimately the only value, standing over and against a truth that always remains transcendent.

It is manifestly a highly relevant philosophical question whether such an approach as that of Position is able to do justice to the questions of our time or whether the point is not, over and against the other, to regard even one's own good will, even while not denying its conditional worth, as questionable, the more so as it is supposed to be the ultimate and highest in one's relationship to the other. Theoretical discourse, however, is scarcely the field in which it is a matter of trying to understand with something other than good will. The problem is precisely the universal theoretizing of the *"heteron"* [Greek "other"] in the discourse, in which intersubjective agreement—that is to say, the judgment of the individual from standpoints which, under finite conditions, can only to a very limited degree be universal—is now to be the decisive criterion. This standpoint can only be valid in the innerness of an inter-subjectivity that is so bundled up in itself that it essentially excludes a "third party."[3]

II

Habermas, too, in his debate with the "French scene" in *The Philosophical Discourse of Modernity* manifestly does not comprehend this problem, despite "good will" (which is to be found here also, in spite of all the many differences with the "universal hermeneutics" of Gadamer) in trying to understand the "French scene." Against the traditional philosophy of reason grounded in the subject Habermas would like to counterpose the model of a rational discourse. He speaks of a "linguistically generated intersubjectivity" in which the ego stands in a "relationship" that allows it "to relate to itself as participant in an interaction from the perspective of alter" (*PDM* 347/297).[4] Obviously what is meant is that the ego experiences itself as an alter over and against an intersubjectivity that is functioning smoothly and which, for this reason, at first excludes it; and this permits it so to use discourse that, instead of an intersubjective bundling that operates to exclude it, it becomes possible to take in the alter, who had been the previously excluded third party.

Now Wittgenstein had already recognized that "human beings, in order to reach accord with each other," also have to agree with each other in "judgments" and not just "over the meaning of the words."[5] This means that a chance of incorporating a third party who was initially excluded from an existing community of discourse only exists when the parties succeed in actually finding an already existing agreement in judgments that was initially unconscious, so agreement in understanding did not appear possible. "A psychoanalysis as interpreted in terms of communications theory" is to point the way for this, according to Habermas (*PDM* 350/300). For Habermas, however, it is only a matter here of investigating "so deeply" that one strikes a common fundament that "would not have been disturbed by the decomposition of bourgeois culture" (156/129), or indeed, since the discovery of such an initially unseen deeper agreement in judgments is a *quaestio facti,* at least to reveal the actual good will involved in this research with the goal of reaching understanding.

Even "the French scene," as Counterposition, will not deny that something like this does occur. Intersubjective communities of discourse generally have a tendency to be open to the assimilation of further persons. The question is only who determines the direction of that openness—"ego" or "alter"—whereby ego may be the already functioning community in which the alter, standing over and against it, had already been experienced as alter in a sense that could be understood by ego. From the Platonic tradition down to and including Gadamer, this question would have been rejected as wrongly posed and answered as follows: neither ego nor alter should determine the direction but the truth, to attain which both sides have to labor with "good will."

The presupposition here, however, is that an objective truth is out there unknown to us, so that it is precisely good will alone that binds us together to seek it; "good will" is now understood as the will to find deeper-lying judgments held in common that are the sought-for, so to speak, relative a priori presupposition for the possibility of finding agreement in understanding. What is overlooked here is that the condition for the possibility of this presupposition is precisely already really to agree in judgments, which is also the presupposition for agreeing with each other about the commonality of judgments. Wittgenstein's thesis about the necessity of agreement in judgments, which we cited above, means that one always, no matter what employment of language one engages in, concedes and affirms "something" with content. Now precisely because in some cases one does not will to concede this because one holds it to be untrue, one wills under these circumstances not to take part in certain discourses. One refuses to accept the conditions for the possibility of this discourse, and that also means that *under such conditions* one does not will to be understood. Likewise, it can happen within an intersubjectivity already found in the discourse that, for the sake of the existence of the conditions for the possibility of that discourse, things are locked out and excluded which certain "thirds" [third parties] hold to be true and possible. For the sake of these conditions, this intersubjectivity will, to use Lévinas' expression, develop an "allergy" to otherness.[6]

Also, the Habermasian thesis that judging subjects, as "those acting communicatively," get "involved in relations to the world" (241/205) still does not get around the fact that precisely action can only grasp itself as possible insofar as it understands itself as something, as something that is isolatable from the totality of events according to pregiven concepts of species of action. It must understand itself as something that has the power or can summon up the energy to initiate and bring to fulfillment that which is resident in the concept of a certain species of action as it itself conceives it, without disruptive outside influences affecting it in any essential way and without any irritation caused by different interpretations. The concept of interaction, like that of intersubjectivity, is again essentially only related to limited interactions about which a clear set of goals and a rationality that in essence corresponds to them is already agreed upon. The foundational judgments held in common must, in being maintained against other possible judgments, be prior to action as the conviction on the basis of which action comprehends itself as possible.

Nietzsche mentions that in forming judgments, above all moral judgments, the point is to isolate the research into the prior history of a deed in such a way that the person making the judgment does not find himself or herself complicitous in it.[7] In other words, there exists a certain interest in defending one's own possibility of judgment (and also the possibility of one's judgment about another whose judgment one wills not to accept without criticism), in not inquiring to a random depth into the possibility of reaching agreement in judgment with others. This is a reality that the "French scene" recognizes. It recognizes that no individuality can summon up at the cost of its own identity, which is the finitely determined ground of its rationality, the good will to be "reasonable" and will to discourse at any price, or at least this price.

Already in Kant it is the other way around: good will, as that which in pure reason is alone that which can be judged good, is rooted in the identity of the subject, namely, by testing out whether its maxims for action as they are formulated in the inner self-understanding of subjectivity can at the same time be thought of as universal law. For the logic of this critical grounding of the good it is unimportant whether this is the subjectivity of an individual subject or an intersubjectivity in agreement with itself. What is important to Kant is that no further discourse on the use of the concepts entering into the maxims and in general into the judgments is needed, such as a discourse about the problem of which of the concrete actions should fall among the concepts for species of action covered in the maxims for action. According to Kant's critique of pure practical reason, if conflicts in interpretation arise, no mere discourse can decide the matter; rather, on grounds of reason only the *Law* as power to compel [*Befugnis zu zwingen*] can do so, and then only in cases where something must be decided because the conflict cannot be endured any more. One must be far from a despiser of democracy to conceive this place for law in reason.

The continuation of this critical position is found more in Nietzsche and in what Gadamer calls "the French scene" than in the model [*Denkmodell*] of intersubjectivity which, for the sake of its unlimited expansion, has to place its fundamental principles unconditionally at anyone's disposal. That this intersubjectivity *ought* to have good will to do so clearly signifies a misunderstanding of the logic of the good in the perspective of critical philosophy.

From this perspective, it would rather have to be conceded that discourses under quite finite conditions are to be carried through rationally to the end only under conditions of very limited purposes, in relation to which an agreement already exists; thus, it must also seem rational to hold back from such discourses if one does not will to share in this agreement, just as it must seem irrational to will unconditionally to incorporate those who do not want to participate. Someone may uncritically suggest that good will is certainly the least one could demand. But this apparently most minimal demand stands under the aegis of an already existing, already decided and not still to be worked out common goal; that is to say, a highest good, namely, general agreement in understanding [*allgemeine Verständigung*] as something achievable under finite conditions— without saying in what regard or why one *unconditionally* should understand each other. It thereby veils the fact that one, for the sake of the pure possibility of agreement, must first accept an agreement in judgments (and if it has to do with an agreement over values, value-judgments) and that then the only further question can be who, when originary dissent [*anfänglichem Dissens*] arises, has to yield and who will determine how deeply one should investigate in order to redeem the presupposition of existing agreement in judgments by the demonstration of real agreement. Only on this can it depend who will maintain his/her starting position. There is no third way here, a way, perhaps, to an agreement in judgments necessary for all and in this sense "deepest." For if depth investigation starting from a dissent at the outset can strike a consensus, then still deeper investigations can also strike a renewed dissent, unless one might believe in a Leader who will take one to the foundational, the deepest Truths, someone who knows before others in what direction to investigate in order to attain the depths and not somehow to move into merely greater superficiality and provinciality (see *PDM* 241). Under the presuppositions of bourgeois culture one could indeed, for example, run into presuppositions just as questionable. At the very least there cannot be found anywhere a consensus about how deep the decomposition would have to reach which would not exclude other possible ways of decomposing.

The concept of intersubjectivity was alien to critical philosophy. It is, above all in its ethical intention, an ideological concept that covertly suggests a direction given in advance, the direction in which one is to question in order to achieve consensus. To speak of the concept of an "ethical community," of beings with an essence in common, is, already according to Kant, still only thinking theocratically. Says Kant, "someone other than the people" would have to be the lawgiver.[8] The metaphor of the depths again suggests precisely this giving in advance of a rational direction of the good will as the concealment of a will to power. This metaphor hides the fact that it is a matter of individual virtue or power to escape the suggestion of such a depth of commonality, in view of the lack of a criterion for objective truth. The provinciality of this suggestion will not be overcome through good will but through the insight that good will exists precisely through the supposition that this overcoming is possible. It will be overcome through an enduring fairness over against the will to power of other persons, through the insight that every will can exist only in its own either individual or intersubjective and provincial way of imagining its possibility. Thus, it cannot be a matter of agreeing with Counterposition as a position and thereby understanding it as also a position; it is a matter, rather, of directing one's attention to what is unavoidably positional/metaphysical in Position's demand for understanding, that is, the demand that we unconditionally ought to understand, or at least ought to will to understand.

III

Nevertheless, Position is right to maintain the presupposition that something held in common is to be presupposed—if understanding is thought to be possible at all. There are a priori conditions of understanding to be presupposed, and if, with all the difficulties of reaching an understanding about the same thing, the discussion at least is to be kept going, a sustained good will to understand is to be presupposed. However, the second premise, which is necessary in order to arrive at the conclusion that understanding is possible, namely, that this condition is fulfilled, does not follow from this. It would only follow if the conclusion were already proven without it. Position is right under the presupposition of that agreement in understanding at which good will aims. Counterposition sees in this the logocentrism of Position. Position wills what it presupposes as possible and therewith something rational, but in doing so it at the same time presupposes something else that lies beyond the power of the will: an already existing commonality in the conditions of understanding. Whether such conditions really are given must always first be shown. It must be seen whether a general will to understand concretely proves its success such that it is able to reach agreement with the other on something specific, or whether it is beyond the boundaries of its capacity to understand because even with the best will it cannot understand. Basically, Counterposition is pointing to the boundaries of a finitely conditioned will and therewith to the otherness of wills standing over and against each other, even in their self-presupposition as good will.

Even the more restricted claim, which asserts that, well, certainly not everything is understandable but here it is a matter of understanding at least something about matter or a person, is open to the same objection from Counterposition. Counterposition would see in this drawing of a boundary between what is comprehensible and incomprehensible in something already the metaphysical preconception of the distinction between what is "essential" in something and what is "inessential" in it, a distinction through which something sets itself in relief as "something" in which "something" then is either understood or not understood. The other's understanding could already see in this an act of appropriation, and, seen from the vantage point of that understanding, a misunderstanding. The counterargument of Position, that such metaphysical preconceptions are unavoidable, for without the prior distinction between the essential and inessential in something there is nothing at all (because not something) to understand, would be taken by Counterposition as merely a confirmation of its argument. Position is saying that in understanding as such lies the impossibility of being able to understand the other without a prior concept, which, in the view of Counterposition, simply means the impossibility of being able to understand the other at all in its being as other. Now of course Position also knows the necessity of prejudice. But Position understands it as prejudice standing over and against something which is already understood as something, so that we supposedly know beforehand, that is, independently of our own standpoint of understanding, what is essential to the thing in itself, as this is what distinguishes it from other things.

If Counterposition thus exists basically—and exclusively, because it can only be a counter position and not itself a position—in holding that understanding, with its good will, is metaphysical, this cannot mean that Position should understand itself other than metaphysically, and thereby better. Counterposition cannot will this. Actually, it can only point to the antinomy in all "good will" to understand, paralleling Kant's exhibition of the antinomies of pure reason. Over and against the other, "good will," too, as pure as it may be before itself, finds itself to be trapped in an antinomy, or else to be for the other just another individual will.

James Risser

4. The Two Faces of Socrates: Gadamer/Derrida

Hermeneutics and deconstruction. Why should we begin this way? Why do we speak of a conjunction? Ostensibly, the conjunction serves to bring together two post-modern approaches to the text. And so we speak of "text and interpretation" as a point of departure for coming to terms with the real possibility of conjunction. There is a public event, the principals are present, the conjunction is cast. But the construction is tenuous at best, a wedge begins to take hold: in the eyes of one of the principals, hermeneutics is not post-modern at all.

As a way of commenting on the exchange between Gadamer and Derrida, let us recast the conjunction. Let us ask again what is brought together when we say "hermeneutics and deconstruction." Is it not the case that the conjunction is rooted in a common quest for liberation? Both hermeneutics and deconstruction can be described as post-Hegelian attempts at freeing language from itself. Both hermeneutics and deconstruction take seriously the playfulness of language, and with it the possibility of liberation from the solidification of meaning in words.

An appropriate expression of this liberation is found in the image of Socrates. Socrates enters the community neither to teach, nor to instruct, nor to prescribe, but to undertake an inquiry that is prior to all positing of knowledge. This prior preparatory task is not skepticism but simply an attempt to shake the discourse loose. The quest for liberation, consequently, takes the form of vigilance: the prior preparatory task is a vigilance against the pretension of knowing. Socrates appears on the scene not to answer but to question, to be vigilant against unquestioned authority that would confuse what appears to be with what really is. Socrates, recognizing the space that separates the human from the divine, takes up this questioning of others in the humility of his own ignorance. For Socrates to be consistent with his own practice, he can never escape the beginning to arrive at a philosophical doctrine; his task is always unfinished.

In contemporary garb, the Socratic figure is the anti-foundationalist thinker. It is the one who does not search for origins as foundations that would have us decide once and for all, at least in principle, what constitutes meaning and truth. It is the one for whom there are no ultimate assurances and thus the one who engages in a probing that always remains at risk. Derrida is one such Socratic figure. His deconstructive critique is a vigilance against the system of signs that leads to a pure presence, to a claim to a stabilized meaning. For Derrida there is no elixir for decidability, but only the sting of interruption. Equally so, the image of Socrates is attributable to Gadamer's hermeneut as well. In fact, it perhaps is more obvious in the case of Gadamer than with Derrida, for Gadamer makes explicit use of the logic of question and answer as a hermeneutic principle. Moreover, Gadamer's dialogical hermeneutics is the hermeneutics of finitude, the hermeneutics that rails against accepting the matter as settled through the objectification of methodological procedure. Gadamer's hermeneut comes to the marketplace armed with the knowledge that the proclamation of the correct interpretation rests on foundations that cannot be supported. Here too we find a vigilance.

There are, consequently, two faces to Socrates; the vigilance has a double sense. On the one hand, there is the vigilance of intervention, the radical probing that neither does not nor *can* not rest. This is Derrida's vigilance. On the other hand, there is the vigilance in the "conversation that we are," the probing that does not rest as long as the conversation continues. Here we find Gadamer's vigilance. Let us examine the exchange between Gadamer and Derrida, then, situated in this space of Socratic vigilance.

The Point of Departure: Text and Interpretation

"Text and Interpretation," the title of Gadamer's own contribution to the exchange as well as the title of the book in which it was published, is in fact a good description for precisely what hermeneutics and deconstruction have in common. For deconstruction, the text is everything; there is nothing outside of the text. But notice how this text is to be considered for deconstruction. It is a text that is no longer simple and nonproblematic. No longer is the text defined by its markings: title, margins, beginning, end, and authorship. The search for principles that would allow one to grasp the real idea of the text has been abandoned. What has been recognized is that the text, as a repository of meaning, as centered, cannot, like the statues of Daedalus, be tied down. The text is always open to a fundamental multiplicity because it is nothing other than a product of a system of arbitrary signs. *Différance* invades the sign.

Neither word nor concept, *différance* is the paradoxical structure that plays on its double meaning of difference and deferral. It refers to the undecidable relation between the event and structure of language:

> One can extend to the system of signs in general what Saussure says of language: "Language [*langue*] is necessary for speech [*parole*] to be intelligible and to produce all its effects, but speech is necessary for language to be established. . ." There is a circle here, for if one rigorously distinguishes language and speech, code and message, schema and usage, etc., and if one wishes to do justice to the two postulates thus enunciated, one does not know where to begin, nor how something can begin in general, be it language or speech. Therefore, one has to admit before any dissociation of language and speech . . . a systematic production of differences, the *production* of a system of differences— a *différance*—within whose effects one eventually, by abstraction and according to determined motivations, will be able to demarcate a linguistics of language and a linguistics of speech (*P* 39–40/28).

The play of difference forbids a simple element from being present in and of itself, referring only to itself. Nothing is anywhere simply present or absent. Consequently, there is no master text that stands firm, guiding, by whatever methodological principle, the access to its innermost secrets.

Corresponding to this notion of a text, the "interpretation" of a text is essentially critique. It is an analysis that displaces the centering found in the text by following certain terms that govern the textual production itself. The analysis that disrupts the structure of the text is in principle interminable; the conclusion is deferred.

Like Derrida, Gadamer would have us shift the centering of meaning from authorship to the text itself. The normative notion of authorial intention represents only an empty space, for what is fixed in writing always frees itself for a new relationship. The new relationship is the event of understanding itself, which is the mediation of difference, without ultimate terminus, within an historical horizon. Here too one is in the grasp of repetition: the reader participates in an event in which the text speaks in the present. There is a master text, the text that is to be understood, but the mastery of this master text is suspect for it is a text that is always multiple: it warrants reinterpretation.

The question that arises in the exchange—the question that is addressed by Gadamer but never explicitly stated by Derrida—is whether the intertwining of text and interpretation in philosophical hermeneutics is simply one more instance of a logocentric metaphysics. This question must be brought to any hermeneutics that sees meaning as something to be discovered. Clearly, Gadamer's hermeneutics does insist on deciding the question of meaning. In fact, Gadamer's hermeneutics appears to be not just one example of a logocentric metaphysics but a very conservative Heideggerian logocentric metaphysics. After all, it is a hermeneutics framed by the notion of tradition such that interpretation is never construed as a breaking free of possibilities, but always something that takes place within the envelopment of what is already handed down.

One cannot help but see in this question something of a defense on Gadamer's part. But the defense should not, like the defense of the church against Galilean science, be construed as someone holding fast to archaic views against a superior position. For if such were the case there would be no point to an exchange. There is something of a "defense" because Gadamer sees the concept of the text as that which "unites and perhaps divides" him from Derrida. The "defense" is one of setting the matter straight, of turning ultimately to the question of linguisticality and deciding if it is a "bridge or a barrier." Behind this, it could be said that Gadamer's defense is one of correcting misinterpretations of his position. Gadamer has said on more than one occasion that Derrida's criticism of hermeneutics is a criticism of the hermeneutics of Paul Ricoeur. As Gadamer sees his own position, we are not faced simply with a choice between practicing an infinite deferral of the signified and a deep probing of a text that seeks *the* meaning of the text. The hermeneutics that engages in reconstruction, which is one way of describing Ricoeur's methodological procedure of explanatory understanding, is not an accurate description of a philosophical hermeneutics. In view of the way in which we have recast what is at stake in the exchange, a serious challenge to Gadamer's position is made only if one risks giving up the vigilance in the very performance of textual interpretation.

Hermeneutic Vigilance: The Communicative Event

There is no question that Gadamer's philosophical hermeneutics accounts for interpretation as a search for meaning. But if we stop with this, Gadamer's position is no different from other traditional theories of interpretation. What distinguishes Gadamer's position is his account of interpretation in which the *fixation* of meaning is problematic. We have only to look at the dialectical character of Gadamer's philosophical hermeneutics to see the issue here.

In "*Destruktion* and Deconstruction," written subsequent to "Text and Interpretation," Gadamer describes his own work as well as Derrida's in the context of Heidegger's effort at leaving behind the language of metaphysics. Heidegger's effort at posing for the first time a non-metaphysical sense of the question of being is described by Gadamer as a "way back from dialectic." His own effort is likewise a step back from dialectic, specifically, a step back from dialectic to dialogue and conversation. It is a step back from thinking as the *logos* of the world situated in subjectivity—Hegel's *logos*—to the Platonic dialectic stripped of its metaphysical encasement. In the Socratic dialogue, Gadamer finds the true carrying out of *anámnēsis*. "What is accomplished in conversation," Gadamer tells us, "is a summoning back in thought which is possible only for the soul fallen into the finitude of bodily existence" (DD 111).

This step back into conversation is stated by Gadamer in a more striking way in his *Philosophical Apprenticeships*:

> In order to locate my first attempts at thinking, I could in fact say that I took it upon myself to save the honor of "bad infinity" [*der "schlechten Unendlich-keit"*]. Of course, in my eyes I made a decisive modification here . . . . [for thinking] is not to be characterized as an endlessly continuing determination of an object-world waiting to be recognized (*PA* 189–90).

The decisive modification, the turn to conversation in which words are there only in the totality of our speaking and answering, is such that, in a sense, the end keeps on delaying its arrival. In conversation there is always a "potentiality for being other that lies beyond every coming to agreement about what is common" (*TI* 30/TI 26). The fact that a potentiality of otherness remains suggests that for Gadamer the text remains plural and not for reasons of an ambiguity of its content. Rather, the text remains plural by virtue of the structure of interpretation itself.

We can think of this interconnection of text and interpretation as a movement of departure and return. The departure must be understood in the context of writing's ideality. In an obvious way, a text attains an ideality in the way it stands apart from the necessary repetition, which links the past with the present, of oral tradition. Writing, unlike speech, is freed from the contingencies of origin. But the issue here is not one of understanding writing on the basis of its supplement, for writing, despite the loss of oral immediacy in which intonation and accent lend themselves more readily to human communication and understanding, has for Gadamer an "astonishing authenticity." "Writing is more than a mere repetition in print of something spoken" (TI 39/TI 34). Ideality, Gadamer tells us, "befits not only the written structure but also original speaking and hearing insofar as their content can be separated from the concrete speech act and can be reproduced."[1] The written structure is essentially a separation from the original language-event. "Reproduction," which can be more or less adequate, is always possible. Thus, the issue here is to see that written texts present the real hermeneutic task. "Even the pure signs of an inscription can be seen properly and articulated correctly only if the text can be transformed back into language." (*WM* 368/352). The ideality of writing, which makes it contemporaneous with every present, is an abstraction from the event (of language itself).

Interpretation, as that which brings written fixed language once again into speech, is, consequently, the event of overcoming the self-alienation, the departure, of writing. The return is to what is meant. But this return is not a reconstruction. Expressed in terms of the dialectical character of philosophical hermeneutics, the return is the new event as the concretion of meaning within interpretation itself. The return is the hermeneutic event of speaking again in a new voice. Speaking is, for Gadamer, an endeavor that continually modifies itself and as such it leaves behind the intended meaning of the speaker. Every production of meaning is one-sided, for language "always refers beyond that which achieves the status of a proposition." Thus, for different reasons than others, Gadamer too recognizes the distinction between *langue* [language] and *parole* [speech]. The spoken word is not to be confused with the system of symbols that constitute language. The activity of language in dialogue is not a system of signs, but "real exchange and work."

The consequence of this notion of language as a speech-event for a theory of textuality is decisive. Interpretation does not proceed on the basis of a free-floating attitude that can discuss the statements of the text as objective information. The text, in other words, "is not to be viewed as an end product the production of which is the object of an analysis whose intent is to explain the mechanism that allows language as such to function at all." (*TI* 35/TI 31). The functioning of language, which is the concern of the linguist, is merely a pre-condition for comprehending what is said. The text must be readable. And then, from out of its readability, it is the subject matter of the text and not the text itself that is the point of concern. Writing needs to be transformed back into speech, that is, the communicative event. "The text is a mere intermediate product [*Zwischenprodukt*], a phase in the communicative event [*Verständigungs-geschehen*]. (*TI* 35/TI 31).

Such an event would seem to be problematic for a theory of text interpretation since the written text, by virtue of its ideality, is something cut off from the give and take of living conversation. What would a conversation with a text amount to? Above all, it would be a conversation that places a certain demand upon the reader as locus of the real exchange and work. A performative dimension is at work in every interpretation.[2]

It is in the context of this performative dimension of textual interpretation that Gadamer emphasizes how both partners in a conversation must have a good will to try to understand one another. This phrase, not to be confused with the will in Kant, captures the overall sense of the conditions for conversation. But in an exchange between the text and a nameless reader the good will seems all the more problematical. Is it not simply a matter of recognizing that the writer of a text wants to impart meaning and thereby has in mind the preview of the other with whom he/she shares presuppositions? Knowing full well that we cannot resurrect the author, the answer to this question would seem to be both a yes and a no. Yes, because what is our writing and speaking if not a community of speakers and writers who wish to be understood? And although this implies that in an exchange we are able to bring about a real understanding—that rupture and break can be brought back to unity, that one can "say the same"—we have not made a naive return to a metaphysics of presence, for the event character of understanding means precisely that there is no mere repetition of the text nor a mere recreation of a text, but a new creation of understanding. The sense of the good will is Socratic: "one seeks . . . to strengthen the other's viewpoint so that what the other person has to say becomes illuminating" (*TI* 59/TI 55). Gadamer considers this essential for every understanding.

But the moment we attempt to probe this dimension of a partner in conversation more deeply, the "no" to our question arises. The intention of a reader is to grasp what is spoken of in the text. In Gadamer's hermeneutic theory this presents a special problem in as much as the reader is always guided in advance by anticipations of meaning. The good will, in this context, is simply the projection of truth, of intelligibility of the text on the part of the reader, that is necessary for the text to speak at all. Without this projection, one enters a circle of having only one's own prejudices confirmed. Gadamer insists that interpretation always fails as the will to mastery.

In *Truth and Method* this projection of intelligibility was characterized as the "anticipation of completion" [*Vorgriff der Vollkommenheit*] (*WM* 278/261). In order to understand at all, a reader presupposes that the subject matter of a text has a perfected unity of meaning. The subject matter, in other words, is regarded *initially* as neither incoherent within itself ("immanent unity of meaning") nor inconsistent with what is true concerning the subject matter ("transcendent expectations of meaning which proceed from the relation to the truth of what is being said"). Naturally a text could be otherwise, but if a text is not regarded as having a perfected unity of meaning there would be nothing to call into question the prejudices guiding the interpretation. A text would say whatever the reader wanted it to say. The perfected unity of meaning thus enables the text to stand as a self-presenting and authoritative whole. From the point of view of the reader, the negative experience that causes the anticipation of completion in a text to fail is simply the change that would not allow the text to speak "be it that we find it boring, empty or ridiculous, sentimental, imitative, or simply not working."[3] Thus a text cannot say anything it wants to and at the same time Gadamer eschews a methodology of a correspondence theory of meaning. The anticipation of completion is more regulative than constitutive of text and reading. A text must be followed according to its meaningful sense [*Sinnsgemäss*] and this is what the communicative situation is directed toward.

Granted, then, that the good will is a condition of the communicative situation and that the understanding of a text is dependent upon the communicative situation, what can we now say about the notion of text? In the coalescing of text and interpretation, the text only emerges in its effect [*Wirkung*]. It has an interpretive free space precisely because what the interpreter follows is its meaningful sense and not the text itself (as literal). Judicial hermeneutics convincingly displays this feature of interpretation. But notice that here, as well as in the interpretation of literary texts, it is always a matter of the attempt to make univocal understanding possible. The free space amounts to a free space of meaningful concretization. Nevertheless, it remains true that the text always holds within itself a fundamental openness. This is the sense of the performative dimension of interpretation. Gadamer writes: "In writing, [where] the openness that is implied in seeking the words cannot be communicated because the text is printed, a 'virtual' horizon of interpretation and understanding must be opened in writing the text itself, one that the reader must fill out" (*TI* 39/TI34).

The Two Faces of Socrates

In view of Gadamer's remarks on text and interpretation, there is no doubt that he sees the work of understanding texts as essentially a work of repetition that does not seek origins. In genuine conversation there is no last word just as there is no first word. One has to wonder what is really so naive about Gadamer's position that would force one to move beyond hermeneutics to deconstruction. The answer, of course, is that Gadamer installs presence: understanding *is* possible. Language is only actualization. Granted that Gadamer is not after meaning in itself, that hermeneutics is not a reconstruction, it is nonetheless logocentric insofar as Gadamer posits coherence, agreement. The productive act of hermeneutic understanding is directed towards saying the same [*homolegein*].

But what if we take this and see if it can work against Derrida? Essentially, this is Gadamer's critique of Derrida's critique. Much of this critique is implicit in what was already said with respect to the communicative event. Rather than beginning anew, let us focus on the critique by returning to the image of Socrates with which we began. Accordingly, we return to our initial question: Is philosophical hermeneutics any less vigilant than that of deconstruction? The question of more or less may be slightly misleading, for the figure of Socrates, as we have seen, shows two faces: intervention and conversation.

The vigilance of intervention is the face of Socrates who enters the community as a gadfly, as an annoyance and a bother; he wants to disrupt and he is disruptive. It is the disruption that allows Socrates to efface the privileged *logoi*. This is the vigilance of Derrida. We can see something of this vigilance of intervention in the questions that Derrida posed to Gadamer's paper. The questions center on Gadamer's claim that genuine conversation requires a good will to try to understand one another. Derrida asks whether the very positing of good will commits Gadamer to a metaphysics of the will as this is understood in the history of metaphysics; that is to say, that Gadamer overlooks the domination that such a notion brings to the text.[4] He also asks about the extent to which a psychoanalytic hermeneutics must enter these considerations of understanding the other. What is behind these questions is for Derrida the necessity of the rupture, the break that constantly wedges itself between what is being said. In the end, Derrida confesses his uncertainty about dialogue ever being able to "say the same."

Consequently, by focusing on the good will, Derrida thinks he has focused on the structure that governs the totality of the phenomenon of understanding. The vigilance of intervention wants to shake free the totality by pointing to what the totality excludes. In this case what is excluded would seem to pertain to the hidden intentions that would conflict with the supposed transparency of the good will. But this does not mean for Derrida that we must replace one kind of hermeneutics for an archeology of the subject. The vigilance as vigilance is only to practice the shaking against the closure of sedimented truth. In his own contribution to the exchange—"Interpreting Signatures (Nietzsche/ Heidegger)"[5]—Derrida did not present an alternative theory of text but continued to probe the issue of domination in hermeneutics. Derrida sees Heidegger's Nietzsche as a figure that has been made to stand still. In understanding Nietzsche as the last metaphysician, Heidegger has made Nietzsche into a partner in his own question.

To really appreciate the seriousness of the vigilance of intervention, it is important to see that the kind of negative conclusion that Derrida would constantly enact does not produce anarchy. For Socrates, the disruptive play is always mindful of the human community. In fact, it could be said that his intervention is in service to the community. Can we not say, then, that the Derridian disruptive play will prepare the way for a new form of community? Such a community would have to be thought in terms of what the disruptive play makes possible, namely, nonexclusion. Only this form of community would we say is truly liberated. Repression enters the system in the form of exclusion and exclusion is precisely what occurs when one seeks unity rather than difference. The community sought must be a community of difference.

At this point one has to wonder if we have failed to keep the two faces distinct, for any reference to community is a reference to unity. Perhaps that is the very question: Can intervention remain outside the community? Is this not precisely what Gadamer asks and what is expressed by the vigilance in the conversation that we are? Socrates is not only the gadfly, he is also the midwife who seeks to bring wisdom to birth, and would have us distinguish sophistry from dialectic. It is a wisdom borne out by the dialectic of question and answer in light of the recognition of humanity's own limitations. Surely in light of what we have seen such vigilance does not fall into the trap of closure and foundation. In fact, one has to see that Gadamer is not Heidegger. Gadamer does not center the text by the question of the meaning of being, but certainly follows Heidegger in seeing that "every word is itself always an answer and gives rise always to a new question" (LD 95).

This is the vigilance of Gadamer. Understanding is always a form of dialogue, a coming to agreement within a structure of openness. And again, conversation is not a talking about something that is already there, but has the structure of an event, a present enactment, which remains unfinished. Any text is a structure that can be taken as a new event; written things must begin to speak again. Every reading that attempts to understand is only a first step and never comes to an end; we need the continuing *effort* to find the common ground. This is what the vigilance of the conversation that we are enacts. Gadamer does install the *logos,* but not a centered one. Gadamer's *logos* is rootless, not tied to a transcendental subject or a methodological procedure. It is a *logos* that is in principle always unfinished. Accordingly, against the naîveté of a reading that sees the logos as simply written there, against the reading of the text that constrains its truth to the mastery of the reader, the hermeneut remains vigilant within the communicative event. Gadamer insists that even Derrida wishes to be understood, otherwise he would neither speak nor write.

The moment of coherence in the conversation that we are, then, is not the moment at which the statue of Daedalus has been secured, but the fulfillment of genuine dialogue as being written in the soul of the one who hears.[6] The coherence is not a sedimentation of meaning but the disappearance of interpretation.

Finally, we need to be aware of the political function in this form of vigilance. We need to see that here too there is a preparation for a form of community. In the conversation that we are, the community would not give way to difference, but rather within the difference seek unity. For Gadamer the ideal of democracy is that there are common opinions, that the other is possibly right. Thus, within the experience of limitation in which full presence constantly eludes the one who wants to understand, there is included all those things that bind us together. In his reply to Derrida's remarks, Gadamer speaks elliptically of the ability to sustain social life through the element of dialogue and how this directs us to human solidarity. Elsewhere, Gadamer has characterized this as participation, a participation that posits the goal of human solidarity.

Charles Shepherdson

5. *Imagine Understanding . . .*

> To understand means that one is
> capable of stepping into the place
> of the other.
> > —Gadamer

> Do we hear, do we understand each
> other already with another ear?
> The ear does not answer.
> > —Derrida

> A voice in the first person
> singular. What an addition to
> company that would be.
> > —Beckett

Imagine a dialogue, then—the one that might in fact have happened, that is yet to come, or that has always already occurred, whether (as Gadamer says) because "one is *capable* of stepping into the place of the other" even if this does not in fact happen, or because (as Derrida says) we have already understood each other (have we not?) "with another ear," even if this has not happened in fact.

Imagine a dialogue between Gadamer and Derrida, then, or perhaps between deconstruction and hermeneutics. We are to understand, it goes without saying, that these names do not always mean the same thing, and that we are speaking of at least three things: the men themselves, the series of writings signed by each that have, for their readers, so many different meanings, and the philosophical movements that now have their own names and their own still more anonymous lives.

Pushing on despite this difficulty, or rather these two difficulties—first (a question of tense), the problem of whether to determine the dialogue as an actual historical *event,* as a *possibility* yet to come, or as having always already occurred in the manner of a pure anteriority, that absolute past that we are still tempted to call a "condition of possibility"; and second (a question of person), the problem of the identity of those who speak in the dialogue—pushing on, however, we are to imagine that they, these two, have talked together, or more precisely that they will have or always already have talked together; for whether they have or have not actually done so, it goes without saying that we are concerned not so much with the empirical fact of dialogue as with its possibility and nature, in the case of these two.

Are we therefore also to imagine that they have heard each other, understood each other, that they have agreed, or even agreed to differ? Are we imagining a dialogue, then, in which one would see them side by side, their commonalities delineated, their divergences clear, their positions thereby situated in a single space? Perhaps. It would be premature to pretend that even the most mundane of comparisons and contrasts can be ruled out as impossible. For on the basis of what difference would one pretend that no differentiation or similitude can be articulated between two thinkers who, however vastly they diverge, are nevertheless both engaged with certain texts, and with questions that lead them both to wonder, first, whether they have, or will have, or have already understood each other, and, second, whether it still makes sense to speak of the other on the basis of a logical or psychological principle of identity? It would be difficult to locate a difference so absolute that no communication, nothing, could be imagined; and if one cannot pretend to such an absolute difference, then to this extent they would indeed be "capable of understanding" and would even have "understood each other already," whether they agree or agree to differ. The most mundane of dialogues will not easily be ruled out.

For example, first and foremost in his response to Gadamer, and even before putting any question to the other, Derrida begins by asking himself if *there is* dialogue, "if anything was taking place here other than . . . unfindable objects" (Response); and he confesses at the end of his introductory remarks that even after he has decided what to say, what questions to put, he is "still asking [himself] this question." Thus, before posing any questions to the other, and even after posing them in fact, it is not clear that there has been dialogue. And yet, again before coming to the questions themselves, he nevertheless also admits that although it is not clear that there has been (or will have been) dialogue, still "we are gathered together here around Professor Gadamer," and "it is to him," Derrida says, "that I wish to address these words, paying him the homage of a few questions." This cannot be dismissed as extrinsic politeness or mere play.

And Gadamer, too, however much he may wish "to understand these questions that have been addressed to [him]," or point out that whoever speaks "wants to be understood"(Reply), has, for his part, burdened us with a similar difficulty. In the "Foreword to the Second Edition" of *Truth and Method* Gadamer finds it necessary once again to "outline the intention and claim of the work," and to stress again that his concern is not to articulate a hermeneutic

method but "to discover and bring into consciousness something that methodological dispute serves only to conceal and neglect" (*WM* xiv/xvi). "My real
concern," he insists, "was and is philosophic: not what we do or what we ought
to do, but what happens to us over and above our wanting and doing" (xiv/xvii).
"This is a question," he says, "which precedes any action of understanding on
the part of subjectivity" (xv–xvi/xviii). Whatever it may be, the relation established in dialogue, and also in any attempt to understand the past, it is not
fundamentally one in which two positions or points of view (hermeneutics and
deconstruction, for example) come into contact. The issue is therefore not at all
the empirical and psychological one of being understood or of wishing to understand, nor yet the exegetical one of delineating similarities and differences (even
if this cannot be ruled out) but the "philosophic" issue that "precedes any
action . . . of subjectivity." We are to recognize, then, that despite all efforts
"to bring into consciousness" (*WM* xv/xvii), as Gadamer puts it, the insight he
has found it necessary "to outline" once again, it is quite clearly the case that
"consciousness" here has lost its status as a name, especially as the name for a
self-knowing subject, and has become a question: "effective-historical consciousness is so radically finite that our whole being, achieved in the totality of
our destiny, *inevitably transcends its knowledge of itself*" (*WM* xx/xxii).

We are therefore explicitly confronted with the difficulty that had already
been presented, without detailed thematization, in the original introduction to
the book. On one hand, Gadamer wishes to articulate or bring into consciousness "that experience of truth that transcends the sphere of the control of scientific method," and to demonstrate "how far the claim to truth of these modes of
experience outside science can be philosophically legitimated" (*WM* xxxvi/xii).
It goes without saying that his purpose is not to secure, apart from science,
certain regions of being such as history and art: regionally, to be sure, he
proposes "to defend that experience of · ruth that comes to us through the work
of art against the aesthetic theory that lets itself be restricted to a scientific
concept of truth"; but he insists that his philosophical goal is "to develop from
this starting point a concept of knowledge and of truth that corresponds to the
whole of our hermeneutic experience" (*WM* xxvii/xiii). It is quite clear, then,
that the issue resides neither with the disciplines of history and art, nor with the
sciences, but with philosophy. What shows itself in the phenomenon of understanding, beyond all the "understandings" that may in fact be positively constituted and articulated, is rather "an experience," he says, "that transcends," as
he puts it, "the control" of scientific method. Thus, the question that will issue
from faithful description of this phenomenon of understanding is: what happens
to philosophy when it is not determined as or even directed toward self-
knowledge, when it "transcends" the "control" of "method" and the ideal of
rigorous science? What happens to philosophy in the experience of seeking

"philosophical legitimation" for something "so radically finite" that it "inevitably transcends its knowledge of itself"? It is Gadamer's question.

Consequently, on the other hand, the very same passages in the original introduction simultaneously confess that, despite this investigation he has undertaken, "the experience of historical tradition goes quite beyond that in it which can be investigated"; furthermore, he continues, the fact "that truth is experienced through a work of art that we cannot attain in any other way constitutes the philosophic importance of art, which asserts itself against all reasoning"; and finally, bringing the *investigation* of this experience into full tension with its *result,* which "goes quite beyond" investigation and "asserts itself against all reasoning," Gadamer adds that this experience "must not only be justified philosophically, but . . . is itself a mode of philosophizing" (*WM* xxvi–xxvii/xii–xiii).

What Gadamer has done, in short, is to force us to imagine dialogue not at all in the mode of exegesis and comparison of viewpoints, but rather in the tension between (on one hand) the hermeneutic understanding that his investigation sought to "justify philosophically," and (on the other hand) the experience that "goes beyond that in it which can be investigated," that "asserts itself against all reasoning," and that nevertheless—perhaps without justification—"is itself a mode of philosophizing." This is why Gadamer acknowledges, in "Text and Interpretation," that "Heidegger completely discarded the concept of hermeneutics because he realized that he would never be able to break through the sphere of transcendental reflection" (p. 23). What we are to understand is that however much he may wish to understand and be understood, and with whatever good will these acts are undertaken, the "philosophical" issue follows "Heidegger's critique of the phenomenological concept of immanence" and "leaves behind the starting point in the subjectivity of the subject" (TI 26). It is also for this reason that Gadamer explicitly acknowledges that *to the extent* that his efforts have been aimed at an expository and critical account of particular theses regarding interpretation—Dilthey's, for instance—he has not fully taken up the question that has issued from his own investigations; and this is what dialogue might well mean: "Since my confrontation with the French continuation of Heideggerian thought, I have become aware that my own efforts to 'translate' Heidegger testify to my own limits and especially indicate how deeply rooted I am in the romantic tradition of the humanities" (TI 24.) Nor is this, on Gadamer's part, mere politeness or extrinsic autobiography, as if he were speaking of some particular exchange of words with the French, for as he goes on to say: "The being-towards-the-text from which I took my orientation is certainly no match for the radicality of the limit experience found in being-toward-death. . . . I can, therefore, understand why the later Heidegger . . . was of the opinion that I never really abandoned the sphere of phenomenological imma-

nence to which Husserl consistently held" (26). And yet, if he has not perhaps
abandoned the sphere of phenomenological immanence, and has not refused
exposition and critique, this does not mean that the question, the "real concern"
which "was and is philosophic" (*Truth and Method,* xvi), the question of imagining dialogue in the tension between his own efforts at positive exegesis or
"philosophical legitimation" and, on the other hand, that which issues from his
exegesis to "*assert itself* against all reasoning," and which he speaks of as "the
unintelligible," simply does not exist. On the contrary: "The finite nature of
one's own understanding is the manner in which reality, resistance, the absurd,
and the unintelligible *assert themselves*" (*WM* xxi/xxiii). What asserts itself
here in and through Gadamer's own phenomenological description of
understanding—is this not what Derrida heard with one or another ear in Husserl: "In the descriptions of the movement of temporalization, all that does not
torment the simplicity and the domination of that form [the *lebendige Gegenwart,* the living present] seems to indicate to us how much transcendental
phenomenology belongs to metaphysics. But one must come to terms with the
forces of rupture. In the originary temporalization and the movement of relationship with the outside, as Husserl actually describes them, nonpresentation or
depresentation is as 'originary' as presentation. That is why a thought of the
trace can no more break with a transcendental phenomenology than be reduced
to it" (*Gr* 91/62).

Let us not imagine, then, that what "asserts itself" will entirely keep Gadamer from repeating, or outlining once again the intention of his work, or from
replying to questions that Derrida, likewise, has not refrained from asking; but
let us also, at the same time, not imagine that their having in fact spoken in this
way means that the philosophical question can simply be forgotten, that it can be
answered by the word "dialogue," or that the question can go without saying. If
Gadamer has insisted upon refusing to speak of understanding without also
allowing the "unintelligible" (in the "Letter to Dallmayr" he writes: "Anyone
who wishes to understand his or her being is confronted by the simple unintelligibility of death," p. 97), Derrida will elaborate the problem that asserts itself in
temporality that Husserl actually describes: "In its greatest formality, this immense problem would be formulated thus: is the temporality described by a
transcendental phenomenology . . . a ground. . . ? Or is the phenomenological
model itself constituted, as a warp of language, logic, evidence, fundamental
security, upon a woof that is not its own? And which—such is the most difficult
problem—is no longer at all mundane?" (*Gr* 98/67).

To say, therefore, that the most mundane of comparisons will not be ruled out
(and have we not just been tempted to open such a comparison?) is not at all to
say that such a dialogue—if this is what we imagine dialogue to be—would be
faithful in the least to the philosophical issue that brings these men or texts or
philosophical movements together, or apart. One might, in other words, fruit-

fully draw up a list, showing that Derrida discusses sexuality, for example, or seeks to enact in his style a kind of play, whereas Gadamer avoids both, preferring a determination of experience that is taken to be presexual, or a more Germanic straightforwardness in exposition; one might helpfully show that the patient attentiveness to the course of history, the contexts and vicissitudes that give, for Gadamer, a limited horizon to the works one encounters, is not shared by Derrida, whose attentiveness to history poses a rather different question. Such a table of comparison and contrast can in fact be made, and even by these two.

If we are not to imagine that the real issue of dialogue could be located within such a table, showing where they agree or agree to differ, might we not perhaps, preferring one (one man, or the series of writings linked to one name, or one movement of thought), take up the resources of that one and bring them to bear upon the other, yielding, for instance, a hermeneutic assessment of the phenomenon of deconstruction, or a deconstructive reading of the hermeneutic effort? It goes without saying that both alternatives would betray the very thinking that one would have imagined oneself to be following.

G. B. Madison

6. Gadamer/Derrida: The Hermeneutics of Irony and Power

The Gadamer/Derrida conversation, if it can be called that—this most "improbable" of encounters—is, to all appearances, one that goes nowhere and that issues in a hermeneutical failure, does not result in the achievement of a common agreement or understanding. This is surely the impression that the listeners who were gathered together at the Goethe Institute in Paris must have had. Such an understanding on the part of the audience would, in any event, I should think, have fitted in well with the possible authorial intention of Jacques Derrida, one of the speakers. For it cannot be denied that it would most definitely be in the interests of an anti-hermeneutical deconstructionist for an interchange between a phenomenological hermeneuticist and an anti-phenomenological deconstructionist to result in a communicative impasse, or a hermeneutical failure, since this would, ipso facto, serve to demonstrate in a concrete way the failure of hermeneutics as a general theory of human understanding, which is one of the things that, I gather, deconstruction is all about.

In his opening remarks Gadamer had asked:

> What, in the final analysis is linguisticality? Is it a bridge or a barrier? Is it a bridge built of things that are the same for each self over which one communicates with the other over the flowing stream of otherness? Or is it a barrier that limits our self-abandonment and that cuts us off from the possibility of ever completely expressing ourselves and communicating with others?[1]

Gadamer and Derrida share a common bond, a common preoccupation—a *locus communis*. This is, of course, language, writing, and textuality. And yet, they seem to inhabit uncommunicating worlds. For while Gadamer insists that language is a "bridge" allowing for communication, Derrida has sought assiduously to convince his readers (and listeners) that language is precisely that which renders forever impossible (indefinitely defers) meaningful self-understanding as well as, to use Gadamer's words, "a genuine mutual understanding [*Verständingung*]."

Throughout his immensely prolific (some might be tempted to say, logorrheic) career Derrida has sought to defend his anti-hermeneutical position, to, in a sense, refute Gadamer's assertion: "Whoever opens his mouth wants to be understood; otherwise, one would neither speak nor write" (Reply). This amounts to a formidable undertaking, indeed an impossible one, philosophically speaking. Derrida's position is one that simply cannot be argued for or demonstrated. Derrida is fully aware of this fact, of course. His position is philosophically impossible, because a philosophical argument or demonstration is one which, *per definitionem*, seeks, by means of various argumentative procedures, to persuade, and to solicit the uncoerced agreement of an interlocutor as to a certain issue or thesis; it is one that seeks to arrive at a mutual understanding as to *die Sache*. Now, if Derrida were to argue for the impossibility of understanding (of decidable meanings) in a philosophical way (if indeed he were even to articulate his position in the form of a thesis—something he is careful not to do), the outcome could only be of two sorts: Either the argument would be a failure; his interlocutor wouldn't have the slightest clue as to what he was talking about (no understanding whatsoever). Or the argument would be successful; his interlocutor would understand him and possibly even agree with him. In either case, however, it would be a failure, even—and especially—if it were successful. For if through philosophical dialogue Derrida succeeded in arriving at a perfectly good common understanding with his interlocutor, this itself would present a lie to what he was arguing for, namely, the impossibility of understanding. Philosophically speaking, therefore, Derrida finds himself in a double bind, as he himself well knows.

Accordingly, Derrida abandons the *via philosophiae* and adopts an altogether different tactic. If his position cannot be demonstrated in a philosophical way, it is perhaps nonetheless possible that it can be demonstrated in a non-philosophical way. If the "truth" of his position cannot be argued for, cannot be *said*, it can perhaps be "shown," can be concretely instanced, made manifest, or pointed out (*de-monstrare*) by means, precisely, of a particular usage of language. The best way to show linguistically that understanding is not possible is to "show" that one does not in fact understand; to "show" that attempts at dialogue inevitably result in failure to arrive at a mutual, meaningful accord. This, I believe, is what Derrida is attempting to show in his reply to Gadamer, in this particular performance of his.[2]

I am not claiming that this was in fact his intention since, as a (phenomenological) hermeneut, I do not have access to the author's intentions, only to the text. I do, however (as a hermeneut), have to try to make sense of the text, of, as Gadamer would say, "the 'intentionality' of the discourse" (*HMP* 396), and I don't readily perceive any other hermeneutical tactic ("strategy" or "protocol," as Derrida would say) for doing so. How else are we to make sense of what in Derrida's response to Gadamer (and in remarks of his elsewhere) is manifest nonsense, a caricaturial misreading of Gadamer and hermeneutics? Can it be anything other than a calculated and deliberate misunderstanding? Let us consider a point or two.

In "the tangle of the web of questions and remarks" (Response) that bore the title, *"Bonnes volontés de puissance,"* Derrida immediately zeroed in on a remark Gadamer had made in his talk the previous evening. In a conversation, Gadamer had said, "Both partners must have the good will to try to understand one another" (TI 33). This is indeed a basic hermeneutical point. As a general rule, one will often not understand another person unless one wants to do so and makes an effort to do so. Without this, one will more than likely simply read one's own presuppositions into what the other is saying and will, accordingly, *mis*understand what he or she is saying. Genuine communication necessitates a continual effort at overcoming the various distortions that are endemic to communicative praxis. Psychoanalysis, which Derrida knows more than enough about, has driven home this lesson to us in a most forceful way. What does Derrida say in response?

With a notable (and no doubt deliberate) lack of "good will" in the hermeneutical sense, Derrida proceeds to accuse Gadamer of endorsing what Heidegger, as he says, "calls the determination that the being of beings is will, or the willing subjectivity." Derrida suggests that to speak of good will is to show that one belongs to "a particular epoch—that of a metaphysics of the will." In effect, as the French title of his reply indicates, Derrida is accusing Gadamer of subscribing to a metaphysics of the "will to power."

An accusation such as this is bound to (calculated to?) strike anyone who is conversant with Gadamer's writings as being thoroughly bizarre. Before saying more about this, however, it might be worth while to take note of a seeming irony at work in Derrida's attack on Gadamer. Derrida accuses Gadamer of being immured in the metaphysics of subjectivity, of promoting a "willing subjectivity," a willing that is a will to power. Most listeners (and Derrida is surely aware of this) will understand "will to power" in the customary sense, as the will to a self-asserting domination. And yet this is a reading of Nietzsche's famous phrase that Derrida, for one, has strenuously objected to. He has attacked Heidegger precisely on this score, for portraying Nietzsche as "the last metaphysician," as the spokesman for an unbridled, subjectivistic will to power. Setting aside all questions as to the appropriateness of Heidegger's reading of Nietzsche, it is clear that what motivated Heidegger was his desire to make a definitive break with subjectivism and the "metaphysics of presence." The fact that Gadamer sided with Heidegger's reading of Nietzsche[3] would seem to indicate, at the very least, that he too has absolutely no desire to defend the metaphysics of subjectivity, that, indeed, the basic purpose of his hermeneutical thinking has been to overcome subjectivism in a decisive way. It is odd, or ironic, that Derrida should rely on a standard reading of Nietzsche, which he himself does not accept, in order to accuse Gadamer of subscribing to something that he himself explicitly rejects (i.e., subjectivism). To be sure, there is a "logic" to all of this. If Derrida were outrightly to object to Gadamer's reading of Nietzsche, he would soon find that their interpretive differences are mediated by a common concern, a common ground, namely, the critique of subjectivism. A genuine conversation aiming at some kind of agreement would inevitably ensue. But this would automatically undermine Derrida's anti-hermeneutical position. Thus, he must pursue the peculiar tactic that he does. For Derrida, it is essential that Gadamer remain "the lost sheep in the dried up pastures of metaphysics" (LD 94).

In his reply to Derrida's reply to him, Gadamer remarked: "I am finding it difficult to understand these questions that have been addressed to me." They are indeed, as we said before, bizarre. It is hard to see how someone who maintains that self-understanding "does not refer to the unshakable certainty of self-consciousness at all," who maintains, on the contrary, that self-understanding is "something unfulfillable, an ever new undertaking and an ever new defeat" (LD 97), could properly be accused of lending support to the metaphysics of presence. As Gadamer himself asks (being close, no doubt, to desperation): "Is this really 'the way of metaphysics'? Is this logocentrism?" (Ibid.). Gadamer nevertheless does make an effort (good will) to understand Derrida's objections, remarking in the process: "I absolutely cannot see that this effort would have anything to do with 'the epoch of metaphysics' " (Reply). Indeed, a non-deconstructive reading of Gadamer would clearly show, I am certain, that Gadamerian hermeneutics is, in regard to metaphysics or what Gadamer refers to in his talk as "the epistemological era" (TI 22), as least as deconstructive as deconstruction.[4] That what we have to do with in philosophical hermeneutics is a thoroughgoing rejection of the metaphysics of presence, of the traditional conception of understanding as coincidence with a pure presence, of truth as mirroring, reproductive adequation, is clearly enough indicated in Gadamer's remark (explicitly addressed to Derrida): "I too affirm that understanding is always understanding-differently [*Anders-verstehen*]" (LD 96).

On the face of it, therefore, it is difficult to make any sense of Derrida's "questions." Derrida must surely be familiar with Gadamer's various writings (it is a first principle of hermeneutics that one should have first read those texts one interprets, in whatever way one does).[5] And he is surely able to construe clearly what is manifestly said therein (to do so is a basic, initial requirement of the deconstructive enterprise). Since hermeneutics works under the assumption that in normal circumstances and in the case of normal people (i.e., those who are not manifest psychopaths or raving idiots), one is attempting to communicate something, that there is something to be understood in what people say, we are accordingly led to ask: What is it that Derrida is trying to say here?

From what has already been said, it is clear that Derrida is not uttering normal philosophical utterances and is not seeking to engage in a normal philosophical dialogue. Derrida is not one of those serious-minded philosophers who "say what they mean and mean what they say." In a spirit of good will, we indeed credit him with not really meaning what he seems to be saying about Gadamer, since, as was mentioned, this is manifest nonsense. Perhaps then, if he does not really mean what he says, he means something else. Now there is a name for that *façon de parler* that consists in saying one thing and meaning something else thereby. It is called "irony."

Should we, therefore, in our hermeneutical attempt to understand Derrida, classify him as an ironist? It is not at all certain, however, that to do so would be to do him a service. The reason for this is that even irony carries with it the hermeneutical presupposition of meaningfulness and mutual understandability. In "Text and Interpretation" (30–51) Gadamer discusses various forms of textuality. One form of textuality, an "oppositional" one, consists of what he calls "antitexts," the prime examples of which are jokes of every kind and irony. When we recall that Derrida is often considered to be a "joking" writer, Gadamer's remarks on antitextuality take on a certain pertinance to the hermeneutical situation at hand. Gadamer writes: " . . . the fact that we do not mean something seriously but rather expect that it will be taken as a joke surely stations this form in the process and event of communication." What Gadamer is saying here is that joking is a "quite classical form of mutual agreement." Irony is another. "For the use of irony presupposes a common set of prior cultural understandings. When one is able to say the opposite of what one means and still be sure that what one really means is understood, this clearly shows one to be in a functioning communicative situation."

Thus, even irony reinforces Gadamer's hermeneutical assumption that "Whoever opens his mouth wants to be understood." Irony is most certainly a form of communication aiming at mutual understanding; indeed, if a speaker does not succeed in communicating to his audience a definite, decidable meaning by means of his irony, he has failed to do much of anything at all. Irony is thus a form of communication, one which for Kierkegaard would fall under the heading of "indirect communication." Its particularizing characteristic, distinguishing it from "normal," straightforward utterances ("The cat is on the mat"), is that it is directed to a specialized audience; by its very nature it deliberately excludes from its sphere of meaningful intelligibility those who are not privy to a particular "set of prior understandings."

Even if we take Derrida as an ironist (in our hermeneutical attempt to make some sense of his utterances), we may still find it difficult to make sense of what he is saying in his response. For as one writer has remarked, Derrida's irony is so supreme that in his case it is not simply a matter of saying one thing and meaning another; his is an irony "in the heightened sense of saying one thing and meaning, or 'wishing to say,' nothing at all."[6] However that may be, Derrida's irony might appear to serve him well in this particular conversational encounter. It would appear to be a superb means for contesting Gadamer's insistence on "good will." For while his ironic, parodying presentation of Gadamer's position renders it very difficult for his interlocutor to understand what he is saying and, accordingly, to respond to him meaningfully in such a way as to carry on the conversation, at the same time it allows him to communicate a definite message to his own specialized audience present at the interchange, this message being, of course, the impossibility of good will in dialogue. However, when all is said and done, it is hard to see this particular conversational gambit as being anything other than a particular exercise in the will to power, indeed a power play to shut one's interlocutor out from the conversation—insuring thereby, and in advance, its failure (and, at the same time, the speaker's own success).

In the final analysis, what Derrida is attempting to do by means of his ironic, parodying, performative utterances is perhaps to teach Gadamer, his philosophical senior, a lesson, a lesson, precisely, in the power plays latent in so-called philosophical dialogue. We know that the main object of Derrida's derision is Gadamer's insistence on good will. Perhaps what Derrida is trying to say, performatively, is something like this: One can, with good will, come to mutual agreements, no doubt about it. But these agreements are in reality *coerced*—by the very nature of the practical situation in which they occur. For the conversational situation is one that is characterized by a constitutional inequality of position, of power, such as the relationship between teacher and student, physician and patient, employer and employee, elderly, well-established philosopher (read: mandarin) and younger, contestatory, anti-philosopher. In cases such as these, the notion of an open dialogue in which the interlocutors share an equal status and seek to arrive at a pure, disinterested agreement, determined by good will alone, is chimerical, and utopic. It is, in fact, the manifestation of a false consciousness and can be productive of nothing but false understanding (no real understanding at all). Thus, the appeal to good will is a diversion, a mask, a cover for the exercise of power, albeit perhaps of an unconscious and nondeliberate sort.

If, *per hypothesis,* this were what Derrida is saying, the irony of it all would indeed be supreme. Derrida's lesson (the hidden power dynamics in the communication process) is a most legitimate one, but it is also one that Gadamer already knows by heart. He does not need any instruction on the subject. Besides being fully aware of the operative forces of domination [*Herrschaft*] subtending our linguisticality, as his *Auseinandersetzung* with Habermas made clear (and as his rectorship at Leipzig no doubt revealed to him in a highly concrete way),[7] he has no idyllic illusions about the ease of achieving understanding and undistorted, mutual agreement; this, he says, requires "a never-ending dialogue"(Reply).[8] "Of course," he replies to Derrida, "we encounter limits again and again; we speak past each other and are even at cross-purposes with ourselves. But in my opinion we could not do this at all if we had not travelled a long way together, perhaps without even acknowledging it" (Reply).

On the power issue Gadamer and Derrida are in agreement to a considerable extent. They do differ though in a crucial respect. Derrida seems to want to reject recourse to good will altogether, viewing it as nothing more than mere camouflage for an exercise in the will to power. What he would put forward in its place is never made clear. Gadamer is not a believer in utopia, nor is he so naive as to think that reliance on good will is sufficient of itself to set aside relations of power and overcome dominating interests. He does think, however, that in the absence of an ideal society and in the absence of perfect equality (a concept that is, as he might say, facticious) good will is the *sine qua non* for building genuine human solidarity; that, without it, only relationships of brute force (masked by ideology) would prevail among men. Thus, the significant difference between Gadamer and Derrida, as this encounter succeeds in showing after all, is the difference between humanism and anti-humanism.

If, in some future encounter, Derrida were to address questions on this whole issue of power to Gadamer, but this time in good will and with the intention of exploring the issue in the hope of coming to a mutual understanding, a genuine and lively dialogue would surely ensue. Much, however, would be at risk in such a conversation; Derrida in particular would be running the risk of alienating that specialized audience which is composed of the addressees of his particular brand of ultra-ironic discourse. After having been exposed for so many years to *"un discours qui ne veut rien dire,"* they might experience some difficulty in understanding when there is actually something that can be understood. Given the vested interests operative in the academic community in general, such a dialogue would be the most "improbable" of all—immensely more improbable than the one which occurred at the Goethe Institute in Paris in April of 1981.

Herman Rapaport

7. All Ears: Derrida's Response to Gadamer

> But it seems to me that I go beyond Derrida's
> deconstruction, since words exist only in conver-
> sation and never exist there as an isolated word,
> but as the totality of a way of accounting, by
> means of talking and answering.
>
> —Hans-Georg Gadamer, "*Destruktion*
> and Deconstruction"

The "Three Questions to Hans-Georg Gadamer" by Jacques Derrida in-
tervene disruptively and can be heard as a splitting of the ear, or, if one prefers,
an earsplitting discourse. That is, Derrida prefers to hear what Gadamer has
said with different ears, as if to say that just as no two pairs of ears ever look the
same, they also never hear in just the same way. "The first question," Derrida
remarks, "concerns what [Gadamer] said to us last evening about good will,
about appealing to one's good will, and to the absolute obligation to desire
consensus in understanding." Such a question, Derrida argues, should challenge
the presupposition that understanding is conditioned not only by an appeal to
good will, but also by a mutual agreement that speakers will make themselves
clearly heard even as they try their best to listen to others. Gadamer's belief that
"the mere presence of the other before whom we stand helps us to break up our
own bias and narrowness, even before he opens his mouth to make a reply" rests
on the assumption that we can all hear with the same ears (TI 26). This is why
Gadamer can say that the appeal by and for an other belongs to experience
generally as "a potentiality for being other [*Andersseins*] that lies beyond every
coming to agreement about what is common" (TI 26).

In *The Ear of the Other* Derrida addresses "the difference in the ear" as an
autobiographical listening to oneself through the ears of an other. Not unlike
Gadamer, Derrida recognizes the potentiality of otherness that can be detected

beyond agreement over what is common, an otherness heard through the ears of someone else. "The ear of the other says me to me and constitutes the *autos* of my autobiography" (*EO* 51). However, this "*autos*" is, as Derrida's pun suggests, vehicular. It moves or transports the locus of the subject in ways that disarticulate subjecthood even to the point of disrupting the hermeneutics of Gadamer. Recall that in *Truth and Method* Gadamer considers hermeneutics a listening to an account from the other, a listening that is open to what we might call the "ear of the other." This interpretive availability "always includes our placing the other meaning in a relation with the whole of our own meanings or ourselves in relation to it" (*WM* 253/238). For Derrida, however, the ear of the other disarticulates the relation with the whole of our own meanings, because it participates in a deconstruction of the "autos" as something with a determinate reference point. Of course, Gadamer's hermeneutics does not presuppose a fixed subject-centered notion of philosophical inquiry; this is precisely what Gadamer is emphatically rejecting. However, in Gadamer the subject takes place as a horizon wherein one can understand or temporarily place the meanings of others. We must comprehend listening, then, as a subordination of the various ears through which we hear to a larger sense of receptivity—Gadamer calls it "dialogue"—in which everything heard can be placed in relationship for the sake of arriving at an interpretation or understanding. However, such a melding of what is heard necessitates a lowering of aural difference, a limiting of what Derrida calls "the difference in the ear," or what I have referred to as the earsplitting.

In *The Ear of the Other,* Derrida explores how philosophical discourse operates like a technological emission or transmission that is irreconcilably split between the collective ears who hear. Hence, Derrida presupposes that in mass media broadcasting we do not ever hear individual voices that are reducible to one specific source. Rather, we hear synthesized voice residues transmitted by someone who impersonates the voice's subject. This impersonation, however, is merely a metaphysical trapping, the illusion that voice emanates from a subject who has the capacity to control or intend expression. Voice, not unlike a musical note, is a construction of overtones and as such is inherently split. Of course, the function of the enunciator or addresser is to harmonize the voices, to bring them into such a relationship that we assume only one person is speaking, that the voice has been listened to, originally, by only one set of ears belonging to the speaker. However, such a voice is never entirely harmonized; in fact, it is always somewhat dissonant or untuned. We become aware of such untunings when we listen to mass media voices from the past, since their tuning depends largely upon conditioning: the repeated appeal to accept voice as a unified tonal construction that we take to be the direct expression of a single addresser. Anyone who listens to outdated radio commercials or even the old radio broadcasts of performances by well-known opera stars will notice the voices within the voices, which is to say, that "différance" of the voice that splits the ear.

Derrida is very sensitive to such a splitting of the ear in philosophy when he considers Nietzsche's discussion of education, because elements of this discussion have been passed on to us through the broadcasting media.

> Democratic and equalizing education, would-be academic freedom in the university, the maximal extension of culture—all these must be replaced by constraint, discipline [*Zucht*], and a process of selection under the direction of a guide, a leader or *Führer,* even a *grosse Führer* (*EO* 27).

Derrida is quick to point out that,

> Doubtless it would be naive and crude simply to extract the word *"Führer"* from this passage and to let it resonate all by itself in its Hitlerian consonance, with the echo it received from the Nazi orchestration of the Nietzschean reference, as if this word had no other possible context (*EO* 28).

However, Derrida thinks it would be "peremptory to deny that something is going on here . . . which passes from the Nietzschean *Führer,* who is not merely a schoolmaster and master of doctrine, to the Hitlerian *Führer,* who also wanted to be taken for a spiritual and intellectual master, a guide in scholastic doctrine and practice, a teacher of regeneration" (*EO* 28).

In other words, Nietzsche's texts take place as a discursive means of broadcasting ideas that split the ears, since this broadcasting involves a political divergence in Germany wherein emerges not only the notion of a *Führer* principle, but the figure of the *Führer* who is himself a broadcasting agency, a figure whose words are extremely earsplitting in the worst sense. Speaking of this sort of utterance, Derrida invokes a "powerful utterance-producing machine" that programs the movements of a divided discourse. This machine does not decipher; rather, it transforms. Certainly, not too much imagination is needed to realize that such a "machine" is the media and that at issue is an apparatus very much like radio through which discursive philosophical fragments are modulated or transformed. Hence, Nietzschean philosophical emissions need to be considered in terms of how they are channeled through an apparatus—specifically, a fascist one—that is set up in such a way that a philosophical discourse necessarily splits the ears. In this sense Derrida pursues the figure of the ear in its larger technological context as amplifier or, to borrow a term from high fidelity language, "speaker."

Indeed, this metaphorical reading of the ear opens up the question of transmission in ways that go against the grain of those who would argue that Derrida is neglecting the most basic differences between texts and contexts. For example, when Nietzsche talks about the *Führer,* this is in no way to be confused with how Hitler uses the term, because the signatures (authorial intentions), events (addresses, times in which the utterances took place), and contexts (philosophy, politics, etc.) are so radically different. Yet, by way of the metaphor of the ear, Derrida suggests that despite these differences, there is something in the supplementary structure of addresser/addressee (the ear, the amplifier, or, in hi-fi terms, the receiver, the speaker) that complicates the determinability of an utterance and disrupts the self-identity of notions like signature, event, or context. Certainly, such self-identity rests on the assumption that one is always hearing with the same ears, that the subject who hears remains constant. This constancy of the ear is a question already raised in Plato's *Phaedrus* when Socrates comments on the broadcasting of discourse as writing, "And once a thing is put in writing, the composition, whatever it may be, drifts all over the place, getting into the hands not only of those who understand it, but also equally of those who have no business with it; it doesn't know how to address the right people, and not address the wrong."[1] Clearly, the emphasis on voice in the *Phaedrus* exists in order to ensure that everyone hears with the same ears.

This orientation to discourse is supported by Gadamer's hermeneutics, exemplified in "Text and Interpretation."

> Plato's presentation of Socrates shows that when leading the conversation Socrates always insisted upon demanding an account from the other and upon leading others back to themselves by convicting them of their pretended wisdom . . .
> (TI 27).

Socrates, Gadamer argues, always allows his interlocutors to hear themselves through his ears or to hear himself through their ears in order that logos can be disclosed as "common to all" rather than the property of one person claiming to speak the truth. However, such a lending and borrowing of ears depends upon the good will between the participants of the dialogue. Socrates assumes such good will even in the face of a very hostile interlocutor such as Thrasymachus in *The Republic.* Socrates himself notices: "And I, when I heard him, was dismayed, and looking upon him was filled with fear, and I believe that if I had not looked at him before he did at me I should have lost my voice" (336d). Yet, Socrates keeps his voice because he allows Thrasymachus to listen to himself through Socrates' ears, to hear himself through the perspective of an other. In this way even someone as utterly self-centered as Thrasymachus is encouraged to hear through ears that are "common to all," an imaginary ear in which meanings are made plain. However, this ear not only places different arguments clearly into perspective by intellectually filtering out their incompatibilities or differences through a certain aural tuning or agreement, but also this ear provides a stable reference point so that the participants in the dialogue can hear themselves in terms of the ears of tradition that are a common ground for understanding. Socrates knows better than anyone that Thrasymachus only represents a tradition that he has only overheard, that Thrasymachus is little else but a pair of ears seduced by a rhetoric of tyranny. And the purpose of the dialogue is not only to listen with this pair of borrowed ears but also to arrive at a better understanding of statesmanship by lending the ear of Socratic philosophy in a spirit of good will.

Nietzsche, of course, listens with ears that are attuned to bad will, and it is he who says, with bad will in mind, that the ear of the other is what signs for a text long after it has been written. Tradition, then, is a signing not by the pen of the author but by the jaded ears of those who read according to their own interests. This suspicion is peculiarly clairvoyant, given the history of Nietzsche's reception in Germany during the thirties, and Derrida's remarks about the National Socialist reading of Nietzsche pertain largely to this insight that those who sign with their ears do not do so in a spirit of good will but, rather, with much more malevolent intent. Addressing Nietzsche, Derrida wonders:

> Is this our situation? Is it a question of the same ear, a borrowed ear, the one that you are lending me or that I lend myself in speaking? Or rather, do we hear, do we understand each other already with another ear? (*EO* 35)

If the borrowing and lending of ears concerns a situation in which bad will can be at issue, this will is not the cause of the splitting of the ear. Rather, ill will, though not always easily distinguishable from good will, ought to be viewed as the effect of splitting.

Derrida develops this structural reading of wills at much greater length in *The Post Card* in which the relationship between Socrates and Plato is discussed in terms of the ear of the other that signs, which is to say, the affixing by Socrates' ear of a signature to Plato's writings. Not only had Derrida discovered such a *mise-en-scène* of Plato speaking into the ear of Socrates in the illumination by the medieval artist, Matthew Paris, but Derrida has also detected that "Plato's eye indeed bespeaks anger" (*CP*/49). Developed at great length in *The Post Card* is how this anger is the effect of intellectual transmission, of listening relays. Read back into the discussion of Nietzsche in *The Ear of the Other* one wonders if the ill will Nietzsche clairvoyantly anticipates in the ears of those who will sign for him is not always already endemic to Western philosophy and to the notion of dialogue itself.

When we turn to Derrida's second question: "What would good will mean in a psychoanalysis?"—or, to put it in a related sense, what does interpretation mean from a psychoanalytic perspective in which splitting has occurred?—we find Derrida remarking, "Such interpretation would perhaps be closer to interpretation in the style of Nietzsche than to that other hermeneutical tradition extending from Schleiermacher to Gadamer." That is, the styles of the Nietzschean dispatch divide or split apart that hermeneutical approach Gadamer invokes in "*Destruktion* and Deconstruction" when he writes,

> One must look for the word that can reach another person. And it is possible for one to find it; one can even learn the language of the other person. One can cross over into the language of the other in order to reach the other. All this is possible for language as language (DD 364/106).[2]

Gadamer's remarks suggest that words can be found in which to bring about an understanding of what is different or other, an understanding based on a measure of good will. Yet, such a hermeneutical approach bears on what from Derrida's view looks very much like an interpretive gesture wherein differences are made to adapt to norms of social consensus. When Derrida, later, cites Gadamer as acknowledging "that experience [*Erfahrung*] that we all recognize" he is wondering to what extent Gadamer's philosophy relies upon the experience of a normative subject. This is a question Paul Ricoeur also raises in "*La tâche de l'herméneutique en venant de Schleiermacher et de Dilthey*" when he suggests that human experience underwrites the Gadamerian enterprise and that it is as action that such experience in dealing with the past "obliges us," in Gadamer's words, "to take experience totally in charge, assuming in some sense its truth."[3] Such action, Ricoeur suggests, presupposes a distance in which the difference between self and other must remain determinate.

Indeed, Derrida's third question, "Is not rather the interruption of *rapport,* a certain *rapport* of interruption, the suspending of all mediation?", is precisely one that takes issue with the self-presentation of experience as it occurs in that dialogue where understanding takes the place of interruption, an interruption crucial, for example, to those who practice the talking cure, which is to say, to those who take French Freudian thought seriously. Derrida recognizes, then, that Gadamer cannot hear that which is earsplitting, because he will not allow himself to listen for the splitting of the ego that is the precondition upon which psychoanalytic interpretation depends and which the counseling techniques of what we call "understanding" routinely fail to recognize. Although it would be mistaken to confuse Gadamer's philosophy with ego psychology, Derrida's point appears to be that Gadamer's hermeneutics has the effect of operating like a normative psychologism that functions in the service of a society concerned with the building and maintenance of values in whose interest one is not likely to think in terms of how one ear signs for another.

Since I am only making an intervention, there are just two questions of my own that I would like to pose. First, I am wondering if Derrida's text is implicitly suggesting that the hermeneutics of Gadamer may be raising interesting ethical questions because it cannot acknowledge the earsplitting of the philosophical dispatch and therefore is vulnerable to the dynamics, political or otherwise, of the ears that sign for us in our name? If it was ethical for Gadamer not to listen with fascist ears during the 1930s—Gadamer's personal and philosophical repudiation of Nazi "nonsense" is well-documented in *Philosophical Apprenticeships*—what are the consequences of this ethical refusal to listen in a philosophical context?[4] Given Derrida's remarks on Nietzsche in *The Ear of the Other* one suspects that the most defensible turning a deaf ear is not unproblematic. Still, how can a philosophy, and especially a hermeneutical project like that of Gadamer, allow itself to be compromised by listening with the morally objectionable ears of a murderous ill will? Does a reading of Derrida's response to Gadamer in tandem with his remarks on Nietzsche in *The Ear of the Other* not demonstrate that in philosophy we may be double binded with respect to the ethical?

My second question concerns the notion of ethics as it pertains to Derrida's reading by way of Nietzsche's ears. I am wondering how the notion of ethics can be posed in terms of what a philosophical dispatch donates? Given the splitting of the ear and the knowledge that "good will" cannot function as a ground for listening, where are we left, ethically speaking? How are we to consider the ethics of the ear of the other, the divisibility of the ears who hear? Certainly this sort of question, as well as Derrida's analysis, is already anticipated by Nietzsche in *Beyond Good and Evil*. But does Derrida make much headway with it, or is his highly metaphorical argument but an amplification of what Nietzsche wrote, for example, in the following passage?

> All sorts of new what-fors and wherewithals; no shared formulas any longer; misunderstanding allied with disrespect; decay, corruption, and the highest desires gruesomely entangled; the genius of the race overflowing from all cornucopias of good and bad; a calamitous simultaneity of spring and fall, full of new charms and veils that characterize young, still unexhausted, still unwearied corruption. Again, danger is there, the mother of morals, great danger, this time transposed into the individual, into the neighbor and friend, into the ally, into one's own child, into one's own fear, into the most personal and secret recesses of wish and will: what may the moral philosophers emerging in this age have to preach now? (*BGE* § 262)[5]

Donald G. Marshall

8. *Dialogue and* Écriture

For this volume, I have been asked to join others in commenting on the "encounter" between Gadamer and Derrida. Unfortunately, the assignment cannot be carried out, since the encounter never took place. Whatever the organizers imagined might take place, the result was hardly worth their efforts in planning. Gadamer presented a comprehensive survey of his views on "Text and Interpretation" and on language in all its forms—a remarkable summary, perhaps too condensed and wide-ranging to be easily taken in, but constructed to make Derrida's task easy by displaying every fundamental position that he might make the target of penetrating criticism. Having had a night to sleep on it, Derrida rose—with what eager anticipation from the audience may be easily imagined—and posed three questions: the first missed the philosophical milieu of the relatively minor term "good will" he picked out of Gadamer's lecture; the second precisely reversed Gadamer's argument; and the third raised what may seem a plausible question about Gadamer's concept of "continuity," though the slightest acquaintance with Gadamer's work would show that Derrida's suspicions about what that concept means or implies are entirely unfounded.[1]

To read so feeble a "response" from the most distinguished French philosopher since Sartre is certainly embarrassing and can be explained only on the assumption that Derrida knows little or nothing of Gadamer's work and was too preoccupied with what he intended to say in his own lecture on this occasion to give much attention to Gadamer's remarks. I have shown elsewhere in a discussion of Derrida's writings on Maurice Blanchot with what exemplary generosity, openness, and finesse Derrida can enter into dialogue and real friendship with a line of thought to which he responds with genial affinity.[2] As someone who has long admired Gadamer, besides disappointment and embarrassment, I felt rather a real alarm: would Gadamer be tempted to take advantage of Derrida's blunders and disgrace himself as a philosopher and a human being by replying with that vindictive triumphalism that makes Derrida's polemics against Searle, Nixon, and McClintock such a painful humiliation to read? Gadamer's reply certainly shows his surprise and bewilderment. But he passes quickly over the first two questions and then works hard to formulate the objection a thoughtful critic might have intended by Derrida's third question, to which he then replies. Having evaded the danger that he might learn something from talking with Gadamer, Derrida was then free to ignore Gadamer completely and display his accustomed deconstructive pyrotechnics on Heidegger on Nietzsche.

I have no illusion that my response to this so-called encounter will be widely shared. The devotees of deconstruction will carry on their collective monologue and assure each other, without bothering to read him, that Gadamer is naive, old-fashioned, metaphysical, insufficiently radical, even—*horribile dictu*—humanist. Derrida will go about his merry way, jetting here and there and ignoring the whole thing. Only those concerned with hermeneutics will find it necessary on principle to continue the effort to bring about some real dialogue. And Gadamer is already in their forefront. Instigated by Fred Dallmayr's effort to "flesh out" this "debate," to make himself the medium for a genuine encounter, Gadamer again tried to take deconstruction seriously. In his "Letter to Dallmayr," Gadamer is in the position of Socrates in the *Apology,* when Meletus is simply unable to sustain even an accusatory dialogue. And like Socrates, Gadamer follows the method of *eumeneis elenchoi,* not only supplying the strongest objections Derrida could make but even framing them in his own style!

In *"Destruktion* and Deconstruction," Gadamer again accepts the core obligation of hermeneutics: "Openness to the other, then, includes the acknowledgement that I must accept as valid some things that are against myself, even though there is no one else who asks this of me" (*WM* 343/324). Beginning from Heidegger's effort to break through the "language of metaphysics" to the experience of thinking that was its origin, Gadamer delineates three paths to move dialectic back "into the open": Heidegger's own venture of seeking guidance from the language of poetry; Gadamer's "path from dialectic back to dialogue, back to conversation"; and Derrida's deconstructive path "through an ontological concept of *écriture,"* that would dissolve "the unitariness of sense as such" by tracing "the background network of relationships of meaning which is the basis of all language." What I wish to do here is simply to reflect a little further on the two paths of hermeneutics and deconstruction, the paths of dialogue and writing, and by displacing these concepts from the questionable interest polemics and the taking of sides have for our era, to lead toward whatever may emerge from that reflection.

In the light of modern philological study, one recognizes in these terms at once the theme of "orality and literacy." Developed by Mathias Murko, Milman Parry, and Albert Lord to explain how the Homeric epics were composed and thus to solve traditional problems of style and authorship, the larger cultural implications of the concept of orality were fully drawn by Eric Havelock and a series of studies ably surveyed by Jack Goody and Ian Watt. The whole subject has been repeatedly surveyed and synthesized by Walter Ong in many books.[3] In these studies, "oral formulaic technique" is no longer simply an epic compositional device, but a technology by which an entire culture is fixed and transmitted. Shaped to the physiology and psychology of human memory, orality requires that individual members of a culture develop into collective agents subordinated to its preservation. An orally transmitted culture must monopolize the memory of individuals and demands constant rehearsal, eliminating any possibility of critical distance or the play of individual consciousness. Doubtless this picture is exaggerated. Different individuals within an oral culture certainly have different levels of responsibility for mastering and preserving the culture as a whole. The legitimating self-understanding of such a culture, which claims that everything is an unaltered inheritance from the ancestors, conceals a ceaseless process of innovation and adaptation. Lévi-Strauss' *Tristes Tropiques* makes clear that the problems of individual leadership are as real in the most "primitive" as in the most "developed" society. We obviously have access to oral culture in antiquity only through surviving texts. We learn of contemporary "oral" cultures through the written reports of ethnographers themselves raised in literate cultures. Only a somewhat abstract projection would show the consistency, the inner solidity of the concept of "oral culture."

In fact the concept of orality is intelligible only in dialectical relation to the concept of literacy. In the transition to literacy and the struggle against the uncritically participatory absorption demanded by orality, Havelock locates the emergence of linear, conceptual thinking; self-consciousness and personality; the separation of knower from known and the conceptualization of a body distinct from a unified spirit or self; critical awareness of language and self-reflection about the customs it records and the very medium of that recording; the separation of information and modes for recording it from linear plots and characters possessing psychological depth; the search for an abstract, conceptually-based certainty, detached from experience and couched in a visual idiom of "clear ideas" or "theoretical insight." Elizabeth Eisenstein's massive *The Printing Press as an Agent of Change* finds the decisive consolidation of all these changes in the invention of printing, as a result of which the means of communication set the invisible boundaries within which modern cultural life transpires.[4]

The obvious difficulty with this opposition of "orality" to "literacy" is not only its irresistible evaluative bias, but its static character. In the spirit of Derrida, one may certainly ask how orality could be subject to so completely external a disaster? Does not the logic of supplementarity demand that orality already contain some trace of that opposite through which alone it can be made intelligible? More relevant to my reflection, is not the linking of orality to dialogue and of literacy to writing in the sense of *écriture* too hasty? For what every student of orality insists on is its monological character. Oral culture does not seek

response, but only repetition. It guards carefully against every tendency to multiply voices and must be simply accepted or rejected in its monological unity.
And on the other side, what Havelock sees as the progeny of writing are the
very concepts of Western metaphysics Derrida sees *écriture* as simultaneously
establishing and subverting, knitting and unravelling.

These complications come to precise focus in the interpretation of Plato's
Phaedrus. Havelock reads Plato as the relentless champion of literacy against an
orality whose self-evidence had been destroyed by Sophistic and by the political
disasters of the fifth century. But in his renowned "Plato's Pharmacy," Derrida
sees Plato as defending the "living" oral word against "dead" writing, severed
from its "father" and available to a promiscuous audience, unstitching the unity
of *logos* in its endless texture and ramifications.[5] Certainly it is puzzling to find
Plato seemingly unaware of the paradoxes in writing against writing and equally
puzzling to find him making the written word the vehicle to preserve the spoken
word of dialogue. In a short essay, *"Unterwegs zur Schrift?"*, Gadamer takes a
different perspective.[6] All writing poses the question whether "there is not in
the use of words always already something like a drive toward fixation." In its
reliance on formulas, orality already exhibits this drive. Similarly, in "Dialectic
and Sophism in Plato's *Seventh Letter,*" Gadamer shows how the unending labor
of dialectic penetrates and transforms mere talk in the Socratic art of conversing.
There is consequently no inconsistency when in the *Phaedrus* Socrates speaks of
a "discourse" (*logos*) "written in the soul of the hearer." In oral formula, in
dialectic, and—I would not hesitate to add—in *écriture,* we find the same opposition to the forms of "antitextuality" (to take up Gadamer's term in "Text and
Interpretation") in the erosive contingency of everyday life, forms in which
language, whether spoken or written, is reduced either to empty talk that simply
clings to a momentary social contact or to an unambiguous vehicle of information. Socratic dialogue is by no means opposed to writing, and certainly not as
"voice" to "graph." Dialogue and writing are dialectically intertwined and together set against "idle talk." The real difference between Gadamer's and Derrida's interpretation (as I have argued elsewhere) is that Derrida, following the
"hermeneutics of suspicion," must separate from the text an essentially neoplatonic metaphysics which, he has to claim, Plato wants to mean, though it is
made impossible by the very vehicle of its expression.[7] Gadamer by contrast
argues that Plato invented his literary form, written dialogue, not as a "clever
hiding place for his 'doctrines,' " but as a meaningful expression of them made
possible precisely by the art of writing. Dialogue here captures the temporality
of all insight, the interplay of the "One and thc indeterminate Two," of *aporia*
and *euporia,* which marks "our fruitful situation halfway between single and
multiple meaning, clarity and ambiguity."

Further to complicate the interplay of the concepts of dialogue and *écriture,* I
want again to displace them into another thematic: Mikhail Bakhtin's "dialo-

gism" or "heteroglossia" and Maurice Blanchot's "literary space."⁸ These two
seem to establish end points in the positioning of literature after the dissolution
of orality first through writing and then through print.

Blanchot seeks to rediscover a guiding necessity for discourse in the situation
of a creator completely withdrawn from the oral situation, determined not only
by its immediate relation to a functioning social world, but also by the passing
over of the work to the process of its reception and preservation by the audience.
In a narrative fiction, the withdrawal of the social world from the author is
followed by the withdrawal of everything in himself that still connects him with
that social world, that is, everything "biographical." What remains is language
itself, and in it the creator must seek the necessity of a work's existence. But
language is purely the power (or impotence) of withdrawing. Withdrawn from
"being-in-the-world," the creator enters the solitude of "literary space," an
interminable opening (*l'ouvre*) where he listens for the "whispering" of the
world. The radical discontinuity of this position is unbearable, and the creator
eventually closes it into a work (*l'oeuvre*), which takes the form of a book
(*livre*). The book does not present the writer's experience of essential solitude in
literary space, but fixes the impossibility of its presence not in a language of
images, but in an image of language.

Bakhtin explicitly asserts that among literary forms, "only the novel is
younger than writing and the book" (*DI* 3). His description of the epic—its
social, impersonal world of tradition, memorializing exemplary heroes set in a
distant but not historical past, incorporating a nonlinear network of stories—
closely parallels the concept of orality. Likewise, he recognizes in Socratic
dialogue an early form of the novel. Equally suggestive is the contrast in "Discourse in the Novel" between the direct word of lyric and the heteroglossic or
double-accented word of the novel. Poetic style is monologic and tends to the
authoritarian, dogmatic, and conservative. Rhythm removes the word from its
immediate social context, unifies it, makes it timeless. It can reflect only social
forms of *longue durée,* and even its polysemy and ambiguity are simply ways of
increasing its internal solidarity, withdrawn from every inferior everyday form
of language. By contrast, discourse in the novel, while not incoherent, always
embodies the dialogical interaction of "cited" languages, rooted in different
national groups, professional groups, generations, and so on. Even the author's
language is simply one among these many voices. Heteroglossia penetrates so
deeply that not only do languages clash with each other, but also the word
within a single language is already divided against itself, double-accented,
"cited."

There is here an obvious affinity between Bakhtin's description of the
"lyric" word and Blanchot's profoundly lyric conception of "writing." Even
more striking, seen through this perspective, Blanchot's conception appears as a
strange transformation or perhaps "afterimage" of orality, a "reoccupation" of

that position, to adopt Hans Blumenberg's term.[9] By contrast, Bakhtin's insistent vocabulary of vocality (dialogue, double-accent, double-voice) explicitly belongs to a possibility that emerges with writing and is fulfilled with the printed book. Linking Bakhtin and Blanchot to Derrida and Gadamer considerably deepens the paradox. For it seems to me obvious that despite Derrida's deep and acknowledged indebtedness to Blanchot (and in some measure even for Blanchot's implicit but unmistakable critique of Heidegger), Derrida's spirit is much closer to Bakhtin's carnivalesque celebration of a diversity and mobility that demolish every standardization, totalization, or system. It is true that Bakhtin's temper seems closest to that of the great nineteenth century novelists, who found the resources for presenting in all its comedy and pathos the many-sidedness of life, while Derrida seems to me closer to the tonality of the Enlightenment, which brought critique to exuberant life in irony, invective, and a lucidity that refuse to be positive but are directed toward destroying and clearing away every authoritative prejudice, even those supporting criticism itself. And the dispersal of monological language is for Bakhtin the consequence of a dialogical interplay of speaking persons and groups, rather than a dissemination along the network of meanings and figures of the words themselves. Nevertheless, the heteroglossia which opens and invigorates language seems to me close to *écriture*'s work of dissemination. By contrast, Gadamer's insistence on the whole of meaning that is glimpsed in and through the endless stream of dialogue brings him close to Blanchot. In just this spirit Blanchot can speak, precisely in the "exergue" of *Literary Space,* of a "center," toward which even a fragmentary book is attracted—a center that is not fixed, but is displaced in the process of composition, yet a center fixed insofar as it remains the same, growing always more central, more exposed; the writer writes through desire and ignorance of this center. I would not hesitate to say that that is no more the language of metaphysics than is Gadamer's talk of the "whole of meaning," the *Sache,* which dialogue keeps in view by the word toward the "whole of speaking."

Nevertheless, I do not intend to invent mere paradoxes. Gadamer's insistence that "language . . . is always simply that which we speak with others and to others" (LD 98), is surely at one with Bakhtin's "dialogism." And where Derrida is close to Blanchot and seemingly farthest from Gadamer is in the suspicion that in understanding and mutual agreement [*Verstehen* and *Einverständis*] hermeneutics confirms the continuity of the understanding consciousness at the price of ceding to the otherness of the other. Derrida could easily have applied to Gadamer's conception of the "event" character of meaning the critique he develops using Blanchot of Heidegger's conception of the "event of Being" [*Ereignis*]. Derrida rests on the exemplary force of Blanchot's narratives, which form themselves around a key event that does not and cannot happen.[10] The "event" (to adopt one of the English renderings of Heidegger's *Er-eignis*) never "ar-rives." In that case, the event of meaning never arrives in dialogue. The "*pas au'dela,*" the "step beyond," is "*pas au'dela,*" "no beyond," a non-step, a "*pas pas,*" the double negation reverberating with the double positive ["*oui oui*"] that shakes the univocal certainty of affirmation and truth. Gadamer stresses that understanding and the common ground of agreement rely on tradition, the stream of all that comes down to us from the past. But if there is no shore, no "*rive,*" and this happening or coming down never touches shore ["*n'arrive pas*"], then meaning never "comes out" [*evenire*]. Participants in a dialogue are "at sea," their feet touching no common "ground." Their wish for meaning [*vouloir dire*] must exhaust itself in the gymnastics of a will to power, checked only by the arbitrary externality of "good will," which conceals or makes up an alibi for what really takes place: not the arrival of Being or meaning, but the power of *logos* Gorgias named, not "disclosure," but deliberate deception [*apatē*—tragedy deceives, Gorgias remarks, and those only are wise who allow themselves to be taken in by the deception].[11]

I have put this in Derrida's style; Blanchot speaks the language of transcendence. To find the necessity of writing, the writer must withdraw from the world, not into another world, but into the other of world. The theologian puts this as follows: God is wholly other—not just "an" other, but other than any other. Blanchot brings this conceptual framework entirely within the sphere of art. And Gadamer has recognized that the artwork represents the sharpest challenge to his attempt to think through understanding within the temporality of finitude. For not only are works of plastic art withdrawn from the flow of experience into their standing as things, but even language in a poem also withdraws, in Blanchot's term, into the image of language, a fixation which refuses the give-and-take, the compromise between the languages of two interlocutors, which marks even the most intent dialogue. In lyric, language seems to speak with an absolute claim that prevents and precludes response on any equal basis and gives us a blow [*Stoss*] from outside the world within which we engage our fellow beings in dialogue. It is true that the fixity of the poem's language, of which Gadamer speaks and which Blanchot assumes, is an artifact of print. Gerald Bruns has rightly pointed out that even in medieval manuscript culture, the poem presents itself as a version with no fixed archetype or *Urtext,* just as under conditions of "orality" the particular poem is improvised in never exactly repeated performances out of an interwoven web of stories, heroes, situations, and verbal formulas.[12] But it should be clear that we have to do here not only with the absoluteness of art, but with the ethical demands of dialogue itself.

Gadamer has stated in his "Letter to Dallmayr" and elsewhere his reply to this challenge. I think it may be more useful than repeating him to refer to some other reflections on dialogue: Martin Buber's "Dialogue" and Emmanuel Levinas' "*Le Dialogue: Conscience de Soi et Proximité du Prochain.*"[13] If Gadamer and Derrida can stand in oppositon precisely because they continue in different directions the one thinking of Heidegger, Buber's work actually precedes Heidegger's and draws not only on the traditions of German philosophy, but also on the independent traditions of Jewish thought, particularly Hasidism. I begin with Levinas, who is consciously poised between Buber and Heidegger. Levinas traces the path that leads the conception of knowledge back into the enclosure of self-knowledge and self-consciousness. Even a conception of dialogue as "reasonable" dissolves the reciprocal otherness of its partners in the priority accorded the goal of "knowledge" or "reason" over the relations of dialogue itself. Echoing Buber (*BMM* 26), Levinas argues that Plato's description of thinking as a "dialogue of the self with itself" is too enclosed, not genuinely open to the other. Levinas argues that thought transcends (its own) world in dialogue insofar as it finds the "surplus," the "beyond" of proximity to the neighbor, better than any self-confirming coinciding with itself. Dialogue is the original mode of transcendence and brings back into philosophy, against Heidegger, the "beyond" of the world, without postulating, in the manner of the metaphysics Nietzsche criticizes, realms "behind" the world. Levinas finds that Buber too often describes the I-Thou relationship as a harmonious copresence face-to-face, but instead, we should find simply in the urgency with which the self rejects self-sufficiency and opens itself to the other the beginning of responsibility and allegiance, of ethics. Dialogue is not simply symmetrical and reciprocal: the self which opens itself to the other becomes "diaconal," active in the other's service.

In fact, I see nothing here inconsistent with Gadamer. His citation of Plato's description of dialogue as thinking intends to show the sense of Greek *logos*-philosophy, not to validate dialogue with the self over that with the other. Gadamer insists that even the "inner word" that Aquinas takes from the Stoics (through the early Fathers) is not formed by a reflective act, but is always already turned toward the other (*WM* 395–404/378–87). Thinking reserved from actual dialogue is unreal. Even Gadamer's references to "consciousness" must be read in the context of the phrase "*wirkungsgeschichtliches Bewusstsein,*" "consciousness open to the effects of history" (in Paul Ricoeur's apt translation) or "historically effected consciousness" (Joel Weinsheimer). Right from the beginning, consciousness is formed not simply in self-reflection, but as a moment in the ongoing dialogue that we are. Even in relation to literary art, Gadamer recognizes that the poem's internal "texture" holds it beyond the stream of historical life, but finds in that "texture's" demand to resound again not its subordination to "voice," but precisely the temporality of that "tarrying" that is basic to all understanding and is open only to those willing to become "all ear."

This is not only consistent with Blanchot's recognition that genuine literary art is not simply the transcendent, but writing that traces the precisely determinate impossibility of *that* to be present in the world. It also resonates with Buber's double insistence that our dialogue with our fellow humans gains its substance only from a relationship with the transcendent that can never be more than intermittent and also that that relationship with the transcendent has no substance unless we find it through dialogue with our fellow humans. God is not beyond dialogue. But in explicit criticism of Kierkegaard's concept of the "Single One," Buber argues that the primacy of the relationship to God does not nullify our relation to the things and persons within a world understood as creation. Buber rejects Nietzsche's concept of the "will to power": power means "simply the capacity to realize what one wants to realize" (*BMM* 151). Only the feeble or the evil seek power in and of itself. Dialogue emerges when two persons exercise what capacity they have to realize together the present being [*Shekinah*]. In this, I do not see that Levinas in fact improves on Buber. Dialogue means that the I serves the other—not that the other is God, but that I and Thou together serve God, discovering transcendence in the "between." This is not either domination or submission, but a way back from "the loss of reality which responsibility and truth have suffered in our time" (*BMM* 41).

Whether the way back lies through a language of dialogue or of *écriture*—whether there *is* a way back is not for us to know. The austere path of a negative theology, especially when animated with stylistic *élan* and dialectic *brio,* has precisely in its double-nature as irresistible a fascination for our era as for the era of the dissolution of Greek philosophy through the advent of Christianity or for the era of medieval thought's self-dissolution through nominalism (so well studied by Blumenberg). But even in an age that hates nothing so much as the middle ground, it may be timely to recall how "here, in Jerusalem, the Hasidim dance the freedom of the heart to the fellowman" (*BMM* 224).

Richard Shusterman

9. The Gadamer-Derrida Encounter: A Pragmatist Perspective

As Fred Dallmayr notes (HD 76), the Gadamer-Derrida encounter promised to be an important event because its figures virtually personify, in hermeneutics and deconstruction, the two major and rival "schools" of contemporary continental philosophy associated with the primacy of interpretation and antagonistic to positivism, whether it be of the empiricist, structural, or Marxist form. In the struggle permanently to replace positivism with an interpretational model of the human sciences, the alliance of hermeneutics and deconstruction would seem crucial, as their violent rift or rupture might prove fatal. Clearly Dallmayr's efforts to promote a closer dialogue and mediation between the two approaches, his hope "to find a mode of interaction balancing hermeneutics and counterhermeneutics" (HD 92), reflect the enormous stakes involved here, not only theoretical but practically social and political.

But this should suggest a point I wish to emphasize: that the importance of the Gadamer-Derrida encounter transcends the arena of continental philosophy; its issues and disseminations are pregnant with significance for Anglo-American philosophy as well. For this philosophy's recrudescent pragmatism does not merely converge in remarkable ways with Gadamerian and Derridean themes. (We may note, for example, that Gadamer's non-foundational, linguisticized, but tradition-respecting hermeneutics nicely dovetails with W. V. O. Quine's conservative "maxim of minimal mutilation" to our inherited web of belief, and with Nelson Goodman's emphasis on tradition's antecedent practice and entrenchment for the projectibility and inductive fruitfulness of categorial predicates; while Derrida's non-foundational hermeneutic scepticism and critique of meaning is remarkably parallelled by Quine's and Donald Davidson's arguments against synonymy and for the indeterminacy of translation and interpretation.)[1] More strikingly, Gadamer and Derrida have been explicitly appropriated and deployed by more radical pragmatists like Richard Rorty and Joseph Margolis whose work both signals and urges the rapprochement of the continental and Anglo-American traditions.[2] From such a nonpartisan but engaged pragmatist perspective, a perspective of neither one nor the other, nor yet of a radically alien other unsympathetic to both, I wish to examine the Gadamer-Derrida encounter.

I shall concentrate commentary on three central, dividing issues that emerge in Derrida's "Three Questions" to Gadamer in the first encounter. These issues are the context of interpretation, consensual continuity versus rupture as the basis or precondition of interpretation, and the nature or possibility of perfect dialogical understanding. With respect to all three issues, pragmatism can suggest a mode of mediation, though perhaps without pretending the superiority that Gadamer thinks any mediator assumes (TI 41).

1. In that characteristic style that implicitly challenges the surface text of its own discourse, Derrida's three questions are in fact many more, a "web of questions and remarks" (Response). His initial question concerning the Kantian metaphysical foundations of the good will to understand does not touch directly on the issues I treat. But it might be taken as suggestively raising the problem of basing the alleged universal will for communicative solidarity and respect for others on the unconditioned will of individual subjects, whose individual autonomy is essential to the Kantian and liberal humanist tradition, to the very Enlightenment tradition that Gadamer's theme of traditional authority and solidarity is meant to oppose. In its suggestion of the dialectical tension between solidarity and the individual will, unity and difference, this question cannot be as irrelevant to Gadamer's project as Gadamer claims, nor all that distant from my concerns here.

2. It is from Derrida's second question regarding the possible integration of psychoanalysis "into a universal or general hermeneutics" (Response) that the issue of the context of interpretation arises. This issue is crucial for both Gadamer and Derrida, since both regard meaning as in some way context-dependent and fluid. For Gadamer this is clear in his insistence that application (always contextual by nature) is an integral part of understanding and not some external appendage to the allegedly prior and independent moments of understanding and interpretation: "Understanding always involves something like the application of the text to be understood to the present situation of the interpreter"; so that "a text is understood only if it is understood in a different way every time" (*WM* 290–92/274–76; see also LD 96). For Derrida meaning is context-bound since it cannot be based on any prior or extra-linguistic signified or positive essence to which language refers. As the product of language's "systematic play of differences," meaning ineluctably changes as these relations must change through

changing contexts of linguistic use, so that language transforms itself even by the act of trying to repeat itself (see *P* 38–41/27–29). "This is my starting point: no meaning can be determined out of context, but no context permits saturation" (LO 81).

If understanding is always dependent on changing context, how can we talk of people in varying contexts sharing the same understanding, as Gadamer wants to (TI 41; Reply); how can we talk of a true understanding as opposed to a misunderstanding? For even two interlocutors in the same concrete dialogical situation bring with them different contexts or horizons of understanding. Deconstruction is willing to doubt the possibility and experience of shared and perfect understanding, as Derrida's third question makes clear. But Gadamer, for whom such understanding is foundational of all "human solidarity, all social stability" (Reply), tries to recover it through two holistic strategies. Both involve larger unities and totalities of interpretive context, ultimately relating to his concept of tradition. Derrida's question of psychoanalysis tries to expose and challenge these strategies by denying the coherence and mediating unity of Gadamerian tradition on which his idea of shared and true meaning rests, suggesting instead that irreducible and irremediable rupture, fragmentation, and conflict characterize the field of interpretive practices we call "tradition." Let me now spell this out.

Gadamer's first strategy for shared understanding is through his idea of the "fusion of horizons" [*Horizontverschmelzung*] of different individuals or contexts. But what for him ensures the possibility that these different horizons can be fused? The answer is that they are already implicitly joined (hence not fully distinct) "in the depths of tradition" (*WM* 290/273); for tradition is portrayed as an all-encompassing and ever-developing, continuous and unified totality: "A single horizon that embraces everything contained in historical consciousness" (*WM* 288/271). Tradition prestructures and thus unites the different understandings of its participants who are both shaped by it and who continually extend and reshape it. It is plausible that Gadamer could ultimately identify "true" with "shared" understanding; for though some of us may share a *mis*understanding, we could not make sense of everyone always sharing a misunderstanding without reverting to a foundationalist realism. In any case, Gadamer offers a second strategy or test for determining the validity of understanding that does not make immediate appeal to the confirming consensus of other human interlocutors. This is the hermeneutical circle's confirmatory yet enriching working-out of one's foreunderstanding in subsequent interpretation of a text.

> A person . . . trying to understand a text projects before himself a meaning for the text as a whole as soon as some initial meaning emerges in the text. The working out of this fore-project, which is constantly revised in terms of what emerges as he penetrates into the meaning, is understanding what is there . . . .

The only "objectivity" here is in the confirmation of a fore-meaning in its being worked out. The only thing that characterizes the arbitrariness of inappropriate fore-meanings is that they come to nothing in the working-out. (*WM* 251–52/ 236–37)

But tradition and its unity are again crucially present in this project: first, because "the anticipation of meaning that governs our understanding of a text is not an act of subjectivity but proceeds from the communality that binds us to the tradition"; and second, because our whole idea of the anticipation and working-out of meaning relies on the principle of "the fore-conception of completion," that "only what constitutes a unity of meaning is intelligible" (*WM* 278/261), that understanding is where "the unity of the whole formation is lighted up" (TI 48). Interpretation strives to make understanding and its unity of meaning more complete, with the ultimate task of "revealing a totality of meaning in all its relations" (*WM* 446/429). This interpretive aim of more comprehensive and unified meaning accounts for the hermeneutic circularity of whole and parts and for "the hermeneutical principle" that in a conflict of interpretations "the larger context should decide the issue" of which is correct (TI 50). Wider than the sentence, work, corpus, genre, or art form—tradition as a whole remains the largest (and ever expanding) context to seek the greatest possible understanding of any text. But since tradition is open-ended and non-totalizable or "objectifiable," this understanding of all the text's relations of meaning is impossible; hence, "interpretation is always a relative and un-completed movement" toward completion (*WM* 446/428).

If for Gadamer the tradition that informs understanding is unified and all-encompassing, Derrida is right to expect that psychoanalysis (like all forms of interpretive understanding our tradition sees as valid) should be able to be inte-grated into a general hermeneutics, as somehow continuous with more ordinary modes of understanding. Gadamer's denial of this is very surprising. For he not only affirms a radical breach between the hermeneutics of suspicion and the hermeneutics of intention, but also presumes that the former could not "lead to mutual understanding" (Reply). This raises serious doubts about the universal scope that Gadamer accorded to hermeneutic understanding, for he once explic-itly held that psychoanalysis, with the unconscious motive, "falls within the larger perimeter of hermeneutics" (*PH* 41). But this admission of a rad-ical rupture between our practices of understanding also deeply challenges any appeal to an all-embracing, common, unified tradition whose *Lebens-zusammenhang* prestructures and ultimately guarantees our shared mutual understanding and the fusion of our different contexts or horizons. It therefore also puts in question (or in opposition) the criteria of comprehensiveness and unity of meaning that formerly served as the twofold measure and aim of valid understanding. For a totality of tradition-endorsed but radically ruptured understandings of a text would preclude the unity of meaning Gadamer requires for intelligibility. It is this aporia that seems to lie behind Derrida's question of whether "enlargement of context" is simply "a continual expansion, or a discontinuous re-structuring" (Response).

If the program of Gadamerian hermeneutics of unity seems here in vulnerable retreat, it need not totally disintegrate into a Derridean field of fragmentation, rupture, and discontinuity. We should remember that unity may admit of degrees and certainly does not require total uniformity, and that the coherence necessary to speak of a common, unifying tradition can be a coherence that embraces conflict and debate, even about the nature of that tradition itself.[3] Too rigid a sense of unity seems to prevent Gadamer from integrating the hermeneutics of suspicion by appealing to the everyday fact that we can and do accept conflicting psychoanalytic and ordinary interpretations of the same act or utterance (e.g. "I did it because I like/hate him") since we have pragmatically workable ways of mediating between these different language-games in a coherent fashion. Gadamer perhaps could better emphasize that the unity of tradition in which we live is far from complete and never guaranteed. Tradition is more a motley patchwork of diverse practices and divergent language-games that we continuously have to struggle to consolidate and hold together, rather than Gadamer's unified and all-embracing "great tapestry which supports us" securely (*WM* 321/302) while we harmoniously continue to weave but never wrench, rip, or forsake it.

Gadamer seems to be moving promisingly in the direction of pluralism when he recognizes the special nature of literary texts and their interpretation, though he must realize that these so-called eminent texts are not foundationally given as such but are so determined by our pluralistic interpretive tradition that reads certain texts in different ways than others in order to serve different purposes. On the other hand, Derrida perhaps might more clearly acknowledge that despite the obvious discontinuities and pluralities in our tradition, there are also some unities and continuities, some agreement and coherence of practice over time (which he admits, in his "Three Questions" to Gadamer, need not be systematic to be coherent), without which effective communication and social interaction on which we all rely would be impossible. Wittgenstein makes this pragmatist point effectively in his discussion of agreement and the following of rules.[4] Derrida is right that there is never any one maximally proper (completely comprehensive and unified) context for interpretation; for what counts as the "proper" interpretive context or interpretive "game" will itself obviously depend on the particular aims of understanding that the interpreter brings with him. But these aims and games are largely tradition-informed, and within most standard ones Gadamer's criteria of comprehensiveness and coherence will have considerable bearing, footnotes as we are to Plato and the metaphysics of form.[5] It is tempting, even if untastefully crude, to trace the Gadamer/Derrida conflict on the unity/fragmentation of our (tradition-given) contexts for interpretation to their biographically different perspectives on tradition's unity: that of a German scholar stably embedded in his country's philosophical and philological traditions versus that of a displaced North African Jew simultaneously assimilating French and German philosophical traditions while still aware of his own ethnic heritage, and therefore particularly sensitive to the decentering of the whole notion of "the tradition."

3. This tradition-traceable tension between unity and rupture, consensus and difference, is similarly reflected in Derrida's third question of "whether the precondition for understanding, far from being the continuity of *rapport* . . . [i.e. Gadamerian consensus or mutual understanding], is not rather the interruption of *rapport,* a certain *rapport* of interruption, the suspending of all mediation?" (Response). What seems particularly penetrating in Derrida's challenge is its implicit appeal to that very alterity of perspective that Gadamer himself sees both as essential to all growth in understanding and as intrinsic to the dialogical nature of understanding. What motivates us to understand or grasp something is that it is not already in our grasp but is seen as somehow outside us, distracting our attention and interrupting our complacent inactivity of thought. Gadamer himself says, "Understanding begins . . . when something addresses us . . . in its own separate validity" (*WM* 283/266). But Gadamer might appeal to Davidson's pragmatist argument that we can make no sense of something's being intelligibly different without being able to map that difference on some common background of coordinates. To try to understand the other or even recognize it as other, we must in some sense understand it through our own terms; in making it at all intelligible we must make it accord in some way with some of our beliefs. For only through *them* can we understand it at all. Yet this agreement, one might rejoin, is not really given but only posited by the interpreter. It might then seem more convincing for Gadamer to see mutual agreement not as the foundational source of understanding but its desired end. In this he would resemble Charles Sanders Peirce who held that inquiry was stimulated by the irritation of doubt (often incited by disagreement) which it seeks to remove by achieving a consensus of belief that provides temporary stasis.[6] This aim of solidarity has been advocated by contemporary pragmatists like Rorty who abandon the ideal of truth for one of consensus, "the desire for as much intersubjective agreement as possible, the desire to extend the reference of 'us' as far as we can."[7]

Yet appealing and noble as solidarity is apt to strike us isolated and alienated selves, this ideal of maximal agreement seems threateningly stultifying and oppressive, ever likely to distort, ignore, or simply stifle the voice of alterity in the name of solidarity. It seems particularly ominous when pursued under the banner of tradition, be it of German "humanism" or American "democracy." Nor need we appeal to Auschwitz and to Adorno's idea of "non-identity thinking" to recognize that Gadamer's "total mutual agreement" is as far from the ideal as from actuality. For this would mean total conformity of thought and hence nothing divergent to stimulate any new thought or understanding at all. Tradition has only succeeded in preserving and extending understanding because of its fruitful frictions and internal debates, whose factions it struggles to hold together in a partial, fragile unity or coherence. Moreover, even if Gadamer is right that we always wish to be understood (and even discounting that large realm of the evasive and duplicitous, I'm not sure this is so), it clearly does not follow that we always seek above all to be agreed with. I think both Gadamer and Derrida should concur that understanding involves both difference and consensus, rupture and continuity. Gadamer's insistence on unity and the authority of tradition encounters Derrida's polarized insistence on discontinuity, free play, and the repudiation of unity as an unwarranted "axiomatic structure of metaphysics" (IS 67). Perhaps James' pluralistic pragmatism (poignantly captured in his oxymoronic sounding notion of a pluralistic universe) provides a possible position of mediation? What the pragmatist sees is "a world imperfectly unified still," and what does she want? "Provided you grant *some* separation among things, some tremor of independence, some free play of parts on one another, some real novelty or chance, she is amply satisfied, and will allow you any amount, however great, of real union."[8]

4. Precious little space remains for the third issue I wish to discuss: the nature of perfect dialogical understanding, whose experience Gadamer affirms as common and Derrida doubts is ever achieved. Derrida seems right if by a perfect understanding of someone's utterance we mean one that could never be deepened, revised, or enlarged. For (as Gadamer would probably agree) no understanding, not even one's self-understanding of what one says, is immune from amplification or revision; and if we can be wrong about what (or all) we meant, we can always be wrong in thinking others were right about it. Yet I think we can all recognize something like the experience Gadamer is suggesting, and we may even be able to give it some sense in pragmatic terms. For just as Wittgenstein showed with the ideal of exactness,[9] the ideal of perfect understanding does not in itself make any sense at all. We need to know "perfect for what?," "in what way perfect?" Gadamer seems right that we experience understandings that answer all our needs, expectations, and hopes to be understood in a particular dialogical context as fully or perfectly as we desire. But this does not mean that this understanding will perfectly answer all such needs, expectations, or hopes in every possible future context, which is what the idea of perfect understanding seems to suggest to Derrida. Nonetheless, hermeneutical understanding operates, as Gadamer repeatedly insists, in the practical realm of *phronesis*; as such its perfect understandings are all imperfect from the absolute standpoint of *theoria*. But surely we would not want to impute that metaphysical gaze to deconstruction.

David Farrell Krell

10. *"Ashes, ashes, we all fall. . .": Encountering Nietzsche*

When I wrote "A Hermeneutics of Discretion" several years ago, I was blissfully ignorant of the Gadamer-Derrida encounter.[1] John Sallis had asked me to contribute to a collection of papers on the theme Heidegger/Nietzsche; my indiscreet hermeneutics of discretion was the result.

Why indiscreet? Because in that piece I claimed that the issue of hermeneutics as such was bound up with the Heidegger-Nietzsche encounter—as though there were not myriad scenes in which the trials and tribulations of interpretation were being played out. I agreed with Derrida's *Spurs* when it asserted, *per impossibile*, that Heidegger's interpretation of Nietzsche encompassed the question of interpretation *per se*: at stake in Heidegger's *Nietzsche*, I wrote, was the very stake of hermeneutics. Yet I resisted the minimalist, anti-hermeneutical strokes of *Spurs*, claiming that even in the case of the forgotten umbrella nothing in Derrida's own text had been left to chance: while deconstruction might eschew the reduction of any text to a semantico-hermeneutical code, its own careful attention to textual strategies seemed to require a crypto-hermeneutics, perhaps an abashed hermeneutics, or at least a hermeneutics of discretion. I concluded that even if hermeneutics appeared to have taken a beating from deconstruction it was still trying doggedly—and admirably—to catch up with the conjunction Heidegger/Nietzsche. And so I came down, as they say, or slipped and fell, on the side of hermeneutics. *Glissez, mortels, n'appuyez pas:* "Gently, mortals, be discreet."

It should not surprise me that Nietzsche, and Heidegger's *Nietzsche,* crop up again and again in the Derrida-Gadamer encounter. And yet it does. Why should Nietzsche, Nietzsche even more than Plato, and Heidegger's *Nietzsche* even more than Nietzsche occupy the shifting ground of this implausible and perhaps quite impossible encounter? Why does Gadamer refer incessantly to Nietzsche, and to Heidegger's *Nietzsche,* as though to an infallible touchstone? Why does

Derrida remain preoccupied with Heidegger's *grand livre* when it is obviously a book that arouses his gravest suspicions? Why, when Gadamer encounters Derrida, and Derrida Gadamer, are both encountering Heidegger—encountering Heidegger encountering Nietzsche?

Although neither Gadamer nor Derrida mentions it, Heidegger juxtaposes to his *Auseinandersetzung* with Nietzsche (the explication or confrontation with Nietzsche in terms of the guiding question of metaphysics) a "going to encounter in thought," *ein Entgegendenken,* that is not prepared to reduce "Nietzsche" to a unity. Derrida, no doubt, remains skeptical. Gadamer, who ought to embrace thoughtful encounter as the very essence of the conversation he believes we are, never celebrates Heidegger's going to encounter Nietzsche. On the contrary, Gadamer announces in almost cavalier fashion, as though it were a secret sin in which he took particular pride, that Heidegger's Nietzsche-interpretation has convinced him utterly. How odd. It never fully convinced Heidegger.

Both Gadamer and Derrida appear to be convinced that Heidegger was convinced about Nietzsche: convinced that Nietzsche was the last metaphysician rather than the last thinker; that he foundered in value-thinking, *Wertdenken;* that a rescue-operation of the "innermost will" of Nietzsche's thinking would secure for him the outermost point in metaphysics' preoccupation with beings as a whole. Was Heidegger so convinced? So convincing?

It is no doubt perverse of me to focus on Nietzsche's eternal recurrence, and Heidegger's, and Heidegger's Nietzsche's, in the Gadamer-Derrida encounter. One ought to take up truly pressing questions such as the following: Is it not striking that in his 1985 text, "*Destruktion* and Deconstruction," Gadamer cites only two ways other than Heidegger's in which one can avoid the "taming" or "domesticating" tendency of dialectic—his own and that of Derrida? Of all the encounters Gadamer has had in his long life, would not this "implausible" one be decisive for post-Hegelian thought? Would not the urgency of the encounter prompt all sorts of questions *en détail,* questions that the texts of the encounter do little to clarify? Questions, for example, like these: How do the conceptions of text, and especially literary text, differ in Derrida and Gadamer? Why does Derrida decline to take up Gadamer's invitation to discuss textuality; why does he restrict himself to questions of will, power, psychoanalysis, and metaphysics? How successfully does Gadamer resist the charge (or is it a self-accusation?) of logocentrism in his notion of language as speech, and speech as conversation? Does not Gadamer have to suffer a bit more patiently the question as to whether or not his own "conversation" appeals always and everywhere to a certain unity, linearity, encompassment, and closure? And yet does not Derrida's most recent thought on the double-yes have to smile on (not at) Gadamer's insistence that "it is only the answer, actual or potential, that transforms a word into a word" (DD 106). Finally is it not strange how the alignment of the fourfold (Heidegger-Gadamer-Nietzsche-Derrida) shifts in the texts of the encounter? When it is a matter of Heidegger's putative logocentrism, Gadamer aligns himself with the accused against Nietzsche and Derrida; when it is a matter of Heidegger's adventurous odyssey through the Presocratics in search of original words for being, Gadamer takes his distance from Heidegger, who now moves closer to Nietzsche and Derrida; when it is a question of Nietzsche, Gadamer embraces Heidegger (or at least one of the heideggers) and bids adieu to Derrida. With Nietzsche, Heidegger's Nietzsche, however, all shifting stops. Why is that? Would this whole series of shifts within the fourfold apply to Derrida as well? Or not at all? Is Derrida's position, the position of this notorious shifter, this thinker so many find so shifty, in fact far more consistent and patient than that of Gadamer, who we thought was Gibralter?

Why is it that when it comes to Nietzsche, to Heidegger's Nietzsche, the shifting stops? That is the sole question I shall take up. My secret hope is that it will prove important for those larger questions—in ways I myself will not be able to grasp.

I

Let me begin by reviewing some of the places in Gadamer's texts where Nietzsche, and Heidegger's Nietzsche, become central. In "Text and Interpretation" (1981) Nietzsche raises his disheveled head as soon as Gadamer invokes the "French scene" he is about to encounter (TI 24). In Gadamer's view, Derrida contrasts Nietzsche to Heidegger: Nietzsche is "the more radical one" when it comes to abandoning the language of metaphysics. Derrida must therefore totally reject [*ganz verwerfen*] Heidegger's Nietzsche-interpretation. What is that interpretation? It discerns Nietzsche's imprisonment in values and valuative thinking. Once Heidegger determines Nietzsche's superficiality [*"Oberflächlichkeit"*—the word, I believe, is Gadamer's, not Heidegger's], he surges beyond Nietzsche to another thinking and a new language. Paradoxically, it is precisely at the point where Heidegger's Nietzsche-interpretation comes to fruition—and it comes quickly, Gadamer will say elsewhere (DD 105), inasmuch as Heidegger and Nietzsche are boon companions only for a brief moment[2]—that Gadamer abandons Heidegger for the stiller waters of Dilthey.

Why must Gadamer abandon not only Nietzsche but also, if one may say so, nietzsche's heidegger precisely at the point where the latter is thought to outstrip the former? Presumably, Heidegger surpasses not only Nietzsche but also Nietzsche's French avatars? If at the end of "*Destruktion* and Deconstruction" Gadamer asserts (112) that his way of escaping Hegelian domesticity goes farther than does deconstruction, how is it that, pulling ahead of Derrida, with both of them still in Heidegger's wake, Gadamer drops back abruptly and deliberately from the turbulence? Gadamer "can understand" why the "later Heidegger" (and presumably Derrida as well, who is now declared to be at one, *einig,* with Heidegger) would complain that Gadamer is trapped in phenomenological immanence; and Gadamer himself confesses his rootedness in the Romantic tradition of the *Geisteswissenschaften* and the humanistic legacy of that tradition (26). How then can he find fault with Nietzsche's "successors" for having bypassed *das Versucherische* of Nietzsche's thought—which both tempts and attempts, which is at-temptation itself? Gadamer notes approvingly the profound ambiguity of Heidegger's Nietzsche-*imago* and insists that Heidegger's own attempt, *Versuch,* surpasses Nietzsche, surpasses Nietzsche's dissolution into value-thinking, by getting back behind the metaphysical provenance of such thinking. Heidegger's own at-temptation leads him back behind—and thus beyond—Nietzsche. Not, however, into the light, but into the inexpungeable darkness of being's mystery: as Schelling is to Hegel, so is Heidegger to Nietzsche, except that Heidegger possesses the "conceptual force" that Schelling lacks. Heidegger has it all. And yet Gadamer must surge beyond Derrida by falling back behind Heidegger with whom Derrida, at least in some respects, is *einig.*

In his "Letter to Dallmayr" and in *"Destruktion* and Deconstruction," Nietzsche—as Heidegger's Nietzsche—is ubiquitous. Gadamer confesses himself as willing sacrificial victim, *ein williges Opfer,* to Heidegger's Nietzsche-interpretation, citing but one aspect of that interpretation: whereas in the earlier lecture, "Text and Interpretation," it was Nietzsche's *Wertdenken* that took center stage, it is now Heidegger's success in "bringing together in thought the will to power and the eternal recurrence" (LD 94) that prevails. Gadamer finds this *Zusammendenken* "fully persuasive and irrefutable," *völlig überzeugend und durchschlagend.* In his "Letter to Dallmayr" (LD 97), it is the challenge to take Nietzsche "seriously enough" that compels Gadamer to his most concise formulation of the hermeneutician's doubt:

> Here we come up against the central problem resonating in all hermeneutic endeavors and which also forms the basis, I think, of Derrida's qualms about my venture in thought: Is there not in hermeneutics—for all its efforts to recognize otherness as otherness, the other as other, the work of art as a blow [*Stoss*], the breach as breach, the unintelligible as unintelligible—too much conceded [*eingeräumt*] to reciprocal understanding and mutual agreement?

This doubt plagues *"Destruktion* and Deconstruction," however confident its rhetoric. And Nietzsche is the carrier of that plague. Heidegger himself must absorb the radical risks of Nietzschean thought in order to achieve his own breakthrough (DD 104). At the end of his odyssey through early Greek thinking stands Nietzsche as the culminating figure, *Endgestalt.* Nevertheless, as we have already heard, the self-destruction of metaphysics as it occurs in and through

Nietzsche can, in Gadamer's view, only result in Heidegger "becoming a fellow traveller with Nietzsche for a short stretch of his own way" (DD 105). Heidegger discovers a new language. And he enables Gadamer to discover that language as such is not the Babylonian captivity of thought but the possibility of passing over into the language of the other. However necessary Nietzsche may have been for Heidegger's breakthrough, Gadamer is at pains to lose Nietzsche in order to find the language that will make himself understood—and to lose Heidegger as well, if necessary, and certainly Derrida. "One must look for the word that can reach another person. And it is possible for one to find it; one can even learn the language of the other person" (ibid.). The formulation is itself awkward, groping, and wholly equivocal: *man kann sogar die fremde, seine, des Anderen Sprache lernen. Seine,* his. His, whose? Not his, meaning one's own, Gadamer would insist, but his, meaning the other's. We others know what he means, do we not? His. Ours. One's own other's own. One's own. Meaning.

> Both then were silent?
> Silent, each contemplating the other in both mirrors of the reciprocal flesh of theirhisnothis fellowfaces.[3]

But silent.

In the circumvention of Babel, which is neither its destruction nor its deconstruction, a penetrating reading of Nietzsche remains at issue. Gadamer wishes to oppose Derrida's reading of Heidegger's *Nietzsche* in order to put his full weight behind Heidegger's own reading of Nietzsche, the one reading that has in fact convinced him altogether, the one reading that is: (1) his reading of (2) Heidegger's reading of Nietzsche. Presuming that Heidegger's reading is one, and that nietzsche does not read heidegger. Let us follow quite closely the final paragraphs of "*Destruktion* and Deconstruction" (DD 113).

In Gadamer's view, the Derrida-Gadamer-Heidegger-Nietzsche encounter has but two sides. "On the one side stands the bewildering richness of facets and the endless play of masks in which Nietzsche's bold experiments in thinking appear to disperse [*zerstreuen*] themselves into an ungraspable multiplicity. On the other side, there is the question one may put to Nietzsche, as to what all the play in this enterprise means [*bedeutet*]." On the one hand, play, mask, and dispersion—perhaps the very dispersion that in *Sein und Zeit* threatens the otherwise cohesive span of a resolute, appropriate Dasein.[4] On the other hand, the question, *What does it mean?* As we shall see, that question reverts to a One: one question, one answer, one significance. The very multiplicity and disparity of readings of Nietzsche will prove embarrassing and will be reduced to a linear progression by which one reading becomes altogether convincing and passes the other by. Nietzsche's own dispersion will consist in the fact that he himself fails to discern [*vor Augen haben*] and to grasp conceptually [*in Begriffe fassen*] the "inner connection between the basic principle of will to power and the noontime message of the eternal return of the same." Nietzsche fails to perceive the unity [*Einheit*] of his own thinking. If Gadamer understands Heidegger correctly, *wenn ich Heidegger recht verstehe,* if in fact Nietzsche fails to descry the unity of his own thinking, the result is that "these metaphors of his last visions look like mirroring facets with no underlying unity," *hinter denen kein Eines ist.* Nietzsche's own dispersion—that is, his blindness to the fact that his thought is not in dispersion but is fundamentally unified—"represents the unified, ultimate position [*stelle die einheitliche Endstellung dar*] in which the question concerning Being itself forgets itself and loses itself." Eternal recurrence of the same finds its (one) meaning in the era of technology (presumably in the rotary motion of the Same) and in consummate nihilism. To think what Nietzsche was unable to think, far from being a regression into metaphysics, represents *Wesen* as a way, as an essential unfolding in which we are able to advance along the path of our own thinking, enhancing the conversation that thinking *is*.

Such conversation seeks new partners, partners of magnitude, partners who are radically other. In 1985, four years after the encounter, Gadamer extends the invitation to begin. Yet it is an invitation issued as a kind of warning, exercising a kind of constraint, making an offer that cannot be refused: "Whoever wants me to take deconstruction to heart and insists on difference stands at the beginning of a conversation, not at its end" (DD 113).

II

Derrida's "Interpreting Signatures (Nietzsche/Heidegger): Two Questions" adopts a starting point different from that of *Spurs*. Whereas the latter accepts Heidegger's own starting point, namely, the will to power *as art*, the present piece interrogates (1) Heidegger's 1961 Foreword to *Nietzsche,* (2) sections 1 and 6 of the 1939 course, "Will to Power as Knowledge," and (3) sections 1 and 12 of the 1937 course, "The Eternal Recurrence of the Same."[5] Presumably, by inquiring into will to power as knowledge and the eternal recurrence of the same Derrida will be touching on that very *Zusammendenken* of the two that Gadamer finds so convincing.

Section 12 of "The Eternal Recurrence of the Same," one of the longest of the 1937 lecture course, proffers a "Summary presentation of the thought [of return]: being as a whole as life and force; the world as chaos." It offers Derrida the chance to focus on a theme that occupies him much of late—that of life, life-and-death, the economy of ashes [*Aschen*] that Nietzsche introduces. Section 1 of "The Will to Power as Knowledge," on "Nietzsche as the thinker of the consummation of metaphysics," will show Heidegger separating off the trivia of Nietzsche's "biography" from the "essence" of his thought; section 6, on "Nietzsche's Alleged Biologism," will allow Derrida to expose Heidegger's resistance to *Lebensphilosophie,* from whose clutches Heidegger would rescue Nietzsche. This section would also enable him to confront an aspect of Heidegger's Nietzsche-interpretation concerning which Heidegger himself is least convinced. For Heidegger is not convinced about whether one should vote "yes or no" on Nietzsche's putative biologism. He is not even convinced about whether one should cast a vote at all whenever it is a matter of mere catchwords. His section on "Nietzsche's Alleged Biologism" ends with the sentence, "We must learn to 'read' " (*N 1* 527/3:47). Derrida does not cite it.

Derrida's two questions concerning the *name* of Nietzsche and the notion of *totality* both turn about the issue of unity, the unity of a signature and of metaphysical inquiry into beings as a whole. When Derrida puts into question the unity of the history of metaphysics as the sole backdrop for Heidegger's *Nietzsche,* he comes very close to voicing the objection that Gadamer voiced against deconstruction of the metaphysics of presence. (A voice, it must be said, that resembles Derrida's own. See LAJ 2–4/1–8.) The history of being in Heideggerian *Destruktion* (presuming that *Destruktion* and *Seinsgeschichte* coalesce in Heidegger) and the history of metaphysics as presence in Derridean *déconstruction*—how do they differ? Gadamer does not pose that question, but appears to accept the Heideggerian history, or at least not to challenge it, whereas the Derridean account of logocentrism and presence arouses his ire. Derrida will later ask: Who said a man carries a single name, and who said there was only one Western metaphysics? Gadamer will reply: You did!

Yet it is clear that if the first unity Derrida wishes to challenge is that of "biography" and the "proper name," the second is Heidegger's "general reading of Western metaphysics." These converge in the third postulated unity, that of Nietzsche's own thought, in the interpretation that Gadamer found penetrating, piercing, all-conquering: *durchschlagend.* Applying to Heidegger a formula that Heidegger applies to Nietzsche, Derrida seeks to think Heidegger's *pensée la plus pensante,* to plumb Heidegger's own *innersten denkerischen Willen.* According to Heidegger's foreword, the *Nietzsche* volumes indicate the path (the unitary trajectory) of Heidegger's thought over the seventeen years that separate the "Letter on Humanism" from the earliest seminars on "the essence of truth." The unities of Heidegger's *Nietzsche* and of metaphysics as such prove to be indissociable from the unity of Heidegger's own *Denkweg*—and for much longer than a brief moment. The very signature of "Nietzsche" is the mark not of a signitory but of a body of thought. Of the "two ways" that Derrida sees opening here (curious that here again, as in the case of Gadamer, there are but two), that of his own *Otobiographies,* in which one must take the risk of seeing the name dismembered or multiplied in masks or simulacra and that of another, which identifies the proper name with the *essence* of the thought and allows the *particularity* of the individual to fall into oblivion, Heidegger surely wanders the second. However, when Heidegger excludes the empirical and goes for the essential [*"Was liegt uns Herr Nietzsche an!"*] his gesture is classically meta-physical, precisely at the point where it ought to be a matter of the consummation of metaphysics and the commencement of another thinking. The political rationale for Heidegger's exclusion of the psycho-biographico-biological in 1939 is of course clear; yet the reduction of the *who?* to a *what?* remains in service to a One, and remains a metaphysical gesture. We recall that the same gesture and appeal loom at the conclusion of Gadamer's "*Destruktion* and Deconstruction," where it is a matter of demanding the One that would lie (truly) behind the Many. In Derrida's view, even the *Zweideutigkeit* of Heidegger's *Nietzsche,* which Gadamer too perceives, derives from Nietzsche's ambiguous position at the crest of the wave of metaphysics—repeating that history, remaining within it, while somehow bringing it to an irrevocable end—which itself, as *the* history of being, is singular.

It is doubtless time to complicate the picture. When Derrida asks of Heidegger whether he is sure that Nietzsche's name and thought are one, when he demands to know who said that occidental metaphysics is one, would we not have to reply as we imagined Gadamer might? Would it not be easy to comb *Of Grammatology* for references to that profound historical necessity by which all the binary oppositions of metaphysics (the one metaphysics) revert to the inside/outside opposition (the one opposition), and to one side of that one opposition, the inside of presence, the presence of *ousia, Anwesenheit, Gegenwart, Vorhandenheit*—as thought by none other than Martin Heidegger? Indeed, who would not fall under such an accusation—that our language and our thinking reduce (to) One? When Derrida asks whether the reduction to unicity and to the propriety gathered in and by the proper name is nothing "more" or "something else" than the desire of the proper name, a desire suppressed by Heidegger, as it were, *in media vita;* when he asks whether any conceivable genealogy would not fall under the same monomania; must he not do so from within the selfsame circle of what he calls an "axiomatics?" If Nietzsche's multiplication of signatures, identities, and masks were to be counterposed to unicity as *la chose, la causa* of Nietzsche's thought, as *der Streitfall,* the definite article, would not a certain resistance to dissemination still be at work in the very counterposition? Derrida's conclusion to his "preliminary remarks" concerning Heidegger's *Nietzsche,* or rather to his own "ulterior" (not "future") reading of that work, his startling image of a fatal rescue-operation in which the falling tightrope walker will be dead before he hits the net (remember that in *Zarathustra* he lived even after smashing against the cobblestones of the marketplace), perhaps the most drastic portrayal of hermeneutic futility, hermeneutic fatality, leaves us with an uncanny suspicion about the chances of either hermeneutics or *Destruktion* or deconstruction. Ashes.

Which brings us to the second of Derrida's questions, the one concerning totality, the totality of beings as a whole in Heidegger's *Zusammendenken* of will to power and eternal return. This conjoining in thought of will to power and eternal recurrence is precisely what convinced Gadamer about Heidegger's *Nietzsche*. Is Derrida also convinced that Heidegger's *Nietzsche* is most concerned to convince us of this conjunction? Is Derrida the simple obverse of Gadamerian coinage, is he simply unconvinced? Whatever the case, is it possible to read the 1937 lecture course quite differently? We shall return to this question in a moment.

Heidegger is of course fully aware that the language of *das Seiende-im-Ganzen* and *die metaphysische Grundstellung* is foreign to Nietzsche, that it is a "Kantian" importation. Nor would it be accurate to suggest that Heidegger's ambivalence as regards Nietzsche's "alleged biologism" arises entirely from his allergic reaction to *Lebensphilosophie*. To be sure, the struggle to liberate his analysis of Dasein from *Existenzphilosophie*, which he needed in order to liberate himself from *Lebensphilosophie*, left its mark on Heidegger long after the 1920s. Nevertheless, throughout the Nietzsche lectures we find Heidegger's own fascination with the "new sensuousness," with "bodying life," with "some body who is alive." *Dasein lebt, indem es leibt.*[6] Thus, Derrida's admittedly surprising revelations concerning the epigraph of Heidegger's *Nietzsche*, which (after Heidegger's excisions) begins with the words "*Das Leben . . . ,*" should not be too hastily interpreted as Heidegger's suppression of life.[7]

Nor does Heidegger's analysis of the guiding question of metaphysics (*die Leitfrage:* What is the being of beings as a whole?) cause him to suppress entirely the thought of *ashes* in Nietzsche, the thought William Butler Yeats called "life-in-death, death-in-life." True, his "Summary presentation of the thought" of eternal recurrence closes by *apparently* accepting the presupposition that one ought to pursue the guiding question ("—presupposing, of course, that we wish . . ."), to see how chaos is *susceptible* of recurrence, to *demonstrate* that doctrine by "proceeding in orderly fashion through the entire labyrinth of Nietzsche's thoughts, mastering that labyrinth as we proceed" (*N 1* 355/2:97). Yet is it a matter of pursuing the guiding question, or is it rather the far more questionable grounding question [*die Grundfrage*] that Heidegger wishes to introduce? Is it a matter of demonstration, penetration, and mastery, or of something far more subtle and—to use Heidegger's own word—susceptible? Had Gadamer been less convinced by Heidegger's *Nietzsche* he might have invited Derrida to ponder these two things:

First, the conclusion to Heidegger's reflection on Nietzschean ashes and dreams of totality, a conclusion Derrida neglects to cite:

> Perhaps two different views of the dead are in play here. If that is the case, then the very possibility of contradiction becomes superfluous. If the dead is taken with a view to its knowability, and if knowing is conceived as a firm grasp on what is permanent, identifiable, and unequivocal, then the dead assumes preemi-

nence as an object of knowledge, whereas the animate, being equivocal and ambiguous, is only a kind—and a subordinate kind—of the dead. If, on the contrary, the dead itself is thought in terms of its provenance, then it is but the ashes of what is alive. The fact that the living remains subordinate to the dead in quantitative terms and in terms of preponderance does not refute the fact that it is the origin of the dead, especially since it is proper to the essence of what is higher that it remain rare, less common. From all this we discern one decisive point: by setting the lifeless in relief against the living, along the guidelines of any single aspect, we do not do justice to the state of affairs—the world is more enigmatic than our calculating intellect would like to admit (*N 1* 342–43/2:85).

Are not Heidegger's thoughts on the *firebrand* much closer to Derrida's own thoughts on the *brûle-tout* than "Signatures" would suggest? From *Feu la cendre,* one brief extract:

> Even so, one must know how to burn. This must be understood. There is also Nietzsche's "paradox"—perhaps Nietzsche is in fact something other than a thinker of the totality of beings—by which the relation of ashes to the whole no longer seems to him to be regularized by the inclusion of parts or by some tranquilizing metonymic logos: "Our whole world is the *ashes* of countless *living* creatures: and even if the animate seems so miniscule in comparison to the whole, it is nonetheless the case that *everything* has already been transposed into life—and so it goes."[8]

Second, the fact that Heidegger's "Summary Presentation of the Thought" in fact constitutes a caesura in his thinking of eternal recurrence. Heidegger interrupts his close reading of the *communications* of eternal return in *The Gay Science, Thus Spoke Zarathustra,* and *Beyond Good and Evil* in order to offer a sketch of its configuration or *Gestalt* in the notes. The 1937 lecture course focuses not so much on eternal return as a metaphysical doctrine of totality as on guarded communication, the telling silence that swathes the figure of Zarathustra. Heidegger himself prevents the thought of the totality of beings from consuming his entire reading of Nietzsche, prevents it here more effectively than anywhere else in *Nietzsche,* by heeding what happens "in the hero's sphere," in Zarathustran solitude, in the gateway *Augenblick* where transition [*Übergang*] is demise [*Untergang*]. Ashes. In Heidegger's own text. " 'For at that instant the full moon, silent as death, rose over the house and then stood still, a round, glowing coal. . .' " (*N1* 439/2:177).

III

Would it not be better for all concerned to be less convinced both by and about Heidegger's *Nietzsche?* For every instance of bold *Zusammendenken* and for every instance of vigorous reduction to One there is in Heidegger's *Nietzsche* a remarkably different gesture: "Yet we must guard against the presumption that we now belong among those who really understand. Perhaps we too are mere onlookers" (*NI* 445/2:181). "A book for everyone and no one, and consequently a book that can never, dare never, be 'read' complacently" (*NI* 289/2:36).

I do not mean to imply that either Derrida or Gadamer reads complacently. Far from it. These two thinkers belong in the fourfold and let it be: Nietzsche-Heidegger-Gadamer-Derrida. Whatever shifts occur in that quaternity help us to see who we are encountering here, to wit:

The most impressive interpreter of our time, the most zealous and least jealous lover of slow reading, the thinker who remains more perspicuous than anyone else about the circle of his own understanding, especially as it expands outward into foreign circles—in short, the supreme *hermeneutician* of the twentieth century: Jacques Derrida.

The most romantic and adventurous of readers and most flexible of conceptual thinkers, the one most open to conversation and debate, the one who shifts the instant his position becomes too rigid—in short, the most *French* of contemporary thinkers: Hans-Georg Gadamer.

Robert Bernasconi

11. Seeing Double: Destruktion and Deconstruction

By calling his essay "*Destruktion* and Deconstruction," Gadamer sets Derrida in opposition to Heidegger. It is clear to Gadamer that *Destruktion* is Heidegger's word, just as the word *déconstruction* is Derrida's. But there will be readers who, on seeing Gadamer's title, will begin to worry that they must be suffering from double vision. What will have brought them to suspect that they are seeing double is the tendency among a number of commentators to use the two words of the title as if they were interchangeable. Some American translators of Heidegger have not hesitated to employ the word *deconstruction* in an effort to capture the sense of both *Destruktion* and *Abbau* as they occur in Heidegger's books and lectures from the 1920s. The difficulty of translating these German words is insufficient as an explanation for what, from a certain perspective, seems to be a blatant misappropriation of Derrida's word. Alternative translations of *Destruktion,* which would avoid recourse to Derrida's word, are available—"destructuring," for example.

But what would justify the claim that *déconstruction* is Derrida's word? The word is not his neologism. As he tells us, when the word came to him "spontaneously" he was able to turn to *Littré* to confirm that it was already "good French" (LAJ 2/2). Nevertheless, it is he who revived and redefined the term. Indeed the 1986 revision of *Le Robert* neglects earlier uses of the word *déconstruction* and illustrates it only with a single quotation drawn from *Of Grammatology.*[1] And even if it is clear that *déconstruction* is Derrida's word in the sense that it is often equivalent to pronouncing his proper name, it is less easy to say at what point it ceases to refer back to him. Derrida has frequently tried to disown the word and particularly the extension it has undergone in other hands. The fame of the word was, he claims, unanticipated by him and even unwelcome to him: "It is a word I have never liked and one whose fortune has disagreeably surprised me."[2] But, given the role he accords to the author's intentions, Derrida knows as well as anyone that such protestations carry little weight.

The assignment of words to proper names raises philosophical questions. The practice is most developed in Heidegger and he provides a suitable context for pursuing these questions a little further. So, for example, whenever Heidegger employs the word *subject* or finds it in a text upon which he is commenting, it is almost always accompanied by a reference to Descartes. *Subjectum* is Descartes' word, much as *idea* is Plato's word and *energeia* is Aristotle's. Not that things are quite so simple in the first case. Subject is a word with a heritage extending back to the Greek *hypokeimenon,* particularly to Aristotle. The fact that Descartes' word can be referred back beyond Descartes to Aristotle—as well as forward to Leibniz, Kant and Hegel, who also contribute to the transformations whereby subjectivity becomes the fundamental concept of modern metaphysics—is used by Heidegger to illustrate the unity of metaphysics. The unity of the history of metaphysics is a constant theme in Heidegger, but not always in the same sense. In *Basic Problems of Phenomenology* (1927), Heidegger presented the unity of metaphysics according to a teleological model that seems to have been borrowed from Hegel (*GP* 103,178/73,127). In the late 1930s, by contrast, the unity of metaphysics was not only articulated epochally, but referred to the history of Being. Even though the word "subject" played a prominent role in the self-understanding of modernity, an examination of Descartes' use of the word shows that he still tended to use it in the manner of medieval ontology. Indeed Heidegger digs deeper and notes explicitly that the word *hypokeimenon* still "resounds" in it (ZW 98/AWP 147).

But there is, on Heidegger's account, an ambiguity in Descartes' use of the word *subjectum.* For in addition to acknowledging the continuity of Descartes' usage with the philosophy that precedes him, Heidegger in the same place asserts of the *Meditations* that "man has become *subjectum,*" something that could never have been said of the Greeks (ZW 98/AWP 148 and ZW 102/AWP 152). This ambiguity, which passes from the word to come to embrace the *Meditations* as a whole, is essential to Heidegger's reading of Descartes. "The ambiguity of the essence of reality in the beginning of modern metaphysics is the sign of a genuine transition" (*N 2* 428/*EP* 25). Similarly with the word *subjectum,* Heidegger finds support for his view that it marks an event in the history of Being in the fact that the word points both forwards and backwards. The effect of referring metaphysics to the history of Being is to withdraw *subjectum* not just from Descartes, but from Aristotle and Leibniz too. That such words are words of Being is an essential part of the background that underlies the way that Heidegger came to identify the name of a thinker with the thought of that thinker in such a way that whatever belonged to the biography or psychology of the thinker fell out of account. In other words, these are some of the reasons why for Heidegger—to recall the passage quoted by Derrida—"the

name of the thinker stands as title for the subject-matter of his thought" (*N 1* 9/
1:xv quoted by Derrida in IS 61).

I shall return to Heidegger's discussion of the fundamental words of metaphysics later, having introduced it now in an effort to complicate what it might mean to say that *déconstruction* is Derrida's word. For the moment, it is important to notice that Derrida himself, in the very place where he tells us that he came upon the word "spontaneously," returns the word to Heidegger. The first reason that Derrida offers for having introduced the word is to translate Heidegger's *Destruktion* and *Abbau*. *Déconstruction* was, at least initially, intended to be some kind of equivalent for *Destruktion*. Indeed in an early essay Derrida had himself employed the word *détruire* only to change it a year later to *déconstruire*.[3] All this might suggest that it was not so inappropriate for Heidegger's English translators to use the word "deconstruction" as a translation of *Destruktion* and *Abbau,* at least if they could ignore what had become of the word after it had passed from Derrida's hands in 1967. This anyway is what Derrida says:

> When I chose this word, or when it imposed itself upon me—I think it was in
> *Of Grammatology*—I little thought it would be credited with such a central role
> in the discourse that interested me at the time. Among other things I wished to
> translate and adapt to my own ends the Heideggerian word *Destruktion* or *Ab-*
> *bau.* Each signified in this context an operation bearing on the structure or
> traditional architecture of the fundamental concepts of ontology or of western
> metaphysics (LAJ 2/1-2).[4]

The phrase "adapt to my ends" may seem to be an invitation to reflect upon the difference between Derrida's "ends" and Heidegger's "ends," but that impression is probably mistaken. It is unlikely that Derrida is inviting a repetition of the kind of operation that Heidegger performed in "The Onto-theo-logical Constitution of Metaphysics," when the latter sought to clarify the difference between Hegel and himself. The differentiation of standpoints was very much at the root of philosophical work for Heidegger in a way it is not for Derrida.[5] It is likely therefore that the phrase "adapt to my ends" is simply Derrida's acknowledgement that his attempted translation of Heidegger's *Destruktion* was not unmotivated. Or, to restate it in Gadamer's idiom, that his interpretation—and all translation is interpretation—takes place within the circle of question and answer.

The questions that dominate Derrida's understanding of Heidegger's *Destruktion* of the history of ontology are questions about philosophy's alleged death, its dying, and its opposition to non-philosophy. (see *ED* 117-18/79). Because Derrida was particularly sensitive to the self-defeating nature of any simple opposition to the previous history of philosophy, he was also highly sensitive to the negative connotations of the French (and English) word destruction. In German these connotations are carried not by *Destruktion*, but by *Zerstörung* (LAJ 2/2).[6] When Gadamer in *"Destruktion* and Deconstruction" patiently explains the difference between Nietzschean *Zerstörung* and Heideggerian *Destruktion*, he only repeats the contrast that Derrida himself employs to explain his choice of the word *déconstruction*. And yet Gadamer labours the point as if he thought it was somehow correcting Derrida. As I shall try to show later, it seems much more likely that Gadamer misconstrued *déconstruction* to be an essentially negative operation, than that Derrida misunderstood what Heidegger meant by *Destruktion*.

Neither Heidegger nor Derrida is entirely innocent of the misunderstandings that have befallen "their" words, but Heidegger's failure is the most surprising for being repeated twice more. Twice Heidegger offered a revised formulation of his relation to the history of philosophy in an attempt to account for changes in his thinking. In the 1930s, the catchword became the "overcoming of metaphysics" and later still he said that "our task is to cease all overcoming and leave metaphysics to itself" (*SD* 25/24). In each case, the rhetoric got the upper hand over what it sought to describe and each of the three phrases is— particularly when taken out of context—more misleading than illuminating. It is curious that Derrida should adapt the word *Destruktion* when his own understanding of his relationship to metaphysics is much closer to that of the later Heidegger than the Heidegger of *Being and Time*. But it is no more curious than Gadamer's own preference for the word "overcoming" when his whole problematic is much closer to what Heidegger called *Destruktion* in *Sein und Zeit* than it ever was to the "overcoming of metaphysics." Just as Heidegger elucidates the destruction of the history of ontology with reference to the "discovery of tradition" (*SZ* 20/41), Gadamer follows Dilthey's talk of "the rise of historical consciousness." In both cases the task set is that of appropriation [*Aneignung*] of the previous history of ontology and not an abandonment of it (*SZ* 220/262).

It could be shown that, like the attribution of a negative sense to Heidegger's *Destruktion*, Gadamer's attribution of a negative sense of deconstruction to Derrida is not altogether without a basis. Nevertheless it is at best a one-sided interpretation of Derrida and, I would want to argue, amounts to a serious misunderstanding. But it is not the only one. It seems that misunderstandings plague the encounter between Gadamer and Derrida so that, at least on the basis of the printed record, the proper verdict would have to be that "the confrontation never quite takes place."[7] But what would a successful encounter mean in this context? Would it be a dialogue resulting in agreement in the sense of mutual or shared understanding? If so, then the encounter would have to be judged by its conformity to an idea of dialogue that is associated with the name of Gadamer. Such a dialogue would be a one-sided dialogue, or no dialogue at all because it would have been from the first designed to confirm Gadamer and his belief in dialogue. Derrida would have found the deck stacked against him and his only option, if he were to retain his identity, would have been to try and frustrate the dialogue from the outset. One could imagine a reading of the texts of the encounter that would develop this hypothesis. It would do so by dwelling on the seemingly peripheral character of Derrida's questions on Gadamer's paper and the fact that Derrida, far from trying to deconstruct Gadamer's texts, fails even to name him in "Interpreting Signatures."

But if the conversation does not really get off the ground, the fault is not one-sided. The fact of the matter is that Gadamer does not show himself to be particularly conversant with Derrida's thinking. Gadamer does not name any of Derrida's texts, any more than Derrida specifies Gadamer's writings.[8] For Gadamer, Derrida was from the outset a proper name representing a position, the critique of logocentrism. Gadamer joins those who attribute to Derrida the argument that it is sufficient for someone to have used certain key words from that language (without the necessary precaution of crossing them out or putting quotation marks around them) for that person to stand accused of being irretrievably and unambiguously metaphysical. Having identified Derrida in this way, it is not surprising that Gadamer tries to make metaphysical language the issue between them. In "Text and Interpretation" he observes that "no conceptual language, not even what Heidegger called the 'language of metaphysics,' represents an unbreakable constraint upon thought" (TI 26/23). Gadamer gives this as his reason for not following Heidegger's path into the strange language of his later texts. But in this context it seems also to be meant as an argument against the stylistic contortions and graphic devices to which Derrida frequently resorts.

And yet it is possible that at a more discreet level a "genuine" encounter awaits us in the printed record. I will suggest that there is a sense in which Derrida's "Interpreting Signatures" addresses Gadamer in such a way that this essay succeeds, in the words of his "Three Questions to Hans-Georg Gadamer," in giving a glimpse of "a quite different way of thinking about texts." In order to show this I must rehearse certain passages from the various papers.

In "Text and Interpretation" Gadamer tries to separate Heidegger and Derrida, just as he does with the title of the later essay "*Destruktion* and Deconstruction." It is almost as if he wants to reserve Heidegger for himself by referring Derrida instead to Nietzsche. Derrida's relationship to Heidegger is summarized in the following vein: "Derrida has argued against the later Heidegger that Heidegger himself has not really broken through the logocentrism of metaphysics" (TI 27/24). Gadamer seems to take it for granted that we know what such a breakthrough would mean for Derrida. He says no more about it than that Derrida regards Nietzsche as more radical than Heidegger and that Derrida believes that Nietzsche did break with the logocentrism of metaphysics by his "positing of meaning in the service of the 'Will to Power'." In any case, as part of this general effort to set Heidegger and Derrida in opposition, Gadamer insists that Derrida "must discard Heidegger's own presentation and critique of Nietzsche." But Gadamer finds in Heidegger's presentation of Nietzsche as "the extreme culmination of that which he called the history of the forgetfulness of Being" something "seductive" that "the French followers of Nietzsche" have not grasped. Gadamer expresses this as, "a deep ambiguity [that] characterizes Heidegger's image of Nietzsche, in that he follows Nietzsche into the most extreme positions and precisely at that point he finds the excesses [*Un-wesen*] of metaphysics at work. . ." (TI 28/25). Beyond the disintegration [*Auflösung*] of metaphysics in value thinking, Heidegger goes back behind metaphysics in a retrospective questioning which "does not do away with the concept of Logos and its metaphysical implications, rather it recognizes its one-sidedness and concedes its superficiality."

In this way, Gadamer places on the agenda both Heidegger's interpretation of Nietzsche and certain views about that interpretation that he ascribes to Derrida. But I shall try to show that Derrida's reading of Heidegger's *Nietzsche* is very different from the caricature Gadamer offers of Derrida's reading both before and after "Interpreting Signatures." Derrida is well aware of certain moments of Nietzsche's texts that resist Heidegger's reading, but far from rejecting Heidegger's reading, as Gadamer claims, Derrida ultimately comes close to Gadamer's own understanding of the ambiguity of Heidegger's *Nietzsche*.

I have suggested that Gadamer holds only a negative understanding of deconstruction. This claim can be made more precise in respect to Derrida's relation to Heidegger. By focusing on Derrida's alleged "critique" of Heidegger's logocentrism and by criticizing Derrida in turn for overlooking the "deep ambiguity [that] characterizes Heidegger's image of Nietzsche," Gadamer somehow overlooks the fact that it is precisely this ambiguity that preoccupies Derrida. The first few pages of "Interpreting Signatures" might seem to confirm Gadamer. There Derrida reminds us how Heidegger insists on the unity of Nietzschean thought, a unity generalized by Heidegger in his claim that every great thinker has only one thought. Derrida refers this unity to two other unities: the unity of Western metaphysics and the unity of the Heideggerian path of thought (IS 248/ 59–60). Without rehearsing the various steps on the way, it may be recalled that Derrida suggests that Heidegger seeks "to rescue Nietzsche from ambiguity" (IS 253/65). But at this point Derrida shows that he does so in a gesture that is itself ambivalent (IS 256/67). I shall quote these passages at some length because they do not seem to be represented by Gadamer's judgment in his letter to Dallmayr that "Derrida rejects the effort of Heidegger's Nietzsche-interpretation from the ground up. He sees in it the logocentric bias of metaphysics from which Heidegger's thinking had futilely tried to escape" (93 above).

That Derrida can be found saying that Heidegger seeks "to rescue Nietzsche from ambiguity," might seem to suggest that Gadamer is correct to accuse Derrida of overlooking "the deep ambiguity" of Heidegger's image of Nietzsche. But can the criticism be sustained in the face of the following passage?

> Heidegger directs this whole interpretation of Nietzsche's essential and singular thinking to the following argument: this thinking has not really gone beyond the end of metaphysics; it is still itself a great metaphysics and even if it points to such an overcoming, it is just barely, just enough to remain on the sharpest crest of the boundary. Or, in other words, to remain in complete ambiguity. This, then, is essential ambiguity! Not just Nietzsche's, as Heidegger sees it, but also Heidegger's own ambivalence with regard to Nietzsche (IS 253–54/65).

Furthermore, this ambiguity is not unique to Nietzsche or to Heidegger's reading of Nietzsche. It structures Western metaphysics itself. "At the very moment of affirming the uniqueness of Nietzsche's thinking, he [Heidegger] does everything he can to show that it repeats the mightiest (and therefore the most general) schema of metaphysics" (IS 254/65). As Derrida realizes, this puts the very notion of Western metaphysics in question. "And likewise, who has said or decided that there is something like a Western metaphysics, something that would be capable of being gathered up under this name and this name only?" (IS 256/67). Could Gadamer have overlooked the significance of these passages if he did not, prior to reading the "Interpreting Signatures" essay, hold a prejudicial view of Derrida's alleged critique of Heidegger? Irrespective of the apparent ease with which Derrida sometimes uses the phrase *Western metaphysics,* sensitivity to Derrida's recognition of the difficulties of the logic of the opposition between metaphysics and what allegedly breaks with it—the inside-outside opposition—confirms that he was aware of the vulnerability of the notion of metaphysics, even while employing it. And just as the name *metaphysics,* as the name for a unity, serves to guard against "the dangers of dissemination" (IS 257/68), so the name *Derrida,* as the title for a critique of logocentrism, functions in Gadamer's essay "Text and Interpretation" to exclude a dialogue with the bearer of that name. In this way, "Interpreting Signatures" after all does address Gadamer directly and precisely in terms of his [Gadamer's] own ends— dialogue and mutual understanding. It does so because it focuses on that which stands in the way of a dialogue (in the Gadamerian sense) between Gadamer and Derrida—the identification of a thinker with a single thought.

But how can Derrida affirm the ambiguity of Heidegger's Nietzsche and at the same time say that Heidegger seeks to rescue Nietzsche from ambiguity? To answer such a question it is necessary to penetrate more deeply into what Derrida is saying about metaphysics in "Interpreting Signatures." And because, as Derrida himself acknowledges, the reading of Heidegger's *Nietzsche* that he offers there is only a preliminary one, it is necessary to look elsewhere for clarification. It is for this reason that I shall now turn to an essay called "Sending: On Representation" (E), which was Derrida's contribution to a French philosophical congress on the subject of representation. Reference to this essay will serve to highlight the general direction—perhaps even the necessities—governing "Interpreting Signatures." Certainly the question Derrida asks of French philosophical language: "Is there such a language, and is it a single language?" (E 22/318) is a similar question to that which leads Gadamer to say "there is no 'language of metaphysics' " (DD 366/107). Neither Gadamer nor Derrida approaches the language of metaphysics as a dead language, a written corpus, trying to fix the sense of certain words as if establishing entries in a dictionary such as *Littré* (E 7/298). Derrida's translation of the language of philosophy breaks with the temptation of securing the fixed meaning of words. Some of his imitators would have us believe that certain words are declared taboo and their presence in a text is sufficient to condemn the text in which they appear, but it is more characteristic of Derrida himself to accord the words on which he focuses the status of undecidables.

The question that Derrida directs to Heidegger in "Sending" is, as in "Interpreting Signatures," focused on the unity of metaphysics. In this case, Derrida is concerned specifically with the unity that embraces the various epochs of the history of metaphysics. He recalls that although the sequence of ages is supposed to be arranged in Heidegger non-teleologically—that is to say not in the Hegelian manner, at least according to an interpretation of Hegelianism "at once strong and classical"—they are nevertheless gathered together under the unity of a destiny of Being (E 12/306). So, for example, the characteristically modern conception of the world as *Vorstellung* or representation was already implicit among the Greeks as the "distant condition, the presupposition, the secret mediation that would one day permit the world to become representation" (E 15–16/312). This is much in the same way that, following my earlier example that was also drawn from "The Age of the World-Picture," *hypokeimenon* is said to "resound" in *subjectum*.

Derrida understands Heidegger to be saying that although each epoch is "sent," it nevertheless belongs to a more powerful and original sending of Being—that of the unity of a history of metaphysics as *Anwesenheit* (E 24/321). The question then arises as to how Heidegger conceives the relationship of *Anwesenheit* to the epoch of representation. Can it be conceived in any way other than in terms of representation (E 16/313; E 25/322)? And this question in turn prompts another: Is Heidegger's reading "challengeable in principle, deconstructed from a historical point of view" (E 25/322)? This question would seem to point in the direction of Gadamer's understanding of Derrida as attempting to provide a critique of Heidegger, but there are in the text various pointers in the other direction. The most important of these arises when Derrida acknowledges as something "Heidegger would recognize" that "the *envoi* of Being was originally menaced in its being-together, in its *Geschick*, by divisibility or dissension (what I would call dissemination)" (E 25/323). In other words, Derrida finds dissemination alongside Heidegger's quest for unity. He thus comes to hear the word *Geschick* in a twofold manner. It can be heard with the emphasis on the gathering of its prefix or with the accent on the dissemination of a sending. In Derrida's double reading it is undecidable between its indivisibility (E 24/322) and divisibility (E 29/324). Thus, *Geschick* cuts across the twin strands of Heidegger's discourse.

Derrida is not thereby developing a counter-position to that of Heidegger. Derrida's word *dissension* is introduced as a translation of Heidegger's *Zwiespalt*. Indeed, earlier in "Sending," Derrida makes the point that "*Anwesenheit* is not simple, it is already divided and different, marking the place of a scission, a division, a dissension (*Zwiespalt*)" (E 19–20). If we return to Heidegger's text, "The Age of the World-View," we find Derrida's source. Heidegger writes:

> Rather man is gazed upon by the being, by that self-opening onto presencing which is gathered within it (the self-opening). To be gazed on by the being, to be fetched into the open, held into it and thereby sustained by it, pursued by its oppositions and marked by its dissension—that is the essence of man in the great age of the Greeks (ZW 83/AWP 131. Translation adapted).

"Pursued by its oppositions and marked by its dissension"—but Derrida does not hear the word *Zwiespalt* as saying the same thing as *Gegensatz*—opposition. The justification for Derrida's reading lies behind that passage in a source he does not cite, the discussion in Heidegger's 1936–37 lecture course on Nietzsche. There Heidegger explores the ambiguity of *Zwiespalt*. It is a scission and also a severance that is at bottom a concordance (*N 1* 219/1:189). Heidegger illustrates this with respect to the relationship between Nietzsche and Plato. There is a dissension in Nietzsche's inverted Platonism only because there is a dissension already in Plato, although in the latter it takes the form of a concordance. In this sense, the possibility of the overcoming of metaphysics is already inscribed in Plato, as much as representation was. Or in the way that *hypokeimenon* resounds in *subjectum*. Of course, insofar as Nietzsche simply reverses Plato, it would not amount to an overcoming. Reversal remains within the oppositional structure. Hence, the importance of what Heidegger calls "twisting free." "How far the twisting free extends with Nietzsche, how far it can go, to what extent it comes to an overcoming of Platonism and to what extent not— these are necessary critical questions" (N 1 242/1:210). Critical questions. Questions arising from a critique, not in the sense of a rejecting and faultfinding criticism, but in the sense of delimitation as de-cision. And de-cision not as a division between what we accept and what we refuse, nor even between what is held to be metaphysics and what evades it, but as a *Zwiespalt,* a dissension, within metaphysics which gives *rise* to double reading.

It may seem that the crucial question is whether the *envoi,* the sending, is gathering or disseminating. But is not Derrida better understood as attempting to displace the alternatives? He may indeed write of "a destiny which is never certain of gathering itself up, of identifying itself, or of determining itself" (E 29/325). And yet he had previously already explicated the sending that does not gather itself together by reference to the way that "it gathers itself only in dividing itself, in differentiating itself" (E 29/324). Gathering and disseminating are not poles of an oppositional structure which are to be rejected outright.

Derrida adds that he "does not know" whether this gathering that disseminates as it gathers—"a destiny which is never certain of gathering itself up, of identifying itself, or of determining itself"—"can be said with or without Heidegger, and it does not matter" (E 29/325). A similar formulation can be found elsewhere concerning precisely the same point: "The concept of onto-theology, if it be admissible, still depends on a unity or an assemblage of the destination (or of the *sending,* the *envoi,* of Being [*Geschick des Seins*]) that seems to me to situate the urgency of a question (in Heidegger, with or without Heidegger, I don't know)."[9] This second formulation serves to clarify what does not matter so that we say more precisely what it is that does matter. Ultimately it does not matter what Heidegger himself thought, in the sense of the author's intention. But what matters very much is that the reading can be sustained as a reading *in* Heidegger, a possible reading of Heidegger's text. The task is not to assign Heidegger, the author, to a place inside or outside metaphysics. Nor is it even to assign Heidegger's texts as metaphysical or non-metaphysical. For the terms of the question rely on the very notion of metaphysics that is itself in question. In both "Sending" and "Interpreting Signatures," Derrida has set himself the task of indicating how it is that we are not obliged to decide whether a text is held by metaphysics or whether it evades it, whether it gathers or whether it disseminates. He helps us to recognize how Heidegger can be read— with or without Heidegger—so that the disseminating, discontinuous, discourse of the words of Being, defies the gathering of the *legein* and doubles with the unifying coherent discourse of presence.

Derrida calls this an attempt "to outline another relation to Heidegger" (E 22/318). Viewed from outside this other relation is liable to be situated in the reading of Heidegger that Derrida adds. It is this reading which comes to be regarded as his contribution and comes to bear his name as Derrida's reading of Heidegger. And many commentators would be inclined to think of the reading as belonging more to Derrida than to Heidegger. In the case of "Sending," the reading at issue would be the one that defines the gathering of the *legein.* By contrast, ten years or more earlier, at the time when the orthodoxy amongst readers of Heidegger was that Heidegger had indeed broken with metaphysics, Derrida was more preoccupied with putting such a reading into question and in consequence the reading that was identified from outside as *his* and so bore his name was his alleged "critique" of Heidegger. Derrida himself refers to this problem when he introduces an apparent distinction between the reading that Heidegger gives and the one Derrida himself gives of that reading, "the one we would make of his own reading" (E 25/323). But how could Derrida sustain the distinction without entertaining the classic epistemological problem of our access to Heidegger's reading independent of our reading of it? The problem arises as soon as an attempt is made to assign the two readings, in this instance, that which draws Heidegger back into metaphysics, and that which attempts to stand out "beyond a closure of representation" (E 29/324). But Derrida—and this is at the heart of double reading—does not attempt to decide what reading is *with* and what reading is *without* Heidegger. And even if one of the readings of a double reading represented the standard reading at a particular time and it was juxtaposed with another, a "novel" reading, then double reading could not be identified with the latter alone but with their juxtaposition. That is why double reading as such is obliged to renounce the posture of critique. Indeed it is only insofar as double reading is understood in this way that it can "twist free" of the metaphysical opposition by what Derrida would call an "interweaving of the two strategies."

In this way, Derrida can never let himself be identified with a particular reading. He reads by juxtaposing readings. Double reading is, one might say, a dialogue of readings. But the conception of dialogue would have to be different from that operative in Gadamer. It is not easy to summarize the account of dialogue that Gadamer offers. The power of his hermeneutics depends on the recognition we accord to his descriptions, but he does not always describe dialogue according to the same model. Nevertheless, if an encounter between Gadamer and Derrida is to take place here, some such summary cannot be avoided. Dialogue, according to Gadamer, is directed towards agreement (*WM* 168/158). It is important to understand that by agreement or shared understanding [*Einverständnis*], Gadamer cannot be taken to mean agreement about content. For him agreement is concerned with the maintenance of a common language. It is therefore not only or even primarily a goal. It is also a precondition. Or, rather, because this is not an agreement that could be struck in advance once and for all, agreement needs constantly to be sustained. It is in this sense that Gadamer is led to the idea of an "endless conversation" or "infinite dialogue."

In his "Letter to Dallmayr," Gadamer says that he finds Heidegger's reading of Nietzsche fully persuasive (LD 94), but Gadamer would not regard his agreement with Heidegger as an exemplary case of understanding. This is because in his hermeneutical theory Gadamer places a value on the experience of being challenged through an encounter with otherness. Can we perhaps not find in the lack of the hermeneutic moment of otherness from Gadamer's reading of Heidegger's *Nietzsche* an explanation for the difficulties Gadamer and Derrida face in their dialogue? Is not this explanation at least as plausible as the explanation that Gadamer himself provides? Gadamer himself attempts to explain to Dallmayr his dissatisfaction with the encounter by saying that the topic of Nietzsche's language did not help them to attain a common ground. Nietzsche is not an appropriate topic for dialogue because "one can read Nietzsche in fundamentally different ways" (LD 93). Gadamer seems thereby to imply, somewhat curiously, that Nietzsche is in this regard a special case, as if other thinkers could be read in only one way.

Of course, had Gadamer been right in his claim that "Derrida rejects from the ground up Heidegger's Nietzsche-interpretation," then the distance between them would have been great indeed. But the difference between them lies elsewhere. It comes to the surface in the course of Gadamer's response to Dallmayr, when the former makes plain his presupposition that what must be sought is a "unitary understanding of Nietzsche" (LD 93). He does not mean by this that Derrida and he must agree on their interpretation of Nietzsche. Nor does he mean that one's attitude should be free from ambivalence. Both Gadamer and Derrida draw attention to Heidegger's ambivalence towards Nietzsche and they both recognize that it has its source in the ambiguity of Nietzsche's relation to metaphysics (94 and IS 254/65). What Gadamer means by a "unitary understanding of Nietzsche" is one which gathers into a unity that which in Nietzsche himself remains dispersed in an intangible multiplicity (DD 372/113). If Gadamer finds Heidegger's interpretation so convincing, it is no doubt because he believes that only Heidegger has succeeded in thinking the inner connection between the will to power and eternal recurrence. What convinces Gadamer in Heidegger's Nietzsche interpretation is what Heidegger brings to Nietzsche.

In this way Gadamer brings the discussion back to the issue raised by Derrida in "Interpreting Signatures," that according to Heidegger there is a unity in Nietzschean thought (IS 247/59). It would be tempting to identify this quest for a unitary understanding of Nietzsche as itself, in Derrida's phrase, "a gesture of classical metaphysics" (IS 250/62). In this way, Gadamer would have elected to keep faith with Heidegger knowing full well that it would render him subject to Derrida's "critique." But Gadamer's defiant gesture misconstrues Derrida's practice against which it is directed. I shall try to clarify this practice later, but first it is necessary to identify a tendency in Gadamer's reading of other philosophers.

In his response to Dallmayr, Gadamer himself helps to identify this tendency when he suggests that the likely source of Derrida's qualms about his work are to be found in the way that he gives too much weight to mutual understanding at the expense of otherness. It is certainly true that Gadamer tends to emphasize the rhetoric of mutual understanding in his responses to Derrida, as if Derrida stood for its opposite. When Gadamer does encounter otherness it leads him to self-doubt. Often Gadamer manages to put this doubt quickly behind him. One of the most common motifs of Gadamer's writing is for him to say that he once found something puzzling or difficult, but that he soon discovered that on further examination it was perfectly obvious. He is thus inclined to reverse the more familiar gesture among philosophers whereby what was taken to be obvious comes subsequently to be thought of as puzzling. But otherness is not simply a complement to agreement. When Gadamer talks about hermeneutics, although he emphasizes what is shared or held in common, it is always subordinated to the hermeneutical experience of a challenge from that which is other. The difficulty is that in practice Gadamer tends to enclose otherness in the circle of self-recognition, according to a gesture that he himself acknowledges owes its inspiration to Hegel. Only rarely is otherness allowed to remain in its otherness.

According to Gadamer, the highest principle of hermeneutics is that one should "always recognize in advance the possible correctness, even the superiority of the conversation partner's position" (S 505/189). Heidegger had already pointed in this direction when he said that "If we want to encounter a thinker's thought, we must magnify still further what is great in him" (*WHD* 72/77). Heidegger does not, except in a very few cases, minimize the thinker with whom he deals. To enter into a dialogue is to leave oneself exposed to "one's doubt as well as to the rejoinder of the other." There are clear instances of such doubt in both "Text and Interpretation" and "*Destruktion* and Deconstruction." For example, Gadamer writes, "I can, therefore, understand why the later Heidegger (and Derrida would presumably agree with him on this point) was of the opinion that I never really abandoned the sphere of phenomenological immanence. . ." (TI 335/26). For the most part Gadamer struggles to keep Heidegger and Derrida apart, but when he experiences the genuine hermeneutic moment of doubt they present themselves to him in unity.

On Gadamer's account, openness to self-doubt is the condition of dialogue. The notion of dialogue here is primarily Platonic, but it also has a Heideggerian source. Looking to defend himself against the charge that his *Kant and the Problem of Metaphysics* did violence to its subject, Heidegger in 1950 appealed to the notion of a "dialogue between thinkers" which is "bound by other laws" than those of historical philology. Similarly, by appealing to the model of a *dialogue,* Gadamer is striving to explain the sense in which a thoughtful encounter with a text does not simply repeat that text like an echo, any more than it constitutes a one-sided projection of an already established position. The hermeneutical notion of a dialogue opens the way to a reading of texts that goes beyond what is explicitly said in them.

How does this appeal to dialogue compare with deconstruction or what I prefer to call "double reading?" Double reading is directed to a "blind spot" in the text, a "not-seen that opens and limits visibility" (*Gr* 234/163), just as Heidegger's readings are directed to the unsaid in what is said. Or, rather, the reading that Derrida adds has this characteristic. He adds it to a first or initial reading that tends to be assigned to the author's intentions, to a standard translation or to a particularly eminent commentator. That "first" reading will often be characterized as "metaphysical," but it can also present itself as "beyond" or "outside" metaphysics in which case it is the task of the "second" reading to draw it back within metaphysics. The juxtaposition of readings serves to mark the multiplicity of readings to which the text is open. The reason why it is presented as a double reading (rather than a plurality of readings) arises from a structural necessity. The double reading is *double* in remembrance of the oppositions, the dualisms, which have served to govern the discourse of metaphysics, and which still govern the question of the overcoming of metaphysics. One of the readings remains *inside* metaphysics, while the other stands *outside*. To maintain only the one or the other would be—following an argument already very familiar from Hegel—to remain bound to the system of metaphysical oppositions. Only by maintaining both can one "displace" that logic. The text is ultimately undecidable between the twin readings.

As a consequence, the practice of double reading calls into question—more precisely, "deconstructs"—the concept of metaphysics. One would have to say, "There never was metaphysics as such."[10] Hence, far from it being the case that Derrida insists on a critique of metaphysics that has the language of metaphysics as its target, the notion of metaphysics has a heuristic or strategic function. This is what Heidegger came to recognize when he found that there never was metaphysics in isolation, but that it always bore its excess within it. The words of Being are in each case an excess both over what has gone before, in terms of which they can never be explained, and over what comes after, so that they can never be given a definitive reading. The distinction between metaphysics and what lies beyond it, cannot therefore be accorded a definitive status. That is why Heidegger is drawn to the conclusion that "a regard for metaphysics still prevails even in the intention to overcome metaphysics. Therefore, our task is to cease all overcoming and leave metaphysics to itself" (*SD* 25/24). Derrida's recognition of the problematic status of the notion of the end of philosophy arises from the same insight. In "Of an Apocalyptic Tone Recently Adopted in Philosophy," Derrida acknowledges that his own talk of closure rather than of end does not save him from the charge of participating in the contemporary form of apocalyptic discourse "whether wanting to or not" (ATRAP 21). In its place, he introduces the notion of an "end without end." Not an end which is never reached, but a gathering in dissemination. The end of metaphysics does not mean the end of metaphysical readings of texts. Nor does it mark the beginning of transgression. The notion of the end of philosophy is a self-destructive notion, one that cannot be sustained within a narrative without the destruction of that narrative, a notion which—as it were—*interrupts* its own discourse. In this way, self-doubt is also found to be an aspect of Derrida's writings, although he may not explicitly identify it as such. When in "Sending" and "Interpreting Signatures" Derrida addresses Heidegger's idea of the unity of metaphysics, he is not addressing something that is simply foreign to him. It should not be forgotten that in such writings as *Of Grammatology,* Derrida had himself proposed a conception of the unity of metaphysics articulated by epochs (*Gr* 145–46/97). The assignment of ideas to their authors is not a simple matter.

Derrida's own readers go astray when they identify *one* of the readings as Derrida's own, because by so doing they upset the "logic" that sustains his procedure. From the historian's perspective Derrida may appear to have simply added one more reading to the catalogue of readings that constitute the history of that text. But this would be to miss the strategy by which Derrida brings the text to the so-called *edge of metaphysics* (undecidable between inside and outside) that gives rise to a "doubling" of the text—in a very different sense from the doubling accomplished by simple paraphrase. If anything is Derrida's own, it is the juxtaposition of readings. There is not, as it were, a single truth to each text that might be said to exhaust it in the sense of being its fulfilment. Nor is there only one single correct reading, so that all others must be false and must therefore be rejected.

The question is whether this does not amount to what Gadamer with reference to Valéry called "an untenable hermeneutic nihilism" (*WM* 90/85). Gadamer, like Heidegger before him, rejected the classic formula that the task of interpretation was to understand the author better than he understood himself. But equally, neither Heidegger nor Gadamer turned to the author's intentions to find the criterion that would legitimate their interpretations. Gadamer seeks to resolve the problem in terms of the claim to truth encountered in a text, the experience of that which asserts itself as truth. Derrida looks instead to the notion of the history of the text. "One must then, in a single gesture, but doubled, read and write. And that person would have understood nothing of the game who, at this, would feel himself authorized merely to add on; that is, to add any old thing. He would add nothing: the seam would not hold" (*D* 72/64). The text is not a meaning hidden behind the words that can by a strenuous effort be uncovered. Every text has a history constituted by the various persuasive, powerful or influential readings offered of it. Each reading is the addition of a new thread, though if there is no basis for it "the seam would not hold." The plurality of readings that underlies double reading is not equivalent to arbitrariness, but is understood positively in terms of the dissemination of the text. The task of confronting this understanding of the text as its constantly expanding history with Gadamer's principle of *Wirkungsgeschichte* lies beyond the present essay, but I hope to have said enough to suggest that that task cannot be engaged except in terms of the "logic" of double reading. For if there is in Derrida what Gadamer would call "a claim to truth," this is where it would be found.

And Gadamer is never closer to that logic than in his attempt to confirm Heidegger's reading of Nietzsche. This is because he can confirm Heidegger only by acknowledging what Heidegger has brought to Nietzsche—a unity that is lacking from his thought. At the same time as he confirms Heidegger, Gadamer must also affirm the dispersal of Nietzsches's texts in their intangible multiplicity. Only then does Heidegger's marking of "the unity of this dispersal" appear as a contribution at all (DD 372/113). Gadamer discovers that he cannot confirm the unitary reading without affirming the disseminating reading. If the so-called unitary understanding of a philosopher seeks to resolve ambiguity, gather into one the dispersed thoughts to be found there, the problem is not that it is supposedly "metaphysical" and so therefore must be opposed. The problem is that by excluding its other, it denies itself.

The difference that emerges from the encounter between Gadamer and Derrida is that the latter knows this better than the former. *Déconstruction* is not opposed to *Destruktion,* but nor can they be equated with each other. That Derrida's word *déconstruction* is a kind of reinscription of Heidegger's word *Destruktion* is an acknowledgement that the former can only be thought in remembrance of the latter. Derrida's relation to metaphysics—or rather, his relationship to what can only ever be called "metaphysics" provisionally—is parasitic on Heidegger's relationship to it. But an important lesson can be learned thereby. Any attempt simply to affirm another reading—as Gadamer initially attempts to do with Heidegger's reading of Nietzsche—tends to be destructive (in the negative sense) of that reading. If Nietzsche is equated with Heidegger's Nietzsche, then Heidegger's contribution—or rather the dialogue between Heidegger and Nietzsche—disappears. Gadamer's agreement with Heidegger works against Heidegger by reducing his thinking to an orthodoxy. Derrida, by contrast, saves Heidegger both from being a proper name in the sense of a representative of a position and from disappearing in the texts he reads. This turns out to be the better way of keeping the Heideggerian space open in the sense of preserving it.

But what does this mean for the encounter between Gadamer and Derrida? Was the encounter between Gadamer and Derrida the failure it at first sight appears? Between whom was the encounter supposed to take place? Was it to be between Gadamer and Derrida as proper names? Or was it supposed to be an encounter between two individuals? Would it have had any bearing on what Gadamer and Derrida each "represent" had Gadamer and Derrida reached some kind of formal agreement in the way that politicians are expected to do at the close of summit meetings? At the end of "*Destruktion* and Deconstruction" Gadamer suggests that "conversation should seek its partner everywhere, just because this partner is other and especially if this other is completely different. Whoever wants me to take deconstruction to heart and insists on difference stands at the beginning of a conversation, not at its end" (DD 372/113). These sentences need to be examined carefully. Before Gadamer will "take deconstruction to heart" there must first be an agreement to continue the dialogue. Does that mean that Gadamer is insisting on receiving a commitment to a dialogue that will continue until agreement is reached? That is not what Gadamer usually understands by dialogue. It is more likely that he means, as explained earlier, an agreement to join an "infinite conversation" (S 504/188). Perhaps he suspects that Derrida is not commited to the idea of an "infinite conversation," but it is possible to find something parallel in Derrida's idea of the history of the text as infinite. Gadamer looks at this point to be trying to shift the burden of the conversation away from himself to the Other, but in such a way that the Other is called upon to compromise his or her alterity from the start. One could well imagine the course such a dialogue might take. It would conform to a model that Gadamer has already observed in Plato. As he says, Socratic dialogue often exposes that "the seeming agreement in which we live and speak quasi-consciously is no real agreement" (S 497/180). In other words, agreement is not confined to being a goal or a precondition. It can also be an illusion. The encounter between Gadamer and Derrida as it is found in the present volume begins with the presupposition that their proper names stand in opposition to each other. The opposition rests on an agreement. They come together as opposed, representing different strands of contemporary thinking. In the course of reading the texts assembled around their names, I find that this opposition becomes an otherness. That should not be regarded as a failure. Philosophy—or, rather, thinking—is not politics.

I do not know how far the things I have focused on in this essay belonged to the intentions of the participants. For example, I have suggested that, by focusing on the way a philosopher's name is used to name the subject matter of his thinking, Derrida counters Gadamer's attempt to restrict the dialogue to a certain image of Derrida. I do not suppose that this was Derrida's intention. I suspect that Derrida had not had the opportunity to read "Text and Interpretation" when he wrote "Interpreting Signatures." But Derrida's intentions here do not matter. Encounters are not limited to what the participants intend; much of what goes on can take place by accident. And what seems to have taken place, at least for this reader of the text, is that Derrida's essay on Heidegger's *Nietzsche* led Gadamer away from his initial focus on what he took to be Derrida's truth-claims and critique, to consider not just the approach which Derrida adopted, but also his own approach. Gadamer still sought a unitary understanding of Nietzsche, but he learned not to efface altogether the dispersal that necessarily underlies it. Perhaps dispersal is also a "precondition," although that word no longer seems appropriate here.

If our attention is limited to the truth-claims of the participants, if we set ourselves the task of differentiating their standpoints, we might well be led to the conclusion that the encounter did not take place. But that would be to confine our expectations to what standardly passes for philosophical debate and both Gadamer and Derrida have—in their very different ways—broken with the standard conception. An encounter between ways of thinking and questioning is much harder to recognize than one that takes place at the level of content, the level of what is said. Perhaps the very failure of Gadamer and Derrida to communicate at the level of content helps direct us to another level. Although thinkers may share a tradition and so share a language, it is also true that they have their own language by virtue of their own words, the words that name them, as *deconstruction* names Derrida enigmatically in his relationship to Heidegger. Is it the task of thinkers to try to come to an agreement across their languages? Could they do so without opting for the flatness of unitary understanding? Or is it enough if at rare moments they intersect with one another and in such a way that the contours of their thinking are highlighted? Is it not enough for that thought to have received new definition—and further dispersal—by the new context in which it appears?

John Sallis

12. Interruptions

Did an encounter really take place? Between Hans-Georg Gadamer and Jacques Derrida, both of whom, indisputably, were present and took part in the colloquium held at the Goethe Institute in Paris in April 1981.

Will the encounter ever have taken place? Even after all the texts subsequent to the event itself have come to compensate for what might have been lacking in the event itself. Including a text signed by Derrida and others by Gadamer. Including also the present text.

Could an encounter ever have taken place without by that very occurrence deciding what would have been in dispute in the encounter, confirming the continuity, the ideal (of) dialogue, that Gadamer so eloquently advocates? Confirming it in deed.

Could an encounter not have taken place without by that very nonoccurrence deciding, in the other direction, what would have been in dispute, confirming what Derrida says about interruption and the suspending of all mediation? Confirming it in deed, as in a Platonic dialogue.

"eine unwahrscheinliche Debatte"

A heterogeneous set of texts: the intertextuality operative in the genealogy of this body of texts is quite complex and will need somewhere to be analyzed. Not only is there a text by Derrida that was added without any explicit connection to the context of the debate, but also there is a contribution by Gadamer that arose not directly from the debate but in the course of a correspondence with Dallmayr. To say nothing of the additional text(s) that Gadamer will have added to the dossier.

And yet, there, in Paris, a *Versuch(ung)*: dialogue in behalf of dialogue: "What we find happening in speaking is not a mere reification [*Fixierung*] of intended meaning, but an endeavor [*Versuch*] that continually modifies itself, or better: a continually recurring temptation [*Versuchung*] to engage oneself in something or to become involved with someone. But that means to expose oneself."

Met with questions, among them the following: "one needs to ask [*on peut se demander*] whether the precondition for *Verstehen*, far from being the continuity of *rapport* (as it was described yesterday evening) is not rather the interruption of *rapport*, a certain *rapport* of interruption, the suspending of all mediation."

If only it were as radically fictitious as a Platonic dialogue, the very occurrence or non-occurrence of the dispute, the encounter, the dialogue, would suffice to settle what would have been in dispute. If only it were not determined by so many factual contingencies, not least of all the language barrier, which, in a supplementary text written three years after the colloquium in Paris, Gadamer mentions as having complicated the desired encounter between Heidegger's two heirs apparent. Derrida could not but be translated into German, Gadamer into French, and both, now into English: barriers that cannot but interrupt the smooth flow of dialogue, interruptions that translation could never simply circumvent and neutralize. The colloquium at the Goethe Institute in Paris was already interrupted from the beginning. However much one might have dreamed of a decisive γιγαντομαχία over the Heideggerian heritage. Der traum ist noch nicht ausgeträumt. Pas encore.

What would be in dispute is disputation itself, or, rather, the possibility of a dialogue that, even if never-ending, would in an essentially continuous movement remain directed to authentic understanding and mutual agreement. It is to such dialogue that Gadamer would reorient dialectic, diverting it thus from the self-presentative speculative method of German Idealism. It would be a matter of turning from the subjectivism of modern philosophy back to the living dialogue of Socratic-Platonic thought, following thus the insight that German Romanticism gained into the dialogical principle. It would be a matter of setting the original dialogical phenomenon of language in place of that subjectivity whose relation to language would be essentially exhausted in its positing of intended meanings. It is a matter too of generalizing the dialogical phenomenon in such a way that language comes to be regarded as mediating all access to the world, a matter of setting forth the dialogical midworld of language in such a way as to prohibit every appeal to an

In the case of the Platonic dialogues one would like to say that nothing is accidental and so to declare, with Leo Strauss, a law of logographic necessity. And one can, heuristically, without also positing behind the text an author that would have exercised over it just such utter control as the *Seventh Letter* declares impossible. The deeds would, then, always declare even what did not quite come to be said. Unlike real (non) encounters, where accidents always interrupt the connection between words and deeds.

Even the words themselves, belong accidentally, it would seem, to different languages: "My encounter [*Begegnung*] with Derrida in Paris three years ago, which I had looked forward to as a conversation between two totally independent developers of Heideggerian initiatives in thought [*ein Gespräch zwischen selbständigen Fortführern Heideggerischer Anstöße*], involved special difficulties. First of all there was the language barrier. This is always a great difficulty when thinking or poetizing strives to leave traditional forms behind und aus der eigenen Muttersprache neue Weisungen herauszuhören trachtet."

And yet, the barrier, Gadamer had insisted in Paris, is not unbreakable: "It seems to me that my own contribution is the discovery that no conceptual language, not even what Heidegger called the 'language of metaphysics,' represents an unbreakable constraint [*einen unbrechbaren Bann*] upon thought if the thinker only allows himself to trust language; that is, if he engages in dialogue with other thinkers and other ways of thinking. Thus, in full accord with Heidegger's critique of the concept of subject, whose hidden ground he revealed as substance, I tried to conceive the original phenomenon of language in dialogue. This effort entailed a hermeneutical reorientation [*Rückorientierung*] of dialectic, which had been developed by German Idealism as the speculative method, toward the art of the living dialogue in which the Socratic-Platonic movement of thought took place."

A matter, of course, only of an ideal (of) dialogue: "Now certainly I would not want to say that the solidarities which bind human be-

allegedly prelinguistic domain, whether one of pure self-consciousness or of positive facts. There would be neither pure consciousness nor perceived things—but, always already, language, linguisticality, λόγος.

The Gadamerian turn to dialogue would thus reenact, in the unity of a single gesture, both the Socratic turn to λόγοι, that δεύτερος πλοῦς of which Socrates tells when in the *Phaedo* he recounts his own history, *and* the Heideggerian subversion of the subject-object distinction (and, hence, of the opposition between idealism and realism) by regress to the more originary phenomenon, Dasein as Being-in-the-world, as disclosedness [*Erschlossenheit*], as originary transcendence.

It is at this point—the point at which the continuity with the Socratic and the Heideggerian moves would be secured—that I would want to interrupt the dialogue gathered around Professor Gadamer. To interrupt it perhaps for the sake of another dialogue, one more inclusive, or, rather, one that in the move to include its other would inevitably be exposed to choosing either appropriation of its other or disruption of itself from within. The interruption would not, then, simply have served to extend dialogue. The bind is that of a dialogue that would put in question the very possibility of dialogue.

It goes almost without saying that the Socratic turn to λόγοι is an engagement not only in dialogue with others but also in the dialogue of the soul with itself. Is there a more direct way to self-presentative subjectivity than that which, beginning with such interior monologue, withdraws it from the externality of language, silencing the soliloquy and submitting all other discourse to it? Could one not more

ings together and make them partners in a dialogue, always are sufficient to enable them to achieve understanding and total mutual agreement. Just between two people this would require a never-ending dialogue."

Still, reorientation to the (ideal (of)) dialogue concurs with and enforces the lending of "a certain primacy to the 'linguisticality' of our experience of the world. Over against the illusion of self-consciousness as well as the naïveté of a positive concept of facts, the midworld [*Zwischenwelt*] of language has proven itself to be the true dimension of that which is given."

A double turn: (1) to language, λόγος, as in the Platonic text: "I thought of that danger, and I was afraid my soul would be blinded if I looked at things with my eyes and tried to grasp them with any of my senses. So I thought I must have recourse to λόγοι and examine in them the truth of beings [τῶν ὄντων τὴν ἀλήθειαν]." (2) But also a turn to an intermediate, a between that is, at the same time, deeper, more originary even than intentionality: "Underneath the entire earlier problem of the 'relation' of 'subject' to 'object' is the undiscussed problem of *transcendence*. . . . The problem of transcendence as such is not at all identical with the problem of intentionality. As ontic transcendence, the latter is itself only possible on the basis of originary transcendence, on the basis of Being-in-the-world."

Thus gathering into the Heideggerian impulses the initial drive to dialogue, gathering these up in hermeneutics. "We are gathered together here around Professor Gadamer. It is to him, then, that I wish to address these words, paying him the homage of a few questions."

First, about the inner dialogue that would have the same essential structure as dialogue with the other: "Just between two people this would require a never-ending dialogue. And the same would apply with regard to the inner dialogue the soul has with itself." Almost a citation from Socrates' discourse with Theaetetus, in which thinking [τὸ διανοεῖσθαι] is called "discourse [λογος] that the soul carries

effectively disrupt the dialectic of self-presentative subjectivity by exposing a breach always already operative within it, an archaic operation of difference within the dialogue of the soul with itself, that is, within discourse in solitary mental life [*in einsamen Seelenleben, de la vie solitaire de l'âme*]? Not simply by turning to dialogue with the other, not even just by insisting on a certain potentiality of otherness [*Potentialität des Andersseins*] within the dialogical relation, but by demonstrating that otherness is always already operative in what one would otherwise have called monologue.

But it is primarily a question of the homogeneity of those Platonic discourses that are called—all too carelessly, no doubt—dialogues. Even if one leaves out of consideration those discourses in which Socrates remains mostly silent or does not participate at all, one still cannot but ask whether the Socratic discourses presented in the Platonic texts are ever simply reciprocal exchanges between interlocutors open to one another and in search, through the exchange, of mutual agreement and common understanding—that is, dialogues in the modern sense of homogeneously textured discussions between persons open to one another. Not only are the Socratic discourses often placed in settings that violate such homogeneity, for example, in a wrestling school or a courtroom. They also take place, almost always, in contexts that are highly determined erotically. Need it be said that the play of eros is one of heterogeneity and of veils rather than of open dedication to common understanding? What such discourses produce is rarely mutual agreement but rather rupture in the discussion, disclosure of the (self-ignorant) ignorance of Socrates' interlocutors, and irony from Socrates himself. It is not, after all, on account of some mutual understanding reached with him that the Athenians sent Socrates to his death. What is produced is more often hostility and confusion than openness and understanding. The Socratic art—is it really a τέχνη?—is not simply one of living dialogue but also one that

on with itself about any subject it is considering."

The question is one of deconstruction, and it would be necessary in this connection to reconstitute almost the entire analysis given in *La Voix et le phénomène*, assembling it perhaps around the following two excerpts: (1) "This self-presence of the animating act in the transparent spirituality of what it animates, this inwardness of life with itself [*cette intimité de la vie à elle-même*], which has always made us say that speech [*parole*] is alive, supposes, then, that the speaking subject hear himself [*s'entende*] in the present." (2) "Auto-affection as an operation of the voice would suppose that a pure difference have come to divide self-presence."

Difference, heterogeneity, is manifoldly in play in the Platonic texts. For instance, in the *Lysis,* which takes place in a wrestling school [παλαίστρα] during the festival of the liar/messenger Hermes. Socrates has asked Hippothales about his favorite: "At this question he blushed; so I said: Oh, Hippothales, son of Hieronymus, there is no longer any need for you to tell me whether you are in love or not, since I am sure you are not only in love but also far along already in your passion. For though in most matters I am a poor useless creature, yet by some means or other I have received from god the gift of being able to recognize quickly a lover or a beloved." Socrates will eventually interrogate Hippothales' beloved, Lysis; and as places are being taken by those who will be party to that discussion, Socrates assumes his purely narrative voice in order to expose Hippothales: "There came up, moreover, the rest of our party, among them Hippothales, who seeing them form into a good-sized group, screened himself behind them in a position where he did not think he could be seen by Lysis—so fearful was he of giving him offense. And thus placed near him, he listened to our conversation."

Or in the *Euthyphro,* in the rupture with which it concludes, Euthyphro rushing off to continue his unholy business of prosecuting his aged father for murder: "Another time, then, Socrates, for I am in a hurry and must be off this minute." Socrates: "What are you doing,

induces radical perplexity, an art that magically casts its spell over others, numbing, paralyzing even those of greatest rhetorical powers. Socratic discourse does not just enliven, often does not enliven at all but kills, produces death. If the Socratic art is indeed a τέχνη, it is a war machine; and Socrates' reputation as a soldier was quite well-deserved.

my friend? Will you leave and dash me down from the mighty expectation I had of learning from you what is holy and what is not, and so escaping from Miletus' indictment?"

Or in the *Apology*, in the outbursts with which the "men of Athens" would interrupt Socrates' defense. To say nothing of that practice that Socrates describes just after the second of such outbursts. Delphi is in question, Socrates seeking a man wiser than himself: "So I considered this man thoroughly—I need not speak of him by name, but he was one of the politicians—and when I considered him and conversed with him, men of Athens, I was affected something like this: it seemed to me that this man seemed to be wise, both to many other human beings and most of all to himself, but that he was not. And then I tried to show him that he supposed he was wise, but was not. So from this I became hateful both to him and to many of those present."

He becomes hardly less hateful to Meno: "Socrates, even before I met you they told me that in plain truth you are a perplexed man yourself and reduce others to perplexity. At this moment I feel you are exercising magic and witchcraft upon me and positively laying me under your spell until I am just a mass of helplessness. If I may be flippant, I think that not only in outward appearance but in other respects as well you are exactly like the flat sting ray that one meets in the sea. Whenever anyone comes into contact with it, it numbs him, and that is the sort of thing that you seem to be doing to me now. My soul and my lips are truly numb, and I have nothing to reply to you. Yet I have spoken about virtue hundreds of times, held forth often on the subject in front of large audiences, and very well too, or so I thought."

Socrates was not otherwise in war, if the drunken Alcibiades is to be believed: against the enemy ("convincing anyone even from afar that whoever cares to touch this man will find he can put up a stout enough defense"); also numbing himself against the hardships ("he stood the hardships of the campaign far better than I did, or anyone else, for that matter").

It is of course with the sophists that Socrates especially must fight, those whom one

Can he, then, be called a man of good will? Can one, then, agree that good will has "a

would like to distinguish from the philosopher, to distinguish, for example, as not being men of good will, open to others and willing to understand them. The difficulty is with the distinction, with making it and with making it stick. With making it, convincingly, before the "men of Athens," in response to accusations supported by ingrained prejudices and accumulated hostility. In defense of life.

The question is, then, whether sophistry can ever be set over against philosophy simply as its other, whether it can in this way be excluded and controlled. Or whether it does not always threaten philosophy from within, whether it does not belong always almost indistinguishably to philosophy, haunting the latter constantly, never simply to be expelled so as to leave intact a domain of openness in which discussion would be governed by the aim of common understanding, a sphere of good will. What if, instead, sophistry were the death that would always already have interrupted the living discourse of philosophy? What if sophistry, in its deceptive appeal to obviousness, were to be thought as corresponding to that counter-essence [*Gegenwesen*—namely, *die Irre*] that Heidegger thinks as belonging to the essence of truth?

And so there must be some question of the continuity with the subversive moves of Heidegger, even with those already fully in play in *Sein und Zeit*. For one cannot but interrupt the virtual identification of Rede with Gespräch, one cannot but break apart—cannot but set *apart* rather than side by side—that moment which, along with Verstehen and Befindlichkeit, goes to constitute Dasein's disclosedness and, apart from it, living discussion with others. To make Rede constitutive for Being-in-the-world, for disclosedness, is not to install living discussion, speaking with others, at the point at which world and meaning would arise. For whatever the relationship of Rede to the other moments, Verstehen and Befindlichkeit—I leave aside this controversial question—Heidegger could hardly have been more insistent on the distinction between Rede, that articulation of Verständlichkeit that is the

good deal to do with the difference between dialectic and sophistics"? Is it not precisely to the difficulty of this distinction that the Platonic texts testify? For example, the text entitled *Sophist,* in which the Stranger and Theaetetus, searching for the sophist, come across the art of cross-questioning [ἔλενχος], which otherwise one would take as characteristically Socratic. Stranger: "But what of this? Who shall we say are those who use this art? I for one am afraid to assert that they are sophists." Theaetetus: "Why is that?" Stranger: "Lest we attach to them too great an honor." Theaetetus: "But it is still the case that the present remarks do bear a resemblance to someone of the sort." Stranger: "So, for example, does a wolf to a dog, the most savage to the most tame."

The connection is also noted by Heidegger in the context of an analysis of the essence of truth, just following the discussion of the counter-essence: "However, in the same period in which the beginning of philosophy takes place, the *marked* domination of common sense (sophistry) also begins. Sophistry appeals to the unquestionable character of the beings that are opened up and interprets all thoughtful questioning as an attack on, an unfortunate irritation of, common sense."

No less questionable than the exclusion of sophistry is the homogenization of the difference between language (living discourse with others) and its existential foundation (what Heidegger calls *"Rede"*). To reorient dialectic to dialogue is not tantamount to taking Heidegger's existential analysis of Rede as one's point of departure. It cannot be simply a matter of comparing dialogue to Rede, setting them side by side ("Wenn ich meinerseits davon ausgehe, dem Existenzial der Rede das Gespräch als das wahre 'Unterwegs zur Sprache' sur Seite zu stellen. . ."). For Heidegger insists on the depth that separates Rede from language in the ordinary sense (*Sprache*): "Das existenzial-ontologische Fundament der Sprache ist die Rede." Conversely: "Die Hinausgesprochenheit der Rede ist die Sprache."

existential foundation of Sprache, and Sprache in the sense of the living discourse that one carries on with others.

Furthermore, because discourse in the ordinary sense is existentially founded on Rede, it is never simply a matter of speaking with others but, rather, for example in the form of assertion, has as its primary signification *Aufzeigen*, ἀπόφανσις: letting something be seen from itself. Communication, speaking *with others*, is only the third of the three significations that belong to assertion.

Rede, the distinctively linguistic moment of Dasein's disclosedness, is so remote from anything like living discourse with others that it is nothing spoken, nothing sounded, at all, but rather a moment of that which precedes all dialogue, all discourse—the silence that will always already have interrupted living, sounded speech. It can also be thought—has been thought—as the death inscribed within living speech, written there and, like all writing, escaping supervision, withdrawing.

If it were a question simply of heritage, it could not but have to do with writing. Which is to say that it could never be simply a question of heritage. But always also of interruptions.

Even in language, appropriately distinguished from its existential foundation, the communicative function is less than primary: "1. Assertion signifies primarily *pointing-out* [*Aufzeigen*] . . . . 3. Assertion means *communication*, speaking forth [*Heraussage*]."

And as for Rede, it is more akin to silence: "*Hearing* and *keeping silent* [*Schweigen*] are possibilities belonging zum redenden Sprechen. In these phenomena the constitutive function of Rede for the existentiality of existence becomes entirely clear for the first time."

The silence within speech: writing.

"Is that not perhaps what the beginning of writing is, a liberation of writing to the draft, or rather to the whirlwind, writing in withdrawal."

John D. Caputo

13. Gadamer's Closet Essentialism: A Derridean Critique

In his recent work *Pragmatism Without Foundations,* Joseph Margolis makes a telling point against Gadamer that provides us with just the right angle for seeing what has gone wrong in Gadamer's "philosophical hermeneutics" from the standpoint of deconstruction. Margolis cites the following passage from *Truth and Method* that he takes—rightly I think—to be a characteristic claim:

> That which has been sanctioned by tradition and custom has an authority that is nameless, and our finite historical being is marked by the fact that always the authority of what has been transmitted—and not only what is clearly grounded—has power over our attitudes and behavior. . . . The validity of morals, for example, is based on tradition. They are freely taken over, but by no means created by a free insight or justified by themselves. That is precisely what we call tradition: the ground of their validity . . . tradition has a justification that is outside the arguments of reason and in large measure determines our institutions and attitudes. (*WM* 264–65/249)

There is, as Margolis rightly suspects, a version of foundationalism in this position, but of a more discrete, less obnoxious form, because it has done its best to accommodate the demands of history and finitude and to keep its distance from an outright transcendentalism. This is a theory of deep truth, which means that tradition—*the* tradition? a tradition? any tradition? what if there are many traditions, or many traditions within *the* tradition?—has the goods, both the *ousia* and the *agathon*. Having a tradition then is primarily a matter of trusting it, of letting it have sway so that it can deliver on its promises. "Read correctly," Margolis points out, "this marks the unmistakable sense in which Gadamer is a closet essentialist. . ."[1] "Closet"—because up front there is a lot of brave talk in Gadamer about history and change, time and becoming—but still "essentialist"—because when the truth is told, that is all just a front for a theology of lasting essences. All you really get from Gadamer, Margolis thinks, is an "historical analogue" to essentialism, that is, everything that essentialism promises, but wrapped in historical form.

In Margolis's view, Gadamer defends a theory of "traditionalism," which is a variation on foundationalism, a crypto-foundationalism, a foundationalism in disguise.[2] Foundationalism thinks that you can actually lay out rigorous theoretical foundations for knowledge and action, that you can really get into a transcendental standpoint. Traditionalism thinks that while there are indeed foundations, they inhabit the marrow of our historical bone, the interstices of our beliefs and practices, and hence are too deep-seated to be laid hold of theoretically or raised to the level of objectification by a transcendental subject. Hence, instead of raising the foundationalist question and being drawn into debates about how to answer it—that is the classical Enlightenment project which these days almost nobody is willing to undertake—Gadamer claims that our foundations lie deeper than we can say, that we are primordially rooted in our tradition before foundationalist questions appear on the scene. Thus, Gadamer is a critic of the Enlightenment not because he is critical of foundations, but because he is critical of raising the *question* of foundations—of the whole foundationalist enterprise.

Like Alasdair MacIntyre (who is, it seems to me, his closest Anglo-American counterpart), Gadamer thinks that foundationalism is bound to come to grief, that is, to Nietzsche. Foundationalism demands a reasoned account, an explicit *logos,* an *Urteil,* about what is so deeply lodged in our bones that it can only show up on the level of a *Vorurteil* which we can never manage to flush out. The best we can do is unfold, lay out [*aus-legen*], the ground upon which we stand, nourish and savor it, but we cannot get *gründend,* foundational, about our ground. If we do, we will pay the price—and that price is Nietzsche: the open admission, indeed the audacious celebration, not far from madness, that all values are the issue of the will to power, that all that remains is a competition among valuations. Being—*ousia* and the *agathon*—has become a value, and that is nihilism. That is why in his debate with Derrida, Gadamer keeps coming back to Nietzsche, complaining again and again about the Nietzsche that has gotten into Derrida's pen. The wages of foundationalism is Nietzsche, *Nietzsche aujourd'hui,* that is, deconstruction.[3]

The historical explanation for Gadamer's closet essentialism lies in Gadamer's attachment not only to Plato, the aboriginal essentialist, but more interestingly to Hegel, whose overtly and robustly essentialist thought had an historical twist. Hegel wanted to show the historical unfolding of essence. To say that *Wesen* is *Gewesen* is not to attack essence but to insist that essence is always the result of historical process. Hegel had nothing at all against essence or *ousia;* he was simply insisting that it be conceived, not abstractly and timelessly, but concretely, in and as a process of historical becoming. Essence is not shot directly from guns in the manner of Schellingian intuition; rather it must submit to dialectical development and unfolding. It must become what it is—through historical hard work—in order to be [*wesen*] what it has been all along [*gewesen*].

The *Wesen* that Margolis is smoking out in Gadamer is deeply Hegelian and it represents a headlong retreat from the radicalization of *Wesen* that was underway in Heidegger. It is a classical metaphysical notion and proof positive of the hollowness of Gadamer's protests that he has followed Heidegger beyond metaphysics (see DD 110). In Gadamer the Hegelian *Wesen* has taken on a little more modesty, has a bit more of its finitude showing (*WM* 339/320), as befits a properly historical being. Chastened by the fire of the Kierkegaardian critique of Hegelian idealism, and then by Heidegger's critique of Husserlian idealism in *Being and Time,* Gadamer has given up on the notion of a parousiological completion of *ousia,* of a definitive historical form for the *Geist,* and of a pure form of reflective consciousness. He puts in its place a pluralized, historicized, non-hierachized multiplication of historical forms and a concretely situated subject. This is another way of saying that Gadamer has broken with Hegel's theology. He does not think that history is relentlessly grinding out the progressively more perfect formation and unfolding of the spirit. He has a much more liberal, tolerant view than that. He thinks instead of multiply "different"—not better—unfoldings of the tradition. The successive applications of the "classic" are not to be rank-ordered. Authors do not have canonical rights over their own works. Things have neither been going all down-hill since the Greeks (Strauss), nor has there been a steady ascent (Hegel); things have just been different. (Cf. *WM* 180–85/169–73). The only sense in which things are getting better is that they are different, that is, differently applicable, applicable to the differences that show up in each epoch (*WM* 289ff./274ff.). Gadamer gives us a very liberal, non-teleological, non-hierarchical version of a fundamentally conservative, traditionalist, essentialist idea.

What Gadamer offers is a theory of deep truth or deep essence—where the function of the "deep" metaphor is twofold: (1) it sees to it that the essence is deep enough to forbid definitive formulations or final, canonical versions—the only canon is the longevity and vitality of the tradition itself, and (2) it insures that beneath the multiplicity of historical formulations and multiple applications there rests an underlying, undying truth, deeper than we can say, too rich to be exhausted in a single try, too deep to be tapped in a single draft, but always keeping watch over the multiplicity of forms, seeing to it that they do not get out of hand. So it belongs to the essence of a Gadamerian tradition that it has to be written again and again, redone ever anew, in a kind of joyous acclamation of our impotence ever to spend its infinite wealth, in an economy of infinite re-serves, of lifetime endowment. That is why Gadamerian hermeneutics is so attractive to theologians—it allows them to develop moderate theories of theo-logical traditions in which theology is neither hide-bound to archaic dogmatic formulations nor forced to throw the dogmatic baby (a terror of a child!) out with the historical bath.[4]

When Gadamer talks about deconstruction he gets very reassuring that he stands with Heidegger and against Nietzsche, in particular with Heidegger's stand against Nietzsche as the last metaphysician, and he insists that his philo-sophical hermeneutics follows Heidegger's lead in overcoming logocentric me-taphysics. There can be no doubt that Gadamer has taken seriously Heidegger's delimitation of transcendental consciousness, that he has made an effort to fol-low Heidegger's critique of subjectivity, which includes Heidegger's critique of Nietzsche. But from a deconstructionist point of view Gadamer's use of Heideg-ger is half-hearted, indeed reactionary, even resistant to the momentum, the direction, the tendency of Heidegger's critique of metaphysics. This more radi-cal, more critical side of Heidegger's project is just what deconstruction wants to keep going. So the conflict between Gadamer and Derrida is in my view a conflict between a right wing and left wing Heideggerianism, between a Heideggerianism that exploits Heidegger's conservative side (his affection for the "truth of Being") and a Heideggerianism that has gotten more ruthless about truth, which will not let us translate *alētheia* with "truth" [*Wahrheit*], even that *Wahrheit* which is too deep for method to get at, too close to us for the objectify-ing gestures of method to grasp.[5]

There is a point in Heidegger's later writings when he gives up on the word *Wahrheit,* on truth as preserving [*verwahren*], and begins to think the sheer happening or event of *a-lētheia,* according to which "there is" only the succes-sive unfoldings of the multiple events of Being, the multiple sending of the epochs. At that point—a point which "philosophical hermeneutics" never reaches—the matter [*Sache*] for thought is not this or that content [*Gehalt*] of the tradition—not even its Greek contents—but the very happening *of* the tradition, the *dare* in the *trans-dare, tra-ditum,* the *Es gibt,* which gives the epochs of presence. Pushed to its most extreme point, Heidegger's thinking is concerned not with the meaning or the truth of Being, but with the *giving or granting* of meaning and truth. In a sense, Heidegger ended up answering his earliest ques-tion, posed to him by Brentano's book on Aristotle—what is the unified meaning of the manifold sense of Being?—by saying that there is [*es gibt*] only the manifold sense, the many senses, the endless unfolding of sense after sense, truth after truth, in a process which he describes as a groundless play, a play without why (*SG* 185–88).

From this point of view, Gadamer's thought has lost its nerve, for its precise concern is with presence, *Anwesen,* the manifold riches of the tradition, the stored up goods and *ousia* that the tradition has to deliver. Gadamer's interest is in how the tradition can deliver the goods, how it can pass on its accumulated wealth, how it can be a living and self-renewing tradition, a good infinite. There is an unmistakable resistance to Heidegger's step back out of the history of presence. Gadamer is always more interested in the gift of the presence—the "present" which tradition makes to us—than in the giving itself, the *es gibt*. To give Margolis' Anglo-American formulation a continental twist: Gadamer's closet essentialism consists in a certain retreat into the classical idea of *Wesen* as deep essence, *essentia*, albeit with historical embodiment, and in an unmistakable resistance to Heidegger's attempt to think *Wesen* verbally, as the sheer coming to presence [*An-wesen*] and passing away [*Ab-wesen*] of the epochs of presence.

That is why Gadamer is simply cutting wide swaths in the air when he criticizes deconstruction. He does not see that Derrida too has taken the step back out of the epochs of presence, of the meaning and truth of Being. For Derrida, as for the late Heidegger himself, Being, meaning, and truth have all become what Derrida would call, in his more Husserlian moments, constituted effects, "granted," let us say, by *différance* in the one case or by *Unter-Schied* in the other. A Gadamerian tradition steams along on a more naive, constituted plane, in a kind of historical-natural attitude. It is quite literally, to deploy the English translation, a history of effects, history *as* effects, history, truth and tradition as effects of *différance/Unter-Schied*. In Heidegger, the step back leads from the epochs of presence to the opening, the open space in which presence emerges, the letting-come-to-presence of presence. In Derrida there is a parallel, albeit different, move to the differential matrix, the spacing, within which the various unities of meaning take shape. Gadamerian hermeneutics and deconstruction operate on different levels. Gadamer's is a philosophy of meaning—of the transmission, communication, preservation, enrichment, and nourishing of meaning. Deconstruction has taken the step back out of meaning into that which grants meaning and at the same time delimits it. Gadamer thinks there are deep deposits of meaning in the tradition into which we have been placed and the task of hermeneutics is to learn how to mine that wealth and to pass it along to the current generation. Deconstruction explains the transcendental naîveté of such a view.[6]

Deconstruction carries out such a radical disruption of essentialism that we might be tempted to say it represents a clean break with foundationalism—were it not for the fact that deconstruction remains suspicious too of all clean breaks. The *Stimmung*, the distinctive key in which philosophical hermeneutics is turned, is one of "trust": trust in language, trust in the good will of a conversation, trust in the deep powers of the tradition to deliver the goods. But deconstruction has a more suspicious eye. In Derrida, language, meaning, tradition, and truth have not dropped from the sky: rather they are taken to be constituted effects, effects that are at once enabled and disabled by the archi-system of tracings in which they are inscribed. Derrida is moved by a Socratic distrust of everything that poses as present, that presents itself as one of the powers that be, powers that try to pass themselves off as present, as being, as substance, *ousia,* especially when they are passed along by men [*sic*] of substance. Like the Socratic sting ray, deconstruction poses disturbing questions rather than trusting what is being handed down. Derrida does not think there is a deep ontology inscribed in the *Muttersprache,* a matriarchal ontology that usually ends up saying that father knows best. He thinks that languages, traditions, meanings, truth, and Being itself are only more or less stable—and hence more or less unstable—unities of meaning, relatively frail concoctions that have acquired hoary prestige, effects that are held together in part by violence, in part by inertia, in part by their usefulness for life.

If Gadamer feels called upon to defend speaking over writing, life over texts, dialogue over reading, when he thinks about Derrida, that is just simply not to the point (see TI 34f.). For Derrida is working at a different and more radical level of *archi*-writing, of textual*ity,* of the quasi-system of inscription that in-habits both speech and its "empirical analogue," writing, both conversation and reading. Archi-writing enables and disables writing no less than speech, written texts no less than conversations. It is a system, or quasi-system,[7] of inscription which insists upon the differential character of tracings or markings which both enables us to speak or write and which skews the attempts of speaking or writing to reach a closure. Archi-writing shows how speech and writing are inhabited by an undecidability that keeps our axioma and postulates, our es-sences and intuitions, our self-evident principles and supreme goods, our au-thorities and institutions, in an unstable state—even as it should keep the rest of us on our toes when these hallowed names are invoked.

Deconstruction is a way of writing from below, of insisting that we never get access to things except by way of a maze of markings. Gadamer has taken half a step in this direction by insisting on the uncircumventability of language for understanding. But Gadamer undoes the good he has accomplished with this move by bending his knee to language, asking us to lay our heads to its breast so that we may hear it rumble with deep truth and the wisdom of the classic.

Deconstruction has its doubts about that. It suspects that deep truths are purchased by deep violence, by excluding what contaminates the system of truth, by repressing what disturbs its unity, by swatting away those who trouble the guardians of truth with bothersome questions. It has an idea that the tradi-tion maintains itself in no small part by reason of its success in erasing the "dangerous memory" of those who have questioned it.[8] It is hard to assume a place in the tradition if one's books have been torched—or if one has not been taught to read or write in the first place. The unity of the tradition is in no small measure a function of the fact that educational systems—Gadamer is fond of the authority of the educator that he rightly connects with the authority of tradition[9]—keep spinning out the same yarn while no one is around to tell the other side of the story. It took a long time for the tradition to swallow the idea of contamination by the vernacular, by the language of the *Vulgus*. Traditions have always thrived on learned languages, learned by the few, the privileged, the initiates. When it comes to theology, deconstruction wants to know why everyone was so frightened of the "heretics," and just what it was that the tradition wanted to exclude. In theology, as elsewhere, deconstruction looks to the marginalized and excommunicated figures, not the classics; the forbidden sayings, not the eternal truths engraved in stone; the suppressed writings, not the ones that sit on the high altar.

For deconstruction, tradition is largely the story of the winners while the dissenters have been excommunicated, torched, castrated, exiled, or imprisoned. It does not matter much whether the tradition in question is that of the state or the university, of literature or philosophy: it always resorts to the same tricks. Traditions have unity and perdurance and an authority that seeps into our bones—just as Gadamer says—but at a price. Deconstruction thinks that the deep unutterable common faith of the tradition is the result of the fact that the traces of dissenters have been erased by the guardians of truth while the historical tracings that gave rise to the tradition in the first place were erased and the illusion created that we have to do here with ageless essences.

It is true that Gadamer has made much of the need for hermeneutic openness to the other—and that is his most profound moment—but he allowed this radical theme to be undermined by a metaphysics of the tradition inspired by Hegel and German Romanticism and by a metaphysics of the dialogical soul inspired by Plato. He has made a useful start in the direction of overcoming the metaphysics of history and of self-consciousness, but he has not had the heart to see it through to the end.

So if Gadamer's philosophical hermeneutics is a closet essentialism with deep roots in the metaphysical tradition from Plato to Hegel, Derrida is engaged in a pitiless critique of essentialism in the spirit of Heidegger's overcoming of metaphysics. If Gadamer is interested in how the metaphysical tradition passes along its stored-up treasures, Derrida is on the look-out for the police state that inevitably accompanies theories of infinite wealth. Philosophical hermeneutics takes a stab at recognizing the finitude and flux that inhabits all human institutions, but deconstruction doubts that hermeneutics has its heart in it. Deconstruction suspects that hermeneutics has something else up its sleeve—or hidden in the closet.

Neal Oxenhandler

14. The Man with Shoes of Wind: The Derrida-Gadamer Encounter

There is no denying that in the long run every one
of these great teachers of a purpose was van-
quished by laughter, reason, and nature: the short
tragedy always gave way again and returned into
the eternal comedy of existence.

—Nietzsche, *The Gay Science*

This encounter between two great contemporary thinkers has an abortive
character, notable in the brevity and tone of Derrida's "Three Questions to
Hans-Georg Gadamer." Derrida does not enter into the discourse of Gadamer;
he places himself totally outside its presuppositions, its conceptual frame and
even to some degree its broader field of implication, although his own work
overlaps much of that very field. Derrida stands outside of Gadamer's position
and subjects it to the cutting edge of irony.

Theoreticians of laughter tell us that it functions by typifying its victim. We
do not see the individual; we see the miser, the clown, the trickster, the social
climber. The man who slips on a banana peel instantaneously changed from an
autonomous and complex being into a grotesque falling object. I suggest that
Derrida's irony, though masked by politeness, operates exactly in this way in his
"Three Questions to Hans-Georg Gadamer." It objectifies, and it typifies Gadamer as the unwitting victim of the metaphysical banana peel.

Yet Gadamer employs his own irony against Derrida. It arises as he continues, with exquisite patience, to explain and justify himself to Derrida, as he
tries to recuperate Derrida within the marvelous flexibility of his hermeneutical
net. His very patience causes Derrida (apparently at that time not in the best of

health) to respond in a way that appears almost intemperate. This encounter reminds me of Kafka's tale *The Penal Colony*. Does not Gadamer, in his openness to Derrida, assume the role of the Officer, who steps into the torture machine and allows it to inscribe the name of his crime ("You Have Committed Metaphysics") on his body? The analogy becomes even more germane when we realize that the Old Commandant, inventor of the machine, is none other than Heidegger himself; while Derrida becomes the alienated Explorer who climbs hastily into his boat and rows away.

Irony aside, the truth of the matter is that Gadamer and Derrida have much in common. Foremost is their common origin in the later Heidegger. In an essay in which he speaks about his student years with Heidegger, Gadamer summarizes that same influence which is acknowledged by Derrida: "Heidegger's thought clearly pushes out beyond the transcendental philosophical direction of reflection. . . . In fact, in the end, the critique of the ontological prejudice involved in the Aristotelian concept of being and substance, and in the modern concept of the subject, necessarily brought about the dissolution of the idea of transcendental reflection itself" (*PH* 204). Derrida, of course, is tempered by Nietzsche, whose metaphorical and often apocalyptic *écriture* is his principal stylistic model, while Gadamer remains within the traditional post-Hegelian mode of expression.

Gadamer's notion of art as play is, once again, a point shared with Derrida, for whom the disseminative play of the text is valorized by its appearance in Plato: "Plato thus plays at taking play seriously. That is what we earlier called the stunning hand Plato has dealt himself. Not only are his writings defined as games, but human affairs in general do not in his eyes need to be taken seriously" (*D* 181/157). Gadamer sees aesthetic consciousness as informed through the play of the work: ". . .it is part of the event of being that occurs in representation and belongs essentially to the play as play" (quoted in *GH* 112). But whereas for Gadamer the play of the work, in manifesting a way of being, conveys "truth," for Derrida there is no closure beyond the ceaseless play of dissemination.

Before pursuing the position on truth and other transcendental notions in the two thinkers, let me add one further element of commonality. Both men see the philosopher's task as the reading of difficult or obscure texts. Gadamer renews philological and psychological hermeneutics along the ontological line proposed by Heidegger; he works toward a broad hermeneutical theory that can account for the fusion of horizons (of writer and reader) within the historical context of the work's creation and reception. Derrida, from his more radical position, constantly suggests solutions to these issues and just as constantly undermines them.

So much for points of confluence, but what of their differences? Even though Derrida accuses Gadamer of falling into metaphysics, I find that the chief conflict between them lies in their attitude toward transcendental terms. Gadamer believes in the possibility of truth ("For what else is interpretation in philosophy but coming to terms with the truth of the text and risking oneself by exposure to it?" *PH* 201) seen as the manifestness or revelation that accompanies something that impresses itself powerfully upon the mind, as the immanent unity of meaning in a text or the self-presentation of a work of art. Here, taste, judgment, and common sense come into play as the means by which consensus may be achieved.

Derrida, whose work may be seen as a sustained endeavor to avoid falling into what Heidegger calls "presence-at-hand," which is the domain of science and traditional metaphysics, allows for no transcendental use of terms; rather, his elaborate etymological and linguistic digressions represent an effort to hollow out and undermine the stability of concepts. That Derrida's principal objection to Gadamer comes in the latter's use of transcendental terms becomes apparent if we look again at the "Three Questions to Hans-Georg Gadamer."

Derrida finds a tilt into metaphysics in Gadamer's use of the term "good will," which he sees as implying a concept of "willing subjectivity" and hence of that transcendental subjectivity so powerfully rejected by Heidegger. Gadamer employs that very same "good will" to try to recuperate Derrida within his hermeneutic, but, given the latter's rejection of the very possibility of consensus, he is doomed to failure from the outset. Derrida's writing, which rests on the principle of undecidability and the structure of *mise-en-abîme,* voids notions normally considered necessary to any philosophical dialogue, such as good will and what Habermas calls "communicative rationality." He writes, "Dissemination endlessly opens up a *snag* in writing that can no longer be mended, a spot where neither meaning, however plural, nor *any form of presence* can pin/pen down [*agrapher*] the trace" (*D* 33/26). It is tempting to suggest that Derrida's voice, which belongs to the same family as the voices of Mallarmé, Proust, and Beckett, reminds us of its presence even while insisting upon its fundamental emptiness, as if to say: *I am here . . . in my lack I exist. . . .* Gadamer has something useful to say on this score: "Nevertheless it is true that a literary text demands to become present in its linguistic appearance and not just to carry out its function of conveying a message. It must not only be read, it must also be listened to, even if mostly with our inner ear. Thus it is in the literary text that the word first attains its full self-presence . . . ." (TI 43).

Although Derrida seems to disallow the conditions necessary for dialogue, which would lead inevitably to metaphysics, he also acknowledges that no one can stand outside his own epoch. In a discussion of Heidegger's fall into metaphysics, he concludes: "This would perhaps mean that one does not leave the epoch whose closure one can outline" (*Gr* 24/12). Does Derrida not then put himself in a position of mastery by assuming the privilege of deciding what is or is not metaphysical? If even Heidegger fell into metaphysics, how can Gadamer (or even Derrida himself) be exempt? Would it not be preferable to see metaphysics less as something we can choose to do or not do, than as an attitude, a position toward reality, a *Weltanschauung* that envelops us, at the very least a horizon which is always visible no matter how we philosophize?

Western metaphysics is seen, by both Derrida and Gadamer, as contaminated by a trance-bound subjectivity, the fatal and inevitable outcome of the medieval rejection of "the primordial Greek experience of Being" (Gadamer) in favor of Christian idealism. This shared agreement on a negative premise might be a common foundation for understanding, were their ways of building on it not radically different. Against the dream of idealism, Gadamer sets a reading practice; while Derrida, one of our greatest readers, brings his reading practice back—to a dream. For he is something of a Romantic, a crusader who carries his message around the world on "shoes of wind," trying to open up a new kind of intellectual and cultural freedom. He sounds the alarm at the appearance of any hypostatizing presence or self-presentation, notions which take on the threatening character associated with the "uncanny." He speaks of a "terrifying, blinding, mortal threat (of that) which presents itself, which obstinately thrusts itself into view" (*Spurs* 30/39). In Derrida's at times apocalyptic style we perceive fundamental obstacles to consensus and to community: this is always something exclusionary about prophets, they have many acolytes but no equals.

> "I have the impression nothing really happened. . . . I could develop a position in response to Gadamer, but that would take a great effort and it is not what I want to do now." (Jacques Derrida in a private conversation, Hanover, NH July 8, 1987)

Derrida, reflecting on his encounter with Gadamer, spoke of it as something that never really happened, largely because he himself was not in a position to make a sustained commitment to dialogue. Derrida is a writer who has passed from the gestatory to the disseminative phase of his philosophical enterprise and now spans the globe, winding an ever broader range of issues into the skein of his discourse. He has become, like Rimbaud, *l'homme aux semelles de vent,* a thinker who, for the time being at least, cannot allow himself the luxury of stopping for a period of time in the intellectual space inhabited by another thinker of his own stature, such as Gadamer. There was a certain wistfulness in his voice, when he replied to my characterization of him: "*Ces semelles souvent deviennent bien lourdes*" ["These shoes often become extremely heavy"]. No doubt the time will come when Derrida will assume the responsibility of developing "a position in response to Gadamer"; until that happens, the comments and studies contained in this volume will have to fill the gap.

Gabe Eisenstein

15. The Privilege of Sharing: Dead Ends and the Life of Language

Chacun de nous est le mystagogue et *l'Aufklärer d'un autre.*

—Derrida, *"D'un ton apocalyptique adopté naguère en philosophie"*

*Darum darf es weder überraschen noch verwun-
dern, wenn die meisten der Hörer sich an dem
Vortrag stoßen. Ob jedoch einige durch den
Vortrag jetzt oder später in ein weiteres Nach-
denken gelangen, läßt sich nicht ausmachen.*

—Heidegger, *"Zeit und Sein"*

*Die Sprache ist wie ein Acker, auf dem das Ver-
schiedenste aufgehen kann.*

—Gadamer, *"Der Weg in die Kehre"**

---

*Translation:

"Each of us is the mystagogue *and* the *Aufklärer* of another."

—Derrida, ATRAP

"Therefore, we must be neither surprised nor amazed if the majority of the audience objects to the lecture. Whether a few will, now or later, be prompted by the lecture to think further on such matters, cannot be foreseen."

—Heidegger, "Time and Being"

"Language is like a piece of arable land: the most varied things can come up out of it."

—Gadamer, "[Heidegger's]
Path to the 'Turn' "

Derrida says that in our best attempts at thinking and speaking clearly, we inevitably assume the position of a mystagogue: we speak in such a way as to take up a privileged position with regard to a certain universe of discourse—discourse governed by the *absence* of some fundamental sense-giving experience possessed or intimated by the speaker alone. What a contrast such a provocative statement makes with Gadamer's advocacy of hermeneutical good faith—with the critical spirit which, while never claiming to be free of all prejudices and hidden agendas, nevertheless strives for ever-increasing honesty about them through dialogue. Gadamer's goal is shared understanding, "conversation that builds up a common language" (DD 106), whereas in Derrida's "apocalyptic" paradigm language rather appears as land whose ownership is in constant dispute, and where furthermore there are no *essential* contents of understanding to be shared.

Gadamer views this apparently skeptical attitude as the result of a one-sided attention to a topic that is also a constant theme of his own studies, namely "the strangeness that arises between one human being and another, always creating new confusion" (DD 106). "But," he continues, "precisely in this fact lies the possibility of overcoming confusion." He takes Derrida's emphasis on the absence of shareable essences as a sign that Derrida is still attacking classical concepts of meaning—concepts which belong within the sphere of dialectics ("as if all speaking consisted merely of propositional judgments—" DD 112), whereas that sphere has already been transcended in his hermeneutics. There concealment and alienation are understood as part of the being of historical language, and what we share in language is not seen merely as propositional knowledge, but first of all as a form of communal coexistence operating on all levels of experience. In this more comprehensive perspective, the provocation that arises from identifying the will to communication with a will to mystification would be absorbed and disarmed. Then one would have to ask, as a matter of responsibility, the question put to Derrida by Francis Guibal, as to whether

> *il est possible d'estimer que la pensée de l'écriture est plus forte dans sa dénonciation de nos rêves mythiques (plénitude, présence, proximité, vie sans mort, etc.) que dans la création du nouveau qui nous appelle. (A 28)*

I find something right about Gadamer's criticism when I consider some of the more polemical parts of Derrida's writings, as for example the critique of Heidegger that equates his view of the "subject matter" [*Sache*] of thought with "thought itself defined as the content of theses" (IS 62). This surely is an oversimplification; the privileged position adopted in Heidegger's discourse is not that of the proposition. But Derrida has shown in his own way just how far beyond the level of theses and propositions we must look in order to appreciate what taking up a position in philosophy really means. And his investigations bear directly on the matter of philosophical responsibility, and the possibility of being "called" in philosophy. I take the question of privilege Derrida raises to be more than a reminder of the interest-bound character of thinking, and more than a reaction to Idealistic notions of meaning. Granted that we can get along without expressing what we strive to share in terms of conceptual or essential unity, there is still a need for a richer characterization of the most *productive* alienations and limitations on sharing, on intelligible coexistence, than is possible within the paradigm of dialogue as unidirectional questioning and answering.

I will try to show how certain features of Derrida's "apocalyptic" paradigm allow for an understanding of alienation and privileged meaning as contributing to the configuration of a larger semiotic field; and I will do this both on the plane of philosophical discourse (part 1) and that of everyday narrative consciousness or existential self-interpretation (part 2). Should this effort be successful, it would follow that figures like Gadamer and Derrida need not be taken as debaters whose case needs to be resolved or amongst whom we must choose sides; for we might come to see them as each playing a role, that is, taking a particular privileged position, within a drama that involves us on more than one level, and as more than just potential contestants. Although their roles are antagonistic, we need not suppose that one is right and the other wrong, or that one has attained a morally superior position. Insofar as we are dealing with a contest, we might still keep in mind Lyotard's maxim: "At the moment of victory one has been imprudent. It is imprudent to win."[1] Therefore, it is appropriate to begin a discussion of privilege with this very debate, or drama, which exemplifies the problem (of sharing) it discusses.

1. Heidegger and the Conversation of the Dead

> . . .And then the foolishness of the body will be cleared away and we shall be pure and hold converse with other pure souls. . .
>
> —Plato, *Phaedo*

1.1 Gadamer's Critique: "The impassable"

One thing defining the context of this contest seems to be a certain filial regard for Heidegger; he appears both as an authority and as someone to be bested through new insights. Although Gadamer defends Heidegger and his Nietzsche-interpretation (not unsuccessfully) against Derrida's attacks, it seems to me that it is Derrida who is actually closer to Heidegger's philosophical practice, precisely with regard to an instinct for the unique and the privileged in thinking. In explaining this I will begin a sketch of some of the positive limitations on the sharing of meaning in philosophy.

Gadamer's distance from Heidegger is signalled in the essay *"Destruktion and Deconstruction"* by the repeated assertion that Heidegger, who spoke so dramatically of the path of thinking, strayed into "the impassable" (*Unwegsam*, DD 104). Gadamer wants to contrast his own path out of dialectic (DD 00) with Heidegger's "adventurous journey into error" that got trapped in "labyrinthian paths" (DD 104). Heidegger's effort to overcome dialectics may have ended in dead ends, but Gadamer asserts that he did pose the question of the meaning of Being in a way that aims at no essence, but only "points in a certain direction for inquiry" (DD 111). My argument will focus on the relationship between this pointing and the labyrinths or dead ends as such, in order to bring out an essential limitation on the language game played by Gadamer vis-a-vis that (or those) played by Heidegger.

Heidegger's own talk of the dead ends or woodpaths [*Holzwege*] is alive with dynamic interpretations of this image, and suggests that in philosophy straying from the main public road is hardly a defect. I cannot help associating the image of the many dead ends, the more or less connected woodpaths, with Wittgenstein's famous image of language as a city built up along different lines and styles in different epochs,[2] and philosophy as a criss-cross journey in which the same points might be re-traversed from different directions (ibid., preface). A certain kind of dead end can form the shell or skin of a living thought-process. But Heidegger's "impassability" has at least this obvious sense: his writing is unreadable except to a privileged few. It is a game with its own rules, and it seems that part of the game is figuring out what the rules actually are. Of course, one might say the same thing about many philosophers; but a clear measure of Heidegger's limited (or as I will say presently, multivocal) communicative intentions, is given in his own descriptions of what he is doing as something to be engaged in by a very few.

An extreme expression of this tendency is his statement that Aristotle was, at least with regard to the phenomenon of time, "the last great philosopher who had eyes to see" (*GP* 00). Taken together with assertions that he is not out to contribute any theories or information, only to share in a certain conversational activity, such statements make Heidegger's relationship to his readers and students (those with whom he wishes to share something) extremely problematic— after all, if past experience is a guide, he would have to wait a few milennia for an equal partner in conversation, that is, someone of the stature of Aristotle and himself! Many a reader has, I am sure, experienced a kind of *embarrassing* reaction to Heidegger's apocalyptic appeal, to the temptation to picture himself a privileged partner in this millennial conversation, Socrates' conversation of the dead. No such embarrassment attaches to Gadamer's writing, which is devoted to the public *life* of language.

Now the conversation of the dead—the projected context of a meaning which would be privileged to ignore the dialogical constraints imposed by one's contemporaries—is a *timeless* one: it lacks the tension, ambiguity, and desire of the actual situations from which it is abstracted. But is a philosopher's regard for the timeless (assuming we can speak this way of some aspect of Heidegger's communicative intentions) to be taken at face value? Or shouldn't such a regard be taken together with the manifold of its accompanying historical concerns so as to see the distinctive temporality it helps constitute? Gadamer says of Heidegger's conversation with the pre-Socratics,

> Although in the end all this was valid enough for the kind of indicative linguistic gesture [*für den Wink der Worte*], that would point off into timelessness, it was not really valid for speaking—that is to say, for the kind of self-interpretation that one finds in the early Greek texts. (DD 105)

To conclude that in the end the author of *Being and Time* was looking only at the timeless is a grave indictment. Here it seems to me that Gadamer's indictment suffers from the same dialectical (cf. DD 108–11) one-sidedness he attributes (perhaps partly correctly, as I said) to Derrida.

Clearly Gadamer does not read Heidegger as if he were just presenting theses. On the contrary, his discussion extends to the most sensuous aspects of Heidegger's language.[3] Nevertheless he reads him *univocally,* from the point of view which aims at "a common thought" [*gemeinsam Gedachte*], whereas Heidegger's text is woven of a multitude of voices and roles with different functions.[4] Heidegger may have pursued a "single thought," as he sometimes said, but the single-mindedness of this pursuit is expressed through the mastery of a great variety of means, which we will consider presently. Thus, not only a *propositional* reading but even a *dialogical* reading in the most subtle sense seems to me to be too restrictive an approach to let us take account of this variety, which we would have to do in order to assess the place and significance of the paths that end with a wink at the timeless. I would start instead from a *narrative* paradigm, not only because it offers hope of understanding the kind of complex play with time which can make use of a timeless gaze,[5] but also because it is helpful for dealing with the cosmic story of the "History of Being," as well as the self-presenting hermeneutic of Dasein whose autobiography is always at issue.

1.2 Philosophical Autonomy and the Narrative Paradigm

> . . .but the philosopher, even when
> by himself, can contemplate truth,
> and the better the wiser he is; he can
> perhaps do so better if he has fellow-
> workers, but still he is the most self-
> sufficient.
> —Aristotle, *Nichomachaen Ethics*

Consider Gadamer's domestication of Heidegger's wild story in the essay "Heidegger and the History of Philosophy":

> Heidegger's attempt to think through the history of philosophy exhibits the violence of a thinker who is driven by his own questions and who seeks to recognize himself in everything. Thus his "destruction" of metaphysics becomes a kind of wrestling-match with the power of this tradition of thought (*HW* 444).

Heidegger's apparent self-absorption, his involvement, as we might say, with his own immortality (or again with the character of his ultimate dead end), occurs within a semiotic space, or involves the playing of a certain language game, into which Gadamer is not inclined to venture or participate, because in granting his own story a uniquely privileged position in his story, Heidegger introduces the most extreme limitations into language with regard to its conceptual development through public discussion. But this is just the aspect that becomes so interesting from the "apocalyptic" perspective.

Although Heidegger was indeed concerned with dialogue and the phenomenon of answering which, as Gadamer insists, "makes a word into a word" (DD 106), he was not *ultimately* concerned with it in a *general* way.[6] He rather aims at a certain peculiarly transformed "answering" which, although rooted in traditional philosophical and religious practices, would gain its full sense only in relation to a historical form of existence quite different from the ones we actually know. Thus, his text reserves a privileged place for this implicit intimation, first approached in terms of the "call of conscience" and being-guilty, later through poetic receptivity, through a sense of actively relaxed waiting, and a variety of other "dead ends." In the context of cultural criticism, it may be hard to accord such language a place on a par with language that has the definiteness and generality of hermeneutics or ethics. But I think this is because the privileged aspect of the text is not seen as an inner articulation of its narrative configuration; instead it is either discarded, in order to focus on the more analytical modes of the text, or it is embraced as the "meaning" of the text. It seems to me rather that this type of suggestive language play is an important component of the great philosophical texts. Derrida recognizes the need to study this component in all its intratextual effects: he thematizes this kind of intimation as the fundamental appeal of all apocalyptic speakers, and refers to it as "Viens," the originless imperative "Come!" (see ATRAP).

In order to designate such language, involved in calling and answering while yet remaining preliminary to the circumstances of its fulfillment, I shall use the old word *protreptic*. In Aristotle's *Metaphysics*, for example, autonomy is symbolized by the self-thinking of God; but it is grounded in the protreptic force exercised by the Greek philosophers on their contemporaries, through channels long since developed by storytellers and orators. In the modern era, the sense of autonomy is bound up with epistemology; protreptic language gets supplanted by transcendental description. Heidegger was one of those who tried to revive the sense of autonomy without resorting to that kind of crutch or facade. We know from Heidegger's discussion of *Ereignis*—the event which "only occurs in the singular" (*ID* 100/36)—that Heidegger's protreptic projection of ideal answering is indeed involved with the "timeless" and with the ineffable; but the voice of this answering is itself installed in Heidegger's larger, temporal narrative. And he does this not just in order to develop the "speculative, dual unity playing between the said and the unsaid" (DD 111), important as that dynamic may be. For the unification or gathering effected by *das Ereignis* is not just speculative but narrative, in the broad sense of a context that can make an event appropriate; the role played by the privileged aspect of the text is not simply a dialogical one: it rather enacts the peculiar autonomy of philosophical meaning.

The result, as has often been remarked, is almost embarrassingly indefinite. To the extent that the peculiar autonomous answering invoked by the Heideggerian text is cut loose from the behavior of particular persons at different identifiable moments, it seems to tend in the direction of Derrida's apocalyptic "addresses without message and without destination, without sender or decidable addressee" (ATRAP 94), divorced, as I think Gadamer might say, from the responsibility of existential self-interpretation. Such being cut loose might be understood in a traditional manner as the "absolution" of particular subjectivity by the universal—an aspect that Gadamer too wants to preserve in his own way as the "*über-sich-hinaus-sein*" which is "*Gespräch-sein*," according to the logic of question and answer. But prior to either the Idealistic transcendence of subjectivity or the hermeneutical incorporation of individuality in the spirit of conversation is the apocalyptic dimension of the absolutely authoritative voice— the voice that establishes a narrative field on the ground of a radical *alterity*, a cognitive-emotional dissonance that first brings into view the limitations that would be overcome in the drama of autonomy, and marks in advance the privilege to be enjoyed.

This recalls Derrida's point that even when the authoritative voice masquerades as the voice of Reason, it can never be made into a communal property, but retains something of the prophetic stance and the intentional asymmetry of its basic situations (ATRAP 66ff.). Its utterance is a shock, a blow, a transforming gesture rooted in the radical incommensurability of differing standpoints. This alterity is essential to protreptic discourse. It may always be possible to accommodate the alterity of the authorative voice within a subtle understanding of how conversation takes us out beyond ourselves, feeding on the creative sparks struck in an *Auseinandersetzung* with a partner in dialogue. This type of description is true to our experience of dialogue from the point of view of a unifying emergent meaning. But it seems to me that this accommodation must always compromise the narrative closure through which the effect of autonomy is produced, to the extent that it does not allow for irreducibly unequal as well as potentially equal linguistic positions; it does not see a semiotic field constituted by the former as well as the latter.

What is meant by "closure" here? Although the closure that establishes the absolute authority of a voice is easiest to represent as a projected temporal limit (as in the most literal understanding of apocalyptic discourse, which precludes an open-ended interpretive life), it would be better expressed as an *internal* limit, a rupture or fold, relating a protreptic meaning (which aims at a temporal opening) to one that is descriptive and final. Unequal linguistic positions are configured by this fold. The fold precludes a simultaneous view of its inner and outer surfaces, that is, the view presented by a synoptic theoretical account. It requires that one should act, should take up a definite position within the narrative field, in order from that situation and mood to authorize one of its dramatic movements.[7]

Now consider this "folded" relationship between new and old, radical alterity and existential self-interpretation, in Heidegger's texts. There we find the apparatus for a hermeneutical identification of new and old (as in the slogan "Origin comes to meet us out of the future"), which can be spelled out in Gadamerian terms; but what happens when we try to apply this to the problematic case of Heidegger's own teaching? We find, again, that his text works on many levels. . . . Unquestionably he has given us much that is new to read in the old texts of Aristotle, Kant, and others. And these new readings are in the service of a new-old or neoclassical attitude towards the practice of philosophy—a restoration of the protreptic dimension so threatened by the institutionalization of philosophy and the adoption of the paradigm of scientific research. But it is just this dimension—the "existential" dimension (with its religious, and specifically Kierkegaardian heritage)—which opens up the radical novelty, the disparity of intentions and the heterogeneity of linguistic functions that convolute the philosophic text and demand we walk its dead end streets. This dimension is attained through insight into the "facticity" of life and the "mineness" of human meaning and experience (e.g. the insight into the paradox of the philosopher, who seems to try to do for everyone precisely that which each can only do for himself); these in turn point to the general question of privilege, which goes beyond that of subjectivity.

The role of the private voice, thought thinking itself, the vision transcending language due to its uniqueness and particularity, is one among the other roles in the multilevelled language game of philosophy. Gadamer refers to it succinctly in the formula of Romanticism: *"Individuum est ineffabile"* (TI 21). From this "ineffability" the most significant consequences have been held to flow. And language play that incorporates this role, must, as I said, be a temporal structure in which the "timeless" moment has its privileged place. So the reader of Heidegger must in the course of a single reading play the roles of philologist, existential hero, conceptual analyst, cultural critic, poet *and* mystic, in order to fulfill the different moments of the text. He or she is supposed to identify with both the narrational and narrated aspects of the story of The History of Being; to actualize the virtual text through reading and rereading—to fill in presuppositions and contextuality for all those parts of the text that are referentially underdetermined. Consequently, the reader must negotiate a position for himself somewhere between or including the embarrassing position of millennial thinker, who would have his own place in the story (being a mouthpiece for being), and that of a mere reader seeking to be well-informed about philosophy (a position rendered nearly senseless by Heidegger's text). Everything depends on the reader's willingness to listen, from a stance defined with respect to the text, for the silent voice of "presencing," that is, for the intelligibility of his present situation within the widest and most authoritative narrative field: the story of his life and world. Thus, the outcome of Heidegger's story is dependent on a kind of private meditation or bearings-taking on the reader's part, marked out nonetheless in a public manner as privileged understanding.

Such a text certainly depends on much interpretive good will or faith. In fact someone might say that language such as I have been describing has too much in common with faith and too little in common with philosophy. But I see this moment of faith as only one pole of a narrative field within which we are involved, that is, we do want to do justice to the protreptic seriousness that lies behind the embarrassment of philosophy, and at the same time we have to put this seriousness in a playful perspective, to relate it to the current movements of society and culture, and so forth. The text is a place where I practice all these different actions—including the most decisive.

Hence, I understand Derrida's apocalyptic paradigm, which I have been applying to Heidegger, as a textual structure deployed through a multiplicity of dramatic moments or roles.[8] The "dead ends" represented in different moments each mark out possibilities of fulfillment by the creative reader—fulfillment that effects an internal rupture in the text, but that nevertheless contributes to the economy of the narrative whole.[9] The text is "open,"[10] not only because it offers a range of interpretive choices or because of its key terms that function with the indeterminacy of symbols, but also because of an internal heterogeneity obtaining between these different readerly enactments, characterized by different kinds and degrees of privilege. Nevertheless it is also "closed," and closable, just in the sense that corresponds to the authority—one could even say truth—of language that is actualized by a free decision to take up a privileged position within it.

In the remaining space I would like to argue that the creative achievements of the ideal reader to whom I have just alluded are nothing extraordinary when taken in a context that is not just dialogical, but one of human sharing in its broadest dimensions. From such a perspective, a perspective that allows for the coexistence of incommensurable standpoints *and* for a sharing based on absence, we can see the hermeneutical good will as operating not just in a "living medium" of language, but in a space in which the "living" and the "dead" aspects of language cooperate. This cooperation permeates every human life.

2. Death in the Life of Language

> *Pour entrer en rapport avec l'autre, il faut que l'interruption soit possible; il faut que le rapport soit un rapport d'interruption. Et, l'interruption, ici, n'interrompt pas le rapport à l'autre, elle ouvre le rapport à l'autre.*
>
> —Derrida, *Altérités*

2.1 An Example of Meaning Which Is Both Shared and Privileged

Let's return to the general notion of shared meaning, and those natural limitations upon it that might complicate the structure of philosophic texts for the hermeneutical approach. At this point, I want to move away from the example of Heidegger's text, in order to focus on a more common kind of anthropological reality shaped by privilege and incommensurability, and in so doing to recall the ordinary application of the notion of privilege: although "privileged meaning" may have seemed to imply a meaning restricted to one person, it more naturally pertains to that shared by a restricted group. In order to develop certain analogies with the preceding analysis, I will limit my discussion to the case of privileged meaning which is shared by only two persons—ones who have said to each other, "till death do us part."

Such persons are the privileged tellers, listeners to, and characters in a unique narrative. This narrative is not private, but they are its privileged interpreters. That is to say, there is one interpretive stance toward the story that can only be adopted by the "characters" themselves, in spite of the fact that the narrative is open to (and may well be affected by) other interpretations. For a necessary ingredient or sub-plot of this story is its continual (re)interpretation and the fluctuating state of harmony between the two privileged interpreters. They say "how it's going," and what they say—or the speech acts they perform by so saying—partly constitutes that which is being interpreted (the marital story).

The "meaning" of such a narrative is of course inseparable from its being lived—and "being lived" here is far less precise than saying the narrative is coextensive with a living-together, a "dwelling" (full of subtleties such as Heidegger has urged us to investigate in this phenomenon). Dwelling is a concept that transcends all metaphysical questions of identity and embodiment because its ground is not in the "substance" of consciousness but in the dramatic, narrative coherence of the day-to-day events with which consciousness finds itself involved. To share an understanding of some linguistic elements in the creative dwelling process (i.e., the verbal self-interpretations) of a marital story is not fundamentally different from sharing the use and experience of other of its private elements, like a bed or a dinner table. Therefore what I am calling narrative here, the understanding of a process of coexistence articulated within that coexistence and organizing it in turn, is a shared framework of meaning, a truly common language; and yet it is one that is shaped all around by exclusiveness and reliance on privilege. Nor is this common language to be viewed as a mere code that could be broken: its privilege is manifest through the necessity of *being in* the story, not of knowing its structure objectively.

All of this only serves, so far, to emphasize that in shared meaning the *universally* intelligible components may not be what is significant—something that can come as no surprise to the finite historical perspective of hermeneutics. But now let me turn to the further mark of the narrative I have chosen to examine, namely, that it is signed by the parting of death. Here I see more than a dialogical meaning; I see an involution of the narrative field analogous to that brought about by Heideggerian dead ends.

The ritual formula of marriage in which death is inscribed can indicate something deeper than fidelity. It can indicate a certain absolute priority of the marital narrative over others with which it is implicated (or other language games which each person plays). The dialogical partners here are not only joined temporarily for an event of common self-interpretation (as happens in any good dialogue), they become permanently indispensable for each other's self-interpretation in a basic way: the story of X becomes part of the story of X and Y and all other stories about X or Y properly belong to the story of X/Y. The sign of death indicates here, as it often does in philosophy, a certain self-sufficiency or autonomy—in the language of *Being and Time*, a *Ganzseinkönnen* or capacity for being a whole, which is experienced both emotionally and reflectively.

And yet this sign speaks of parting, thus indirectly of the mysterious disparity between the kind of whole that depends on sharing, on being-together, and the kind of whole which *excludes it* . . . it speaks therefore of the way these incommensurable realities are folded together. If I am justified in seeing more than a predictive or contractual meaning in the formula "till death do us part," more than a knowledge of the fact that humans die combined with an expectation of fidelity—if the formula is rather to be taken as a sign of a kind of narrative sensibility shaped by (not mere knowledge about but) *being mortal*—then its interpretation requires something like the apocalyptic paradigm as it was applied to Heidegger. Just as the philosophical narrative allows the reader to take up different positions while yet being bound by the privileged character of one of them, so we can only do justice to the inevitable rupture in the shared marital narrative by seeing the interweaving of both its final and open, dead and living aspects.

The disruption of death entails an asymmetrical dispersal of roles across the narrative field, which is nevertheless dramatically unified through what I would suggest is the protreptic character of this asymmetry itself. Here death is not merely a metaphor for all bygones, as Gadamer suggests in his critique of Heidegger's protreptic conception of "being-towards-death" (*"Der Weg in die Kehre,"* HW 109); nor is it just the projection of a futural limit (even one which brings out the "thatness" of existence in a special way) . . . for in the course of time this parting does occur within the experience of the partner who lives on— who lives, that is, still within the privileged narrative framework, in spite of being aware that it is finished in a most obvious way. In this case the connection between being-towards-death and the death of an other is by no means comprehended merely analogically: neither the thought that "this will happen to me too," nor the symbolic installation of the departed in an order to which I too belong, touches upon the peculiar autonomy of meaning that is generated by this ultimate deferral.[11] Anyone whose life story has been disrupted in this way knows something about conversing with the dead, and the strange privilege it confers.[12] The ambiguity attaching to the living self-interpretation has been, in a certain sense, removed (although interpretation continues to move, like the Aristotelian idealization, in a circular path).

My claim is that it is appropriate to see this interpretive closure as *already* marking the *living* marital narrative that precedes it, in accordance with what I have said regarding involution. This basic mode of human sharing depends on the narrative encompassing of privileged voices within a space unified by a protreptic call—by the sense of autonomy, that is, which is generated by this very privilege; by the heterogeneity and alterity of narrative dead ends. I offer the "completed" marital narrative as an example of involution not on the basis of the ritual formula alone, but because the magical binding-together of heterogeneous sense, which is both theme and substance of this narrative, is at bottom one with the privilege attaching to a conversation with the dead (that is, with death's involution of the narrative field). Here the Derridean understanding of death, that is, the apocalyptic paradigm as a whole, reveals its fruitfulness.

2.2 Death and the Coexistence of Incommensurables

> *C'est un rapport fou, un rapport sans rapport, qui comprend l'autre comme autre dans un certain rapport d'incompréhension. Ce n'est pas l'ignorance, ni l'obscurantisme, ni la démission dévant aucun désir d'intelligibilité. . . .*
> —*Altérités*

Derrida has shown in various ways how a complex mutual enfolding of life and death permeates the production of meaning, in that the life of linguistic beings is driven by the generation of works that fix and therefore transcend their fluid and ambiguous basis. Put more simply, "who I am" is determined not by the shifting subjectivity that is "expressed" in my speech and other behavior, but just by the relative stability achieved in such "expressive" works themselves—in their very detachment from living self-presence. With this detachment, of course, comes the openness to interpretation affecting everything public; "fixed" expressions take on lives of their own. Hence, the paradox that the linguistic means for "*l'amortissement de la mort*" (*Gl* 187), or the denial of absolute loss, inevitably work to subvert their purpose (i.e. they do not completely preserve an original intention or fixed meaning), not in spite of but precisely *because* of their detachment; and that conversely this semiotic life-force apparent in the "detached" sign was already active in the original process of "expression." Consequently the external limit of mortality or loss is thoroughly internalized: the very gesture of self-expression is a movement of loss and alienation—not in a dialectical sense, but in the manner of an infinitely varied interweaving. The "original intention" is articulated in the particular historical terms of its deformation, limitation, and interruption.

The apocalyptic paradigm pertains to all expression insofar as it seeks to retain control over its future interpretation, through innumerable contracts, strategies, and ruses, including that of declaring the absolute closure of its narrative field.[13] Saint John's book that warns its readers against making any alterations, or Plato's which complains of its separation from his voice, are only extreme examples of this pervasive tendency. If this apocalyptic dimension could be removed entirely it would eliminate all authority in language, every instance of true teaching, and the very phenomenon of truth itself; for the controlling impulse in question is no mere egotism, but rather belongs to the movement of detachment (or *différance*) that necessarily presents the sign as a re-iteration in the first instance, and thus as always already installed in an order which gives it authority.

On the other hand, the boundless intensification of interpretive control leads to dogmatism, to the death of meaning in still another sense. Thus, talk about the apocalyptic dimension ultimately aims at a negotiation with its own apocalyptic, dogmatic, and dialectical tendencies—aims, that is, at a problematic of interpretive *balance* between privilege and accommodation. What seemed to be at stake in the question of privilege was the democratic openness of dialogue, the fusing of horizons, etc.; the autocratic refusal to fuse appears first as mystical or perhaps just skeptical and thus nihilistic, from the point of view of an open dialogue . . . until we recall how the open spaces of some of the most common empirical dialogical realities are organized by local fusions that exclude other possible fusions in specific ways. Then we have to consider the reciprocal relations obtaining between fusion and exclusion, and the mirroring of the latter *within* the former.

To continue for a moment in political terms, democracy is not just the mutual orbiting of equal voices or interpretive centers bound by a single interpretive interest; it is rather the dynamic balancing of many unequal voices, not only disagreeing but often talking across one another and aiming at different, occasionally overlapping goals. Their speeches are often incommensurable, and thus the whole of the linguistic field which concerns us is not subject to scientific or purely structural analysis; but it seems to me that studies of what Derrida has identified as belonging to property, signature, etc. (i.e. all that is unique and privileged in the meaning) can provide lessons in what might be called the "dynamics of incommensurability": getting used to viewing language not as a homogeneous dialogical space but rather as a heterogeneous narrative one must broaden our thinking about factical coexistence in a socially productive way. What I have called the "involution of a narrative field" extends to various interweavings of voices in tensed equilibrium—particularly to the problematic balancing of authority and openness in speech. Rather than attempting a dialectical resolution of authority and openness or necessity and freedom, we might look instead for a suitable interweaving of roles, for example, the inclusion of a discourse addressed to the privileged within one addressed to the underprivileged, or, returning again to my example, the inclusion of a discourse addressed to the dead within one which is addressed to the living.

The example of the marital narrative shows how the urgent, ambiguous works of our symbolic life may be framed by an ultimate disruption which, far from completing their meaning teleologically, confers upon their privileged interpretation an authority based instead of awareness of the *incompleteness* of the finished narrative. In other words, one finds in this incompleteness—in the contingency that has been sealed by death—a self-sufficiency "not to be outstripped" because the persistency of the incompleted and thus uncomprehended past continually announces the irrevocability of the narrative bond. One sees, from the perspective of the narrative closure, the absolute value of things that were only *present* within a structure of ambiguity, desire, and expectation. The fact that "life goes on" for the widowed person and one narrative framework becomes a part in others only emphasizes how the understanding is bound to elements that can never be made commensurable with a future interpretation. The fusion of horizons that had always seemed perfectible before, now stands revealed as the mask of a radical finitude.

And yet isn't it just this sense of finitude, attaching absolute value to experiences in spite of their radical ambiguity and imperfection by casting them within the framework of an all-important story, which we know in the realm of personal relations as love? Love embraces the particularity and imperfections of its object at the same time that it, as it were, steps into the picture (i.e. accepts the force of a narrative bond by relating to it as teller, listener, and character). Then one heeds not only what is said by the other, but also *who she is* as determined from within the horizon of self-interpretation that grants absolute value to the contingent. Her expressions become not just *means* in an open process of dialogical self-interpretation but *ends* of our pure appreciation. At the same time these "ends" have the indeterminacy and "sense of direction" that characterizes the protreptic call.

These observations on the limitations of sharing can be extended to many other types of coexistence. The conversation of adults and children provides an example of unequal linguistic positions wherein a constant revolving and interweaving of seriousness and play must be accomplished. The privileged position taken by a teacher, who contrary to our wishes is sure to have some students incapable of ever entering into dialogue on an equal basis, provides more analogies: here too there is the possibility of enfolding the meaning (i.e. the teaching) which from the ungifted student's point of view is an ideal or "dead" one, within a broader narrative framework—in other words the model suggests that the teacher should speak in such a way as to anticipate incompetent as well as competent interpretation, trying to be fruitful on both levels, and indeed to combine both levels within a higher perspective. Such a suggestion would belong to the sphere of responsibility that Derrida sees as "exceeding the limits of ethics," because it concerns "respect for the singularity or for the call [*appel*] of the other" (*A* 71). This view of teaching conflicts with our usual view in which the meaning of a teaching is identified with the state of mind that it aims at bringing about; instead the suggestion is that we step back to consider a more complex and heterogeneous narrative sort of meaning, in which states of mind and moments of insight play only a limited—albeit privileged—part. In all such cases, the embarrassment attaching to the adoption of a privileged position is not necessarily to be taken as a sign that something is wrong, but as an essential part of the dynamic governing the privilege of sharing.

Abbreviations

Note: In the body of the text, many citations have been given in parentheses in order to reduce footnoting. Citations of French and German books and articles will in most cases give both the page(s) in the German or French, followed by a slash, and the page(s) in the English translation, if available. The names Heidegger, Gadamer, Derrida, and Nietzsche have been abbreviated as M H, H-G G, J D, and F N in the table of abbreviations below.

A   J D and Pierre-Jean Labarrière. *Altérités*. Paris: Éditions Osiris, 1986.

AF   *Die Aktualität der Frühromantik*. Ed. by Ernst Behler and Jochen Hörish. Paderborn: Ferdinand Schöningh: 1987.

ATRAP   J D. "Of an Apocalyptic Tone Recently Adopted in Philosophy." Trans. John P. Leavey, Jr., in *Semeia* 23 (1982).

AWP   M H. "The Age of the World Picture," a translation of ZW in *QCT* 115–54.

BMM   Martin Buber. *Between Man and Man*. Trans. Ronald Gregor Smith. New York: Collier Macmillan, 1965. First published in 1929.

BW   M H. *Basic Writings*. Trans. and ed. David Krell. New York: Harper and Row, 1977.

CFS   *Cahiers Ferdinand de Saussure*. Publication began in 1941.

CMN   Giorgio Colli and Mazzino Montinari, eds. *Nietzsche Werke: Kritische Gesamtausgabe*. Berlin: Walter de Gruyter and Co., 1968 et seq.

CNP   J D. "Comment ne pas parler: Dénégations." *Psyché* 535–95. Originally presented at Jerusalem in English as "How to Avoid Speaking" (1986).

Cours	Ferdinand de Saussure. *Cours de linguistique générale* (1908/9). Critical edition by Tullio de Mauro. Paris: Payot, 1972, 1980².
CP	J D. *La Carte postale de Socrates à Freud et au-delà.* Paris: Flammarion, 1980. Trans. by Alan Bass: *The Post Card.* Chicago: University of Chicago Press, 1987.
D	J D. *La dissémination.* Paris: Éditions du Seuil, 1972. Trans. by Barbara Johnson as *Dissemination.* Chicago: University of Chicago Press, 1981.
DD	H-G G. *"Destruktion* and Deconstruction" in this volume. In some cases two page references will be given. In these cases, the first refers to the German original, *GW 2* 361–72, the second to the page in the present volume.
DD	H-G G. *Dialogue and Dialectic: Eight Hermeneutical Studies on Plato.* Translated, with an introduction, by P. Christopher Smith. New Haven: Yale University Press, 1980.
DE	J D. *De l'esprit: Heidegger et la question.* Paris: Galilée, 1987.
Derr	Christopher Norris. *Derrida.* Cambridge: Harvard University Press, 1987.
DI	Mikhail Bakhtin. *The Dialogic Imagination.* Ed. Michael Holquist and trans. Caryl Emerson and Michael Holquist. Austin: University of Texas Press, 1981.
DSPSL	H-G G. "Dialectic and Sophism in Plato's *Seventh Letter,"* pp. 93–123 in *DD.*
DuD	H-G G. "Destruktion und Dekonstruktion," pp. 361–72 in *GW 2.*
E	J D. "Envoi," *Actes du XVIIIème Congrès des Sociétés de Philosophie de Langue Française.* Paris: Vrin, 1980. Trans. Peter and Mary Ann Caws, "Sending: On Representation," *Social Research,* 49,2(1982).
E	Jacques Lacan. *Écrits.* Paris: Éditions du Seuil, 1966. Trans. Alan Sheridan. *Écrits: A Selection.* New York: W. W. Norton, 1977.
EC	Ferdinand de Saussure. *Critical Edition.* Ersten Band, containing three previously unpublished handwritten lectures. Wiesbaden: Harrassowitz (first volume), 1974 (sec-

ond volume). See footnote 10 of Manfred Frank's essay, *TI* 198.

ECN   Volume 2 of the Saussure critical edition, which contains the *Notes*.

ED   J D. *L'Écriture et la différance*. Paris: Seuil, 1967. Trans. A. Bass: *Writing and Difference*. Chicago: University of Chicago Press, 1978.

EGT   M H. *Early Greek Thinking*. Trans. David F. Krell and Frank A. Capuzzi. New York: Harper and Row, 1975.

EHG   Lawrence K. Schmidt. *The Epistemology of Hans-Georg Gadamer: An Analysis of the Legitimization of* Vorurteile. New York: Peter D. Lang, 1985, 1987².

EO   J D. *The Ear of the Other—Otobiography, Transference, Translation: Texts and Discussions with Jacques Derrida*. Ed. by Christie V. McDonald. Pp. 1–38 contain "Otobiographies: The Teaching of Nietzsche and the Politics of the Proper Name," trans. Avital Ronell. New York: Schocken Books, 1985.

EP   M H. *The End of Philosophy*. New York: Harper and Row, 1973. Translates *N 2* 399–490 (final three sections).

FJ   J D. *La faculté de juger*. Paris: Édition de Minuit, 1985.

FLC   J D. *Feu la cendre*. Paris: Des femmes, 1987.

GH   Joel C. Weinsheimer. *Gadamer's Hermeneutics*. New Haven: Yale University Press, 1985.

Gl   J D. *Glas*. Paris: Galilée, 1974. English trans. John P. Leavey, Jr. Lincoln: University of Nebraska Press, 1986.

GOA   F N. *Werke*. Grossoktavausgabe. Leipzig, C. G. Naumann, 1905ff.

GP   M H. *Die Grundprobleme der Phänomenologie*. Frankfurt am M.: Klostermann, 1975. Trans. by A. Hofstadter as *The Basic Problems of Phenomenology*. Bloomington: Indiana University Press, 1982.

Gr   J D. *De la grammatologie*. Paris: Éditions de Minuit, 1967. Trans. by Gayatri Chakravorty Spivak, *Of Grammatology*. Baltimore: The Johns Hopkins University Press, 1976.

GS   F N. *The Gay Science*. Trans. Walter Kaufmann. New York: Random House, 1974. Citations are by section rather than page.

GW 2   H-G G. *Gesammelte Werke*. Vol. 2: *Hermeneutik II*. Tübingen: J. C. B. Mohr (Paul Siebeck), 1986.

H   M H. *Holzwege*. Frankfurt am Main: Vittorio Klostermann, 1950.

HB   M H. "Über den »Humanismus«: Brief an Jean Beaufret, Paris," pp. 53–119 in *Platons Lehre von der Warheit: Mit einem Brief über den »Humanismus.«* Bern: Franke Verlag, 1947. English translation, "Letter on Humanism," pp. 193–242 in *BW.*

HD   "Hermeneutics and Deconstruction: Gadamer and Derrida in Dialogue," by Fred Dallmayr in this volume. Reprinted, omitting his summary of the encounter, from his *Critical Encounters: Between Philosophy and Politics*. Notre Dame: Notre Dame University Press, 1987, pp. 130–58.

HD   *Hermeneutics and Deconstruction*. Edited by Hugh J. Silverman and Don Ihde. Selected Studies in Phenomenology and Existential Philosophy 10. Albany: State University of New York Press, 1985.

HDial   H-G G. *Hegel's Dialectic: Five Hermeneutical Studies*. Trans. and introduced by P. Christopher Smith. New Haven: Yale University Press, 1976.

Hk   M H and Eugen Fink. *Heraklit: Seminar Wintersemester 1966/67*. Frankfurt: Vittorio Klostermann, 1970. English: *Heraclitus Seminar 1966–67*. Trans. Charles H. Seibert. University, Alabama: University of Alabama Press, 1979.

HL   H-G G. "Hermeneutics and Logocentrism." Translation in the present volume of "Hermeneutik und Logozentrismus," published as "Frühromantik, Hermeneutik, Dekonstruktivismus," in *AF*, pp. 251–60.

HMP   *Hermeneutics and Modern Philosophy*. Edited by Brice R. Wachterhauser. Albany: State University of New York Press, 1986.

HuK   Friedrich Schleiermacher. *Hermeneutik und Kritik*. With a supplement of philosophical texts, edited and introduced by Manfred Frank. Frankfurt: Suhrkamp, 1977.

HW   H-G G. *Heideggers Wege*. Tübingen: J. C. B. Mohr (Paul Siebeck), 1983.

ID   M H. *Identity and Difference*. Trans. Joan Stambaugh. New York: Harper and Row, 1969. Contains the German text, pp. 79–146. References to the German will be to this same text rather than the Neske, 1957, German original.

IS   J D. "Interpreting Signatures (Nietzsche/Heidegger): Two Questions" in this volume. French original text unpublished. First published in German translation, pp. 62–77 in *TI*. The present translation is from the unpublished French text kindly furnished to us by Professor Derrida through the good offices of Philippe Forget. Our translation previously appeared in *Philosophy and Literature* 10,2 (October 1986): 246–62.

KPM   M H. *Kant und das Problem der Metaphysik*. 4th ed., enlarged; Frankfurt: Klostermann, 1973.

LAJ   J D. "Lettre à un ami japonais," *Le Promeneur* 42 (Mi–Octobre 1985): 2–4. Trans. "Letter to a Japanese Friend," pp. 1–8 in *Derrida & Différance*. Ed. D. Wood and R. Bernasconi. Evanston: Northwestern University Press, 1988.

LD   H-G G. "Letter to Dallmayr" published for the first time in this translation with the kind permission of Professor Dallmayr and Professor Gadamer.

LO   J D. "Living On: Border Lines," trans. James Hulbert, pp. 75–176 in H. Bloom et al. (eds). *Deconstruction and Criticism*. New York: Seabury, 1979.

M   J D. *Marges de la philosophie*. Paris: Éditions de Minuit, 1972. English: *Margins of Philosophy*. Trans., with notes, by Alan Bass. Chicago: University of Chicago Press, 1982.

N   M H. *Nietzsche*. 2 vols. Pfullingen: Günther Neske, 1961. Page references by volume and page to the English translation in four volumes edited by David F. Krell (New York: Harper and Row, 1979–87) will be given after the German. Volume titles for the four English volumes are as follows. I: *The Will to Power as Art*, 1979; II: *The Eternal Recurrence of the Same*, 1984; III: *The Will to Power as Knowledge and as Metaphysics*, 1987; and IV: *Nihilism*, 1982.

O	J D. *Otobiographies.* Paris: Galilée, 1984. Partial trans. see *EO.*
P	J D. *Positions: Entretiens avec Henri Ronse, Julia Kristeva, Jean-Louis Houdebine, Guy Scarpetta.* Paris: Éditions de Minuit, 1972. English: *Positions.* Trans. and annotated by Alan Bass. Chicago: University of Chicago Press, 1981.
PA	H–G G. *Philosophical Apprenticeships.* Trans. R. R. Sullivan. Cambridge: MIT Press, 1985.
PDM	Jürgen Habermas. *Der philosophische Diskurs der Moderne: Zwölf Vorlesungen.* Frankfurt am M.: Suhrkamp Verlag, 1985. English translation by Frederick Lawrence. Cambridge: MIT Press, 1987.
PH	H–G G. *Philosophical Hermeneutics.* Trans. and ed. David E. Linge. Berkeley: University of California Press, 1976.
Préj	J D. "Préjugés," in *La faculté de juger.* Paris: Éditions de Minuit, 1985.
Psyché	J D. *Psyché: Inventions de l'autre.* Paris: Galilée, 1987. 650pp. In addition to "Geschlecht I and II" it contains CNP, E, LAJ, and RM.
QCT	M H. *The Question Concerning Technology and Other Essays.* Translated with an Introduction by William Lovitt. New York: Harper and Row, 1977.
QS	J D. "The Question of Style," in *The New Nietzsche: Contemporary Styles of Interpretation.* Ed. David Allison. New York: Dell, 1977.
Reply	H–G G. "Reply to Jacques Derrida" in this volume. The German text will be found in *TI* 59–61 under a title formulated by editor Philippe Forget: "Und dennoch: Macht des Guten Willens," and a French translation by Philippe Forget appeared under the title, "Et Pourtant: Puissance de la Bonne Volonté (Une Réplique à Jacques Derrida)," in *RIP* No. 151 (1984): 344–47.
Response	J D. "Three Questions to Hans-Georg Gadamer" in this volume. The original French text is titled "Bonnes Volontés de Puissance (Une Réponse à H-G G)" and may be found in *RIP* No. 151 (1984): 341–43. The German trans-

lation, by Friedrich A. Kittler, "Guter Wille zur Macht (1)," appears in *TI* 56–58.

RIP   *Revue internationale de philosophie.* Publication began in 1946.

RM   J D. "Le retrait de la métaphore," *Psyché* 63–93. Translation: "The *Retrait* of Metaphor," *Enclitic,* 2, 2 (1978): 5–33. Essay from an encounter with Ricoeur.

RP   *Research in Phenomenology.* Publication began in 1971.

S   H-GG. "Selbstdarstellung," in *GW 2,* pp. 479–508. Translated as "On the Origin of Philosophical Hermeneutics," in *PA.*

Schib   J D. *Schibboleth: Pour Paul Celan.* Paris: Éditions Galilée, 1986.

SD   M H. *Zur Sache des Denkens.* Tübingen: Niemeyer, 1969. Trans. J. Stambaugh as *On Time and Being.* New York: Harper and Row, 1972.

Searle   John Searle. "Reiterating the Differences: A Reply to Derrida," *Glyph* 1 (1977): 198–208.

SG   M H. *Der Satz vom Grund.* Pfüllingen: Neske, 1965.

Spurs   J D. *Éperons: Les styles de Nietzsche.* Paris: Flammarion, 1978. Trans. Barbara Harlow. *Spurs: Nietzsche's Styles.* Chicago: University of Chicago Press, 1978.

SZ   M H. *Sein und Zeit.* 10th edition. Tübingen: Max Niemeyer Verlag, 1963 [unchanged from original 1927 edition]. Trans. John Macquarrie and Edward Robinson as *Being and Time.* New York: Harper and Row, 1962.

TI   H-G G. "Text and Interpretation" as it appears in this volume. When two sets of pages are given, the earlier will be to the German original in either *TI* 24–55 or *GW 2* 330–60.

TI   Philippe Forget, ed. *Text und Interpretation: Eine deutsch-französische Debatte mit Beiträgen von JD, Philippe Forget, Manfred Frank, H-G G, Jean Greisch und François Laruelle.* Ed. Philippe Forget. Munich: Wilhelm Fink Verlag, 1984 [UTB 1257].

TM   Rodolphe Gasché. *The Tain of the Mirror: Derrida and the Philosophy of Reflection.* Cambridge: Harvard University Press, 1986.

TT	J D. "The Time of a Thesis: Punctuations," in *Philosophy in France Today*, ed. Alan Montefiore. Cambridge: Cambridge University Press, 1983.
TuI	H-G G. "Text und Interpretation" as it appears in *TI*, pp. 24–55, or in *GW 2*, pp. 330–60.
US	H-G G. "Unterwegs zur Schrift?" in *Schrift und Gedächtnis: Beiträge zur Archäologie der literarischen Kommunikation*, ed. Aleida and Jan Assmann and Christof Hardmeier (Munich: Wilhelm Fink, 1983), pp. 10–19.
US	M H. *Unterwegs zur Sprache*. Pfullingen: Neske, 1959. Trans. Peter D. Hertz. *On the Way to Language*. New York: Harper and Row, 1971.
VEP	J D. *La Vérité en peinture*. Paris: Flammarion, 1978. Trans. Geoff Bennington and Ian McLeod. *The Truth in Painting*. Chicago: University of Chicago Press, 1987.
VP	J D. *La Voix et le phénomène*. Paris: PUF, 1967. Trans. D. Allison, *Speech and Phenomena*. Evanston: Northwestern University Press, 1973.
WBI	H-G G. *Wer bin ich und wer bist du?: Kommentar zu Celans "Atemkristall"*. Frankfurt: Suhrkamp, 1973.
WHD	M H. *Was Heißt Denken?* Tübingen: Niemeyer, 1954. Trans. F. D. Wieck and J. Glenn Gray. *What is Called Thinking?* New York: Harper and Row, 1968.
WIM	M H. *Was ist Metaphysik?* 9th ed. Frankfurt am Main: Klostermann, 1965. Also pp. 1–19 in *Wegmarken*. Frankfurt am Main: Klosterman, 1967. English trans. by David F. Krell in *BW* 95–112.
WM	H-G G. *Wahrheit und Methode: Grundzüge einer philosophischen Hermeneutik*. 2nd ed.; Tübingen: J. C. B. Mohr, 1965. English: *Truth and Method*. Ed. Garrett Barden and John Cumming. New York: The Seabury Press, 1975.
WP	F N. *Der Wille zur Macht*. Ed. Walter Kaufman. *The Will to Power*. New York: Random House, 1968. Citations are by aphorism number rather than by page.
ZW	M H. "Die Zeit des Weltbildes," in *H* 69–104.

Contributors of Commentaries

Robert Bernasconi is author of *The Question of Language in Heidegger's History of Being* (1985) and has written articles on Hegel, Derrida, and Levinas, as well as Heidegger. He has co-edited several volumes with David Wood, including *Derrida and Différance* (1985) and *The Provocation of Levinas: Rethinking the Other* (1988). For a dozen years professor of philosophy at the University of Essex, Bernasconi in 1988 accepted an endowed chair in philosophy at Memphis State University.

John D. Caputo's most recent book is *Radical Hermeneutics: Repetition, Deconstruction, and the Hermeneutic Project* (1987). In addition to many articles related to post-metaphysical philosophy, he is author of *The Mystical Element in Heidegger's Thought* (1978) and *Heidegger and Aquinas* (1983).He is professor of philosophy at Villanova University.

Fred Dallmayr is author of books and articles on the intersection between continental philosophical and political thought, including *Language and Politics: Why Does Language Matter to Political Philosophy?* (1984) and more recently *Critical Encounters: Between Philosophy and Politics* (1987). He is professor of government and international studies at the University of Notre Dame in Indiana.

Gabe Eisenstein is presently an assistant professor of philosophy at Portland State University, on leave from Research and Development at the Hewlett-Packard Corporation. His current research is on the problem of narrative unity and philosophical interpretation.

Philippe Forget was the editor of *Text und Interpretation* (1984). His introductory essay there, "Leitfäden einer unwahrscheinlichen Debatte" ["*Leading Threads of an Improbable Debate*"], deals with the Gadamer-Derrida encounter and other essays in the volume. A co-author of *Textverstehen und Übersetzen* (1981), Forget is professor of German literature at the Sorbonne in Paris.

Manfred Frank has written books on Schelling, on Schleiermacher's hermeneutics, and also several books on contemporary hermeneutics. His *What is Neostructuralism?* (German 1983, English 1988) critically explores Nietzsche, Foucault, Deleuze, Derrida and others. He is presently professor of philosophy at the University of Tübingen.

David Farrell Krell has written *Intimations of Mortality: Time, Truth and Finitude in Heidegger's Thinking of Being* (1986) and *Postponements: Woman, Sensuality, and Death in Nietzsche* (1986). Co-editor with David Wood of a volume *Exceedingly Nietzsche: Aspects of Contemporary Nietzsche Interpretation* (1988), Krell is editor and co-translator of a collection of Heidegger's basic writings, of a volume of essays by Heidegger on early Greek thinking, and also of the four-volume translation of Heidegger's *Nietzsche*. He is professor of philosophy and chairman of the department at DePaul University in Chicago.

G. B. Madison has written a book on the phenomenology of Merleau-Ponty (French 1973, English 1981), edited a volume of essays in honor of Paul Ricoeur (1975), as well as having written *Understanding: A Phenomenological-Pragmatic Analysis* (1982), *The Logic of Liberty* (1986), and *The Hermeneutics of Postmodernity: Figure and Themes* (1988). Madison is professor of philosophy at McMaster University, Hamilton, Ontario, Canada, and has since 1986 published the *Bulletin* for *The Canadian Society for Hermeneutics and Postmodern Thought*.

Donald G. Marshall is author of numerous articles on literary theory and its history and with Joel Weinsheimer he did the revised translation of Gadamer's *Truth and Method* forthcoming from Crossroad/Continuum. Recently he edited *Literature as Philosophy/Philosophy as Literature* (1987). He is professor of English at the University of Iowa.

Neal Oxenhandler has written a number of books and articles on French literature, film, and literary criticism, including *Scandal and Parade: The Theatre of Jean Cocteau* (1957) and *Max Jacob and "Les Feux de Paris"* (1964). He is a professor of French literature at Dartmouth College.

Herman Rapaport has written *Milton and the Postmodern* (1983) and *Heidegger and Derrida: Reflections on Time and Language* (1989). He is professor of comparative literature at the University of Iowa.

James Risser has published a number of articles in the fields of hermeneutics and contemporary philosophy, among them "The Disappearance of the Text: Nietzsche's Double Hermeneutic," in volume 15 of *Research in Phenomenology* on the theme "Nietzsche/Heidegger" (1985). He is currently working on a book on Gadamer. He is an associate professor of philosophy at Seattle University.

John Sallis has written *Phenomenology and the Return to Beginnings* (1980), *Being and Logos: The Way of Platonic Dialogue* (1975), *The Gathering of Reason* (1980), *Delimitations: Phenomenology and the End of Metaphysics* (1986), and *Spacings—of Reason and Imagination in the Texts of Kant, Fichte, Hegel* (1987). He is editor of *Deconstruction and Philosophy: The Texts of Jacques Derrida* (1987) and also editor of *Research in Phenomenology*. He is professor of philosophy at Loyola University of Chicago.

Richard Shusterman has written *The Object of Literary Criticism* (1984) and *T. S. Eliot and the Philosophy of Criticism* (1988) and edited *Analytic Aesthetics* (1989). He is presently associate professor of philosophy at Temple University.

Charles Shepherdson has written on Kant, Heidegger, Foucault, and Lacan in philosophy and on the Romantic and post-Romantic lyric in English literature. His dissertation (Vanderbilt, 1986) related Heidegger to the interpretation of lyric poetry. He is presently the Henry A. Luce Fellow in Humanities at the Claremont Graduate School and teaches in the departments of English, Philosophy, and European Studies.

Josef Simon has written a half dozen books on philosophy and/of language beginning with *Das Problem der Sprache bei Hegel* in 1966. Among eight books Simon has edited or co-edited are three on Nietzsche: *Zur Aktualität Nietzsches* (1984), *Nietzsche und die philosophische Tradition* (1985), and *Kunst und Wissenschaft bei Nietzsche* (1986). In addition he has written numerous articles on Hamann, Kant, Hegel, and the philosophy of language. In English, one of his articles on Nietzsche appeared in *Studies in Nietzsche and the Judaeo-Christian Tradition,* ed. J. C. O'Flaherty, T. F. Sellner, and R. M. Helm (1985). He is professor of philosophy at the University of Bonn.

Notes

Introduction

1. See "Plato's Pharmacy," *D* 69–197/63–171, and "The Ends of Man," *M* 129–64/ 109–36.

2. See Manfred Frank's essay in this volume and also his "Avant-propos," *RIP* No. 151 (1984): 329–31. There he asserts that hermeneutics and deconstruction are "the two most important currents of European thought since World War II" and also have a good deal of common ground. He singles out five significant common elements: the "linguistic turn" as a theoretical foundation; the "critique of the crisis running through modern thought"; the denial of an "absolute spirit" or timeless self-presence and an affirmation of finitude; the fact that both go back to the diagnosis by Nietzsche and Heidegger of "Western rationalism," also the thesis of its closure; and finally, the emphasis in both on the primordial significance of aesthetic phenomena, especially literature and literary criticism.

3. The exact dates of this meeting were April 25–27, 1981. A second "encounter" took place in early February 1988, this time under the aegis of the French Department at the University of Heidelberg. It featured Gadamer and Derrida on "Heidegger and Politics." The topic drew a large crowd (See Günter Zehm, "*Wenn es um Heidegger geht, reicht der Hörsaal nicht aus,*" *Die Welt*, February 8, 1988, p. 3) but involved no appreciable further dialogue on hermeneutics and deconstruction.

4. See Philippe Forget, "Leading Threads of an Improbable Debate" ("*Leitfäden einer unwahrscheinlichen Debatte,*" *TI* 7–23), editor's introduction to *Text und Interpretation*. This volume serves as the primary source for our encounter papers. It also includes other papers presented at the same symposium by François Laruelle, Jean Greisch, Philippe Forget, and Manfred Frank. In order to focus our volume on the encounter between Gadamer and Derrida and the issues it raises, we have not included these other papers except for a shortened version of the paper by Manfred Frank.

5. This exchange was tape recorded and transcribed, thus providing a written record.

6. In the French publication of the encounter in *RIP* Gadamer's presentation was titled "*Le défi herméneutique.*" ["The Challenge of Hermeneutics"]. The German publication of Gadamer's paper in *TI* is a considerably expanded version of his original presentation.

7. See also Derrida's remarks on the biographical reading of Nietzsche in *O/EO.* See also his *DE,* ch. 8.

8. A remark that echoes Derrida's comment on another debate, that between himself and Searle: "What I like about this 'confrontation' is that I don't know if it is quite taking place, if it ever will be able, or will have been able, quite, to take place; or if it does, between whom or what?" "Limited, Inc abc. . ." in *Glyph* 2 (1977): 172.

9. See "Roundtable in Autobiography," trans. Peggy Kamuf, in *EO* 86–87.

10. For Derrida's thoughts about the treatment of the word "deconstruction" in the hands of others, see, for instance, *EO* 85–86, *CNP* passim, "The Time of a Thesis" (TT), or Christopher Norris, *Derr* 14 and passim; and the interview (with photographs) of Derrida in the special tenth anniversary issue of *Art Papers* on "Poststructuralism, Postmodernism, Postmodernity," Robert Cheatham, "Jacques Derrida (Interview)," *Art Papers* 10, 1 (1986): 31–35. Special issue available from Atlanta Art Papers, Inc., P.O. Box 77348, Atlanta, Ga 30357.]

11. See *Spurs,* for example, 112/113, 125/126 where he is critical of hermeneutics.

12. See *M* 162–63/134–35; *ED* 427–28/292–93.

13. See *A* 85.

14. Commentators were provided with copies of the encounter documents as well as the "Letter to Dallmayr" and "*Destruktion* and Deconstruction." "Hermeneutics and Logocentrism" came into the hands of the editors too late to be circulated to the commentators.

15. See especially his *Was ist Neostrukturalismus?* (Frankfurt: Suhrkamp, 1984); trans. Sabine Wilke and Richard Gray as *What is Neostructuralism?* (Minneapolis: University of Minnesota Press, 1988).

16. See his *Das individuelle Allgemeine: Textstrukturierung und Interpretation bei Schleiermacher* (Frankfurt: Suhrkamp, 1977).

17. *Das Sagbare und das Unsagbare: Studien zur neuesten französischen Hermeneutik und Texttheorie* (Frankfurt: Suhrkamp, 1980), and more recently *Die Unhintergehbarkeit von Individualität: Reflexionen über Subjekt, Person und Individuum aus Anlaß ihrer "postmodernen" Toterklärung* (Frankfurt: Suhrkamp, 1986).

18. Nietzsche said he became uneasy when someone claimed to understand him, for this implied that that person was intellectually his equal. Nietzsche said that he "did his best to be difficult to understand." See *Beyond Good and Evil,* secs. 27, and 24–44.

19. Nevertheless, Gadamer advised us that when he and Derrida again shared the podium in February of 1988 for a discussion of the topic "Heidegger et la Politique," sponsored by the French Department of the University of Heidelberg, it turned out to be more of a media event than a genuine conversation. See note 3 above.

20. For a basically favorable exploration of the political dimensions of Gadamer's early thinking, see the forthcoming book by Robert Richard Sullivan, *The Early Gadamer.*

21. Regarding Derrida's exegetical ties with Hebrew tradition, see Susan Handelman, *Slayers of Moses* (Albany: SUNY Press, 1982). For a view of Derrida from the perspective of another non-Gadamerian hermeneutics, see Thomas M. Seebohm,

"Deconstruction in the Framework of Traditional Methodical Hermeneutics," *Journal of the British Society for Phenomenology*, 17, 3 (1986): 275–88, and from still another German perspective, Hubertus Busche, *"Logozentrismus und Différance: Versuch über Jacques Derrida,"* *Zeitschrift für philosophische Forschung*, 41 (1987): 245–61.

22. Elsewhere, Marshall gives a lengthier discussion of issues involved in this debate in the context of Plato: "Deconstruction, Sophistic and Hermeneutics: Gadamer, Gorgias, Plato, and Derrida," *Journal of Comparative Literature and Aesthetics*, 9, 1–2 (1986: 83–108). Other articles on the encounter of possible interest include: Ernst Behler, "Deconstruction versus Hermeneutics: Derrida and Gadamer on Text and Interpretation," *Southern Humanities Review* 21, 3 (1987): 201–23; Richard E. Palmer, "Improbable Encounter: Gadamer-Derrida," *Art Papers*, 10, 1 (1986): 36–39; and Diane Michelfelder, "Derrida and the Ethics of the Ear," forthcoming in a *SPEP* volume from the fall 1987 meeting.

I, 1: Text and Interpretation

1. There is no equivalent in English for *"für etwas Verständnis haben."* We have rendered it "to have an appreciation for something," but *Verständnis* suggests also to sympathize, to comprehend, to have insight into something. It also involves such considerations as those Gadamer immediately raises here—of language, community, and the happening of understanding in conversation.—Trans.

2. Gadamer adds the following footnote in *GW 2* 332: "See the collection of my studies on the later Heidegger, *Heideggers Wege* [*HW*]: *GW 3.*" Unless otherwise indicated, the footnotes which follow were added by Gadamer in *GW 2* and are listed here with the kind permission of the publisher as editorial footnotes with appropriate citation of *GW.*—Eds.

3. *GW 2* 334 footnote: Cf. "Correspondence Concerning *Wahrheit und Methode:* Leo Strauss and Hans-Georg Gadamer," *Independent Journal of Philosophy* 2 (1978): 5–12.

4. See *WM* 450/432.—*TI* editor's note.

5. *GW 2* 335 footnote: Already in 1959 I sought to show this in "On the Circle of Understanding," an essay dedicated to Heidegger which is contained in the present volume [*GW 2* 57–65].

6. *GW 2* 339 footnote: See Moritz Schlick, "Über das Fundament der Erkenntnis," in his *Gesammelte Aufsätze 1926–1936* (Vienna: Gerold & Co., 1938), pp. 290–95; 300–309.

7. *GW 2* 339 footnote: For references to recent theory of science, see Weinsheimer, *GH.*

8. *GW 2* 340 footnote: See Erich Rothacker, *Das "Buch der Natur": Materialien und*

Grundsätzliches zur Metapherngeschichte. Edited from the posthumous papers, by W. Perpeet. Bonn: Bouvier, 1979.

9. See *WM* 370/353ff. and esp. 373/356, where Gadamer concludes, "The concept of the original reader is crammed full of unreflected idealizing [*Idealisierung*]."

10. From the beginning of the next paragraph to the end, the present translation follows *TI*, except that a few additional footnotes from *GW 2* have been indicated. This portion of the essay appears in English translation for the first time. See translators' headnote.—Eds.

11. *GW 2* 350 footnote: Cf. an essay of mine which has appeared more recently, "The Hermeneutics of Suspicion," pp. 54–65 in *Hermeneutics: Questions and Prospects,* ed. Gary Shapiro and Alan Sica, Amherst: University of Massachusetts Press, 1984.

12. In this regard, see the various essays on literary theory which I have collected together in volume 8 of my *Gesammelte Werke* (*GW*).

13. This sentence was added to TI in *GW 2* 354–55, with the following footnote: "See Max Warburg, *Zwei Fragen zum Kratylos.* Neue philologische Untersuchungen 5. Berlin: Weidmann, 1929.

14. "Shakespeare und kein Ende," in Johann Wolfgang Goethe, *Sämtliche Werke,* Artemis-Gedenkausgabe, Vol. 14, p. 757.—*TI* editor's note.

15. Mörike's poem runs: [with interlinear, literal translation added]
    Noch unverrückt, o schöne Lampe, schmückest du,
    Still undisturbed, oh beautiful lamp, thou adornst
    An leichten Ketten zierlich aufgehangen hier.
    On a light chain gracefully hung here.
    Die Decke des nun fast vergeβnen Lustgemachs.
    The ceiling of a now almost forgotten pleasure room.
    Auf deiner Weiβen Marmorschale, deren Rand
    On your white marble skin, whose border
    Der Efeukranz von goldengrünem Erz umflicht.
    The ivy wreath of golden green metal woven round
    Schlingt fröhlich eine Kinderschar den Ringelreihn.
    A troop of children joyfully twist in the ring dance.
    Wie reizend alles lachend, und ein sanfter Geist
    How attractive everyone laughing, and a gentle spirit
    Des Ernstes doch ergossen um die ganze Form—
    Of seriousness indeed suffuses the whole form—
    Ein Kunstgebild der echten Art. Wer Achtet sein?
    An artistic shape of the authentic kind. Being noticed by whom?
    Was aber schön ist, selig scheint es in im selbst.
    But what is beautiful shines blissfully in itself.

The interchange between Emil Staiger and Martin Heidegger to which Gadamer alludes here is documented in Emil Staiger, *Die Kunst der Interpretation* DTV 4078 (1971 and 1955, by permission of Atlantis Verlag, Zürich and Freiburg), pp. 28–42.—*TI* editor's note.

I, 4: Interpreting Signatures

1. Derrida elsewhere treats this theme. Cf. *O/EO*. Also of interest are *De l'esprit: Heidegger et la question* (*DE*) and the 650–page recent collection, *Psyché: Invention de l'autre.* —Trans.
2. Martin Heidegger, *Nietzsche*, trans. Pierre Klossowski (Paris: Gallimard, 1971).
3. *N* 1:9/1:xv. Translator's note: Where Derrida provides a French translation, we have translated from the French rather than simply use Krell's translation. Where German text is presented untranslated, we have sometimes used the Krell translation and sometimes supplied our own. Throughout this essay, as throughout the volume, we give the pages of the original source first, then those of the English translation. See our list of abbreviations for names of the four volumes in the English translation of Heidegger's *Nietzsche*.
4. The point Derrida is making relies on the French sounds, so we have not translated. A translation would be something like: "He wants Nice, he venices, he wants Nietzsche" All of these expressions sound enough alike in French to invite the play on words.
5. This is the interpretation proposed by Derrida in *O/EO*.
6. French "exergue." See the significant reference in *EO* 11: "Between the Preface [of *Ecce Homo*] signed F. N., which comes after the title, and the first chapter . . . there is a single page. It is an outwork, an *hors d'oeuvre,* an exergue or a flysheet, whose topos . . . strangely dislocates . . . the time of life's *récit.* . . ."

II, Prelude: Hermeneutics and Deconstruction

1. Giambattista Vico, *The New Science,* trans. and ed. Thomas G. Bergin and Max H. Fisch (New York: Anchor Books, 1961), pp. 88 (section 405).
2. Compare on this score especially the debate between Gadamer and Habermas in *Hermeneutik und Ideologiekritik* (Frankfurt-Main: Suhrkamp, 1971); see also Dieter Misgeld, "Critical Theory and Hermeneutics: The Debate between Habermas and Gadamer," in John O'Neill, ed., *On Critical Theory* (New York: Seabury Press, 1976), pp. 164–83, and Thomas McCarthy, "Rationality and Relativism: Habermas's 'Overcoming' of Hermeneutics," in *Habermas: Critical Debates,* ed. John B. Thompson and David Held (Cambridge, MA: MIT Press, 1982), pp. 57–78.
3. (Translation slightly altered, as will be the case hereafter in many of the citations from German and French). See also Heidegger's "The Origin of the Work of Art" (*H* 7–68/*BW* 143–87).
4. In Gadamer's portrayal, transformative rupture is particularly pronounced in the case of literature or written texts (156/145): "Literature has a unique and incomparable mode of being; it presents a specific problem to understanding. There is nothing

so strange or alien and at the same time so demanding as the written text. Not even the encounter with speakers of a foreign tongue can be compared with this strangeness. . . . Writing and what partakes of it, literature, is the intelligibility of mind transferred to the most alien medium. Nothing is so purely mental trace as writing, but also nothing so dependent on the understanding mind."

5. The last statement clearly illustrates Gadamer's ambivalence: his oscillation between an ontological "event" or "happening" (in Heidegger's sense) and the stress on intelligible "meaning" or significance. Gadamer, it is true, tends to construe this oscillation in a Hegelian (dialectical) vein, which is further evidence of his idealist moorings. Revealingly, both his critique of "aesthetic consciousness" and his defense of the "ontology" of artworks terminate in a discussion of Hegel; see *WM* 93–95/87–89; 158–61/147–150.

6. Compare also QS 178–80.

7. The treatment of Nietzsche as philosopher-artist finds support, of course, in the fragments assembled under the title "The Will to Power as Art" in *WP*, especially fragments 794—"Our religion, morality, and philosophy are decadence forms of man. *The countermovement: art.*"—and 811: "In all philosophy hitherto the artist has been lacking." The latter fragment, among others, is cited by Derrida, who adds: "Before art, the dogmatic philosopher, a maladroit courtesan, remains—like a second-rate scholar—impotent, a sort of old maid" (*Spurs* 77).

8. Compare also QS 186, 188.

9. Compare on this point also Gadamer's *HDial* and *DD*.

10. Regarding the issue of "truth" compare especially Robert D. Cumming, "The Odd Couple: Heidegger and Derrida," *Review of Metaphysics* 34 (1981): 487–522. See also Charles A. Pressler, "Redoubled: The Bridging of Derrida and Heidegger," *Human Studies*, 7 (1984): 325–342.

11. The shift of emphasis between the two volumes is particularly underscored by Hannah Arendt, *The Life of the Mind*, vol. 2: *Willing* (New York: Harcourt Brace Jovanovich, 1978), pp. 172–73.

12. In *Spurs*, the possibility of a matrical arrangement or "congruence" is even advanced as "the thesis of the present communication" (57).

13. See also Nietzsche, "Thus Spoke Zarathustra," in Walter Kaufmann (ed.), *The Portable Nietzsche* (New York: Viking Press, 1968), p. 328. On suffering compare also this passage (p. 199): "Creation—that is the great redemption from suffering and life's growing light. But that the creator may be, suffering is needed and much change. Indeed, there must be much bitter dying in your life, you creators." By resolutely bypassing this domain, Derrida sometimes seems more like the jester than the tightrope walker described at the beginning of *Zarathustra*. Note also Zarathustra's comments (p. 311): "There are many ways of overcoming: see to that *yourself.* But only a jester thinks: 'Man can also be *skipped over.*' "

14. Kaufmann, *The Portable Nietzsche*, p. 139.

15. Ibid., p. 156.

16. In my view, a closer reading of Heidegger shows that, far from constituting an undecidable vortex of being and nothingness, *Ereignis* is the "giving" of affirmative

potency which sustains being (with its attendant non-being) in being; see his "Time and Being" (*SD* 16–22/16–22). For an explicit effort to distinguish ontology from undecidability or indifference, compare Heidegger, *Schellings Abhandlung "Über das Wesen der menschlichen Freiheit"* (1809), ed. Hildegard Feick (Tübungen: Niemeyer, 1971), pp. 123, 184–90. [This work is now available in English: *Schelling's Treatise on the Essence of Human Freedom,* trans. Joan Stambaugh (Athens: Ohio University Press, 1985).—Eds.]

17. For a brief sketch of the contours of a "recollective ethics" see my *Twilight of Subjectivity: Contributions to a Post-Individualist Theory of Politics* (Amherst: University of Massachusetts Press, 1981), pp. 250–54.

18. The Gadamerian linkage of hermeneutics and praxis is stressed by Richard J. Bernstein, *Beyond Objectivism and Relativism: Science, Hermeneutics, and Praxis* (Philadelphia: University of Pennsylvania Press, 1983), esp. pp. 109–69.

19. Compare Hubert Dreyfus, "Beyond Hermeneutics: Interpretation in Late Heidegger and Foucault," in *Hermeneutics: Questions and Prospects,* ed. Gary Shapiro and Alan Sica (Amherst: University of Massachusetts Press, 1984), pp. 66–83.

II, 1: Letter to Dallmayr

1. "Attempts and enticements" in this sentence translates *Versuchen und Versuchungen.* The play on the word *Versuch,* which means to attempt, and *Versuchung,* which means a temptation, is lost in the translation. This and all subsequent notes to the "Letter to Dallmayr" are by the translators.

2. See "The Onto-theo-logical Constitution of Metaphysics," *ID* 107–43/42–74.

3. Basically, *Existenz* is Dasein's sense of its future possibilities of being.

4. "To make something known," or in Cairns' *Guide for Translating Husserl* (The Hague: Nijhoff, 1973), "giving cognizance of, (making known); that of which cognizance is given, (what is made known). Not 'manifestation.' " And *kundgebende Funktion* is, for Cairns, "cognizance-giving function." However, in *VP* we find Derrida rendering *"kundgebende Funktion"* felicitously as *"la fonction de manifestation"* (41) and translating *Kundnahme* as follows: *"la saisie de la manifestation [Kundnahme]* est une simple perception de la manifestation *[Kundgabe]. . ."* (43; ch. 3, sec. B).

5. "Unterwegs zur Schrift?" in *Schrift und Gedächtnis: Beiträge zur Archäologie der literarischen Kommunikation,* ed. Aleida and Jan Assmann and Christof Hardmeier (Munich: Wilhelm Fink, 1983), pp. 10–19.

6. Gadamer suggests in *"Destruktion* and Deconstruction," that *Destruktion,* in Heidegger's usage, does not mean destruction but rather a destructuring of hardened concepts that retrieves the lost dimensions of meaning which these terms formerly possessed in living language. Because no English word exactly corresponds to what is involved in *Destruktion,* we leave it untranslated throughout this volume.

II, 2: *Destruktion* and Deconstruction

1. Echoing the *Aeneid* 1, 33: *"Tantae molis erat Romanam condere gentem"*—"Such was the cost in heavy labor of founding the Roman nation."—Trans.

2. For remarks by Derrida on *Destruktion* and the relation of this word to "deconstruction" see *EO* 86–87.—Eds.

3. In German, *ent*- means "away," "un-," or "dis-," and *fern* means "far" or "distant," thus the two together mean an overcoming of distance.—Trans.

4. This echoes Hölderlin's famous line, *"ein Gespräch wird sind. . ."*—"We are a conversation"—from the fragment *"Versöhnender, der du nimmergeglaubt. . ."* where it occurs in the following lines: "Mankind has experienced much,/Named many of the heavenly,/Since a conversation we are/And hear from one another" (trans. Geoff Waite).—Eds.

5. See "Der Spruch des Anaximander," in *H*, esp. 329ff./"The Anaximander Fragment" in *EGT* esp. 42ff.—Eds.

6. See HB 71/*BW* 207, referring back to a citation of *SZ* 42/67 in Sartre's *L'existentialisme est un humanisme* (Paris: Nagel, 1970), p. 21/*Existentialism and Human Emotions* (New York: Philosophical Library, 1957), p. 15.—Eds.

7. See *WM*, opening section: "The Significance of the Humanist Tradition for the Human Sciences." Also: "Sense is directional!"—Eds.

8. Virtuality is used here in the sense that an image on the face of a mirror is a "virtual" rather than a real image.—Eds.

II, 3: Hermeneutics and Logocentrism

1. "Zur dialektischen Bedeutung romantischer Ironie," *AF* 85–95. In the course of his remarks Professor Gadamer comments on several other papers presented at the colloquium. The titles of these papers in *Die Aktualität der Frühromantik* will be indicated in notes by the translators, who wish to thank Professor Ernst Behler for providing us with a prepublication table of contents and also allowing us to compare our text with his galley proofs of Gadamer's paper. All notes here are by the translators.

2. " 'Intellektuelle Anschauung.' Drei Stellungnahmen zu einem Deutungsversuch von Selbstbewußtsein: Kant, Fichte, Hölderlin/Novalis," *AF* 96–126.

3. "Der Töne Licht: Zum frühromantischen Programm der Wortmusik," *AF* 191–207.

4. Gadamer is presumably referring here to Ernst Behler's paper at the colloquium, "Friedrich Schlegels Theorie des Verstehens: Hermeneutik oder Dekonstruktion?" *AF* 141–60.

5. See his *Aesthetische Erfahrung und literarische Hermeneutik* (Munich: Fink, 1974)/ *Aesthetic Experience and Literary Hermeneutics*, trans. Michael Shaw (Minneapolis: University of Minnesota Press, 1982).

6. At this point in the manuscript, handwritten emendations by Professor Gadamer were not readable on the xerox copy supplied to the translator, so Professor Gadamer sent another copy, retyped, which actually revised slightly the formulations published in *Die Aktualität der Frühromantik*. For the benefit of specialists, the translators provide the revised German text:

> In der Tat ist es nicht mehr bedingt, etwa durch das, was der eine oder der andere meint oder dabei denkt, noch teilhaben an dem, was im Geist des Schöpfers vor sich ging. Das ist das Wesen der kommunikativen Kraft des Werkes, daß sich darin allein das Gemeinsame konstituiert. So glaube ich, daß Derrida in gewissem Sinne den gleichen Weg von Heidegger aus eingeschlagen hat, wie ich. Aber mir scheint, daß er ihn durch eine ontologisch ungeklärte Abhängigkeit von dem semantischen Ausgangspunkt seiner Sprachbetrachtung markiert hat. Die Unausweichlichkeit der hermeneutischen Fragestellung, die wahrlich nichts mit Feststellung des richtigen Sinnes zu tun hat, als ob dieser feststünde und als feststehender erreichbar wäre, ist das Thema meiner Auseinandersetzung mit Derrida. Die Differenz ist in der Identität. Sonst wäre die Identität keine Identität. Denken enthält Aufschub und Abstand. Sonst wäre Denken kein Denken.

III, 1: Argument(s)

1. "Guter Wille zur Macht I" and "Und dennoch: Macht des guten Willens." Notice how Derrida continually addresses Gadamer by his title of Professor. To anyone who remembers Derrida's remarks on the Schapiro-Heidegger confrontation (cf. "Restitutions" in *VEP*, especially p. 315), the polemical charge here is obvious. Lessing had previously, with a stronger sense of irony, used such a tactic towards Gottsched. Gadamer, on his part, offers "Monsieur": faithful, in such contexts, to academic courtesy and urbane civility.

2. Except to mention that this should be read in conjunction with a text that has since been published: *Otobiographies* [*O*], and to risk an interpretation of the orthographic play (*oto* for *auto*) related to our discussion: one can "read" o-t-o in a double chiasma starting from the axis of the *t*: (t-o-)t(-o-t), the thought of life-death hidden in a title.

3. This is a critique that I summed up in Gadamer's terms at the end of my "Leitfäden einer unwahrscheinlichen Debatte" [Intro to *TI*], without hiding my adherence to Frank's *argument*.

4. Cf. *Glas* [*Gl*], specifically with regard to a choice of ground in Hegel's work: "This choice is far from innocent. It holds not only for theoretical afterthoughts but also

for unconscious motivations which one must put in play and to work [*en jeu et au travail*], *without any preliminary theoretical grasp being possible*" (*Gl* 6, *italics mine*).

5. For example, this structural tendency of hermeneutics, which would open itself up to everything that presents itself to it, is the condition for the authenticity of its experience: "The hermeneutical experience must take as a genuine experience everything that becomes present to it. It does not have prior freedom to select and discard" (*WM* 439/420). It remains to be seen if deconstruction presents itself to it. Here let us simply risk this thought: Deconstruction does not present itself. This could also constitute an "experience."

6. "*Hôte*" can mean either "host" or "guest."—Trans.

7. It even turns out that Gadamer himself trangresses his own descriptions of the hermeneutical experience constitutive of the "good will": one of his arguments consists in saying that in a situation where two conversational partners speak different languages, there always comes a time, even if the partners understand a little of each other's language, when they end up communicating in the same tongue. From the experience of the Paris encounter, though, we know otherwise: Gadamer, after attempting to answer Derrida in French, carried on his response in German.

8. By simply underlining the "la" of "la psychanalyse," as for example in this sentence: "*La* psychanalyse est ici présentée en *continuité*," Forget is able to put a stress (a stress that unfortunately disappears in translation) on the alleged unity of "psychoanalysis."—Trans.

9. Etymologically, "to be delirious" means "to come out of a *lira,* a furrow": the very thing that receptively welcomes good seeds, but also "good" writing, as Socrates maintains in the *Phaedrus.*

10. Deconstruction doesn't deny unity. It knows that the desire for unity is nothing less than desire itself. What it doubts is the possibility of assuming unity, and, a fortiori, unity itself as a presupposition.

11. In itself, this is a debatable argument. At the very least, it can be put into question from the basis of certain texts of Nietzsche's. For example, when Nietzsche writes that he writes in order to be understood only by a few, that also means that he writes in order not to be understood. As for Derrida, one of the motives/motifs of his writing is to "cloud with confusion" ["*s'ennuager*"].

12. Jürgen Habermas, *Zur Logik der Sozialwissenschaften* (Frankfurt am Main: Suhrkamp, 1970), p. 283.

13. In French in the German text. ["*Es gibt préjugés légitimes*"—*WM* 255/240.] Does the legitimacy of legitimate prejudices express itself more clearly in a foreign language that one prejudges by saying that it displays Cartesian self-consciousness more clearly than other languages?

14. In any case, we know that with respect to the idea of beauty Freud has contradicted this affirmation. Cf. his *Über Vergänglichkeit.*

15. Indeed, this is the root of the German word *befangen* [*in Urteilen befangen,* in the grip of prejudice, from *fangen,* to seize or take captive.]—Trans.

16. In "Über die Frage: Was heisst Aufklärung," from *Was ist Aufklärung?* (Stuttgart: Reclam, 1974). [The passage that Forget goes on to cite is on page 7; (the italics are also his.—Trans.]

17. *Was ist Aufklärung?*, p. 7 [translation mine (DM)]. This passage also shows us that the defense of prejudice is not limited, as Gadamer thinks or presupposes, solely to the Christian current in the Enlightenment.

18. Cf. supra my comments about " *'la' psychoanalyse.*"

19. This problematic is set forth from a perspective similar to that put into play in his description of the "fusion of horizons," and so falls prey to a similar critique.

20. Cf., for example, Rainer Warning, *Rezeptionsästhetik*, UTB 903 (Munich: Fink, 1975), pp. 21ff.

21. This pair forms the very basis of the phenomenological and logocentric movement. It is indeed the organizing thesis of the recent great work of Jürgen Habermas, *Theorie des kommunikativen Handelns* (Frankfurt: Suhrkamp, 1983) [English trans.: *Theory of Communicative Action* (Boston: Beacon, 1987)].

22. "For are not all of them based on history, written or verbal? And don't we adopt history on the basis of belief and trust—isn't that right? And where is our belief and trust least in doubt? Isn't it with our own people? Those to whom we are tied by blood? Those who have given us proofs of their love ever since we were little? . . . . How could I believe my forefathers less than you believe yours? Or the other way around. Could I ask you to accuse your ancestors with lies so as not to contradict my own? Or the other way around. The same thing is true of Christians. Isn't that right?" Lessing, *Nathan der Weise*, [*Nathan the Wise*], III/7 [trans. mine, DM].

23. In French, *leurre herméneutique.* One can hear, in this phrase, a reference to Lacan—and, more directly, both *leurre* [lure] and *leur* [their].—Trans.

24. Gadamer responds here to an argument that I have sketched out in my introduction to *Text und Interpretation* (see *TI* 13). I want to thank Richard Palmer for sending me Gadamer's letter before publication, which allowed me here to further develop my argument.

25. Cf. on this point the first lines of Derrida's "Signature Event Context" (*M* 367/309).

26. Préj 94. Here at the same time we find confirmation of the hypothesis—contested by Gadamer—which claims his hermeneutics has a tie of kinship, certainly concealed but structuring (and concealed because it is structuring), to the ideological-scientific perspective of a *code* (which, according to his very principle, is never decipherable).

27. Cf. Roland Barthes, *Critique et vérité* (Paris: Seuil, 1966), p. 74.

28. *WBI* 62ff. Bernhard Boschenstein has already devoted a critical study to Gadamer's interpretation of this poem: cf. "Die notwendige Unauflöslichkeit," in *Zeitwende*, 6 (1985): 329–344, especially 334ff. But Boschenstein does not address the citation added to the interpretation, and, as a last resort, he imposes his own interpretation in a confused way by grounding his argument on some confidences of Celan (336), thereby falling back within the type of commentary he is critiquing.

29. ". . .in a complete turn-around of intelligible reality . . . the poet himself calls himself a 'flag'" (*WBI* 63). The identification is clearly relativized in his conclusion ("certainly the 'song-secured flag' [*liedfeste Wimpel*] does not only mean the poet and his perseverance in hope, but the last hope of all creatures" [*WBI* 64]), but the effect this has is to trivialize the poem into a humanistic message and turn the poet into a messenger of what is human: therefore the identification keeps on working. In the "Afterword," Gadamer states his opposition to any kind of identification: "I must settle things: the figure of this 'you' [*Du*] is this figure itself and not this or that, a lover of humanity or anyone else or the absolute Other" (p. 118). On this point, see Jacques Derrida's remark: "You, the word 'you' can address itself to the other just as well as to myself, to oneself as another. Each time, it exceeds the economy of discourse, its being with itself" (*Schib* 93).

30. Gadamer, following what he has had to say in *WBI* about the conditions of writing, quotes the poem from memory.

31. *Jäh* also signifies an abrupt slope; one can speak of an "abrupt abyss" [*jäher Abgrund*]. With respect to "*aufgetan*" ["opened up"], one can refer to the meaning that this word has in more than one place in Nietzsche's writing; for example, in the poem "The Mysterious Boat" (precisely in relation to an abyss); or again in *On the Genealogy of Morals,* each time with the dimension of a new knowledge, a new space for thinking.

32. Following the expression "to take the bit in one's teeth" [*prendre le mors aux dents*]—in other words, to run wild, to set off on a foolish course. This note could also be read as an invitation to reread the poem on the basis of what Jacques Derrida has specifically said about "*mors,*" heard with a sure ear.

33. Cf. Lucette Finas, "Salut," in *Esprit,* "Lecture I: L'espace du texte," 12 (1974): 871–901. [The reader is additionally referred to Philippe Forget's review of Jacques Derrida's *Schibboleth: Pour Paul Celan,* titled "Neuere Daten über Paul Celan, *Celan Jahrbuch I,* ed. Hans-Michael Speier (Heidelberg: Carl Winter Universitätsverlag, 1987), 217–22.—Trans.]

34. I am referring here to several remarks concentrated on pp. 96 of Gadamer's "Letter to Dallmayr": "What is writing if it is not to be read? . . . Even so, I only read a text with understanding when the letters are not just deciphered but when the text begins to speak, and that means when it is read with appropriate modulations, articulations, and emphases. . . . I really would like to know what understanding— and also, by implication, reading with understanding—has to do with metaphysics."

III, 2: Limits of the Human Control of Language

1. In: *Das individuelle Allgemeine: Textstrukturierung und -interpretation nach Schleiermacher* (Frankfurt: Suhrkamp, 1977), and above all in *Was ist Neostrukturalismus?* (Frankfurt: Suhrkamp, 1983)/English: *What is Neostructuralism?* (Minneapolis: University of Minnesota Press, 1988).

2. Friedrich Schleiermacher, *Hermeneutik und Kritik,* with a supplement of philosophical texts, edited and introduced by Manfred Frank (Frankfurt: Suhrkamp, 1977).

3. On this problem see the illuminating introduction offered by Michel Foucault to Antoine Arnauld and Claude Lancelot, *Grammaire générale et raisonée* (Paris, Republications Paulet, 1969), esp. pp. IXff.

4. *The Order of Words* (New York: Random House, 1970), p. 220. French given by Frank: "un des plus radicaux sans doute qui soit arrivé à la culture occidentale pour que se défasse la positivité du savoir classique, et que se constitue une positivité dont nous ne sommes sans doute pas entièrement sortis." *Les mot et les choses* (Paris: Gallimard, 1966), p. 232.—Eds.

5. "La linguistique a pour unique et seul objet la langue invisagée en elle-même et pour elle-même." *Cours,* 2nd ed., p. 317.

6. "Dans la langue, il y a toujours un double côté que se correspond: elle est sociale/individuelle.[. . .] Formes, grammaire n'existent que socialement, mais les changements partent d'un individu" (F. de Saussure, *Cours de linguistic générale* (1908/9). Introduction, ed. by R. Godel, in *CFS* 15. Cf. *Cours,* 2nd ed., p. 231: "Rien n'entre dans la langue sans avoir été essayé dans la parole, et tous les phénomènes évolutifs ont leur racine dans la sphère de l'individu" (cf. p. 138, also).

7. "Reiterating the Differences: A Reply to Derrida," *Glyph* 1 (1977), 199. Hereafter abbreviated as "Searle."

8. For reasons of space, we could only include about half of Frank's very suggestive essay. At this point we skip pp. 190–206 and translate a few paragraphs from pages 206–209, omitting the concluding remarks, pp. 209–13. The reader interested in a fuller statement of Frank's position is referred to his *What is Neostructuralism?* cited in footnote 1 above.—Eds.

III, 3: Good Will to Understand and the Will to Power

1. Nietzsche, *Nachlaß, KG* VIII 1 [182] (*KSA* 12, 51).

2. "And what kind of man am I? One of those who would gladly be refuted if anything I say is not true, and would gladly refute another if what he says is not true, but who would be no less happy to be refuted myself than to refute. . . ." Woodhead translation, Plato, *Collected Dialogues,* ed. E. Hamilton and H. Cairns (Princeton: Princeton University Press, 1964).—Trans.

3. German: "*Dritte.*" In response to a translator query, the author provides the following (translated) explanation of the term: "The expression is certainly hard to translate. One speaks in German of 'thirds' over and against a society to which 'third' does not belong, even when it is not a matter of any exact number. I chose this term for its connotations to the logical thesis of the 'excluded third.' In Position the 'third' does not actually appear but only the other as that which Position hopes to include."—Letter to translator dated August 21, 1987.

4. Since the German term "*Alter*" is translated with "alter" by Frederick Lawrence in the Habermas text cited, I have retained this translation in the ensuing paragraphs. According to Webster's *New International Dictionary*, "alter" or "alterum" are used specifically in philosophy to mean "Other—applied to that which is distinguished from the ego." In Habermas' usage, it would seem to mean something like a dialogical "other," a person or persons whose perspective(s) the ego attempts to imagine.— Trans.

5. Ludwig Wittgenstein, *Bemerkungen über die Grundlagen der Mathematik*, ed. G. E. M. Anscombe, Rush Rhees, G. H. von Wright, vol. 6 of an 8-volume German edition of his works (Frankfurt: Suhrkamp Verlag, 1984), p. 343.

6. Emmanuel Lévinas, *Die Spur des Anderen*, ed. W. N. Krewani (Freiburg/Munich: Alber Verlag, 1983), p. 211. [Perhaps a translation of *Le Temps et l'autre* (Montpellier: Fata Morgana, 1979).—Trans.]

7. See Nietzsche, *The Wanderer and his Shadow* (Part II of *Human, All too Human, GO* 2, 56ff.), aphorism 28.

8. Cf. *Die Religion innerhalb der Grenzen der bloßen Vernunft* [*Religion within the Limits of Reason Alone*], vol. 6 of *Kants Werke*, Akademie-Textausgabe (Berlin: De Gruyter, 1977), pp. 98ff.

III, 4: The Two Faces of Socrates: Gadamer/Derrida

1. Hans-Georg Gadamer, "Philosophy and Literature," trans. Anthony J. Steinbock, *Man and World*, 18 (1985): 247.

2. Gadamer takes this term from Austin. In *How to Do Things with Words*, Austin distinguishes between performative and constative utterances. Constative utterances describe a state of affairs and are true and false. Performative utterances perform the action to which they refer and are neither true nor false. See Jonathan Culler, *On Deconstruction: Theory and Criticism after Structuralism* (Ithaca: Cornell University Press, 1982).

3. "Philosophy and Literature," p. 253.

4. Note Forget's title in *TI* for Derrida's response to Gadamer and also for Derrida's essay: "Guter Wille zur Macht(I)" and "Guter Wille zur Macht(II)."

5. Since Derrida's French manuscript, forwarded by Derrida to the translators, did not carry this title but simply read [retaining Derrida's capitalization], "Interpréter les Signatures (Nietzsche/Heidegger): Deux questions," the editors have deleted Forget's added title. This also applies to Derrida's earlier "Three Questions for Hans-Georg Gadamer," where we deleted Forget's title, "Guter Wille zur Macht (I)."—Eds.

6. See Plato, *Phaedrus*, 274b–278b.

III, 6: Gadamer/Derrida: The Hermeneutics of Irony and Power

1. TI 27. Gadamer's use of the word "completely" ("completely expressing oneself") is unfortunate. He himself furnishes a corrective for this infelicity when earlier on in his text he says: "My own efforts were directed toward not forgetting the limit that is implicit in every hermeneutical experience of meaning" (TI 25).

2. In his reply Gadamer remarks: "Is he really disappointed that we cannot rightly understand each other? No indeed, for in his view this would be a falling back into metaphysics. He will, in fact, be pleased, because he sees in this private experience of disillusionment a confirmation of his own metaphysics" (Reply).

3. "When Heidegger thought the will to power and the eternal recurrence of the same together, I found this a fully persuasive interpretation" (LD 94).

4. For a detailed attempt to show that this is the case, see my essay, "Beyond Seriousness and Frivolity: A Gadamerian Response to Derrida" in Madison, *Figures and Themes in the Hermeneutics of Postmodernity* (Bloomington: Indiana University Press, 1988).

5. I should think that this would count as one of the "classical exigencies" which, Derrida says, even an active, deconstructive reading of texts is obliged to respect. See *Gr* 227/158.

6. Allan Megill, *Prophets of Extremity* (Berkeley: University of California Press, 1985), p. 284.

7. Of this particular "apprenticeship" Gadamer writes: "In this period I learned a good deal, and not only about the game of politics. There has always been something like this in the small world of academia, and the rules of the game have been known since Machiavelli and are everywhere the same. . . . When I went to the West two years later, as a professor at Frankfurt, I was more than a little perplexed by the illusions I still found in the academic politics there." Speaking of his failed attempt to convince the communist authorities not to transfer philosophy to the fine arts academy at Leipzig, Gadamer remarks: "This was in my eyes a crushing result of this attempt to reach understanding." The failure on his part to achieve good will understanding was surely underlined for him by his arrest and brief imprisonment: "The story of my four-day incarceration in the Leipzig jail on Bismark Street would make a novel in itself. For someone who had never been in prison and had never been a soldier, it was utterly instructive, serious and comical at the same time" (*PA* 104–120).

8. In this regard see the following remarks directed at Habermas: "Does hermeneutics really take its bearings from a limiting concept of perfect interaction between understood motives and consciously performed action (a concept that is itself, I believe, fictitious)? . . . Take for example the interest in political and economic domination. In the individual life, the same thing applies to unconscious motives, which the psychoanalyst brings to conscious awareness. Who says that these concrete, so-

called real factors are outside the realm of hermeneutics? . . . The principle of
hermeneutics simply means that we should try to understand everything that can
be understood." "On the Scope and Function of Hermeneutical Reflection," in
PH 30–31.

III, 7: All Ears: Derrida's Response to Gadamer

1. *Plato: The Collected Dialogues,* ed. E. Hamilton and H. Cairns (New Jersey:
   Princeton University Press, 1961), p. 521 (passage 275e).
2. Gadamer's original text reads as follows: "Man muss das Wort suchen und kann das
   Wort finden, das den anderen erreicht, man kann sogar die fremde, seine, des
   Anderen Sprache lernen. Man kann in die Sprache der Anderen übergehen, um den
   Anderen zu erreichen. All das vermag Sprache als Sprache."
3. Paul Ricoeur, *De texte à l'action* (Paris: Seuil, 1986), p. 99.
4. See *PA* 69–85, esp. 75: "That I had failed to see any danger in this pale instrument
   [Alfred Rosenberg's *The Myth of the Twentieth Century*] is easy to understand. It
   was a widespread conviction in intellectual circles that Hitler in coming to power
   would deconstruct the nonsense he had used to drum up the movement, and we
   counted the anti-Semitism as part of this nonsense" (p. 75).
5. F. Nietzsche, *Beyond Good and Evil,* trans. W. Kaufmann (New York: Random
   House, 1966), pp. 211–12.

III, 8: Dialogue and *Écriture*

1. Gadamer's discussion of "Verwandlung ins Gebilde," translated as "transformation
   into structure," brings out the difference between "Verwandlung" and "Verän-
   derung," translated as "change." What "changes" remains fundamentally the same.
   What is "transformed" becomes at once and entirely something else, which is its
   true being, in contrast to which what it was was null. See *WM* 105ff., esp. 106/99ff.,
   esp. 100.
2. "History, Theory, and Influence: Yale Critics as Readers of Maurice Blanchot," in
   The Yale Critics, ed. Jonathan Arac et al. (Minneapolis: University of Minnesota
   Press, 1983), pp. 135–155.
3. For Havelock, see *Preface to Plato* (Cambridge, Mass.: Harvard University Press,
   1963), *The Literate Revolution in Greece and Its Cultural Consequences* (Princeton:
   Princeton University Press, 1982), which collects essays published from 1966–
   1980, and *The Muse Learns to Write: Reflections on Orality and Literacy from
   Antiquity to the Present* (New Haven and London: Yale University Press, 1986). For
   Goody and Watt, see Watt, "Introduction," pp. 1–26, and Goody and Watt, "The

Consequences of Literacy," pp. 27–68 in *Literacy in Traditional Societies,* ed. Jack Goody (Cambridge: Cambridge University Press, 1968). Walter Ong's most recent survey is *Orality and Literacy: The Technologizing of the Word* (London and New York: Metheun, 1982).

4. Subtitled *Communications and Cultural Transformation in Early-Modern Europe* (2 vols.; Cambridge: Cambridge University Press, 1979).

5. Published in *Tel Quel* in 1968, collected in *D* 69–197/61–171.

6. In *Schrift und Gedächtnis: Beiträge zur Archäologie der literarischen Kommunikation,* ed. Aleida and Jan Assmann and Christof Hardmeier (Munich: Wilhelm Fink, 1983), pp. 10–19.

7. See my "Deconstruction, Sophistic and Hermeneutics: Gadamer, Gorgias, Plato, and Derrida," *Journal of Comparative Literature and Aesthetics,* 9, 1–2 (1986): 83–108.

8. Blanchot, *L'Espace littéraire* (Paris: Gallimard, 1955). Bakhtin, *The Dialogic Imagination,* ed. Michael Holquist, trans. Caryl Emerson and Michael Holquist (Austin: University of Texas Press, 1981).

9. See *The Legitimacy of the Modern Age,* trans. Robert M. Wallace (Cambridge, Mass.: MIT Press, 1983), pp. 463–66 and passim.

10. See Derrida, "Pas I," *Gramma,* nos. 3–4 (1976), 111–215.

11. See particularly the analysis of Gorgias by Mario Untersteiner, *The Sophists,* trans. Kathleen Freeman (New York: Philosophical Library, 1954), especially pp. 108–114. I have tried to follow out some of the issues in "Deconstruction, Sophistic, and Hermeneutic: Gadamer, Gorgias, Plato, and Derrida," cited in note 7.

12. See G. Bruns, "The Originality of Texts in a Manuscript Culture," in *Inventions: Writing, Textuality and Understanding in Literary History* (New Haven and London: Yale University Press, 1982), pp. 44–59.

13. Buber's "Dialogue" is in *BMM* 1–39. Levinas' essay is in *Esistenza-Mito-Ermeneutica: Scritti per Enrico Castelli,* ed. Marco M. Olivetti (*Archivio di filosofia*; 2 vols. Padua: CEDAM-Casa Editrice Dott. Antonio Milani, 1980), II, 345–57.

III, 9: The Gadamer-Derrida Encounter: A Pragmatist Perspective

1. See W. V. Quine, *From a Logical Point of View* (New York: Harper and Row, 1961), 46; *The Web of Belief,* with J. S. Ullian (New York: Random House, 1970), 43–44; *Ontological Relativity and Other Essays* (New York: Columbia University Press, 1969), 25–68; Nelson Goodman, *Ways of Worldmaking* (Indianapolis: Hackett, 1978), 97, 128, 138; and D. Davidson, *Inquiries into Truth and Interpretation* (Oxford: Clarendon, 1984). These and other affinities between such pragmatist thinkers and Gadamer and Derrida are discussed in more detail in chapters 7 and 8 of my *T. S. Eliot and the Philosophy of Criticism* (New York: Columbia University Press,

1988); and in S. Wheeler, "The Extension of Deconstruction," *Monist* 69 (1986), 1–21; and "Indeterminacy of French Interpretation: Derrida and Davidson," in E. LePore (ed.), *Truth and Interpretation* (Oxford: Blackwell, 1985), 477–94.

2. I refer, of course, to Rorty's *Philosophy and the Mirror of Nature* (Princeton: Princeton University Press, 1979); *Consequences of Pragmatism* (Minneapolis: University of Minnesota Press, 1982); and J. Margolis, *Pragmatism without Foundations* (Oxford: Blackwell, 1985).

3. A. MacIntyre makes this clear in *After Virtue* (London: Duckworth, 1981), 206–209.

4. See especially *Philosophical Investigations* (Oxford: Blackwell, 1953), para. 198–242.

5. For more on the idea of different interpretive games and their different logics and aims, see R. Shusterman, "The Logic of Interpretation," *Philosophical Quarterly*, 28 (1978), 310–324. For an illustration of how the twofold criterion of comprehensiveness and coherence motivates very different interpretive logics and practices, see chapter five of my *T. S. Eliot and the Philosophy of Criticism*.

6. See *The Collected Papers of Charles Sanders Peirce* (Cambridge, Mass.: Harvard University Press, 1931–35), 5.394–443.

7. R. Rorty, "Objectivity or Solidarity," in J. Rajchman and Cornell West (eds.), *Post-Analytic Philosophy* (New York: Columbia University Press, 1985), 5.

8. See W. James, *Pragmatism and Other Essays* (New York: Simon and Schuster, 1963), 71–72.

9. *Philosophical Investigations,* para. 88.

III, 10: "Ashes, ashes, we all fall. . ."

1. See *RP* 15 (1985): 1–27.

2. Is the Heidegger-Nietzsche encounter only a brief one, or does it begin in the early 1900s and end only in 1976? See Krell, *Intimations of Mortality: Time, Truth, and Finitude in Heidegger's Thinking of Being* (University Park, PA: The Pennsylvania State University Press, 1986), chaps. 6 and 8.

3. James Joyce, *Ulysses,* ed. Hans Walter Gabler et al. (New York: Random House, 1986), p. 577, 11. 1182–84.

4. See Martin Heidegger, *Sein und Zeit,* 12th ed. (Tübingen: M. Neimeyer, 1972), sections 64 and 72; on *Zerstreuung,* see esp. pp. 56, 129, 172, 310, 323, 347, 371, and 389–90. See also Jacques Derrida, "Geschlecht: Différence ontologique, différence sexuelle," in Michel Haar, ed., *Martin Heidegger* (Paris: Cahiers de l'Herne, 1983), pp. 419–30; also available in *Livre de poche,* pp. 571–95, and *Psyché* 395–414. English trans. in *RP* XIII (1983): 65–83.

5. For sections cited here see *N 1* 9–10/l:xv–xvi; *N 1* 255–59/2:5–8; *N 1* 339–56/2:82–

97; *N 1* 473–81/3:3–9; and *N 1* 517–27/3:39–47. Ed. note: For titles of the four volumes see list of abbreviations.

6. See the references in *Intimations,* p. 190n. 16, but add to them: *Hk,* 234/146.

7. Notice that Gadamer's reference (105) to the motto chosen for "The Will to Power as Art" (*N 2* 11/1:1), "Well-nigh two thousand years and not a single new god!" is *not* the motto for Heidegger's *Nietzsche-Rezeption* as a whole. As for "*Das Leben. . .*": I confess that I did not check this opening epigraph from *In media vita* when I translated *N 1* twelve years ago, nor in the intervening years, so that Heidegger's excisions caught me by surprise. I did manage to indicate a far more serious case, involving *WP* 617; see *N 1* 27/1:19 and *N 1* 466/2:201–2. Yet, I would resist Derrida's suggestion—as I resisted Lacoue-Labarthe's in "A Hermeneutics of Discretion" that Heidegger generally neglects or even "effaces" the more subtle aspects of a text, such as its punctuation (see IS 66). Quite often in *Nietzsche* Heidegger insists that we read every mark of punctuation, every piece of italic, and so on. As usual, with Heidegger the matter is complicated. On the complex question of Heidegger and the philosophy of life, see the papers and discussions by Jacques Derrida and myself in "Reading Heidegger," *RP,* 17, (1987).

8. *FLC* 51–53: "—Encore faut-il savoir brûler. Il faut s'y entendre. Il y a aussi ce 'paradoxe' de Nietzsche . . . etc." Note that the text of *GOA,* XII, no. 112 (= *CMN,* M III 1 [84] 1881), cited by both Heidegger and Derrida, has not been translated well in my translation of *Nietzsche* (*N 1* 342/2:84). ". . .that *everything* has already been transposed into life and so departs from it." The German text reads: ". . .*so ist alles schon einmal in Leben umgesetzt gewesen, und so geht es fort*" (Studienausgabe, *9,* 473, ll. 1–2). *Fortgehen* can of course mean departure; but the *so* suggests that the sense here is one of *continuance, Fortsetzen.* The French edition has ". . .et continuera de l'être ainsi." The translation now proposed tries at least to preserve the ambiguity: ". . .that *everything* has already been transposed into life—and so it goes." Finally, the passage ends with a sentence-fragment that all concerned have heretofore omitted: "If we assume an eternal duration, and consequently an eternal mutation of matter—"[.] If we do so assume, would the whole of being be eternal the return *of the same*? Let us not forget that [*CMN*] M III 1, contains Nietzsche's most vigorous critique of the presupposition he regards as eminently metaphysical, that of *des Gleichen.* For Nietzsche it remains a matter of ashes. (See pp. 260–62 of my "Analysis" at the end of vol. 2 of the English edition of *N.*)

III, 11: Seeing Double: *Destruktion* and Deconstruction

1. *Le Robert* agrees with *Littré* that *se déconstruire* has a nineteenth century usage. But it does not cite the quotation from the Preface to Villemain's *Dictionnaire de l'Académie* (1835) that Derrida himself found in *Littré.* Instead, *Le Robert* quotes Darmesteter's observation that although Villemain may have used the form *se*

déconstruire in the Preface to his dictionary, Villemain still did not see fit to legitimate his own usage of it by including it as an entry in the dictionary itself. So even where there are authorities to decide such things, it is obviously no simple matter what is and what is not "good French."

2. J. Derrida, "The Time of a Thesis: Punctuations" in *Philosophy in France Today*, ed. Alan Montefiore (Cambridge: Cambridge University Press, 1982), p. 44.

3. J. Derrida, "De la grammatologie (II)" *Critique* 22, Jan. 1966, p. 36. Cf. *Gr* 99/68.

4. The reference to *Abbau* is slightly puzzling as it does not appear at all in *Sein und Zeit*. The word is prominent in *Basic Problems of Phenomenology* but that text had not appeared at the time of *Of Grammatology* (1967). Derrida would, of course, have known Husserl's use of the word, but this is not under discussion at the present place.

5. "Davoser Disputation zwischen Ernst Cassirer und Martin Heidegger," *KPM* 267.

6. See also Gadamer's "Letter to Dallmayr" where he spells out the difference between the two words. It is as if Derrida is accused of not being aware of this as the sense of Heidegger's *Destruktion*. According to Gadamer, Nietzsche was engaged in a self-destruction (*Selbstzerstörung*) of metaphysics (DD 364; 00) and so on this matter again Gadamer finds Derrida closer to Nietzsche than Heidegger. It should also be noted that there is at least one exception to Gadamer's account insofar as Heidegger does use the word *Zerstörung* for his relationship to western metaphysics in his notes for the Davos lecture (*KPM* 245).

7. The phrase is Searle's from "Reiterating the Differences: A Reply to Derrida" *Glyph 1* (Baltimore: John Hopkins University Press, 1977), p. 198.

8. In an essay dated 1985 (and thus perhaps written between TI and DD), Gadamer acknowledges learning a great deal from Manfred Frank about "Neostructuralism," i.e., Derrida. "Zwischen Phänomenologie und Dialektik: Versuch einer Selbstkritik," *GW* 2 15.

9. Letter to John Leavey, 2 January 1981, *Semeia* 23, 1982, p. 61.

10. Cf. "there never has been THE style, THE simulacrum, THE woman" (*Spurs* 139), and "there never was perception" (*VP* 116/103).

III, 13: Gadamer's Closet Essentialism: A Derridean Critique

1. Joseph Margolis, *Pragmatism without Foundations: Reconciling Realism and Relativism* (Oxford: Basil Blackwell, 1986), p. 76.

2. Margolis, pp. xviii.

3. It is no accident that in both "Text and Interpretation" and "*Destruktion* and Deconstruction" Gadamer situates deconstruction in the context of Nietzsche. It is part of our thesis that this is a cover, and that he does not concede the extent to which its true context is Heidegger's critique of metaphysics, which would include philosophi-

cal hermeneutics itself within its sweep, even as it undoes Heidegger's own reading of Nietzsche.

4. See, for example, David Tracy's *The Analogical Imagination* (New York: Crossroads, 1981) and his more recent attempt to make use of deconstruction within a fundamentally hermeneutical standpoint, *Plurality and Ambiguity: Hermeneutics, Religion and Hope* (New York: Harper & Row, 1987).

5. I develop the opposition between left wing and right wing Heideggerianism in my *Radical Hermeneutics: Repetition, Deconstruction and the Hermeneutic Project* (Bloomington: Indiana University Press, 1987). See also Thomas Sheehan, "Derrida and Heidegger," in *HD* 201–18.

6. See, for example, Derrida's critique of Richard's *L'univers imaginaire de Mallarmé*, a hermeneutic reading of Mallarmé, in "The Double Session" in *D* 277ff./246ff., and his critique of the conservative side—the "onto-hermeneutical" side—of Heidegger in *Spurs*.

7. See Rodolphe Gasché's masterful exposition of Derrida's "quasi-transcendentals" in *The Tain of the Mirror: Deconstruction and the Philosophy of Reflection* (Cambridge: Harvard University Press, 1986).

8. I take this expression from the political theologian Johann Baptist Metz, *Faith in History and Society,* trans. David Smith (New York: Seabury, 1980).

9. For an instructive illustration of the difference between Gadamer and Derrida, compare Gadamer's remarks on educators in *WM* 264–65/249 with Derrida's "The Principle of Reason: The University in the Eyes of Its Pupils," *Diacritics*, 13 (1983), 3–20.

III, 15: The Privilege of Sharing

1. Jean-François Lyotard, *Just Gaming,* trans. Wlad Godzich (Minneapolis: University of Minnesota Press, 1979), p. 40.

2. Ludwig Wittgenstein, *Philosophical Investigations* (Oxford: Basil Blackwell, 1953), §18.

3. Cf. "Der Weg in die Kehre," which includes a discussion of the line "Nur was aus Welt gering, wird einmal Ding," with attention to rhyme and other poetic elements. The passage concludes, however, "Man kann sich fragen, ob solche Sprachbrechungen und Sprachzeugungen ihr Ziel erreichen, und dies Ziel ist natürlich, sich mitzuteilen, kommunikativ zu sein, im Wort Denken zu versammeln, uns in Wort auf ein gemeinsam Gedachtes zu versammeln" (*HW* 115). The discussion of the material aspects of language in TI 42–51 also reveals the concreteness of Gadamer's notion of dialogue.

4. Then again, it isn't that Gadamer doesn't notice the differences I have in mind, but that he hierarchizes the different aspects for purposes of the kind of intellectual discipline in which he chooses to work.

5. This phrase is the title of an important chapter of Paul Ricoeur's *Time and Narrative,* vol. 2, translated by Kathleen McLaughlin and David Pellauer (Chicago: University of Chicago Press, 1984).

6. Gadamer certainly realizes this—see the discussion below of Heidegger's abandonment of the scientific role. Nevertheless, it should be mentioned that the model I am proposing allows for the role of ontologist or language analyst to help constitute the text *as well,* and I think this role is occasionally present even in late Heidegger.

7. On the distribution of force amongst the narrative poles of the teller of, listener to (or "narratee"), and character in a narrative discourse, see "The Three Pragmatic Positions" in *Just Gaming* (op. cit.). Lyotard's negative references to "autonomy" would not conflict with my use of the term here; indeed the point I am trying to make about the involution of the closure in which the effect of autonomy is produced would be concretely illustrated by his hermeneutical maxim quoted above.

8. Derrida himself characterizes the apocalyptic voice as a narrative voice, which he wants to distinguish, following Blanchot, from the voice of an identifiable narrator (ATRAP 25). He also speaks of a "narrative sending" [*"envoi"*] that involves an "interlacing of voices and sendings in the dictated or addressed writing," and of a differential reduction or gearing down of voices and tones that perhaps divides them beyond a distinct or calculable plurality" (87).

9. Ricoeur, op. cit., on "concordant dissonance" in Part I, section 1.

10. Cf. Umberto Eco, *The Role of the Reader* (Bloomington: Indiana University Press, 1979). On the manifold means of fictional narrative for specifying and/or creating an ideal reader, cf. Ross Chambers, *Story and Situation: Narrative Seduction and the Power of Fiction* (Minneapolis: University of Minnesota Press, 1985). Derrida gives his own version of textual openness in *A* 29: "Aucun texte n'a la solidité la cohérance, l'assurance, la systematicité requise si la réponse de l'autre ne vient l'interrompre, et l'interrompant, le faire résonner."

11. Now of course *Being and Time* is quite insistent that the being-towards-death which is made manifest through the key mood of *Angst* is "non-relational," contrary to what I am suggesting. I see the "unsurpassable" [*unüberholbar*] autonomy of the death relation as pertaining to a variety of possible narrative structures; and just as *Angst* can be seen as a negative modification of the fundamental boredom which reveals "what-is-in-totality" (*cf. WIM* 334), so I see a corresponding modification of the joy in the presence of a beloved which is said to accomplish the *same* revelation of totality (ibid.), as well as still other analogous possibilities.

12. As in all cases of privileged meaning (e.g. the literal understanding of apocalypse), there is the opportunity here for a one-sidedness in which the narrative embedding of meaning is ignored. Schelling, who lost his wife at the age of 34 and went through a period of metaphysical "research" into the "spiritual world," provides us with a fascinating if enigmatic example of such onesidedness. See the discussion in Karl Jaspers' *Schelling: Grösse und Verhängnis* (Munich: R. Piper, 1955).

13. Again, I refer to Ross Chambers' studies (cf. footnote 10 above), which show how much more subtle these strategies may be than to simply give the favored interpretation (which of course would be far less effective than getting the reader to come up with it on his or her own).

Index of Names*

Adorno, Theodor W., 220
Alcibiades, 255
Anaximander, 105, 110
Arendt, Hannah, 300
Aristotle, 99, 100–101, 103, 114, 122, 234, 272, 274, 275
Arnauld, Antoine, 307
Assmann, Jan and Aleida, 311
Austin, J. L., 308

Bakhtin, Mikhail, 209–11, 311
Barth, Karl, 119
Barthes, Roland, 305
Beaufret, Jean, 115
Beckett, Samuel, 17
Behler, Ernst, 297, 302
Benn, Gottfried, 95, 143
Bernasconi, Robert, 15, 233–50, 313–14, 292
Bernstein, Richard J., 301
Blanchot, Maurice, 210–11, 311, 316
Blumenberg, Hans, 211, 214, 311
Boehme, Jacob, 108
Bormann, Alexander von, 122, 302
Boschenstein, Bernhard, 305
Bruns, Gerald, 212, 311
Buber, Martin, 13, 119, 212–13, 311
Bubner, Rudiger, 119, 302
Büchner, Georg, 147
Bultmann, Rudolf, 119
Busche, Hubertus, 297

Cairns, Dorian, 301

Caputo, John D., 16, 258–64, 292, 314–15
Cassirer, Ernst, 28, 98
Celan, Paul, 45, 144–48, 305–306
Chambers, Ross, 316
Cheatham, Robert, 296
Cohen, Hermann, 98
Culler, Jonathan, 308
Cumming, Robert D., 300
Cusanus, Nicolaus, 108

Dallmayr, Fred, 5–6, 75–92, 215, 244, 292, 299–301
Davidson, Donald, 14, 215, 220, 311
deMan, Paul, 114
Descartes, René, 234
Dilthey, Wilhelm, 22, 23, 25–26, 49, 122, 189, 236
Dreyfus, Hubert, 301

Ebner, Ferdinand, 119
Eckart, Meister, 108
Eco, Umberto, 316
Eisenstein, Elizabeth, 208
Eisenstein, Gabe, 17, 269–83, 315
Euthyphro, 254

Fichte, Johann Gottlieb, 108, 120
Finas, Lucette, 148, 306
Forget, Philippe, 2, 4, 10, 111, 129–49, 292, 295, 303–306
Foucault, Michel, 11, 152, 307

*Gadamer, Derrida, and names in the List of Abbreviations are not included here.

Frank, Manfred, 11, 111, 120, 130,
    150–61, 292–93, 295–96, 304, 306–
    307
Freud, Sigmund, 304

Gasché, Rudolphe, 315
Goethe, Johann Wolfgang, 298
Goodman, Nelson, 215, 311
Goody, Jack, 207, 311
Greisch, Jean, 295
Guibal, Francis, 270

Habermas, Jürgen, 12, 97, 136, 170,
    305, 308
Haecker, Theodor, 119
Handelman, Susan, 296
Hardmeier, Christof, 311
Hartmann, Nicholai, 98
Havelock, Eric, 208
Hegel, Georg Wilhelm Friedrich, 7, 16,
    24, 27, 97–98, 103–4, 108, 110, 119,
    125, 139, 151, 157, 169, 184, 194,
    208–10, 228–30, 234, 238, 245–46,
    259–60, 264, 300, 303
Heidegger, Martin, 1, 3, 7, 9, 15–16,
    24, 27–28, 50, 52, 58–71, 92–94, 98,
    100, 115–17, 120, 145, 151, 189,
    223–24, 234, 252, 256, 261, 271–72,
    273–74, 276–77, 279, 298, 301
Held, David, 299
Henrich, Dieter, 119
Heraclitus, 105, 123
Herder, Johann Gottfried von, 102
Hermes, 254
Hippothales, 254
Hölderlin, Friedrich, 100–101, 302
Humboldt, Alexander von, 151
Husserl, Edmund, 8, 11, 16, 94–95,
    102, 110, 112, 115, 120, 122, 124,
    189–90

Jaeger, Werner, 100
James, William, 221, 312
Jaspers, Karl, 316
Jauss, Hans Robert, 123, 303

Kant, Emmanuel, 52, 168–169, 172–73,
    234, 308
Kaufmann, Walter, 300
Kierkegaard, Søren, 90, 97, 104, 110,
    117, 119–20, 122, 214, 260, 276
Krell, David Farrell, 15, 222–31, 293,
    312

Lacan, Jacques, 106, 130–31, 134, 151,
    156, 159, 305
Lancelot, Claude, 307
Laruelle, Francois, 295
Lawrence, Frederick, 308
Leibniz, Gottfried Wilhelm, 234
Lessing, Gotthold E., 142, 303, 305
Levinas, Emmanuel, 13, 97, 119, 171,
    212–13, 308, 311
Lévi-Strauss, Claude, 208
Lipps, Hans, 28
Lord, Albert, 207
Lyotard, Jean-Francois, 271, 315, 316
Lysis, 254

MacIntyre, Alisdair, 259, 312
Madison, G. B., 13, 192–98, 293, 309–
    10
Mallarmé, Stephane, 17, 45, 145, 148,
    151
Mann, Thomas, 105
Margolis, Joseph, 14, 216, 258–60, 314
Marshall, Donald G., 206–14, 293, 297,
    310
Megill, Allan, 309
Mendelssohn, Moses, 305
Meno, 255
Metz, Johann Baptist, 315
Misgeld, Dieter, 299
Montefiore, Alan, 314
Morris, Charles, 124
Mörike, Eduard, 49, 298
Murko, Mathias, 207

Natorp, Paul Gerhard, 98
Nietzsche, Friedrich, 3–5, 11–12, 15,
    24–25, 27, 53, 56–71, 81–82, 87–89,

93, 96–97, 105, 109–10, 115, 135,
151, 162–66, 168, 171, 184, 194, 201,
203–5, 213–14, 224–25, 227–30, 237,
241, 249, 259, 296, 300, 304, 307–8,
310

O'Neill, John, 299
Ong, Walter, 208, 311
Overbeck, Franz, 100
Oxenhandler, Neal, 17, 265–68, 293

Paris, Matthew, 203
Parmenides, 101, 105
Parry, Milman, 207
Paul, 116
Peirce, Charles Sanders, 124; on consensus of belief, 220
Plato, 24, 55–56, 98–99, 101, 116, 202–3, 209, 241, 264, 266, 281, 307–308, 310
Pressler, Charles A., 300
Proust, Marcel, 17

Quine, W. V. O., 215, 311

Rapaport, Herman, 13, 199–205, 293, 310
Richard, Jean-Pierre, 314
Ricoeur, Paul, 56, 204, 213, 310, 316
Rimbaud, Arthur, 17; and man with shoes of wind, 268
Risser, James, 12, 176–85, 293, 308
Rorty, Richard, 14, 220, 216, 312
Rosenberg, Alfred, 310
Rosenszweig, Franz, 119
Rothacker, Erich, 298
Russell, Bertrand, 28

Sallis, John, 16, 222, 251–57, 293–94
Sartre, Jean-Paul, 110–206, 302
Saussure, Ferdinand de, 11, 124, 151, 154, 158–159, 161, 178, 307
Scheler, Max, 102
Schelling, Friedrich Wilhelm Joseph, 25, 316

Schlegel, Friedrich, 118–19, 122–23
Schleiermacher, Friedrich, 11, 22, 26, 53, 122, 137–38, 151, 307
Schlick, Moritz, 297
Schmidt, Dennis J., 21
Searle, John, 155, 307, 314
Seebohm, Thomas M., 297
Shapiro, Gary, 298
Shepherdson, Charles, 12, 186–91, 294
Shusterman, Richard, 14, 215–21, 294, 311–12
Sica, Alan, 298
Simon, Josef, 11, 162–75, 294, 307–308
Socrates, 16, 119, 164, 176–85, 202, 207, 253–55, 263
St. John, 281
Staiger, Emil, 50, 144–45, 298
Stambaugh, Joan, 301
Steinthal, Hermann, 151
Strauss, Leo, 252
Sullivan, Robert R., 296

Thompson, John B., 299
Tracy, David, 314
Trakl, Georg, 134
Trendelenburg, Friedrich, 98

Ullian, Joseph Silbert, 311
Untersteiner, Mario, 311

Valéry, Paul, 247
Vico, Giambatista, 76, 298
Virgil, 103, 302

Warburg, Max, 298
Warning, Rainer, 305
Watt, Ian, 207, 311
Weber, Max, 99
Weinsheimer, Joel, 213
Wheeler, Stephen, 312
Wittgenstein, Ludwig, 28, 221, 308, 315

Zehm, Günter, 295

Index of Works

A, 17, 270, 283, 296, 316
Aeneid, Virgil, 302
Aesthetic Experience and Literary Hermeneutics, H. R. Jauss, 303
AF, 302
After Virtue, A. MacIntyre, 312
"All Ears: Derrida's Response to Gadamer," H. Rapaport, 13, 199–205, 310
Analogical Imagination, The, David Tracy, 314
"Analysis" [of *N*], D. F. Krell, 313
Apology, Plato, 207, 255
"Argument(s)," P. Forget: Notes, 10, 129–49, 303–6
"Ashes, ashes, we all fall . . . ': Encountering Nietzsche," D. F. Krell, 15, 222–32, 312–13
ATRAP, 17, 246, 269, 275–76
"Auf eine Lampe," E. Mörike, 49, 51, 144, 298
"Avant-propos" (to the encounter as published in *RIP*), M. Frank, 295
AWP, 234, 240, 241

Begmerkungen über die Grundlagen der Mathematik, L. Wittgenstein, 308
"Beyond Hermeneutics," H. Dreyfus, 301
"Beyond Seriousness and Frivolity," G. B. Madison, 309
Beyond Good and Evil, F. Nietzsche, 205, 231, 296, 310
Beyond Objectivism and Relativism, R. J. Bernstein, 301
BMM, 213, 214, 311

"Buch der Natur," Das, E. Rothacker, 298
BW, 299, 302

CFS, 159
"Clues to an Improbable Encounter," P. Forget, 130
CMN, 313
Collected Papers of Charles Sanders Peirce, 312
Consequences of Pragmatism, R. Rorty, 312
"Correspondence Concerning *WM*: Leo Strauss and Hans-Georg Gadamer," 297
Cours, 307
CP, 203
"Critical Theory and Hermeneutics," D. Misgeld, 299
Critical Theory, On, J. O'Neill, 299
Critique et vérité, R. Barthes, 305

D. 247, 266–67; "Plato's Pharmacy" in, 295
"Davoser Disputation," H, 314
DD, 5, 6, 7, 11, 15, 102, 130, 144, 179–80, 199, 204, 207, 223, 225–27, 229, 233, 245, 260, 270–72, 275, 296, 300, 314; conversation that seeks its partner everywhere, 248; conversation that builds up a common language, 270; G demands at the conclusion the One behind the Many, 229; G tries to separate H and D, 237; G: "There is

no language of metaphysics," 240; G: "What does N's ungraspable multiplicity and play all mean?" 226;

DD, 300

"Deconstruction in the Framework of Traditional Methodical Hermeneutics," T. M. Seebohm, 297

DE, 296, 298

Deconstruction, On, J. Culler, 308

"Deconstruction, Sophistic and Hermeneutics," D. G. Marshall, 297, 311

"Deconstruction versus Hermeneutics," E. Behler, 297

"Défi hérmeneutique, Le," H.-G. Gadamer, 295

"Derrida and Heidegger," T. Sheehan, 314

Derr, 296

"Derrida, Jacques (Interview)," R. Cheatham, 296

DI, 210

"Dialectic and Sophism in Plato's *Seventh Letter*," H.-G. Gadamer, 209

Dialogic Imagination, The, M. Bakhtin, 311

"Dialogue and *Écriture*." D. G. Marshall, 13, 206–14, 310–11

"Dialogue: Conscience de Soi et Proximité du Prochain, Le" E. Levinas, 212

"Double Session, The," J. Derrida, 315

E ("Sending"), 240–43, 246; D asks if there is a French philosophical language, 239–40; D attempts "to outline another relation to H", 242; D's question to H is focussed on the unity of metaphysics, 240; in E and IS, D helps us to recognize how H can be read so that disseminating discourse doubles with unifying discourse of presence, 242

E. 131, 134, 159

Early Gadamer, The, R. R. Sullivan, 296

EC, 159–60

ED, 8, 9, 235, 296

EGT, 302

Either/Or, S. Kierkegaard, 90,

Elements of a Unified Doctrine of Knowledge, J. G. Fichte, 120

Eliot and the Philosophy of Criticism, T. S., R. Shusterman, 311–12

Encyclopedia of the Philosophic Sciences, by F. Hegel, 103, 108

"Ends of Man, The," J. Derrida, 295

EO, 200, 203, 205, 296, 298

EP, 234

L'Espace littéraire, M. Blanchot, 311

"Eternal Recurrence of the Same, The," F. Nietzsche, 227

"Ethics of the Ear, The" D. P. Michelfelder, 297

Euthyphro, Plato, 254

"Existentialism is a Humanism," J.-P. Sartre, 110, 302

"Extension of Deconstruction, The" S. Wheeler, 312

Faith in History and Society, J. B. Metz, 315

Figures and Themes in the Hermeneutics of Postmodernity, G. B. Madison, 309

FLC, 313, 231

From a Logical Point of View, W. V. Quine, 311

"Fundament der Erkenntnis, Über das," M. Schlick, 297

"Gadamer's Closet Essentialism: A Derridean Critique," J. D. Caputo, 16, 258–64, 314–15

"Gadamer-Derrida Encounter: A Pragmatist Perspective, The," R. Shusterman, 14, 215–21, 311–12

"Gadamer/Derrida: The Hermeneutics of Irony and Power," G. B. Madison, 13, 192–98, 309–10

"Gadamer's Closet Essentialism: A Derridean Critique," J. D. Caputo, 16–17, 258–64, 314–15

Genealogy of Morals, F. Nietzsche, 306
"Geschlecht: Différence ontologique, différence sexuelle," D, 312
GH, 266, 297
GI, 281, 303
GOA, 12, 313
"Good Will to Understand and the Will to Power: Remarks on an 'Improbable Encounter,' " J. Simon, 11–12, 162–75, 307–8
GP, 234, 272, 314
Gr, 190, 229, 235, 245, 266–67, 309, 314
"Grammatologie (II), De la," in *D,* 314
GS, 66, 71, 231, 265; living creature a kind of dead creature, 69
Guide for Translating Husserl, D. Cairns, 301
GW 2: 297–98, 314; 3:297; 8:298

H, 104, 299, 302. *See also* "The Privilege of Sharing: Dead Ends and the Life of Language." ("Dead Ends" is a translation of the term *Holzwege.*)
Habermas: Critical Debates, ed. J. B. Thompson and D. Held, 299
HB, 302
HD, 5, 75–92, 215
HDial, 300
"Heidegger and the History of Philosophy" in HW, 274
"Heidegger et la Politique," symposium with G and D, 296
"Hermeneutics and Deconstruction: Gadamer and Derrida in Dialogue," F. Dallmayr, 5, 75–92, 299–301
"Hermeneutics of Discretion, A," D. F. Krell, 313
"Hermeneutics of Suspicion, The," H.-G. Gadamer, 298
Hermeneutics: Questions and Prospects, by G. Shapiro and A. Sica, 298
"Hermeneutics of Suspicion, The," H.-G. Gadamer, 298
"Hermeneutic Task from Schleiermacher to Dilthey, The," P. Ricoeur, 204

Hermeneutik und Ideologiekritik by K.-O. Apel, C. v. Bormann, et al., 299
"History, Theory and Influence," D. G. Marshall, 310
HL, 5, 7–9, 11, 114–25, 296, 302–3
How to Do Things with Words, J. B. L. Austin, 308
HuK, 307
HW, 274, 297, 315

ID, 275, 301
"Igitur," S. Mallarmé, 45
"Imagine Understanding . . . ," Charles Shepherdson, 12–13, 186–91
"Improbable Encounter," R. E. Palmer, 297
Individuelle Allgemeine, Das, M. Frank, 296, 306
Inquiries into Truth and Interpretation, D. Davidson, 311
"Intellektuelle Anschauung: Kant, Fichte, Hölderlin/Novalis," M. Frank, 302
"Interruptions," by John Sallis, 16
Intimations of Mortality, D. F. Krell, 312–13
Introduction to Aristotle, by M. Heidegger, 117
Introduction to Literacy in Traditional Societies, I. Watt, 311
Inventions, G. Bruns, 311
IS, 4, 58–74, 87, 221, 231, 238, 239, 244, 246, 270, 299; a different starting point from that of *Spurs,* 227; by focussing on N in IS, D led G away from his initial focus on D's truth-claims to consider not just D's approach but his own, 250; does address G because it focusses on that which stands in the way of a dialogue between them, the identification of a thinker with a single thought, 239; does address G and suggests "a quite different way of thinking about texts," 237; does not present an alternative theory but probes the domination of hermeneutics, 184

Just Gaming, J.-F. Lyotard, 315–316

KPM, 245, 314
Kunst der Interpretation, Die, E. Staiger, 298

LAJ, 228, 233, 235
LD, 4, 5, 7, 93–101, 184, 190, 195, 211–12, 216, 244, 301–2; G a willing victim of H's N-interp, 225, 243; G does not take N seriously enough, 225; G here in the position of Socrates in the "Apology," 207; G incorrectly asserts that D rejects H's N-interpretation "from the ground up," 238
"Leading Threads of an Improbable Debate," P. Forget, 295, 303
Legitimacy of the Modern Age, The, H. Blumenberg, 311
"Leitfäden einer unwahrscheinlichen Debatte," P. Forget, 130, 295, 303
"Lenz," by G. Büchner, 147
"Letter to John Leavy," J. Derrida, 314
Letter to the Thessalonians, 116
Life of Friedrich Nietzsche, The, E. Förster-Nietzsche, 63
Life of the Mind, The, H. Arendt, 300
"Limited, Inc. abc. . . ," J. Derrida, 296
"Limits of the Human Control of Language," M. Frank, 11, 150–61, 306–7
Literature Revolution in Greece, The, E. Havelock, 310
LO, 217
Logical Investigations, E. Husserl, 95, 115
"Logic of Interpretation, The," R. Shusterman, 312
"Logozentrismus und Différance," H. Busche, 297
Lysis, by Plato, 254

M, 9, 296, 305
Magic Mountain, The, T. Mann, 105

"Man with Shoes of Wind: The Derrida-Gadamer Encounter, The," N. Oxenhandler, 17, 265–68
Meditations, René Descarte, 234
Meno, Plato, 255
"Meridien," P. Celan, 147
Metaphysics, Aristotle, 99, 275
"Mit erdwärts gesungenen Masten," P. Celan, 45–46, 146, 306
Muse Learns to Write, The, E. Havelock, 310
"Mysterious Boat, The," F. Nietzsche, 306
Myth of the Twentieth Century, The, A. Rosenberg, 310

N, 15, 58, 63, 69–70; N, 228, 230–31, 234, 238, 298, 312–13; French preface, 60–61; preface, 59; H's path of thought over seventeen years, 228; H's quest for the essence loses the particularity of the individual, 228
Nachlaß, F. Nietzsche, 307
Nathan the Wise, G. Lessing, 305
Neostructuralism?, What is, M. Frank, 296, 306–7
New Science, The, G. Vico, 76, 298
New Testament, 116
Nietzsche, The Portable, W. Kaufmann, 300
"Nietzsche's Alleged Biologism" in *N*: H ambivalent about, 227
Nichomachaen Ethics, Aristotle, 273–274
"Notwendige Unauflöslichkeit, Die," B. Boschenstein, 305

O, 296, 303; dismemberment or unity?, 228
"Objectivity or Solidarity," R. Rorty, 312
"Odd Couple: Heidegger and Derrida, The," R. D. Cumming, 300
Ontological Relativity and Other Essays, W. V. Quine, 311
"Onto-theo-logical Constitution of Me-

taphysics, The," M. Heidegger, 235, 301

Orality and Literacy, W. Ong, 311

Order of Words, The, M. Foucault, 152, 307

"*Ousia* and *Grammè*," 114

P, 158, 217

PA, 13, 205, 309-10

"Pas I," J. Derrida, 311

PDM, 170, 171, 173

PH, 218, 267, 309-10

Phaedo, Plato, 253

Phaedrus, Plato, 209, 308; discourse written in the soul of the hearer, 209; emphasis on voice insures that all hear with the same ears, 202

Philosophical Investigations, L, Wittgenstein, 312, 315

"Philosophy and Literature," H.-G. Gadamer, 308

Philosophy and the Mirror of Nature, R. Rorty, 312

Philosophy in France Today, A. Montefiore, 314

Physics, Aristotle, 117

Plato: The Collected Dialogues, ed. E. Hamilton and H. Cairns, 307, 310

Plurality and Ambiguity, David Tracy, 314

Politics, Aristotle, 117

Pragmatism and Other Essays, W. James, 312

Pragmatism Without Foundations, J. Margolis, 258, 312, 314

Preface to Plato, E. Havelock, 310

Préj, 10, 136, 305

Printing Press as an Agent of Change, The, E. Eisenstein, 208

"Privilege of Sharing: Dead Ends and the Life of Language, The," G. Eisenstein, 17-18, 269-83, 315-16

Prophets of Extremity, A. Megill, 309

Psyche, 298, 312

QS, 300

Radical Hermeneutics, J. D. Caputo, 314

"Rationality and Relativism," T. McCarthy, 299

"Reading Heidegger," D. F. Krell, 313

"Redoubled: The Bridging of Derrida and Heidegger," C. A. Pressler, 300

"Reiterating the Differences," J. Searle, 307, 314

Religion innerhalb der Grenzen der bloßen Vernunft, Die, I. Kant, 308

Reply, 2, 55-57, 187, 193, 195, 197, 217-18, 303, 308-9; concentrates on D's third question, 206

Republic, The, Plato, 202-3

Response, 2-4, 13, 199, 219-20, 267, 303, 308; a pragmatist solution to each of the three questions, 216; all three questions hasty, misguided, 206; does enlargement of context involve a continual expansion or a discontinuous restructuring?, 219; "manifest nonsense," a deliberate misunderstanding as a strategy for teaching Gadamer a lesson, 194; the three questions are a whole "web of questions and remarks," 216

Rezeptionsästhetik, ed. R. Warning, 305

Role of the Reader, The, U. Eco, 316

"Roundtable in Autobiography," J. Derrida, 296

RP 15, 222

S, 245, 249

Sagbare und das Unsagbare, Das, M. Frank, 296

"Salut," L. Finas, 306

"Salut," S. Mallarmé, 45, 148

Schelling, K. Jaspers, 316

Schellings Abhandlung über Freiheit, M. Heidegger, 301

Schib, 144; review of by P. Forget, 306

"Schlegels Theorie des Verstehens," E. Behler, 302

Schrift und Gedächtnis, ed. A. and J.
  Assmann and C. Hardmeier, 311
SD, 236, 246, 269, 301
"Seeing Double: Destruktion and Decon-
  struction," R. Bernasconi, 15, 233–50,
  313–14
"Sending." *See* E.
Seventh Letter, Plato, 252
SG, 261
"Shakespeare und kein Ende," J. W.
  Goethe, 298
"Signature Event Context," J. Derrida,
  305
Slayers of Moses, S. Handelman, 296
Sophist, Plato, 256
Sophists, The, M. Untersteiner, 311
Spruch des Anaximander, Der, M.
  Heidegger, 110, 302
Spur des Anderen, Die, E. Lévinas, 308
Spurs, 3, 83, 86–87, 89, 227, 268, 296,
  300, 314, 315; for D, H's N-interp
  encompassed the problem of interpreta-
  tion per se, 222
Story and Situation, R. Chambers, 316
Symposium, Plato, 255
SZ, 94–95, 100, 116, 157, 236, 256,
  257, 302, 312, 316; makes clear H did
  not have in mind presence-metaphysics,
  122; Protestant theology clung to *SZ*'s
  pathos and call for authenticity against
  H's later view, 120

Tain of the Mirror, The, R. Gasché, 315
Texte à l'action, De, P. Ricoeur, 310
Theaetetus, Plato, 254
Theory of Communicative Action, J.
  Habermas, 305
Thrasymachus, Plato: his purpose was to
  arrive at a better understanding of
  statesmanship by lending the ear of
  Socratic philosophy, 203
"Three Pragmatic Positions, The," J.-F.
  Lyotard, 316
Thus Spoke Zarathustra, F. Nietzsche,
  69, 89, 229, 231, 300

TI, 3, 145, 163, 179–83, 189–90, 195,
  199, 202, 217–18, 237–38, 245, 263,
  267, 277, 297–98, 309, 314–15; G
  tries to separate H and D, saying D
  opposed H's N-critique, 237–38; some
  places in TI where N becomes central,
  224–25; summarized by Simon, 163–
  64
TI, 2, 93, 129–30, 145, 163–66, 179–83,
  303, 305, 309
Time and Narrative, P. Ricoeur, 316
"Töne Licht, Der," A. von Bormann,
  302
Tristes Tropiques, C. Lévi-Strauss, 208
Truth and Interpretation, ed. E. LePore,
  312
TT, 296, 314
Twilight of Subjectivity, F. Dallmayr, 301
"Two Faces of Socrates: Gadamer/
  Derrida, The," J. Risser, 12, 176–85,
  308

UK, 299
Ulysses, J. Joyce, 312
"Understanding, On the Circle of," H.-
  G. Gadamer, 297
*Unhintergehbarkeit von Individualität,
  Die,* M. Frank, 296
L'univers imaginaire de Mallarmé, J.-P.
  Richard, 314
US, 96, 209, 301

VEP, 303
VP, 16, 95, 114, 254, 301, 314

"Wanderer and his Shadow, The," F.
  Nietzsche, 308
"Was heißt Aufklärung, Über die Frage,"
  M. Mendelssohn, 305
Ways of Worldmaking, N. Goodman, 311
WBI, 146, 306
Web of Belief, The, W. V. Quine and J. S.
  Ullian, 311

"Weg in die Kehre, Der," H.-G. Gadamer, 269, 280, 315

"Wenn es um Heidegger geht, reicht der Hörsaal nicht aus," G. Zehm, 295

WHD, 108, 245

WIM, 316

Wissenschaftslehren, J. G. Fichte, 120

WM, 1, 5, 6, 10, 77, 79–80, 85–86, 91–92, 111, 118, 130, 136–39, 156–57, 180, 182, 187, 189–90, 200, 207, 213, 216–19, 247, 258, 260, 297–98, 300, 302, 304, 310; not vulnerable to the empty speech critique, 131; tension between investigation and result, 189; the constant ambiguity in, 158

WP, 300, 313; world is the ashes of living creatures, 69

"Dialektischen Bedeutung romantischer Ironie, Zur," R. Bubner, 302

ZW, 115

ZW, 234, 241

Zwei Fragen zum Kratylos, M. Warburg, 298

"Zwischen Phänomenologie und Dialektik," H.-G. Gadamer, 314

Index of Terms and Topics

Note on abbreviations: To conserve space, Gadamer, Derrida, Heidegger, and Nietzsche will be abbreviated G, D, H, and N, and hermeneutic(s) and deconstruction, h. and d. Also, the indexed word when reappearing within the entry will be abbreviated to its first letter.

Abbau (dismantling), 9
Absolutely authoritative voice, 275
Action: Ricoeur on, 204
Aestheticism: D's relation to, 91
Aesthetics: not divorced from ethics, 91
Agreement in judgments: presupposition for a. in understanding, 170–71
Agreement in understanding, 174; did not arise as a problem prior to the Enlightenment, 152; ominous dimensions of, 220; requires prior a. in judgments, 172
Alētheia (truth), 94; not "truth", 261
Alienation: D's "apocalyptic paradigm" and, 271
Alter (alter): translation of, 308; ego and the perspective of in Habermas, 170. *See also* Linguistically generated intersubjectivity
Alterity: established by the authoritative voice, 275; in D, 18; in protreptic discourse, 276; stifled by solidarity, 220. *See also* Otherness; Hermeneutics of deconstruction
Ambiguity: code model sciences cannot handle, 155
Analytic philosophy of language, 154
Anamnesis (recollection): as a presupposi-

tion of dialogue, 110; Socratic dialogue and, 111, 180
Angst (anxiety): non relational or not nonrelational, 316
Answer: all speaking calls for, 131, 156; transforms word into word, 106, 223
Answering: H's peculiar transformation of, 274–75
Anticipation of completion, 135; assumes a potential perfected unity of meaning, 182
Anticipation of meaning: not a matter of subjectivity but tradition, 218
Antitexts, 37–38; G's remarks on a. apply to D, 196
Anwesen (property): H understands *Wesen* as, 110; meaning of, 122
Anwesenheit (presence): not simple, already divided and different, 241
Apocalyptic: dimension in D, 18; discourse, 276; perspective and H's privileging of his own story, 274; speakers and the originless imperative, "Come!" 275; style contains obstacles to consensus and community, 268; autonomy of a. voice, 18, 316
Apocalyptic paradigm: aims at a balance between privilege and accommodation,

282; definition of, 277; risks loss of democratic openness, 282; tendency to dogmatism and death of meaning, 282; D's a. p. shows how philosophical discourse and existential understanding have contributed toward a larger semiotic field, 271; fruitfulness of, 281; applied H, 277; pertains to expressions seeking to retain control over their future interpretation, 281; Plato and St. John as examples of, 281; removal would eliminate authority in language, 281; the sign as a reiteration in an order that gives it authority, 281; and "till death do us part", 280

Archi-writing: inhabits both speech and writing, conversation and reading, 263

Argument for authority: truthful prejudices and, 139. See Prejudices, legitimate

Aristotle: became concrete through H's interpretation, 122; his conversation with H across the millenia, 272; the effect of his practical philosophy on G, 117; the last philosopher with eyes to see, 272; his metaphysics not acceptable to H, 116; noted that *ousia* means farm property, 122; a precondition for dialogue about H, 114; the need to return to but also abjure, 100

Artwork: gives a blow, 212; h. and H's view of the a., 94; self-presentation of, 267; speaks for itself and in itself, 123. *See also* Work

Ashes, 222, 227; as death-in-life, 230; in H's text, 231; in N, 313; H's guiding question leads him to suppress the thought of ashes in N, 230–31; world as ashes of living creatures, 231

Ausdruck (expression) and *Bedeutung* (meaning) in Husserl, 115

Auseinandersetzung (confrontation), 2; and the alterity of the authoritative voice, 276; G and Habermas in, 197

Authorial intention, 202; artwork does not go back to, 123; as criterion of

legitimate interpretations, 247; as deformed and limited by the detachment of the work, 281; G close to Schlegel, 123; neither H nor G seek to understand the author better than he understood himself, 247

Authority: dialogue and openness in speech, 282; of language and the closability of the text, 278; of prejudice and Forget's critique of, 135, 141; of tradition and the authority of educator, 264

Autonomy: of apocalyptic voice, 18; ancient form is grounded in the protreptic force of Greek philosophers, 275; H tried to revive autonomy without transcendental description, 275; modern form bound up with epistemology and transcendental description, 275; of philosophical meaning, 275

Bedeutung (meaning), 115. See *Ausdruck*

Befindlichkeit (condition), 256

Being 25, 94, 104; Aristotle and, 116; arrival of, 212; D and, 263; dissemination and, 241; Greek understanding of, 100, 241; Greek understanding fatefully rejected, 268; H and, 23, 100, 104, 105, 110, 112, 179; history of, 228, 234; Husserl and, 112; language and, 25; metaphysics and, 228; N and, 163, 259; N versus H on, 163; narrative and the history of, 273; temporality of, 100; the truth of, 253; truth as the eventing of, 261; understandability, 163; words of, 246

Being-in-the-world, 253, 256

Being-toward-death: as the metaphysical pair of quidditas and manner of existing, 70; D's effort to escape from, 87, 89; G's critique of H's protreptic conception of, 280

Being-toward-the-text: parallel to Being-toward-death, 25–26

Bible, Lutheran: brought innovations into philosophical language, 121

Bildung (cultivation, education): ethical implications of, 91

Calculative thinking: H's critique of, 116
Celan's poetry: G as interpreter of, 11
Center: writer writes through desire for and ignorance of the, 211
Christianity: H and, 116; self-understanding in, 119
Closure of a corpus: concept of, 53, 276
Code model: in grammar, language game, and structure, 155; Lacan and G reject it as a model for conversation, 156
Coexistence of incommensurables: death and, 281
Collocution, 56
Come!: the fundamental appeal of all apocalyptic speakers, 275
Communicative event, interaction, rationality, situation, understanding: c. e. in relation to texts, 41; c. i. a limited concept, 171; D's writing and c. r., 267; importance of c. s. in judicial h., 35–36; c. s. and use of irony, 12, 37; c. u., 7; will to power as counter-concept to c. u., 165
Concordant dissonance: Ricoeur on, 316
Conflicts in interpretation: Kant on, 172; tradition in, 218
Consciousness: H's critique not a complete breakthrough, 104; reflective c., 260
Consensus: assumption of, 133; demand for, 10, 13; as extremely hypothetical, 151
Context, 202; maximally proper context for interpretation, 219; meaning for D as context-bound, 216
Conversation, 8, 10, 99, 223; clarification of meaning and, 165; code-model not adequate to, 156, 161; as a step back from dialectic, 110, 180, 207; G's view of, 5, 9; between h. and d., 6; as an individual universal, 153; as infinite, 249; as never ending, 95; language as, 106; must leave room for an answer,

154; not defined by intentionality, 118; seeks new partners, new others, 113, 227, 248; potentiality for being other in, 164, 180; prerequisites for, 151; self-understanding developes in c. with tradition, 157; shared understanding and, 270; something comes to language in c. but not the speaker, 122; substance-metaphysics and, 111; we are a, 110, 156; c. with a text contains a performative dimension, 181; D's deboundarized c. with a text, 158; c. with tradition does not entail a collective subject, 130
Conversing with the dead: confers a strange privilege, 273, 280; H and, 271; Socrates' c. across millenia, 272
Critique of ideology, 39–40. *See also* Pretexts

Dasein (being-there, existence): essence of, 110; futurity in, 116
Dead ends (*Holzwege*): H's turn to privileged forms of language, 274; as possible moments for the creative reader, 277; as shell of a living thought-process, 272; as Wittgenstein's image of a city, 272
Death: and the coexistence of incommensurables, 281; D's understanding of, 281; linguistic efforts at denial of, 281; the living marital narrative and, 279–80; protreptic asymmetry of, 280; ultimate deferral, 280
Deconstruction, 1, 2, 7, 8, 114, 228; definitions of d. in Littré and Robert, 313, 314; G's objection to metaphysics of presence parallels that of D, 228. *See also* Deconstruction *and;* Deconstruction *as;* Deconstruction *and Derrida;* Deconstruction *and Gadamer;* Hermeneutics and deconstruction
Deconstruction *and:* D's apocalyptic paradigm of interpretation, 17; the deconstructive reading of h., 191; marginalized figures, forbidden sayings,

suppressed writings, 264; the transcendental naiveté of h. of meaning, 262; d. suspects deep truth of violence and suppression, 263

Deconstruction *as:* a break with foundationalism, 262; a path back from dialectic, 109; a peculiar construction based on a misunderstanding of *Destruktion,* 121; a pitiless critique of essentialism, 264; D's critique of perfect understanding, 221; D's path back from Hegelian dialectic, 207; D's word, 233–35; encouraging disengagement, 92; same as H's *Destruktion* or not, 15; translating *Destruktion* and *Abbau,* 233; a radical disruption of essentialism, 262; going completely beyond Husserl, 120; the true context is H's critique of metaphysics, 314; only N aujourd'hui, 259; a sustained endeavor to avoid falling into "presence-at-hand", 267; containing parallels to Quine and Davidson, 14; denying a deep ontology in the *Muttersprache,* 263; effort to keep the radical side of H going, 261; exploring what the tradition wanted to exclude, 264; taking the step back into that which grants meaning in the tradition, 262; a way of writing from below, 263; "a word I have never liked," 234; wanting to know why everyone feared "heretics," 264; denying the presupposition of unity, 304

Deconstruction *and Derrida:* D adapted the early term *Destruktion* yet his own position is closer to the later H who had deserted the term, 236; D changed *détruire* in an early essay a year later to *déconstruire,* 235; D himself returns the word to H, 235; D intended it to translate *Destruktion* and *Abbau,* 235

Deconstruction *and Gadamer:* G's claim to go beyond, 112; G's interpretation of d., 236, 261; G parallels D in denying metaphysical realm of meanings, 112

Democracy: a dynamic balancing of unequal voices, 282

Derrida: apocalyptic paradigm, 271, 277; fruitfulness of his understanding of death, 281; supreme hermeneutician of the twentieth century, 232; view of language broadens our thinking about factical coexistence, 282; name functions for G in IT solely for the critique of logocentrism, 239; position cannot be argued for, 193; position is really a counterposition, 166, position is shown through irony, 193; D has qualms about G's h. as losing the other, 225, 244; method of reading is double reading (author's intentions and then beyond or outside metaphysics), 245–46; his juxtaposition of readings, 247; the supreme hermeneutician of the twentieth century, 232; as a Romantic crusader trying to open up a kind of intellectual and cultural freedom, 268; said "I have the impression [regarding the encounter] nothing really happened. . . .", 268; spirit is closer to Bakhtin than to Blanchot, 211; view of teaching respects the call of the other, 283; voice in same family as the voices of Mallarmé, Proust, and Beckett, 267; actually wanted to be understood, 57, 166. *See also* Deconstruction; *Destruktion;* Derrida's interpretations (next entry); Gadamer's interpretations; Gadamer-Derrida encounter

Derrida's interpretations: as double reading first of author's intentions and then beyond or outside metaphysics, 245–46; as juxtaposition of readings, 247; the supreme hermeneutician of the twentieth century, 232; of H, 3, 8, 90, 242–43; of H's interp. of N, 87–88, 94, 163; of N a common ground with H, 94; of N more radical than H's, 163; of texts as bringing the text to edge of metaphysics, 247. *See also*

Derrida; *Destruktion;* Hermeneutics; Language; Hermeneutics and deconstruction

Destruktion (polishing a term, a tradition, in order to retrieve its premetaphysical dimensions), 7, 10, 114, 228, 235–36; a definition of, 301; d. of the concept of consciousness, 104; D's interpretation of, 235–36, 302; versus dialectic, 108; G sets *Destruktion* in opposition to d., 233; G's reproach to D seems to be based on assuming that *déconstruction* is used negatively by D, 236; G's use of d. closer to early H than the later H, 236; goal of d. is a h. task, 100; H and, 99–100, 121, 236, 274; meaning of, 121; d. of the language of academic metaphysics, 121; related to death of philosophy question, 235; related to overcoming and ceasing to overcome metaphysics, 107, 236; not related to any quest for origins, 100; pathos of, 98; Plato engaged in d., 101. *See also* Deconstruction; Language of metaphysics

Dialectic: 55; versus d., 108; Hegel and, 7, 24, 101, 111; H and 108–109; h. reorientation of, 23, 252; Western metaphysics and, 110; Platonic d., 101, 179; of recognition, 108; rests on speculative structure of language, 111; Schlegel's irony and Hegel's d., 119; self-knowledge in the Being of the other (Hegel), 27; speculative method and, 252; three paths back from d., 109–10, 179, 207; wordplay and, 45

Dialectical hermeneutics, 98; G does not object to this label, 121

Dialogical midworld, 252

Dialogical principle, reading, understanding: d. p. arises in a deeper form in the epoch of German romanticism, 164; d. r. still too restrictive for reading H, 273; nature of d. u., 221

Dialogue, 2, 6, 8, 23; a carrying out of *anamnesis*, 111; not an answer to the philosophical question, 190; needs a lowering of aural difference, 200; d. between D and G, 243; d. between thinkers not bound by laws or philology, 245; breaks up bias and narrowness, 26; Buber and Levinas on, 212; participants never find common ground, 212; two contrasting conceptions of d. in G and D, 12; as endless conversation, 243; D's concept of, 243; D's critique of, 16, 165; D's reluctance to enter into d. with G, 10–11, 17, 171–72; 196, 267; D's view of language is based on a narrative rather dialogical paradigm, 282; a d. that puts in question the possibility of d., 253; as living dialogue, 23, 53; Bakhtin's dialogism and Blanchot's literary space, 209; as place of difference between h. and d., 11; and *écriture*, 209, 214; as "empty speech", 158; ethical demands of, 89, 212–13; G's concept of, 245; G on d. similar to Blanchot, 211; Platonic basis of G's claims about d, 16; goes beyond Hegel, 26; relates G to early Romantics, 118; good will and will to power in, 165–66, 170; H not concerned with it in a general way, 274; ill will in, 203; impediments to d. between G. and D., 12; Lacan and, 131; Levinas and, 213–14; living dialogue, 252; logocentrism and, 8; Logos is common to all, 164; metaphysics of presence and, 95; model of, 5; moment of coherence the fulfillment of, 185; more important to G than H's ownness and fallenness, 117; dissolves the otherness of the partners, 213; mediating otherness in, 27; not metaphysical, 213; mutual agreement and, 252; openness to self-doubt a condition of d., 245; orality and, 208; potentiality for being other, 26; Plato's model of, 1; reading as d., 47; reorienting dialectic is not taking

Rede as a point of departure, 95, 256; Shekinah and, 214; soul's d. with itself, 253; leaves behind subjectivity of subject as starting point, 26, 252; transcendence in the between, 213–14; needs to go beyond unidirectional questioning and answering, 271; needs to allow for the irreducibly unequal, 276; universality of d. a prejudice of h., 143; knowing one has been understood in d., 54; intertwined with writing, 209. *See also* Conversation; Dialogical principle; Empty speech; Mutual understanding

Différance, 5, 7, 8; risks aestheticism, 90; found in Aristotle's concept of time, 112; auto-affection presupposes a pure d. dividing self-presence, 254; being-present-with rests on, 160; manifold in Platonic texts, 254; a relation between the event and structure of language, 178; reuse of a sign rests on, 160; of the voice that splits the ear, 201

Dilthey: concept of structure, 49; G's starting point for critique, 25; on temporal structure of understanding, 49; on *Wirkungszusammenhang,* 49

Displacement, 160. *See also* Meaning

Dissemination: D finds d. alongside H's quest for unity, 241; d. endlessly opens a snag in writing that cannot be mended, 267

Double reading: D cannot let himself be identified with a particular reading, so he reads by juxtaposing readings, a dialogue of readings, 243; d. r. is double in remembrance of the dualisms governing the discourse of metaphysics, 246; d. r. deconstructs the concept of metaphysics, 246; d. r. does not attempt to decide what reading is with and without H, 243; d. r. renounces the posture of the critique and thus "twists free" of the metaphysical opposition,

243; is directed to a blind spot in the text, 245

Dwelling: creative d in the marriage relationship, 279; grounded in the narrative coherence of everyday events, 279

Ear of the other: disarticulates our relation with the whole of our own meanings, 200; ethics of, 205; signs for a text long after it is written, 203; I lend it to myself in speaking, 203

Eastern thought: H's efforts and explorations in vain, 104–105

Écriture, 109, 118, 124; contains opposition to antitexts, 209; D's path back from Hegelian dialectic, 207; G claims to parallel, 112; return to not required, 118. *See* Writing

Education: *Bildung* as universal task, 91. *See also Bildung*

Effective-historical consciousness (*wirkungsgeschichtliches Bewußtsein*): more being than consciousness, 121; not consciousness, 100; radically finite, 188

Eminent text, 41–42. *See* Literary text

Empty speech, 106; avoids the repression constitutive of discourse, 131; still calls for an answer, 131, 156; Lacan's critique of e. s. parallel to G's, 156. *See also* Lacan

End of metaphysics: does G fail to take it seriously, 96

End of philosophy: a self-destructive, interruptive notion that cannot be sustained within a narrative without destroying it, 246

Energeia: Aristotle's word, 234

Envoi: gathering that disseminates as it gathers, 242; of Being, 241

Epistemological archeology, 154

Ereignis (E-vent) 100; definition of, 300–301; the gathering effected by E. not speculative but narrative, 275

Essentialism, closet: based on G's attachment to Plato and to Hegel, 259; G's talk about history and change "just a front for lasting essences," 259

Eternal recurrence, 94; H's interpretation of, 4; is it the manner of being of beings as a whole? 70

Ethical community: a theocratic idea, 173

Ethics: D's neglect of, 5; dialogical good will not related to, 55; Levinas find face-to-face relationship the beginning of allegiance and responsibility, 213; N's ethical fervor disregarded by D, 89; consequences of e. refusal to listen, 205

eumeneis elenchoi 132, 207. *See also* Good will; Dialogue

Exegesis: not a problem prior to Enlightenment, 152

Exergue: D on, 298

Existenz: definition of, 301

Experience: is it not a metaphysical concept, 53; of being understood, 54

Experience of dialogue: unifying emergent meaning vs. radical alterity, 276

Experience we all recognize: G's familiar phrase seems to imply a normative subject, 204

Fascism: G's deaf ear to, 13, 205. *See* Nazis and Nazism

Finitude: implications for h. of f. in H, 24; of one's own understanding, 190; fusion of horizons and, 283

Foundationalism, 258–59; G thinks that foundationalism is bound to come to grief, 259; G's h. as a version of, 258; the wages of f. is N, 259

Fundamental ontology: unable to overcome self-reference, 104

Fusion of horizons, 41, 130; becomes appropriation by subject or tradition, 158; implicitly joined in the depths of tradition, 217; is contested by Counterposition (D), 167; masks a radical

finitude, 283; necessary, 119; reciprocally related to exclusion of otherness, 282; structure of, 305

Führer: N's f. and the Nazi's f., 201

Gadamer, Hans-Georg, *passim;* as the most French of contemporary thinkers, 232; as too eager to fault Enlightenment anti-prejudice, 139; his defense of speaking over writing not to the point, 263; his distance from H is signalled by his rejection of H's turn to poetic language, 272

Gadamer, Hans-Georg, his interpretations: of H show G's limits, 189, 272–73; Forget's critique of, 143–44; of Paul Celan, 45

Gadamer, Hans-Georg, interpretations of Derrida, 75–125; as a person who views anyone using certain key words as irretrievably metaphysical, 237; as a proper name representing critique of logocentrism, 237; as having an ontologically unclarified dependence on the semantic starting point, 125; as pursuing a path from H very much like my own, 124; as too much dependent on the concept of the sign and whole tradition of semantics and semiotics, 124. *See also* Gadamer-Derrida encounter; Gadamer's hermeneutics

Gadamer and Derrida: contrasting views on education, 315; difference lies in G's assumption of the need for a unitary understanding of N, 244. *See also* Hermeneutics and deconstruction; Gadamer-Derrida encounter

Gadamer's hermeneutics: a dialogical hermeneutics, 177; a h. of finitude, 177; a philosophy of the mining of meaning, 262; a very liberal and non-hierarchical version of a fundamentally conservative and traditionalist idea, 260; contains a tension between investigation and result, 189; contains too rigid a sense of unity if its excludes h. of suspicion, 219; denies any single, correct interpretation, 177; D has qualms about the fate of otherness in G's h., 225; does exclude conflict and debate, 219; dovetails with Quine, 215; exploits H's conservative side, 261; fixation of meaning is problematic in, 179; from the standpoint of d., 258; gives everything essentialism promises wrapped in historical form, 259; gives up parousiological completion of *ousia,* a definitive form for Geist, pure reflective consciousness, 260; is as deconstructive as d., 195; is at pains to lose N, and H, and D in order to find a language to make himself understood, 226; is attractive to theologians, 261; is disrupted by D's multiplication of ears, 200; is naive, old-fashioned, metaphysical, insufficiently radical, and humanist, 207; is right about uncircumventability of language but wrong about deep truth and the wisdom of the classic, 263; its key is trust in language and the deep powers of tradition, 262; its openness is undermined by Hegelian, Romantic and Platonic metaphysics, 264; listened with the morally objectionable ears to Nazism, 205; offers pluralized and nonhierarchized historical forms in a situated subject, 260; operates like a normative psychologism in the service of society, 204; raised h. from intentionality to existential ontology, 102; raises ethical questions, 204–205; seen from a deconstructionist point of view, 261–62. *See also* Gadamer; Hermeneutics; Hermeneutics and deconstruction

Gadamer-Derrida encounter, interpretations: a conflict between ways of thinking and questioning not contents of thought, 250; as a dialogue on behalf of dialogue, 251; as already interrupted at the beginning, 252; as event, 2, 4, 5, 76, 186, 248; as nonevent, 5, 6, 8, 192, 206, 236, 251, 265; 268; genealogy of its texts needs analysis, 251; really a quarrel, 129; served to highlight the contours of each thinker's thought, 250; significance of, 18, 215; two biographically different contexts involved, 220; we need not choose sides, 271

Gadamer-Derrida encounter, issues involved in: 83, 84, 188; a conflict between ways of thinking and questioning not contents of thought, 250; common ground between D and G, 131–32, 268; differences and difficulties in, 13, 93, 94, 248, 250, 252; importance for Anglo-American philosophy, 215; opposition becomes otherness, 249; political implications, 13, 77, 91, 92; pragmatist perspective on, 216; two focii, 14, 15; two biographically different contexts involved, 220; undiscussed questions in, 223, 224

Gadamer-Derrida encounter, D's approach to: D counters G's attempt to restrict the dialogue to a certain image of him by rendering problematic (in IS) the use of a name as naming the subject-matter of a thinker's thought, 249; D does not enter into the discourse of G but places himself outside it, 265; D had not had time to develop a position in response to G, 268; D is trying to teach G a lesson, 13; D knows its failure would prove his point, 251, 192; D's reply to G is nonsense, 194; D's approach compared to G's, 166; D subjects G to the cutting edge of irony, 13, 196, 265; D's understanding of G in, 13; on D's preliminary remarks, 187; successful encounter would have stacked the deck against D, 236; the dialogue-frustrating character of D's questions, 237. *See also* Derrida;

Destruktion; Deconstruction; Hermeneutics and deconstruction; Second Gadamer-Derrida "encounter"
Gadamer-Derrida encounter, G's approach to and view of: a deeply meaningful experience for G., 13; G an advocate of tradition in, 163; fleshed out through reference to other works by G, 77–83; G believes that German version suffers from translation, 93; G makes metaphysical language the issue between them, 237; G not sensitive to D's "ear-splitting" discourse, 13; G puts debate back on ethical ground in saying that D and N want to be understood, 135; G seems not particularly conversant with D's thinking, 237; G's theme the unavoidability of the hermeneutic standpoint, 125; G wants to legitate the experience of truth and D does not, 188. *See also* Derrida; Gadamer; Gadamer's hermeneutics; Hermeneutics and deconstruction
Ganzseinkönnen (capacity for wholeness): experienced in marriage, 279
Gebilde (cultivation), 49, 79
Geist (spirit, mind), 260
Geisteswissenschaften (human sciences), 77, 91
Generational grammar, 154
Gerede (talk), 106
German Romanticism, 264
Geschick (fate, destiny): D's double reading of, 241
God: H's reading of N's "So many centuries and no new God!" 105
Good will, 10, 11, 12, 89, 135; the antinomy in, 175; assumes a common will, 168; assumes the intelligibility of the text, 182; assumes that truth is what the understanding understands about an always transcendent truth, 169; close to the spirit of N, 89; coerces agreement, 197; D's doubts about, 165, 267; in dialectic and

sophistic, 256; ethical implications of, 91, 205; foundation of human solidarity, 198; metaphysical, 267; operates between living and dead aspects of language, 278; G overlooks the domination in, 183, 194; in psychoanalysis, 53; in reading H, 277; in the perspective of sharing, 278; related to Kantian g. w., 4, 55, 168, 172, 216; not a matter of whether one understands or not, 168; Plato on g. w. in dialogue, 4, 55, 307; Socratic g. w. seeks to strengthen the other's viewpoint, 182; a threat to identity, 169, 172; too much to ask, 172
Grammatikè: concept of, 33

Habermas, Jürgen: does not understand the problem, 170; psychoanalysis in terms of communications theory, 170; his objection to h., 97. *See also* Mutual agreement in understanding
Hasidism, 213
Hegel: says the artwork imposes itself like a command, 125; "bad infinity" defended by G, 124, 180; insists that essence be conceived historically, 259; his dialectic is found in G's concept of understanding, 157; G resists his infinite mediation, 98; his *Logic* furnished G food for thought, 98; reads Plato as champion of literacy, 209; on recognition of authority, 139; finds self-knowledge in the Being of the other, 27; *See* Hegel in Index of Names
Heidegger: and the term *Abbau,* 9; radical alterity and existential self-understanding in, 276; his apocalyptic appeal provokes an embarrassed reaction, 272; his significant insight is that Being withdraws, 25; debate with Staiger sought a single meaning, 145; D's interpretation of *Destruktion,* 15; D a more faithful follower of H, 16; D's interpretation of, 24, 58–71; D closer

to H with regard to "the unique and privileged in thinking," 271; D finds H less radical than N, 24; H is more radical than N, 3; H juxtaposes his N encounter with a "going to encounter in thought", 223; G and D share filial regard for H, 271; G's interpretation of D's interpretation of *Destruktion,* 15; G's interpretation of H half-hearted and reactionary, 16, 261; G's effort rooted in Romantic tradition and humanistic heritage, 24; cultural implications of his h. circle, 92; his critique of Husserlian idealism influenced G, 260; as not guilty of the Husserlian form of logocentrism, 115; relation to his own immortality, 274; his impassability means his writing is for a privileged few, 272; his concept of interpretation a critique of phenomenology, 30; influence of Kierkegaard on, 117; sensuous aspects of his language, 273; criticized the language of metaphysics in h., 98; finds Greek logocentrism in modern self-abandonment, 27; trapped in metaphysics, 24; interpretation of Plato does not convince G, 116; political consequences of, 16; readings seek to restore a protreptic dimension, 276; relation to his readers and students problematic, 272; the religious impulse in, 116; return to Greek origins pointless and fruitless, 104–105; texts require interpretive good will, 277; texts work on many levels, 276; his critique of the concept of the subject, 252; the unity of his path of thought and his interpretation of N, 59–60. *See also* Heidegger's interpretation of Nietzsche

Heidegger's interpretation of Nietzsche, 58–71, 231; ambiguity in H's image of N, 229, 237; an ambiguous attempt at rescue, 65, 67, 69; ambivalent about N's putative biologism, 228; D actually comes close to G's understanding of the ambiguity in H's interpretation, 238; D does not miss H's ambivalence, 239; D focuses on a moment of summation in H's discussion of eternal recurrence rather than H's close readings of N's texts, 231; D raises the question of H's unitary understanding, 244; D rejects it; G a willing victim of, 93–94; D saves H from being a proper name for a position, 248; D sees H as trying rescue N from ambiguity, 238; D sees it as making N stand still, 184; D tries to free himself from, 115; D's criticism of, 83, 86; D's reading also totalizes, 87–88; H does not really conjoin will to power and eternal recurrence, 230; errs in presenting eternal recurrence as a thought about totality, 70; errs in seeing the will to power as a doctrine N understood to be "true," 167; fails to reshape the concept of autobiography, 64; H's interpretation of N in the G-D encounter, 222–23; G's reading of, 226–27, 248; G can confirm H's interpretation only by recognizing that H himself brought the unity to N's thought and this affirms the dispersal of N's texts, 247–48; G contrasts himself to D on, 113; G finds a seductive element in it that was missed by the French interpreters of N, 238; G finds it persuasive, 115; G reduces H's thinking to an orthodoxy, 248; G stands with H and against N, 261; G supporting H on N refutes D's charge of subjectimism and philosophy of will, 194; H a fellow traveller only a short distance, 105; H and G have logocentric illusions, 96; H criticises the Nazi edition of N's works, 63; H does not claim that N himself puts will to power and eternal recurrence together, 113; H not sure that N's name and thought are one, 229; H not so convinced of unity or so convincing, 223; shifting stops in H's text, 224; H's N-interpretation as focus of the G-D encounter, 222–23; H wanted to corroborate N's view of the Greek tragic age, 105; H welcomed N's breaking of the spell of dialectic, 105; H's attack on philosophy of life an indirect attack on Nazism, 63; H's seeing N as the "last metaphysician" makes N a partner in H's own question, 184; historical and political factors behind it, 63; implies the question of beings as a totality, 70; issue of h. at stake in, 222; metaphysics in, 59, 62; at the crest of Western metaphysics, 58; as end of Western metaphysics, 63; becomes metaphysical at just the moment of finding N the last metaphysician, 229; as not a falling back into metaphysics, 113; misses the content and specificity of N's thought, 63; name and signature in, 59–60, 61, 63; name as cause of N's thought?, 60–62; name as keeping metaphysics' dream of unity, 67; name as naming what N thought, 61–62, 66–67; name contains a plurality which calls H's N-interpretation into question, 68; over-looks how problematic for N is any doctrine teaching the universal, 167; question of life and N's alleged biolo-gism at cent of, 66–67; a guiding question versus a grounding question in, 230; attacks standard interpretation of N as philosopher-poet, 63; does not suppress life, 230; the structuring role of the totality of beings in, 69; the thought of totality does not at all con-sume H's entire reading of N, 231; the totality of beings is will to power and it is eternal recurrence, 70; the unity of the history of metaphysics and, 59, 228

Heideggerianism: left wing and right wing, 16, 261

Hermeneutic: h. approach to texts con-trasts with philology and linguistics, 31; h. assessment of deconstruction not viable, 191; Dallmayr's criticism of h. consciousness, 77, 85; G's advocacy of h. good faith, 270; narrative paradigm

and h. of Dasein: 273; h. nihilism, 247; h. retrieval, 9; d. of h. "self-consciousness," 133; unavoidability of h. standpoint, 125; h. turn in phenome-nology parallel to early Romanticism, 122

Hermeneutical circle, 163; Being-in-the-world and, 23; cultural implications, 92; Dilthey and, 22; phenomenological immanence and, 26; overcoming the subject-object bifurcation, 23; in text interpretation, 217

Hermeneutical experience: experience of living dialogue problematical, 53; full extent not recognized by neoKantians nor Dilthey, 22; G transgresses his own descriptions, 304; limit implicit in, 25; not reduced to empty word in WM, 111; not related to metaphysics of presence, 95; of art, 23; of history, 23; of a that which is other, 245; openness a condition of its authenticity, 304; in tension with that which asserts itself against all reasoning, 189; transcends control of scientific method, 188; universality of, 95, 143

Hermeneutical good will: limits of, 135; suspends the moment of critique, 135

Hermeneutics and deconstruction, 1, 4, 7; agree that understanding involves difference and consensus, 221; a rela-tionship of alterity, 9, 16; areas in common, 2, 6–8, 12, 17, 131–32, 151, 157, 176–78, 192, 266, 295; imagine a dialogue between, 186; difference(s) between, 5, 7, 9, 11, 17, 76, 83–84, 133, 151, 191, 221, 244, 262–63, 266; operating on different levels, 262; difference between G and D is that D attributes neoplatonic metaphysics to Plato but G finds Platonic dialogue made possible by the art of writing, 209; Manfred Frank's view of, 151; implications for the "global city," 91–92; James as a mediator between, 221; linking orality and dialogue, writing

and literacy, 207; in opposition, 2, 84;
practical-political implications, 76; as
"two paradigms", 17; both h. and d.
as the falling tightrope walker in *Zarathustra,* 229. *See also* Alterity; Archi-
writing; Deconstruction; Derrida;
Dialogue, Gadamer; Gadamer-Derrida
encounter; Heidegger's interpretation of
Nietzsche; Hermeneutics; Otherness
Hermeneutics, 253; definition of, 152;
    D's interpretation of, 8; development
    of, 3, 21; dialectical, 7; dialogue and,
    5, 84; "double-reading" h, 15; empha-
    sis on tradition, 14; Hebrew models of,
    18; Hegel in, 16; Heideggerian existen-
    tialism in, 16, 22; history of classical
    h., 23; short history of, 152; inexhaust-
    ibility of meaning in, 24; intential h.
    and existential ontology, 77; Krell
    stands with the underdog, 222; neoor-
    thodox models of, 18; P. de Man and,
    114; 111; Platonism in, 16; political
    implications of, 12, 17, 76, 185; psy-
    choanalysis and 134, 135; Romanticism
    in, 16, 21; significance of judicial text
    interpretation, 35, 36; "single-reading"
    h., 15; status and range of, 85; on the
    unity of said and unsaid. *See also*
    Dialogue; Gadamer; Hermeneutic;
    Hermeneutical circle; Hermeneutics *as;*
    Hermenuetics, contributions of; Herme-
    neutics, criticisms of; Hermeneutics
    and deconstruction
Hermeneutics *as:* a critique of Kantian
    subjectivist aesthetics, 77–78; a critique
    of specular self-presence, 158; a cri-
    tique of idealism and methodologism,
    22; a form of deconstruction, 9; a
    longing for "deep truths",16; a model
    of interpretation rooted in existential,
    historical, finite existence, 16, 22–23; a
    modification of Hegelian dialectical
    model, 157; not the art of nailing
    someone down, 118; not tied to H's
    fundamental ontology, 94; not unavoid-
    able, 9

Hermeneutics, contributions of: critique
    of historicism in, 23; encourages cul-
    tural openness, 91, 92; offers the di-
    alogical paradigm of interpretation, 17;
    G renews philological and psychological
    h, 266; status and range of, 85; empha-
    sis on tradition parallel to Quine and
    Goodman, 14; prior to Romanticism h.
    only a form of decoding language, 152;
    universality of h. experience, 22
Hermeneutics, criticisms of: abandoned
    by H, 23, 189; subordinates artworks
    to understanding and self-consciousness
    (Dallmayr), 80; D criticizes H's exege-
    sis, 83; D criticizes onto-h. in *Spurs,*
    81–83; no dialogue between h. and
    neostructuralism, 150; G's ambivalence,
    84–85; G tries but fails to follow the
    later H, 94; G's ontological turn half-
    hearted, 84; individuality a barrier in,
    21; must remain impervious to Laca-
    nian interpretation, 134; logocentric
    and phonocentric, 117, 178, 183;
    people wish to go beyond it, 183;
    phenomenological immanence, 26, 85–
    86, 104, 190, 245; prejudice and, 135–
    37; highest principle is to recognize the
    possible correctness of the partner's
    position, 245; concedes too much to
    reciprocal understanding, 225; lacks a
    reliable principle of selection, 141;
    contains no standpoint for seeing our
    limitations, 85; goal of solidarity ques-
    tionable, 12; is framed by a notion of
    tradition such that interpretation is not
    a breaking free, 16, 179; universality-
    claims conflict with finitude claims,
    84; not universal in G because based
    on prejudice and exclusions, 142; the
    issue of woman in D's critique of onto-
    h., 81–83
Hermeneutics of discretion: nothing in
    D's text is left to chance, 222
Hermeneutics of facticity: transforms the
    meaning of h., 25; G claims he retains,
    25

Hermeneutics of suspicion: causes D to attribute a neoplatonic metaphysics to Plato, 209; G's denial of surprising, 218; contrasts with h. of intention, 56; mutual understanding and, 218

Heteroglossia: affinity with dissemination, 211; embodies the interaction of "cited" language, 210

Historicism: G seeks to criticize, 25

History of reception: we do not need to know every use and misuse a work of art has been through, 123

History: as the effect of différance/*Unter-Schied*, 262

Holzwege (forest paths). *See* Dead ends; H

Husserl: D's interpretation of, 16; self-understanding goes beyond, 120; theory of signs, 122

Husserlian neoKantianism: H's critique prepared by, 25

hypokeimenon (substance) 234

Idea: Plato's word, 234

Ideal answering: H's protreptic projection of, 275

Ideal reader: his/her creative achievements in the context of human sharing, 278

Identity: lost in a common reciprocal understanding, 169; self-identity rests on the subject hearing with the same ears, 202

Ill will: N anticipated i. w. in the ears of those who sign his works, 203

Incommensurability: death and the coexistence of incommensurables, 281; in the marriage relationship, 278–83; D's studies of property and signature can provide lessons in the dynamics of i. 282; of standpoints, 18, 282

Individuality: D emphasizes the individuality on each side, 167; steps aside for generality in D and Saussure, 159; failure of G and D to deal with, 11; importance in Romantic h., 21, 277;

ineffable i. temporal with a "timeless" moment, 277; F. Schleiermacher and M. Frank on, 11, 153–54; Romanticism and the ineffability of, 277

Infinite conversation, 249. *See also* Conversation

Inner ear: when reading what is written, 124

Inner word: is still turned toward the other, 213. *See also* Ear of the other

Intentionality: only possible on the basis of originary transcendence, 253. *See also* Hermeneutics

Interpretation: constitutes the structure of Being-in-the-world, 30; concept of, 28–30; as decentering critique, 178; as critique of the search for what is "really" in the text, 30; h. significance of judicial i., 35–36; philosophical h. guilty of logocentric metaphysics?, 178; the rise of the term in N, 29; not a straightforward enterprise, 75; contains a performative dimension, 181; in philosophy, 267; problem of i. per se encompassed in H's N-interp., 222; in psychoanalysis, 53; reinterpreting interpretation, 133; returns to what is meant but is not a reconstruction, 180; task of understanding the author better than he understood himself rejected by both H and G, 247; ultimate goal to reveal a totality of meaning, 218; brings written text to speech, 180. *See also* Hermeneutics; Text; Textuality

Interruption: crucial in French Freudian psychoanalysis, 204; i. of rapport a rapport of i., 251; i. of rapport takes issue with the self-presentation of experience in dialogue, 204

Intersubjectivity: a concept alien to critical philosophy, 173; contrary to Kant, N, or the "French scene," i. places its fundamental principles at anyone's disposal, 172; does ego or alter determines the openness of intersubjective communities? 170

Irony: in antitexts, 37; allows D to confuse G as to what he is saying and still communicate to his own specialized audience, 196–97; D means to teach G a lesson in the power plays latent in philosophical dialogue, 197; D's use of, 17, 265; since D makes no sense, he must be being ironic, 195–96; D relies on a reading of N he himself does not accept in order to accuse G of a subjectivism G explicitly rejects, 195; G's irony assumes the role of the Officer takes in Kafka's *The Penal Colony*, 266; h. of, 116–119; rests on mutual understanding which D denies, 196; objectifies and typifies its victim, G, 265

Iterability, 159; as prerequisite for language, 155

Kehre (turn) 23; not in Fichte, 120; hazardously radical paths leading nowhere, 104

Kierkegaard, Søren, 90, 97, 104, 110, 122, 260, 276; Buber's criticism of, 214; G's reappropriation of, 120; G chastened by K's critique of Hegel, 260; influence on H's interpretation of texts, 117; K's turn to Socrates not misguided, 119

Kundgabe (announcement, making manifest), 95

Lacan: critique of empty speech, 106, 130, 156; G agrees with, 158; 130–31; signifiers without signifieds, 134. *See* Lacan in Names Index

Language, 253; authority of, 278; code model in language theory, 154; concealment and alienation in, 270; D's view of, 2, 263; death in the life of, 278; G's view of 2, 5, 6; G at one with Bakhtin's "dialogism," 211; G follows the later H's view of 94; G recognizes the distinction between *langue* and

parole, 181; G seeking a language is at pains to lose N, H, and D, 226; H and privileged forms of, 274; H discovers a new language, 26; H introduces extreme limitations into, 274; in philosophical thought, 28; in relation to literacy, 208; moved to center-stage in H's transformation of phenomenology, 122; mutual agreement necessary to, 56; of mysticism brought innovations into the German language, 121; priority of natural language over scientific, 28; no language to evoke a new God, 105; other person's language learnable, 226; phenomenology's forgetfulness of, 102; philosophy of language moves beyond sign theory and linguistics, 28; prelinguistic domain, 253; priority of, 1, 11, 28; protreptic use of, 275; self-presentation of language in literature, 42; withdrawal into the image of language (Blanchot), 212. *See* Code model; Language *as:* Language of metaphysics; Midworld of language

Language *as:* the basis of dialectic, 111; bridge or barrier, 11, 21, 27, 85, 105–106, 164, 179, 192, 226, 252; conversation, 106; dialogical, 26; forgotten in understanding, 32; like a piece of farmland, 269; freed by H from the grip of *Identitätsphilosophie.* 103; a heritage from the preceding moment, 161; necessary for speech to be intelligible, 178; neglected by Hegel, 102; neglected by neoKantians and first phenomenologists, 28; not a Babylonian captivity of the mind, 105–106. 226; not easily circumventable, 105; not homogeneous dialogical but heterogeneous narrative space, 282; not the same as its existential foundation, *Rede.* 256; object of philosophical reflection, 103; preshaping our thinking, 99; reconceived in the Romantic, 153; a sharing in communal coexistence on many levels, 270; speech-event important to theory of textuality, 181; system of signs, 56; understood in structuralist terms, 154; without deep truth and the wisdom of the classic, 263

Language of metaphysics, 7; its concepts part of the fate of the West, 101; Fichte and Hegel tried to overcome scholastic m., 108; G cannot follow H's critique of, 98–99; G continues to speak it, 98; G's discussion with H, 121; H still speaking it, 24; H's effort to overcome, 24, 103–104, 179, 207; H's use of poetry to step back from, 24, 207; resides for N in language not in what one says in language, 168; not a dead language for either G or D, 240; not an unbreakable constraint on thought, 23, 237, 252; poetic presence escapes, 47; there is no, 98, 106–107, 121

Lebensphilosophie (life-philosophy), 230; H's resistance to, 228.

Levinas, Emmanuel, 13, 119, 171, 308, 311; critizes Buber's I-Thou relationship, 213; on dialogue, 212–13; on the problem of the other, 97

Life and death: shows how the life of linguistic beings produces works that fix and transcend their fluid basis, 281. *See also* Ashes; Death; Nietzsche

Linguisticality, 6, 21, 85, 192, 253; bridge or barrier, 11, 21, 27, 85, 105–106, 164, 179, 192, 226, 252; displaces the illusion of self-consciousness, 29; primacy of, 253; G aware of the forces of domination subtending, 197

Linguistically generated intersubjectivity: allows ego to take the perspective of an other, 170. *See also* Alter

Linguistics: dialogical h. and, 11

Linguistic turn, 154; in Anglo-Saxon thinking, 102

Listening: Dilthey on musical l., 49; similarity to reading, 48

Literacy, 13; Havelock identifies with linear conceptual thinking, self-consciousness, and awareness of language, 208

Literary text, 40; as text in authentic sense, 41–42; basis for new self-understanding, 57; demands to become present and listened to, 267; interpretation of, 41; poetic word versus play on words in, 45; unique rightness of, 49; special character of, 42–43; strikes us a blow, 57; syntax in, 43; different temporal structure of, 48 *See* Literature, Poetic text

Literature: its unique mode of being, 299–300; writing and, 208

Logic of question and answer: a hermeneutic principle, 177. *See* Answer

Logocentrism, 3, 94, 223, 228, 238; accusation peculiar when applied to H, 116; D reads H through Husserl, 112; D's critique of H's l., 24, 113; D sides with N against H, according to G, because he believes that N broke through the l. of m., 237–38; dialectic not a relapse into, 101; G's critique conflicts with model of Platonic dialogue, 84–85; G's h. not guilty of, 178; G replies to D's charge of l., 117–18, 195; Greek thought reflects, 95; H fails to break with, 163; H finds Greek l. in modern self-abandonment and self-insistence, 27; H guilty of, 97; H's critique of l. not itself logocentrism, 95; hermeneutics accused l. of by D in *VP.* 117; in N, 27; Plato Aristotle can be accused of, 116

Logoi, 110; Plato paid obeisance to, 101; Socratic intervention disrupts the privileged logoi, 183; Socrates' recourse to, 253

Logos, 110, 253; as something common to all, 202; as what the parties in a dialogue have in common, 164; G's l. is finite and foundationless and untranscendental, 185; logos-philosophy does not validate dialogue with self over dialogue with the other, 213; metaphysi-

cal concept of, 112; sense of distance
and time in, 117
Love: attaches absolute value to finite
experiences in an all-important personal
narrative, 283; embraces the particularity of its object, 283; has a sense of
direction like the protreptic call, 283

Meaning: anticipation of perfection of,
182; arises in effective-historical consciousness, 157; communality of, 164;
a focus in humanities and social sciences, 75; continuity of m. implies
metaphysics, 96; D has shown how a
mutual enfolding of life and death
permeates the production of, 281; D's
attack still directed to classical concepts
of, 270; D's discourse means nothing
at all, 198; D's view of meanings, 263;
displacement of sense and, 160; event
of m. never arrives in Blanchot, 211;
fixation of meaning problematic in G,
179; fulfillment of m. requires empty
intentions, 106; G as insistent on deciding the question of, 178; the hermeneutic search for, 3; more m. in individual
moment than in its elements in the
chain of signifiers (Saussure), 159;
interplay with sound, 45, 46, 47; language not graspable on the basis of,
115; narrative m. more complex and
heterogeneous than dialogical, 283; no
m. out of context, 217; nonidentity of
meanings, 151; Platonic ideal of, 8;
play of m. in literary text, 44; privileged meaning, 271; repeatability of, 7;
search for, 6; sense or m. is directional,
111; unity of, 1, 182, 218; in the
service of will to power, 24. *See also*
Privileged meaning.
Meaning of Being: H's later thought not
concerned with, 261; not an essence
but a direction, 111
Metaphor: in poetry, 46
Metaphysics, 228, 238; ambiguity in the

beginning of modern m., 234; causes
H to suppress the thought of ashes in
N, 230; refers to the history of Being's
withdrawal, 234; Christian form of, 94;
concept does not apply to Plato, 116;
as defined by H (being of beings without the Being of beings), 69; dialogue
leads to, 267; in N in process of disintegration, 94; disintegrates in N into
value thinking, 238; "double reading"
of, 246; D reduces all the binary oppositions of m. to one side (presence),
229; D's relation to "m." is parasitic
on H's relation to "m.," 248; m. not
the target of D's critique, 246; end of
m. not the end of metaphysical readings
of texts, 246; G denies falling into, 94;
G as following H in the overcoming of,
94; G as lost sheep in the pastures of,
94, 195; going beyond, 9, 109–10;
Greek thought already on the path of,
94; H and, 3; H's concept of, 116; H's
critique of m. applies to h., 314; H's
discussion of fundamental words of,
235; H does not seek to do away with,
238, 246; H as going back behind,
110; H on m. in *N*, 59; if even H fell
into m., how can G or even D be
exempt, 267–68; hermeneutics and, 3;
nothing in language is free of, 168; for
N m. resides in language, 168; logocentrism of, 163; as onto-theology, 116;
project of, 3; rationalist versus imagina-
tive (Vico), 76; rationalist versus imagi-
native (Vico), 76; self-destruction of
m. in N, 225; history of the word
"subject" illustrates the unity of m.,
234; Western m. contaminated by
subjectivity according to both G and D,
268; unity of, 240. *See also* Gadamer;
Heidegger; Language of metaphysics;
Logocentrism; Metaphysics of presence
Metaphysics of presence, 8, 94, 228; as
imputed to H and G, 95; G's treatment
of self-understanding refutes the charge
of, 195

Midworld of language: the true dimension of what is given, 253

Mise-en-abîme: D's writing rest on m. a. and voids the notions necessary to dialogue, 267

Modernity: metaphysics of, 2; the subject a key term in its self-understanding, 234

Mutual understanding: agreement in, 252; Blanchot suspicious of, 211; is there an obligation to desire consensus?, 199; D's argument self-defeating if it succeeds in disproving, 193; D seeks to disprove, 193; D's use of irony presupposes the m. u. he is denies in G, 196; do we understand each other already with another ear?, 203; m. agreement in u. ultimately excludes a third party, 169; G has no illusions about the difficulty of achieving undistorted m. u., 197; not a naive notion, 56; otherness of the other in, 225; possible or impossible?, 193; presupposes social stability, 57; rarely the product the Socratic discourse, 254; difficult to erect universal claims on m. agreement in u., 169

Mystagogue: D says that in thinking, we inevitably assume the position of a, 270; has a privileged position, 270

Name: holds things together in the face of dissemination, 68; in regard to N not single name, 67; D on the name of N, 228; a new nonmetaphysical approach to the problematic of the, 62; thinker's name as naming the subject-matter of his thought, 62, 235

Narrative field of marriage: disrupted through the protreptic asymmetry of death, 280; involution of, 282

Narrative: philosophical autonomy and, 273; language as heterogeneous n space not the homogeneous space of dialogue, 282; natural language regains the center of philosophy, 28; death in marriage n.

frames the works of our symbolic life, 278, 282; marriage n. must be seen in the interwovenness of life and death, 280; absolute priority of marriage n. over other narratives, 279; n. paradigm helpful in dealing with the "history of Being," 273

Nazism, 201; G's repudiation of Nazi "nonsense" still problematic, 205; Nazism in H's N-interpretation, 63

Negative theology: irresistibly fascinating in our era, 214

Negotiation: as alternative to dialogue, 10

Neo-Kantianism, 98, 110

Neostructuralism, 11, 296, 306–7

Nietzsche: not a common ground for dialogue between G and D, 93; conceptual artistry could not satisfy H, 105; D on N, 5, 58–71, 81–82; D denies N's self-understanding, 89; D finds N more radical than H, 24; D questions H's interpretation of, 15; D tries to free himself from H's interpretation of, 115; D's and H's interpretation of N both questioned by Krell, 15; D's interpretation of N discards H's, 24; as a destiny, 162; and *écriture.* 109; eternal recurrence not a thought about totality, 70; French followers miss significance of the seductive in, 25, 163; French followers actually closer to understanding N, 168; at the crest of Western metaphysics, 58; not the last metaphysician because not a thinker of beings in their totality, 70; overcoming or trapped in metaphysics, 24, 109–10; dissension exists in N's inverted Platonism only because it already existed in Plato, 241; G as not taking N seriously enough, 96; G defends H's interpretation of, 15; H on N, 3, 4, 12, 15, 25; H's starting point for critique, 25; H as a fellow traveller with N only a short stretch of his way, 225; H goes beyond N's dissolution of metaphysics into values-thinking, 25; the interest in

defending one's own possibility of
judgment, 171; life and death are not
the whole nor are they opposites, 71;
metaphysical *Grundstellung*, 70; not the
regression into metaphysics to think
what N was unable to think, 227; name
and signature of, 59–61; name as cause
of N's thought, 60–61; as carrier of the
plaque-question of otherness, 225;
styles of N divide and split apart the
hermeneutic approach, 204; has no
trust in thought of totality, 69; eternal
recurrence not a thought about totality,
70; thwarts totality by including the
whole in the part, 71; no such thing as
the truth of N's text, 87; does not want
to be understood, 11, 57, 135, 162,
166, 304; contradicted himself by
writing to be understood, 135; D and
N both wrong about not wanting to be
understood, 57; not yet understood,
162; on the unity of N's thought, 59;
failed to descry the unity of his own
thinking, 227; the will to power as an
instrument to critique G's view of
dialogical good will, 165; Buber rejects
N's will to power, 214; N shows will to
power to be a substrate in self-sacrifice,
27; *See also* Heidegger's interpretation
of Nietzsche; Metaphysics; Understanding; Unity
Nonpresentation: as originary as presentation, 190
Nous: Heraclitus and Plato had similar
conceptions of, 123
Novel: embodies dialogical interaction of
"cited" languages, 210; younger than
writing and the book, 210

Objectivity: in text interpretation, 218;
moral aspect in research, 120
Ontology of substance: G tries to shake
off, 111
Ontotheology, 94; still depends on the
Geschick des Seins, 242

Openness of the text: related to different
degrees of privilege, 278
Orality, 13; Blanchot's conception of
writing an afterimage of orality, 210;
developed by Murko, Parry, Lord,
Havelock, Ong, et al., 207; dialogue
and, 208; intelligible only in relation to
concept of literacy, 208; requires individuals to become transmittters of
culture, 208
Original reader: concept of, 298
Other, 9; potentiality for being o. in
conversation, 180; problem of the
universal theorizing of the o. in discourse, 169; any action presupposes a
distance between self and o., 204; ear
of the o. says me and constitutes the
autos of my autobiography, 199; God is
other than any other, 212; presence of
o. breaks up bias and narrowness, 26,
199; the self which opens itself to the
other becomes "diaconal," 213; Plato's
description of thinking as dialogue with
self not open to the o., 213; speech of
the, 157; taking o. seriously really only
a method of taking people in, 166;
teacher respects the call of the other,
283; o. can help one find what is
"really there" in a text, 164; understanding the o., 220; D on understanding the o., 53; injustice to o. in having
to understand him/her in one's own
concepts, 168; o. can no longer require
me to understand him because it would
require a surrender of my identity, 169;
words can bring about an understanding
of the o., 204. *See* Otherness
Otherness, 1; Blanchot suspicious that
hermeneutic continuity of understanding
cedes otherness, 211; conversation and,
27; D shows otherness already operative
in monologue, 254; D tries to show the
challenge of other wills, 174; D's
qualm about h., according to G, 225;
dialogical overcoming of, 18; essential
to dialogue and growth in understand-

ing, 220; dialogue goes beyond agreement about what is common, 164; when heard through the ears of someone else, 200; when G encounters o. it leads him to self-doubt, 244; on Hegel's claim to have overcome o. dialectically, 97; hermeneutic challenge of, 92, 97; impenetrability of, 164, 174; in "monologue," 16; potentiality for being o., 254; reveals a limitation of Greek models of thought, 27; G tends to enclose o. in a circle of self-recognition, 245; understanding covers up o., according to D and Levinas, 119, 166

Ousia (substance), 260; as the presence of what is present, 107; concept enhanced by language connection to *oikos*. 100, 107

Overcoming metaphysics: already inscribed in Plato, 241; double reading gives a reading inside metaphysics and another reading beyond metaphysics, 246; G's claims ring hollow, 260; H later said his task was "to cease all overcoming and leave metaphysics to itself", 236; H's call for, 116; H's return to Greek origins unsuccessful, 104, 105; not a Gadamerian theme, 116; not possible according to N, 168

Phenomenological immanence: as a description of understanding, 26; D on, 86; fundamental ontology unable to overcome, 104; problem of p. i. in G, 85; G defends himself against, 26; H and D against G, 245; hermeneutics as still within the sphere of, 190

Phenomenology: H's reshaping of, 110, 122; concept of interpretation as critique of, 30; Platonism of p. as transcended by self-understanding, 120; phenomenology of religion as taught by H, 116

Philosophical meaning: peculiar autonomy of, 275

Philosophy: there is no Christian p. or pagan p., 68; crisis in philosophy of reflection, 154; what happens to p. when it transcends rigorous science, 188

Phonocentrism: G denies D's objection of, 113. *See also* Logocentrism

Phronesis (practical understanding), 100

Pietism: related to self-understanding, 119

Plato: as anticipating the ambiguity of dissension (*Zwiespalt*), 241; as champion of literacy (Havelock) and defender of living word (D), 209; as an example of apocalyptic paradigm in his complaint about separation of writing from voice, 281; concept of metaphysics does not apply to, 116; on the metaphysics of the dialogical soul, 264; plays at taking play seriously, 266; Pythagorean element in, 116; relation to Socrates in terms of the ear that signs, 203

Platonic dialogues: nothing accidental in, 252; contain heterogeneity and veils, not mutual dedication to understanding, 254

Play on words: 44–46; critique of G's discussion of, 144

Play: G on, 78, 79, 80; overcomes self-centeredness, 89; a point shared by G and D yet they see it differently, 266; transformative quality of, 88

Pluralism: G moves in the direction of, 219

Poem: fixity of a p.'s language an artifact of print, 212; G's view of p. consistent with Blancot's, 213; texture and tarrying in, 213

Poetic style: tends to be autoritarian and conservative, 210

Poetic text: Dilthey on interpretive mediation, 49; entering into, 57; interpretation of, 46; Mörike's "Auf eine Lampe" as example of, 50, 51; not a matter of self-confirmation, 57; reading meditative poetry a solitary process, 48

Post-Hegelianism, 157
Postmetaphysical thinking: challenge of Hegel, 103
Post-modern: hermeneutics and the, 176
Pragmatism: Anglo-American p. able to mediate the claims of h. and d., 14, 216
Prejudice: as in favor of authority, 139–40; as legitimate, 137–38; question of p. in hermeneutics, 135; rehabilitation of, 10. *See* Hermeneutics
Presence at hand. *See Vorhandenheit*
Presocratics: H's return a journey into error, 104–5
Pretexts: as distorted communication, 39–40; definition of, 39–40; dreams as, 39–40; ideologically slanted texts, 39–40; in psychopathology of daily life, 39–40; require a h. of suspicion, 40
Private voice: part of the language game of philosophy, 277
Privilege: embarrassment of, 283; general question related to facticity and subjectivity, 276; the free decision to take a privileged position in language, 278; p. of sharing, 283. *See* "Privilege of Sharing"; Sharing
Privileged meaning: D's "apocalytic paradigm" allows for an understanding, 271; goes beyond subjectivity, 277; in the marriage relationship, 278–83
Proper name, 228
Proper, the, 90
Propositional judgments: G reproaches D with equating all speaking with p. j., 270
Propositional logic: H critical of p. l. in *SZ*. 115
Protreptic: alterity essential to p. discourse, 276; call from the beloved to lover as, 283; p. asymmetry of death dramatically unifies the narrative field, 280; definition of p. language, 275; D's use of language as p., 17; p. meaning versus descriptive and final meaning, 276

Protreptic dimension: attained through insight into facticity, 276; an "existential" dimension (following Kierkegaard), 276; H seeks to restore, 276; opens up the radical novelties and disparities which convolute philosophic texts, 276
Pseudotext, 38
Psychoanalysis: in terms of communications theory, 170; ear splitting and, 203; G once explicitly held that p. was within the larger perimeter of hermeneutics, 218; integratability of p. into a general or universal h., 216, 218; nonvoluntarist hermeneutics and, 134–35; reinterpreting, 133–34. *See* Psychoanalytic hermeneutics
Psychoanalytic hermeneutics: a disruptive question of D, 53, 183; in radical contrast to hermeneutics, 55

Question and answer: the logic of, 111
Question: community of the, 8; ontological character of, 6

Reading, 118; similar to listening, 48; plurality of readings and the dissemination of the text, 247; temporal structure of, 47–48; D on the track of traces found in, 112; r. without regard to understanding, 149 *See* Recitation
Recitation: art of reciting texts, 47; r. of meditative poetry a solitary process, 48
Recovery from metaphysics: H's call for, 116. *See* Overcoming metaphysics; *Verwindung*
Rede (speech): the death inscribed within living speech, always withdrawing, 257; as existential foundation of language, 256; contains hearing and keeping silent, 257; never simply a matter of heritage, but also interruptions, 257; not primarily communication but letting something be seen from itself, 256; remote from anything like living discourse, r. is nothing sounded or spoken

at all, 257; not the same as *Sprache*. 256

Responsibility: D sees r. as exceeding the limits of ethics, 283; D's investigations bear directly on philosophical r., 271; and the possibility of being "called" in philosophy, 271

Rhetoric: contains bursts of empty words, 38, 106

Romantic irony: lacks social and pedagogical thrust of Socratic irony, 119. *See* Irony

Romanticism: and its formula, "individuum est ineffabile", 277; insights into the dialogical principle, 252. See Individuality; Dialogue

Rupture: a necessity for D, 183; one must come to terms with, 190

Sache (the subject or matter): the being of a, 6; in conversation something comes to language, not persons, 122; dialogue keeps in view, 211; s. of thinking for D, 9; s. of N's thinking, 61–62; s. of the text not the text itself is of concern, 181; s. of thought becomes the happening of tradition, 261, 270

Schriftlichkeit (scripturality), 41

Scientific knowledge: twentieth century linguistic critique of, 29

Second Gadamer-Derrida "encounter," 295

Selbstverständnis (self-understanding), 7, 97; the concept of, 97; stands in a context of involvements, 157; H's and Fichte's similar, 120; goes completely beyond Husserl's first *Logical Investigation*. 120; is rendered possible or impossible by language, 193; not the way metaphysics, 97; s. of modernity, 234; in oral culture it preserves and adapts, 208; transcends the Platonism of phenomenology, 120; connection with Protestant and Pietistic tradition, 97; always puts oneself in question, 119;

always refers itself to the speech of the other, 157; reflects theme of *différance*. 118; refutes D's accusations of a metaphysics of presence, 195; stands in opposition to self-consciousness, 95; evolves in reference to a tradition, 157; transcending the horizon of, 86

Self-alienation: in modern thought, 98

Self-consciousness, 253; cannot see its own ground, 157; loses credibility as the ground of self-certainty, 29; critique of s. by H, N, Freud, 29; denial of s. common to G and D, 131–32; illusion of, 253;

Self-expression: a movement of loss and alienation, 281

Self-knowledge: in the Being of the other, 27

Self-understanding. *See Selbstverständnis*

Semantic innovation: code model sciences cannot handle, 155. *See* Code model sciences

Sending: D and, 316. *See* E in works index

Sharing: G's goal a conversation that builds up a common language, 270; s. a perspective that allows for incommensurable standpoints and a sharing based on absence, 278; need for a richer characterization of productive alienations and limitations on, 271, 283; s. meaning in the marriage relationship, 278–83; shared understanding ultimately true understanding, 217; s. universally intelligible components may not be what is significant in some contexts, 279. *See also* Understanding

Sign: concept of, 8; nonprescribability of, 151; cannot guarantee its own identity, 160, 161; must be interpreted, 115; repeatability of, 159; wrongly taken by Anglo-American philosophy as an ur-phenomenon, 122

Signature, 202; ear of the other signs for a text long after it is written, 203; politics of, 59

Social coexistence: D's view of language broadens our view of, 282

Social sciences: limits of language in, 99

Socrates, 207, 254–55; allows his interlocutors to hear themselves through his ears, 202; a man of doubtful good will, 255; an image of liberation from solidification of meaning, 176; dialogical other par excellence?, 164; encourages Thracymachus to hear himself through ears common to all, 202; G takes position of S in Gorgias, 166; glad to be refuted if wrong, 166; teaches us one must believe one could be wrong, 119; and the turn to logoi, 253; two faces of, 176–85

Socratic dialogue: induces perplexity rather than mutual agreement, 255; makes S. hateful to other rather than inducing agreement, 255; something more than good will in play here, 16

Socratic irony: social and pedagogical thrust of, 119. *See* Irony; Socratic vigilance

Socratic vigilance: D moved by Socratic distrust, 263; D prepares for a new form of community?, 184; D's form of s. vigilance one of intervention, 177, 183; two forms of, 176; G's form of s. vigilance is dialogical, 177; can intervention remain outside the community?, 184; political implications in both forms, 185; against the pretension of knowing, 176

Solidarity: participation in dialogue undergirds human solidarity, 185; Rorty as an advocate of, 220

Sophistry: interprets all thoughtful questioning as an attack on common sense, 256; belongs to philosophy, 256; may belong to the essence of truth, 256

Sophists, 255

Sorge (care), 104

Speaking: in H, s. means letting something be seen from itself, not just speaking with others, 257; temporal structure of, 47. *See Rede*

Speculative, the: philosophy and history try to bring the s. to presentation, 163

Structuralism: G agrees with critique of, 112; leaves behind the individual use of language, 154

Structure: concept of, 49. *See Gebilde.* *Verwandlung ins Gebilde.*

Subject-matter. See *Sache*

Subject-object distinction: H's subversion of, 253

Subject: in Descartes man becomes subjectum, 234; in H, s. always refers to Descartes, 234; key role in self-understanding of modernity, 234; multiple applications illustrate the unity of metaphysics, 234; becomes a word of Being, 234

Subjectivism, 5; critique of s. a common ground between G and D, 195; Hegel's objective spirit overcame s., 104

subjectivity: denial of, 11; dialogue leaves behind starting point of, 26; H's critique of, 23; question of privileged meaning goes beyond, 277; D disrupts self-presentative s. by showing otherness even in monologue, 253–54

Substance: D is suspicious of men of substance, 263

Supersubject: G posits tradition as a, 158

Teaching: D's view of, 283

Temporality: in phenomenology, 190

Text, 40; authentic sense of the word, 41; authority of, 2; concept of, 27, 33; countertexts (see antitexts, pseudotexts, pretexts), 37–38; definition includes picture, architecture, even a natural event, 130; notion of dialogue opens the way to a new model of reading a t., 245; reading of difficult texts is the philosopher's task for both G and D, thus both renew h., 266; D questions G's concept of, 53; D's defintion of and conversation with, 158; D's quite different way of thinking about, 54, 177; for D every t. has a history constituted by the various readings that have been offered of it, a parallel to G, 247; G and D both focus on the text rather than the author, 178; notion of t. for G, 182–83; G sees concept of text as dividing him and D, 179; G vigilant against reading that constrains the text to the mastery of the reader, 185; G's being-towards-the-text no match for the radicality of H's being-towards-death, 189; G's interpretation of, 144; summation by G on interpreting nonliterary texts, 41; hermeneutical circle in confirmatory understanding of t., 217; h. consequences of the printed t., 34, 35; h. significance of early lack of punctuation in, 37; presents the real hermeneutic task, 180; interwovenness of text and interpretation, 31; logocentric concept of, 3; meaning in, 3; meaning not hidden behind the words, 247; openness of t. related to privilege, 278; interpreting orders, laws, contracts, 35, 36; "original reader" of a t. a vague concept, 33; personal letter not a text, 34; poem has no urtext in medieval manuscript culture, 212; a post-modern approach to, 176; privileged aspect enacts the autonomy of philosophical meaning, 274–75; punctuation in, 36–37; "readability" of translated texts, 31–32; recitation of, 47–48; relation of interpreter to nonliterary text and to audience, 41; relation of t. to reader, 41; scientific communication bypasses t., 33; temporality of t. undermines copresence, 159; tradition at work in interpretation of, 218; truth in, 2; understanding a t. always involves application, 216; unity of meaning allows t. to stand as a self-presenting and authoritative whole, 182; history of

the word t., 30–31, 33. *See also* Interpretation, Literary text; Textonomics; Text *as;* Textual autonomy; Textual grammar; Textuality

Text *as:* a firm point of relation, 164; a transcript, 35; closed and closable, 278; containing an ideality that makes it contemporaneous with every present, 180; mutely exposed to differing interpretations, 165; not dependent on author's intention (G agrees w. D), 96

Textonomics, 141

Text theory, code model in, 154. *See also* Code model

Textual autonomy: H's autonomous answering paralleled by D's apocalyptic addresses without message or destination, 275

Textual grammar: D on, 159

Textuality: why does D decline to take up G's invitation to discuss t., 223

Theology: d. wants to know why why everyone was so frightened by "heretics," 264

Thinking: as a conversation, 227; as a dialogue of self with itself which is not open to the other, 213; as something be to engaged in a very few, 272; as the dialogue of the soul with itself, 254

Time consciousness: Husserl's analysis of, 115

Time: Augustine had already broken the riddle of, 112; concept of, 115; as dwelling, 110; D seeks recovery of time in Aristotle, 112; experience of is the basis of presence, 112; Husserl failed to solve problem because of his Greek concept of Being, 112; the sense of tarrying in, 110

Timelessness: the gesture toward, 273; H looking at, 273, 275; ineffable individuality and the "timeless" moment, 277. *See* Individuality

Totality: boredom reveals what-is-in-totality, 316; concept of, 69; D on t. in

N, 228; D's critique of, 87, 88; D's vigilance seeks to break free of, 184; *écriture* shatters, 109–110; task of interpretation is to reveal a t. of meaning, 218; key to H's interpretation of N, 58; life-death deprives totality of its status, 71; Trace: thought of the t cannot break with nor be reduced to transcendental phenomenology, 190

Tradition as: as banishing the narcissism of a self-reflexive subject, 157; as basis for fusion of horizons, 217; as effect of différance/*Unter-Schied*. 262; as having a justification outside the arguments of reason, 258; as having an authority that is nameless, 258; as having erased the dissenters from its "ageless essences", 264; as in need of fruitful internal frictions, 221; as like code-model sciences with regard to ambituity and innovation, 155; as more a motley patchwork than "the great tapestry that supports us", 219; as rendered powerless by Enlightenment prejudice, 136; as resting on rupture, fragmentation, and conflict (D), 217; as resting on shared true meaning (G), 217; as signed by jaded ears attuned to their own interests, 203; as the story of the winners, while the dissenters have been excommunicated, torched, castrated, exiled, or imprisoned, 264

Tradition, 2; can stifle alterity, 220; cannot handle ambiguity or semantic innovation, 155; conversation with, 111; Ds view of, 263; emphasis on t. does not assert a supersubject, 111; need not exclude conflict and debate, 219; maintains itself by erasing the dangerous traces of those who question it, 263; in G indistinguisable from supersubject, 158; for G an all-encompassing and ever-developing, continuous and unified totality, 217; for G t. has to be written again and again, 260; happening of t. as the *Sache* of

thinking, 261; prestructures and unites participants in it, 217; relies on languages learned by the few, 264; two traditions in contrast (G, D), 220; unsurpassability of, 157

Traditionalism: a variation on foundationalism, 259

Transcendence: ontic and originary, 253; problem of transcendence not same as problem of intentionality, 253; an undiscussed problem today, 253

Transcendental terms: D's principal objection to G lies in his use of, 267

Transformation into structured form. *See Verwandlung ins Gebilde*

Translation as interpretation, 32

Truth: 94; as authoritative but not authority per se, 139; of beings, 253; H's later thought not concerned with t. of Being, 261; Deep Truths imply a Leader who will take one to them, 173; D's view of t., 263; t. as effect of différance/*Unter-Schied*. 262; elimination of apocalyptic paradigm would abolish truth itself, 281; the eventing of: h. dimension in which Being manifests itself, 25; as constituted in the fusion of horizons, 156; G offers a theory of deep t., 260; G rejects t. as adequation, 195; G sees t. as adequation, 140–41, 143; as guide in dialogue from Plato to G, 170; H-N-D on, 86–87; objective truth presupposed by G, 171; no criterion for objective truth, 173; the search for, 6; the problem of transcendent t. and commensurate understanding, 169; t. as what understanding understands, assuming a good will and a transcendent truth, 169. *See also Aletheia*

Truth of the text: G believes in the possibility of truth, revelation, immanent unity of meaning, the self-presentation of the work of art, 267

Type-token distinction: applies to all elements of language, 155

Undecidability, 5; D's writing rests on the principle of, 267; neglects the ethical, 89; u. of meaning, 2

Understanding: agreement in, 154; and the art of construing, 48; assimilates the other to oneself, 119, 167; cannot understand everything, 163; commensurate u. presupposes transcendent truth, 169; common u. really means making one's own u. prevail, 165; D's critique of, 81; D's misunderstanding of, 118; deindividualizes, 162; event of u. represents a new relation to text, 178; the demand for, 173; G offers a metaphysical interpretation of, 167; G's picture of u. a target of critique, 165; good will in, 132; justness impossible in, 167; real issue is justice in, 169; in a marriage, 283; reading with u. does not entail a metaphysics of presence, 96; struggles continually against the ontological difference, 163; problem of u. the other, 220; preconditions for, 53; the task of, 24; temporal structure of (Dilthey), 49; textual u. as a work of repetition that does not seek origins, 183; the issue of a true understanding, 217; problem of texts which are understood differently, 165; G's claim that N and D and anyone who speaks or writes wants to be understood, 165–66, 187, 193, 221, 304. *See also* Agreement in understanding, Alterity, Good will, Mutual understanding, Other, Otherness, Privileged meaning, Sharing.

Understanding *as:* like a sudden blow, 48; always depending on the changing context, 217; always involving application to present situation of the interpreter, 216; always understanding differently, 96, 118; requiring distance, 163; an experience transcending scientific method, 188–89; an Hegelian *Aufhebung* not a reconstruction of meaning, 157; event, 1; because of its event-character not metaphysical 182;

dialogical, 220; having to include the unintelligible, 190; imagining the other into one's own worldpicture, 165; standing in the for the other, 96, 186; metaphysical, 174; not a matter of metaphysics of presence, 118, 182; not a matter of will or good will, 168; not a progressive, linear process, 167; operating in the realm of phronesis, 221; presupposing a will to mutual understanding, 56; transformed by H into the foundation for an ontology of Dasein, 102

Unity: of a biography and proper name, 228; of a destiny of Being, 240; of meaning allows the text to stand as a self-presenting whole, 182; of H's general reading of Western metaphysics, 228; D proposed a u. of metaphysics articulated by epochs, 247; of metaphysical inquiry into beings as a whole, 228; versus multiplicity in N and the interpretations of N, 226–27; D in *Gr* reduced all oppositions to one opposition, 229; of a signature and proper name, 228; of N's thought really the u. of H's *Denkweg*, 228; of the history of metaphysics, 228, 240; H borrowed teleological model of metaphysical u. from Hegel, 234; of tradition maintained by suppression of opposition, 263; G discovered that he cannot confirm the unitary reading without affirming the disseminating reading, 248

Universality of hermeneutics, 143. *See* Dialogue, Hermeneutics; Hermeneutical experience

Unsaid: the speculative unity of said and unsaid, 275

Validity in understanding: two strategies G offers for testing understanding, 217; two measures of v. u. called into question, 218

Validity of morals: based on tradition, 258

Verständigungsgeschehen (event of understanding), 21
Verständigungssituation (situation of
understanding): not a barrier, 165
Verständnis 21; no English equivalent,
297
Verstehen (understanding) 21, 75, 256;
meaning of, 118. *See also* Understanding
Verwandlung ins Gebilde (transformation
into structured form), 80, 97
Verwindung (recuperation from metaphysics), 168. *See* Overcoming metaphysics
Vigilance: against unquestioned authority,
177. *See also* Socratic vigilance
Virtuality: definition of, 302; language as
purely a, 153; of the word, 112
Virtue: Meno on, 255
Vorhandenheit (presence at hand): stems
from a primodial understanding of
"Da", 115, 122
Vorstellung (Ideation): modern but already
implicit among the Greeks, 240

Wahrheit (truth): in later writings, H
gives up on W, 261
Wesen: G's *Wesen* a retreat from H's
radicalization of w., 260; H's concept
of, 110; H represents w. as a way, a
path, 227; and *ist Gewesen,* 259; Sartre
misquotes H on, 110
Will to power, 94; counterconcept to
commensurate understanding, 165; D's
implied reference relies on an interpretation of this term that he himself has
objected to, 194; for N there are "no
wills," nothing universal, 167; it is
wrong to interpret w. p. as a doctrine
of N, 167
Wirkungsgeschichte (effective history): of
SZ and Fichte's *Elements,* 120
Wirkungsgeschichtliches Bewußsein: can
be translated as consciousness open to
the effects of history, or historically
effected consciousness, 213
Word: every word an answer leading to
another question, 184; Bakhtin's lyric
word has affinity with Blanchot's conception of "writing," 210; character of,
7; concept of w. should be separated
from its grammatical sense, 124; a
more strict definition empties it of
meaning, 107; mysterious character of,
95; a mysterious multiplicity, 112; play
on words, 44, 144; the question of
whether language let itself be grasped
on the basis of w., 115; self-
presentation of w. in literature, 42;
spoken, as that which says something,
124
Work: hermeneutic autonomy of, 123,
125; Schlegel and the h. concept of,
123. *See* Artwork
Writing: Blachot's conception of, 210;
beginning of w. is a liberation to the
draft, the withdrawal, 257; literacy
and, 208; cannot avoid sound and
meaning, 96; closeness to speaking, 95;
D's thought on w. stronger in its denun-
ciation of dreams than in new creation,
270; Socratic dialogue as not opposed
to, 209. See also *Écriture;* Writing *as*
Writing *as:* the art of constructing a text
that can return to speech, 96; the broadcasting of discourse, 202; dialectically
intertwined with dialogue, 209; freed
from the contingencies of origin, 180;
requiring the inner ear to read it, 124;
requiring to be read, 118, 124–25;
shattering metaphysics and meaning,
109; the silence within speech, 257;
still demanding interpretation, 118

Zwiespalt (dissension): H explores the
ambiguity of Z in N, 241; not same as
Gegensatz (opposition), 241